THE

Newbery &
Caldecott
Medal Books
1986–2000

*A Comprehensive
Guide to the Winners*

The Horn Book

Association for Library Service to Children

AMERICAN LIBRARY ASSOCIATION
Chicago and London   2001

When available, book covers are from original printings.

Text excerpts: *The Whipping Boy* © 1986 by Sid Fleischman; *The View from Saturday* Reprinted with the permission of Atheneum Books for Young Readers, an imprint of Simon & Schuster Children's Publishing Division from *The View from Saturday* by E. L. Konigsburg. Copyright © 1996 E. L. Konigsburg; *Shiloh* Reprinted with the permission of Atheneum Books for Young Readers, an imprint of Simon & Schuster Children's Publishing Division from *Shiloh* by Phyllis Reynolds Naylor. Copyright © 1991 Phyllis Reynolds Naylor

Cover design by Dianne M. Rooney
Text design and composition by ALA Production Services

Printed on 50-pound white offset, a pH-neutral stock, and bound in 10-point coated cover stock by McNaughton & Gunn

The paper used in this publication meets the minimum requirements of American National Standard for Information Sciences—Permanence of Paper for Printed Library Materials, ANSI Z39.48-1992. ∞

Library of Congress Cataloging-in-Publication Data

The Newbery and Caldecott medal books, 1986–2000: a comprehensive guide to the winners / the Horn Book and Association for Library Service to Children.
    p. cm.
Includes bibliographical references and index.
ISBN 0-8389-3505-2
1. Newbery Medal—Bio-bibliography. 2. Caldecott Medal—Bio-bibliography.
3. Children's literature, American Bio-bibliography. 4. Picture books for children—United States—Bio-bibliography. I. Horn Book, Inc. II. Association for Library Service to Children.
Z1037.A2N492 2001
011.62'079—dc21   00-053430

Printed in the United States of America.

05   04   03   02   01   5   4   3   2   1

Contents

Preface

Nothing pleases me more than to introduce the present volume in the continuing series of the Newbery and Caldecott Medal books, first published by the Horn Book, Inc.

It is altogether fitting and proper that the Association for Library Service to Children (ALSC), which administers and presents these most prestigious awards, and the Horn Book, Inc., which reviews and compiles biographical essays on the winners, publish this work together. It's a mystery why this hasn't been done before. But wonder no more! This collaboration brings together the right organizations at the right time to provide a wealth of information for librarians, scholars, families, and the curious.

What sets these award-winning creators and their books apart from other authors and illustrators? How do these works reflect changing attitudes about books for children? How do they reflect the changing nature of society and its mores? Authoritative contributors to this volume address these questions as they consider the medal books of the twentieth century's closing decades.

Maria Salvadore, Coordinator of Children's Services for the District of Columbia Public Library in Washington, D.C., brings practical and academic expertise to her analysis of the Caldecott books as she reviews the wide variety of artwork that stimulates the imagination of readers of all ages. She has been adjunct faculty teaching children's literature at the University of Maryland, book reviewer for the *Horn Book Magazine*, member of the Caldecott Committee, and chair of the committee that selected Allan Say for *Grandfather's Journey*. She is widely respected for her use of children's literature, especially picture books, in programming for children, parents and caregivers, prospective parents, teachers, pediatricians, and the incarcerated—an approach for which she is cited in many publications on librarianship.

Kathleen T. Horning brings a unique and positive contribution to distinguished literature for children in this review of Newbery winners, one shaped by her experience in both the practical and academic spheres of children's literature. She is currently a librarian at the Cooperative Children's Book Center, a library of the School of Education, University of Wisconsin–Madison. Previous to this she worked for nine years as a youth services librarian at the Madison (Wisconsin) Public Library. Author of *From Cover to Cover: Evaluating and Reviewing Children's Books* (HarperCollins, 1997), she is well known for conducting group discussion in the evaluation of children's literature. She has been a member of the Newbery Award Committee and chaired the committee when it selected Sharon Creech for *Walk Two Moons*.

Years of experience as a professional book reviewer stand behind Roger Sutton, editor in chief of the Horn Book, Inc. He began in the profession as a public librarian and was a reviewer and later editor for the *Bulletin of the Center for Children's Books*. He has served on the Newbery Committee. Well known for his many articles on the importance of high quality literature for youth, he brings eminent qualifications to his review of the period's wealth of excellent children's books beyond the medal winners.

ALSC appreciates Roger Sutton's willingness to have the Horn Book, Inc., collaborate in continuing the original series. We thank the essayists for their excellent contributions. We also thank Rebecca Singer, ALSC Communications Manager, for shepherding this project to publication and Patrick Hogan, Editorial Director of ALA Editions, for his openness in taking on this project, which we see as a major contribution to the field of children's literature and the continuance of an exemplary series.

And we especially thank you, the reader, for your interest. Your ideas for improving the work in the next volume are welcome.

Susan Roman
former Executive Director
Association for Library Service to Children
American Library Association

Looking beyond the Winner's Circle

Roger Sutton

Not to put too fine a point on it, the Newbery and Caldecott Medals reward exactly *two* of the thousands of eligible children's books published each year. Winning a medal or, to a lesser extent, being designated a Newbery or Caldecott honor book automatically gifts a book with attention, a readership, and a leg up on longevity. But what about those books that achieve these same rewards despite being passed over by the medal committees? This essay is an attempt to highlight some of those titles from the past fifteen years that, thanks to sustained critical attention, insistent promotion by librarians and educators, and enthusiastic response from children themselves, made and continue to claim a significant place in American children's literature.

This is not an attempt to second-guess the medals. Each Newbery and Caldecott Award committee seeks the most distinguished books of that year; they specifically do not in their deliberations draw comparisons with books published in previous years, nor obviously can they see the future. Nor are the committees honoring popular appeal.

In evaluating the books of 1985, for example, the Newbery committee could not have known of the enduring affection children would demonstrate for Phyllis Reynolds Naylor's Alice McKinley, introduced that year in *The Agony of Alice* and, fourteen years later, star of her own Web site. Nineteen eighty-five also saw *The Runner*, an entry in Cynthia Voigt's acclaimed Tillerman series, and *Jackaroo*, the first of Voigt's popular quasi-Medieval series set in The Kingdom. Other significant young adult titles published in 1985 include Richard Peck's *Remembering the*

Roger Sutton is the editor in chief of The Horn Book, Inc. He has been a librarian and critic of children's books for twenty years and served on the 1999 Newbery committee.

1

Good Times, Hadley Irwin's *Abby, My Love,* and Zibby Oneal's *In Summer Light.* At the beginning of her too-short career, the late Pam Conrad published the historical novel *Prairie Songs,* and Virginia Hamilton turned her attention from fiction to compile *The People Could Fly,* a handsome collection of folktales illustrated by Leo and Diane Dillon, her first of several books drawn from African-American folklore. While *multiculturalism* was not quite the vogue word it would become a few years later, Valerie Flournoy and Jerry Pinkney's *The Patchwork Quilt,* a story of African-American family bonds, would become a key volume in increasingly culturally diverse picture-book collections. David Schwartz and Steven Kellogg's *How Much Is a Million,* a picture book that actually allowed children to count one million stars, was a prime mover for trade books "across the curriculum," extending the use of stories to math and science classrooms.

In 1987 Arthur Yorinks and Richard Egielski's *Hey, Al* became possibly the most surprising Caldecott choice of this era; history and children have been kinder to William Steig's *Brave Irene,* Amy Hest and Amy Schwartz's *The Purple Coat,* and Patricia C. McKissack and Rachel Isadora's *Flossie and the Fox.* The first of Joanna Cole and Bruce Degen's Magic Schoolbus series, *The Magic School Bus Visits the Waterworks,* was published this year. Other nonfiction standouts include three groundbreaking photo-essays: *Thinking Big, the Story of a Young Dwarf* by Susan B. Kuklin; *The Children We Remember: Photographs from the Archives of Yad Vashem, the Holocaust Martyrs' and Heroes' Remembrance Authority, Jerusalem, Israel* by Chana Byers Abells; and *Being Born* by Sheila Kitzinger and Lennart Nilsson. Mary Downing Hahn published the ghost story *Wait till Helen Comes,* which would receive numerous children's-choice state awards, and for young adults Chris Crutcher's *Stotan!* and Cynthia Voigt's *Izzy, Willy-Nilly* would also become enduring favorites. M. E. Kerr's *Night Kites* was the first novel—for children or adults—to confront the tragedy of AIDS.

If *Hey, Al* was the darkest horse to win the Caldecott Medal in this era, then Brock Cole's *The Goats* was in 1987 the most surprising omission from Newbery mention. Reviews hailed *The Goats,* Cole's first novel, as a masterpiece, although even at the time there were mutterings about certain events in the book that would later lead it to regular appearances on ALA's annual Banned Books List. Another title that would go on to censorious wrath was Eve Merriam and Lane Smith's *Halloween ABC,* and Chris Van Allsburg got creepy with his sinister deconstruction of the alphabet book *The Z Was Zapped.* More happily,

James Marshall gave us his wacky *Red Riding Hood,* Jane Yolen and Jane Dyer introduced *Piggins,* and Julius Lester and Jerry Pinkney published the first volume of their mischievous new readings of Joel Chandler Harris's Uncle Remus stories.

In 1988 Robert Cormier's *Fade,* Maurice Sendak's edition of the newly discovered Grimm tale *Dear Milli,* and David Macaulay's *The Way Things Work* demonstrated each of these grandmasters at his most ambitious; only the Macaulay was received with general acclaim. Walter Dean Myers consolidated his Newbery Honor win for *Scorpions* with *Fallen Angels,* a Vietnam novel, while Virginia Hamilton took her genius in yet another direction with her biography *Anthony Burns: The Defeat and Triumph of a Fugitive Slave.* Impressive debuts were made by Iktomi in Paul Goble's first picture book about the Plains trickster hero and by Lois Lowry's Sam Krupnik, who moved from the supporting cast of the Anastasia books to center stage in *All about Sam.*

Nineteen eighty-nine brought us the oft-maligned wolf telling his side of the story in *The True Story of the Three Little Pigs by A. Wolf* by Jon Scieszka and Lane Smith; other picture-book crowd-pleasers included Jan Brett's *The Mitten,* Rosemary Wells's *Max's Chocolate Chicken,* and *Chicka Chicka Boom Boom* by Bill Martin Jr. and John Archambault, illustrated by Lois Ehlert. Two memorable YA heroines appeared in eponymous titles, Brock Cole's *Celine* and Francesca Lia Block's *Weetzie Bat,* and a third, Dicey Tillerman, made her farewell in Cynthia Voigt's *Seventeen against the Dealer,* the last of the author's books about the Tillerman family. Farewells were also made to author Sylvia Cassedy, whose last novel, *Lucie Babbidge's House,* was posthumously published.

In 1990 the somber legacy of war was explored in two picture books, Sheila Hamanaka's *The Journey,* about the internment of Japanese Americans during World War II, and Eve Bunting and Ronald Himler's *The Wall,* wherein a boy seeks out his grandfather's name on the Vietnam Veterans Memorial. Significant fiction debuts were made by Annette Curtis Klause with *The Silver Kiss* and Gary Soto in *Baseball in April; Julius, the Baby of the World,* was also born, fathered by author-illustrator Kevin Henkes. Fatherhood got a more controversial spin with Michael Wilhoite's *Daddy's Roommate,* a gay-themed picture book that has subsequently been challenged in school and libraries across the country along with the similar *Heather Has Two Mommies* by Leslea Newman, published the previous year.

Katherine Paterson published a hefty historical novel in 1991, *Lyddie*, as well as *The Smallest Cow in the World*, an entry in the under-appreciated beginning-reader genre. Susan Jeffers's pictures for *Brother Eagle, Sister Sky: A Message from Chief Seattle* were widely acclaimed as beautiful, but the authenticity of the text became increasingly questioned in subsequent years, particularly after the book's appearance on the *New York Times* bestseller list. Barbara M. Joosse and Barbara Lavallee's *Mama, Do You Love Me?* was a more straightforward success and a harbinger of a flock of similarly themed picture books particularly successful in the retail market. *In the Tall, Tall Grass* by Denise Fleming was a hit among preschoolers; Alice McLerran and Barbara Cooney's *Roxaboxen*, Laura Rankin's *Handmade Alphabet*, Allen Say's *Tree of Cranes*, and Arthur Dorros and Elisa Kleven's *Abuela* were all handsome productions for somewhat older picture-book audiences.

The 1992 quincentenary of Columbus's "discovery" brought forth many books with a decidedly revisionist view of American history; most notable—and artistically promising—was Michael Dorris's first novel for children, *Morning Girl*. *Children of the Dustbowl*, also by a writer new to children's books, Jerry B. Stanley, was the nonfiction standout of the year, although probably the one most welcome by teachers was Pat Cummings's *Talking with Artists*, in which popular illustrators finally gave the lowdown on where they got their ideas. In the picture book *Martha Speaks*, Susan Meddaugh gave children a brand new heroine to cheer for: Martha, the talking dog. Both Cummings and Meddaugh would go on to produce successful follow-ups to their inspired originals.

Impressive novels in 1993 included *The Boggart*, with Susan Cooper writing in a lighter vein than usual, Vera B. Williams's exuberant first novel *Scooter*, Virginia Euwer Wolff's experimental *Make Lemonade*, and Kyoko Mori's harrowing debut *Shizuko's Daughter*. Popular writer Gary Paulsen struck two tones, richly funny with the autobiographical *Harris and Me* and austerely brutal with *Nightjohn*, the first-person narrative of a Southern slave. Virginia Hamilton also confronted this dark historical legacy in *Many Thousand Gone: African Americans from Slavery to Freedom*, while Tom Feelings celebrated the African-American experience with his dramatic paintings for the poetry anthology *Soul Looks Back in Wonder*. Contemporary tragedy was intensely evoked in Maurice Sendak's *We Are All in the Dumps with Jack and Guy*, a radical allegory of homelessness drawn from two little-known Mother Goose rhymes.

Paula Danziger introduced her popular Amber in 1994, in *Amber Brown Is Not a Crayon*, and Jack Gantos's Jack made his first appearance in *Heads or Tails*. Young adult books with gay themes began a resurgence this year, most notably with Marion Dane Bauer's *Am I Blue*, a collection of short stories by notable YA writers, and M. E. Kerr's *Deliver Us from Evie*, a novel. For slightly younger readers, Jacqueline Woodson's *I Hadn't Meant to Tell You This* told a darkly lyrical tale of the interracial friendship between two troubled girls, and Patricia Polacco's *Pink and Say*, a picture book for older children, retold an old family story of the bond between two Civil War soldiers, one white, one African-American. Christmas was notably celebrated in two picture books: Patricia and Fredrick E. McKissack's *Christmas in the Big House, Christmas in the Quarters*, illustrated by John Thompson, described the contrasting holiday traditions of masters and slaves on an antebellum plantation; Robert Sabuda's pop-up *The Christmas Alphabet* revealed many elegant surprises.

Along with the crowd-pleasing Caldecott winner, *Officer Buckle and Gloria*, bestselling picture books of 1995 included Caralyn Buehner and Mark Buehner's tongue-in-cheek etiquette guide, *It's a Spoon, Not a Shovel*, and Jon Scieszka and Lane Smith's third collaboration, *Math Curse*, a smart-alecky send-up of textbook learning. Two major books on African-American themes appeared: Tom Feelings's *The Middle Passage*, a wordless, lavishly produced picture book on the slave trade, and Rita Williams-Garcia's *Like Sisters on the Homefront*, a tough story of two disparate cousins growing up together. Author-illustrator Lynne Rae Perkins made a distinctive entrance with *Home Lovely*; short-story writer Judith Ortiz Cofer claimed her place with *An Island Like You*. Prolific photo-essayist Bruce MacMillan was at his best with *Nights of the Pufflings*, an account of children's assistance with puffling migration in Iceland; Avi introduced mouse-heroine *Poppy*, the first volume in a popular animal fantasy series.

While children's books by movie stars and other celebrities were published with numbing regularity throughout the decade, Jamie Lee Curtis's adoption story *Tell Me Again about the Night I Was Born*, illustrated by Laura Cornell, was a fresh breeze in 1996. Great popular success was found by two children's book veterans as well: Kevin Henkes for *Lilly's Purple Plastic Purse* and Rosemary Wells for her pictures for Iona Opie's compilation *My Very First Mother Goose*. Betsy Byars brought real distinction to the beginning-reader genre with *My Brother, Ant*, illustrated by Marc Simont, and Katherine Paterson published a gripping historical yarn with special appeal for boys, *Jip: His Story.* Andrew Clements's *Frindle*, about a boy who successfully contrives a new word for *pen*, would go on to receive many children's-choice awards. Helen Bannerman's controversial folk hero Sambo received two makeovers this year: *Sam and the Tigers* by Julius Lester and Jerry Pinkney and Fred Marcellino's *The Story of Little Babaji.*

In 1997 children's book buzz was growing over "bleak books," most notably Brock Cole's long-awaited *The Facts Speak for Themselves*, a grim tale about a thirteen-year-old girl who watches the murder of her adult lover by her mother's boyfriend, and Norma Fox Mazer's *When She Was Good*, a sad story about a girl with a severely disturbed and abusive older sister. The questions these books raised were not new (think back to *The Chocolate War*) but demonstrated again the ambivalent feelings we have about children's books that "dare to disturb the universe." Happier innovation was found in Chris Raschka's *Mysterious Thelonius*, a picture book that found visual expression for jazz in colors, and in Walter Wick's *A Drop of Water*, which demonstrated the unique properties of H_2O in a series of stunning photographs.

Many were surprised that the 1999 Newbery committee named only one honor book; other notable contenders published in 1998 included Joan Abelove's *Go and Come Back* and Kimberly Willis Holt's *My Louisiana Sky*, both debut novels of real promise. Among nonfiction standouts were Russell Freedman's *Martha Graham: A Life in Pictures*, Anita Lobel's memoir of the Holocaust *No Pretty Pictures*, and Sandra Jordan and Jan Greenberg's portrait of contemporary painter Chuck Close in *Chuck Close Up Close*. While 1998 was not a strong year for picture books, William Steig gave families a new game to play together with *Pete's a Pizza*, and with *Look-Alikes* Joan Steiner offered them a new way to see their surroundings through her eye-fooling ready-made collage dioramas of familiar scenes. And perhaps folk artist Kathy Jakobsen gave us the best millennial gift; her paintings for Woody Guthrie's song "This Land Is Your Land" truly stretch from sea to shining sea in a cross-country evocation of Americana.

Any critic will have figured his or her own selection of what should have, could have, and would have made the list *if-I-had-been-on-the-committee* in any given year's Newbery and Caldecott announcements. This is as it should be: any book award program needs to recognize that naming the winners is only the beginning of the debate and that such debate is in fact the evidence for the importance of the award.

Caldecott Medal Books 1986–2000

Maria B. Salvadore

The picture book remains an integral, increasingly rich part of the children's book spectrum at the start of a new century. As it evolves, the picture book is perhaps a more prevalent form within the field of children's literature, more daring, perhaps more confusing. One thing remains constant, however. Since established in 1938, the charge of the Caldecott Award committee endures: to identify the most distinguished picture book published during the preceding year, the picture book that is likely to be as commanding to tomorrow's reader as it is to the reader in the year the book is honored.

The late twentieth and early twenty-first centuries provide a different context for children and their books; early childhood is accepted as a critical time in development. Correspondingly, there is a greater recognition of the powerful and positive influence of early exposure to language and literature. It has been argued that the very nature of American society is changing directly related to the proliferation of electronic media (including communication technologies, television, and computers). In examining Caldecott Medal books from 1986 to 2000, one would agree.

During this period, there is an expansion in artistic styles and media used, a sea of change in content, and a shift in the audience

Maria Salvadore has served as coordinator of children's service for the District of Columbia Public Library system, responsible for the overall administration of service to children and families. She has also served on or chaired various book award committees including the Washington Post/Children's Book Guild Nonfiction Award, the Boston Globe/Horn Book Awards, Golden Kite, and the Caldecott Committee.

for the picture book. Picture books of the late twentieth century appear to be moving away from simplicity of line and theme toward lush, sophisticated graphics and design; away from story toward psycho-emotional content through a deluge of images and sophisticated themes. Further, they reflect a change in the audience for the picture book, once regarded as books for the youngest reader.

Not only do these changes indicate a shift in the view of children in the late twentieth century, they mark a shift in market forces. Additionally, they indicate the ability to reproduce art and illustration in myriad ways. When examined in the aggregate, these factors exemplify what Neil Postman has suggested is the "disappearance of childhood." Postman contends that the concept of childhood experienced its heyday from the mid-nineteenth century to the mid-twentieth century. Literature designed especially to engage, not just indoctrinate, children emerged, including the work of Randolph Caldecott.

We have become a pictorial, highly visual society in which it is no longer possible to maintain secrets of adulthood. These secrets, knowledge once taboo to children, were previously accessible to children only when they learned to read. Adulthood and childhood have become blurred, confused, merged as tastes and markets converge. Lines between adult and child audiences for the picture book continue to gray.

The Caldecott Medal has celebrated its sixtieth anniversary and begins its seventh decade. The culture of this period can be characterized by hypervisual stimulation through an explosion in technology, requiring no understanding of what is being depicted. The immediacy of pictures evokes an emotive response from viewers, regardless of age or experience. To be understood, to be more than simply perceived, however, images must be put into a context, most often gained through experience.

Unlike television and other electronic media, the picture book provides an opportunity to investigate meaning and understanding in depth. Instead of presenting a rapid series of often disjointed or unrelated images, the picture book at its best provokes a rhythm, a sense of visual continuity, of movement from a beginning to an end. The eye can linger, return, develop an individual pace. Use of line, texture, and color contribute to meaning, as do composition, perspective, artistic style, medium. These elements are further refined, altered when packaged in the form of a book. The ability to follow a series of images by turning pages, feeling texture and weight of pages, viewing images, simply exploring a book, is based in the individual's maturity. It sets up a multisensory, interactive experience over which the reader has control.

During this period, Caldecott Medal books seem to have fallen into categories that include retellings of traditional material, social commentary, nostalgia, and pictorial biography; fantasy and humor are present but less prevalent. The criteria for the award specify that there "are no limitations as to the character of the picture book except that the illustrations be original work." A broad and exciting range of artistic styles and media has been presented during this period.

Carefully researched and thoughtfully rendered in the style of Italian Renaissance painters, Paul Zelinsky's *Rapunzel* requires a sophisticated reader to appreciate the presentation of architectural detail, authentic costumes, and specifically styled portraiture and landscapes that provide the setting for the traditional Grimm love story, which is complete with interesting subplots including the birth of twins to Rapunzel and her lover. This picture book not only provides a retelling of a familiar story but also serves as an introduction to Renaissance art.

The humor and wisdom of a traditional Yiddish folksong are introduced in *Joseph Had a Little Overcoat* by Simms Taback. Mixed-media illustrations use bold color and broad forms to follow Joseph as he "makes something out of nothing" over and over again. As his old and worn overcoat is reduced to a button, so die-cuts become increasingly small until they disappear entirely, leaving what Joseph himself had: a story about his overcoat. The simple text and illustration reminiscent of folk art call to mind the culture and time in which this universally appealing tale is set.

Ed Young also chose traditional literature in his retelling of a Chinese folktale, an Eastern version of the Red Riding Hood story, *Lon Po Po*. Pastel and watercolor illustrations are formatted in panels inspired by Chinese art. They effectively produce shadows to portend evil, heighten tension, and tell the story. Words become almost secondary to the pacing, tone, and tension of the illustration, which can be appreciated on many levels but which requires the reader to be accomplished in interpreting light, dark, and visual movement across the page.

Meticulously rendered three-dimensional paper cutouts are used to illustrate *Golem*, a careful retelling of the harsh tale of the clay giant brought to life by a rabbi to save the Jews of sixteenth-century Prague. As is the traditional story, the illustrations are necessarily severe, unsettling, violent. David Wisniewski's use of color is as disconcerting as the empathy one develops for the Golem, a Frankenstein-like character. The reader must bring a sense of history to the book and, as in *Lon Po Po*, the ability to interpret the presentation of dark illustrations, both literally and figuratively.

It is interesting to note that although not originally intended exclusively for children, illustrated retellings have made traditional tales accessible to children as well as to adults much as televised news makes real-life events accessible to all. Now even these events have been introduced in picture-book form.

The dissonant color, unyielding lines, grim faces, and harsh backgrounds of *Smoky Night* illustrated by David Diaz provide an unyielding reality, a definite social commentary. Highly textured, semi-abstract acrylic paintings placed on mixed-media collages produce a gritty, urban tone as the text describes the Los Angeles riots from a child's point of view. The child narrator and a Korean shopkeeper come together in their concern for their cats that survived the fire. The cats become the metaphor for community healing as they are depicted cozily napping on the final double-page spread. The expressionistic art is effective but appears to be a series of individual images tied together, forcing the reader to fill in the emotional context created by this disturbing social history.

Also in a realistic vein is *Hey, Al*, the story of a janitor, Al, and Eddie, his dog, both miserably unhappy in their cramped apartment. The detailed illustrations by Richard Egielski portray a dully colored, slightly warped, one-room home from which the two escape when liberated by a large, mysterious, and colorful bird. They travel to a lush "island in the sky" where they get more than they bargained for when they begin to transform into birds themselves. Al and Eddie struggle to make their way safely back to their apartment where Al begins to add color to his life by painting the walls bright yellow. The adult point of view is apparent through the theme, in the depiction of Al as a man (not a boy), and in the subtle shift of tone that may pose a challenge for young readers. It could be argued that the carefully designed illustrations require life experiences beyond what most young readers bring to this book, obfuscating the delineation between adult and child.

Several Caldecott Medal books look back to provide a glimpse of times remembered. While there is danger in presenting times past, there is also potential for enduring stories, universal experiences between generations. Unsentimental presentations remain fresh and engaging.

A little girl and her father venture out on a still winter night to go owling in an *Owl Moon*, illustrated by John Schoenherr. Varying perspectives of the snowy landscape are made more dramatic with shadows, white space, lacy outlines of winter trees, and the dramatic appearance of the Great Horned Owl, which ultimately responds to their call. Though it lacks story, one responds to the effective visual presentation of the frozen night and the warmth exuded by parent and child made dramatic and real through handsome watercolors. Evocative illustrations provide a tacit emotional appeal.

In *Song and Dance Man*, the attic becomes a stage upon which Grandpa, a one-time song and dance man, now performs for his grandchildren. The transformation is created by bursts of color in indistinct lines and the sheer joy in Grandpa's performance. The palette used by illustrator Stephen Gammell creates a warmth reflected in the relationship between the slightly frumpy grandfather and his grandchildren. This causes a gentle kind of happiness that is easily shared. As in *Owl Moon*, Gammell's illustrations exude an emotional glow, easily understood as empathy is created.

Mirette on the High Wire by Emily Arnold McCully introduces another memorable intergenerational relationship. Madame Gateau and her vivacious daughter, Mirette, work hard to make their guests comfortable at their boarding house. Mirette not only befriends the great artist Bellini but also helps him overcome his fear of the high wire as she demonstrates her own hard-earned skill. Nineteenth-century Paris is shown through almost impressionistic watercolors, heightened dramatically by play of light. The artist's use of perspective enhances the suspense on well-composed pages. Readers thrill to the theatricality of the paintings as Mirette and Bellini walk the tightrope toward each other.

Picture books are not bound by subject and are often difficult to classify. *Snowflake Bentley*, illustrated by Mary Azarian, introduces the life of Wilson Bentley, a self-taught scientist who in the early twentieth century perfected the technique for photographing individual snowflakes. Vermont cold and snow are vividly realized through the strong line of hand-colored woodcuts. The illustrations and format allow the presentation of two distinct levels of information. The broader narrative of Snowflake Bentley's life is told in the main portion of each page; sidebars decorated with delicate impressions of snowflakes provide greater factual detail. Here, illustration and format are used to guide the reader's eye as they augment emotional content and present a pictorial biography.

Illustration and format achieve a similar effect in another more highly imagined biography. Allen Say's strikingly realistic, exquisitely rendered watercolors and understated text chronicle a Japanese immigrant's travels to a new land in *Grandfather's Journey*. In documenting the journey, distinct cultures are contrasted through the creation of what appears almost as a family album of portraits and landscapes. Say presents a universal experience through the journey of one family, perhaps based in his own family's experience. The emotional impact of this story is in the authenticity of emotions portrayed, understood best by a mature reader.

All ages appreciate the simplicity of pure comic silliness in the text and illustration of *Officer Buckle and Gloria*. This slapstick story presents a safety officer and his companion dog, Gloria, teaching children important but all-too-often-ignored safety tips. Gloria's antics animate Officer Buckle's otherwise dull safety information and help him realize the importance of "Safety Tip #101: Always stick with your buddy." Peggy Rathmann's cartoonlike line and wash illustrations take the text to another dimension, building both story and visual humor while conveying a certain ageless wisdom.

A very different style is used to effectively create rollicking humor in *Tuesday*, illustrated by David Wiesner. Words are not needed nor are they used to convey the surprise, drama, and humor on a Tuesday evening when frogs rise from the pond on lily pads to cavort in town. The exaggerated features of the frogs' delight and the distress of others are unmistakably presented in seemingly realistic watercolor illustrations that note movement in either vertical or horizontal inserts on full page or double-page spreads. The pure zaniness of the fantasy is achieved through the incongruity of the situation. What is likely to happen next—pigs are rising—is certain to captivate as well as cause a chortle among a broad range of readers.

Incongruity is used as well in *Polar Express*, but for a very different effect. Chris Van Allsburg carefully crafts a seemingly realistic, placid street scene upon which a train appears mysteriously, inexplicably, one snowy Christmas Eve. A child from a house on that tree-lined street joins other children on a memorable journey. Soft line, striking use of light, and dramatic perspective augment the enigmatic quality of the story as the train speeds off to the North Pole where Santa awards the first gift of Christmas to the boy. The magic of believing, the beauty of the landscape, the juxtaposition of unlikely images combine with a good story to create a book with timeless and ageless appeal.

The complexity of David Macaulay's *Black and White* does not allow for visual complacency but instead requires tremendous reader involvement. Four distinct stories begin, intersect, and ultimately intertwine to create—perhaps—only one story after all. In fact, the title page includes a "warning" regarding this, playfully recommending careful inspection of words and pictures. Subtle differences in style of illustration (and in media used), color, perspective, and typeface gradually blur as stories about commuting parents, a traveling child, Holstein cows, and a robber come together over train tracks, visually and textually. Is it real or a fantasy? It is likely that the reader's experience will make that determination.

David Macaulay contends "illustration is a process of selection of that which needs to be seen from all that can be seen." Similarly, Caldecott Medal books help identify books that should be examined and revisited. The influence of Randolph Caldecott will continue to be felt. The medal that bears his name is not only one of the best-known but is among the most consequential awards given to children's books. Rightfully so, since Caldecott has been credited with the creation of the modern picture book. He instinctively created drama in the movement of image and word across and through pages, demonstrating the joy and exuberance in picture books.

Artists of the latter part of the twentieth century have changed the picture book through scope of artistic styles and media made possible by technological advances. These developments have freed artistic expression, beckoning artists to use different media for reproduction. In addition to watercolor, pen and ink, and lithographs, artists of this period have used full-color paper cutouts, placed acrylic paintings on mixed media collages, mixed watercolors with collage, and more. The ability to create and reproduce a mélange of styles in picture-book format should not overshadow the delight and verve that are the hallmark of Randolph Caldecott.

Unlike Caldecott's work, however, where image and word could be readily interpreted by the uninitiated reader, art and theme of many of the more recent medal winners require the reader to bring greater experience to the book. There is danger in highly produced books. Story and illustration become secondary to the process of book production. Even more dangerous, these books are likely to elude the child audience. Readers must have something with which to empathize in order to relate, often missing in an overproduced picture book in which compelling visual imagery becomes the sole value.

Advances in technology have allowed an apparent ease in the reproduction of art used in picture books to generate a considerable array of handsome, varied books. It has also created a narcissism in illustration, even an arrogance, in which books scream out to audiences. The picture book becomes a commodity to sell to any comer, no longer a multisensory experience to which an individual seeks to return. In this regard, children's books emulate the electronic media as the differentiation between adulthood and childhood—and the symbolic world of each—becomes indistinct. Pictures evoke a visceral response, not a reasoned, informed response, from those who view them.

Regardless of the subject, tone, or theme, books that appeal to succeeding generations are books that achieve what Randolph Caldecott did so well. These are books that surprise and delight, that can be read and reread, books in which text and illustration complement and extend the other in gratifying ways.

A picture book, according to Barbara Bader in *American Picturebooks from Noah's Ark to the Beast Within*, is "text, illustrations, total design; an item of manufacture and a commercial product; a social, cultural, historical document; and foremost an experience for a child." Picture books at their best achieve greatness when the triumph of language and the exuberance of art converge. The caution for the coming century is to remember that beyond a product, beyond a social and historical document, that the picture book remains foremost an experience for a child.

Newbery Medal Books 1986–2000

Kathleen T. Horning

More than seventy-five years after the establishment of the Newbery Medal, it can be confidently said that no single factor has had a greater impact on twentieth-century American children's literature than this award for distinguished writing. The Newbery Medal has certainly fulfilled Frederic Melcher's vision of raising the quality of children's literature by recognizing authors and publishers who produce better books. The mere fact that the Newbery Award winners are studied, criticized, argued about, and assigned to children suggests that the medal is highly regarded by all who care about children and children's books. That the committee's decision each year is widely anticipated, thoroughly discussed, and routinely second-guessed by children's literature aficionados attests to the medal's significance, even in the minds of its most vocal critics.

In writing a retrospective critique of past award winners, one has a distinct advantage that no Newbery committee has ever had: time. It is far easier to reflect and write about the Newbery Medal winners five or ten years after they were awarded than it is to choose a single book

Kathleen T. Horning is a librarian and coordinator of Special Collections at the Cooperative Children's Book Center, a library of the School of Education at the University of Wisconsin–Madison. For nine years she was also a children's librarian at Madison Public Library. She is the author of From Cover to Cover: Evaluating and Reviewing Children's Books *(HarperCollins, 1997) and is a regular reviewer for the* Horn Book Magazine. *With Ginny Moore Kruse and Megan Schliesman, she co-authored* Multicultural Literature for Children and Young Adults. *She has served on or chaired several book award committees, including the Americas Award, Batchelder, Coretta Scott King, Newbery, and ALA/ALSC's Notable Children's Books.*

each year to set apart and hold up as the best writing we can offer children. It is a responsibility that each committee takes very seriously, knowing that their decision will have an enormous impact on what children will be encouraged to read and what authors will be encouraged to write. In making that choice, however, each Newbery committee has had an advantage that no outsider will ever attain: context. No matter how well-read an outsider to the process may be, he or she will never be able to replicate the intensity of the committee's critical process—the reading, contemplation, rereading, discussion, and deliberation over the hundreds of eligible books in a given year. As individuals we may disagree with a particular committee's final decision, but as librarians we have learned to trust and respect the process.

In her essay "Newbery Medal Books, 1976–1985" (*Horn Book Magazine*, 1986) esteemed critic Zena Sutherland made some predictions about the future Newbery winners: "There are some ways in which the Newbery selections, whether of the decade past or those to come, have been and always will be the same. As a small sample of all the books published, they will never reflect all the trends or innovations of their decade; nor are they apt to include those trends that reflect the popular culture, like the etiolated adolescent romance that is written to formula and is, alas, so appealing to pre-teen readers. It is unlikely that future winners will have language or concepts that adults, or some adults, find offensive even if the contemporary realistic novel continues to dominate the list of selections. Despite the improvement in the quality of most nonfiction books it would be a surprise if one were selected for the Newbery Medal. Two changes that are more likely to take place are the selection of books, at least some, for younger readers, and given the steady improvement in the quality of fanciful writing in the United States, the inclusion of more fantasy titles as winners or Honor Books."

These last two predictions turned out to be right on target. At the end of the 1980s we saw Newbery winners that were clearly accessible to younger readers, such as *Sarah, Plain and Tall* by Patricia MacLachlan, *The Whipping Boy* by Sid Fleischman, *Number the Stars* by Lois Lowry and, to some extent, Paul Fleischman's *Joyful Noise*. In the 1990s the selections for the most part returned to the realm of literature for the upper age range of the Newbery Medal's audience, defined as children through age fourteen. With the establishment of the Michael L. Printz Award for young adult literature in 2000, it will be interesting to see what, if any, the impact will be on the Newbery selections or terms.

While only *The Giver* by Lois Lowry can be placed in the broad category of science fiction/fantasy, when one looks at the honor books there are several that qualify, including *Dragon's Gate* by Laurence Yep, *The Ear, the Eye and the Arm* by Nancy Farmer, *The Thief* by Megan Whelan Turner, and *Ella Enchanted* by Gail Carson Levine. But surely fanciful elements enter into both *Maniac Magee* by Jerry Spinelli and *Holes* by Louis Sachar to such an extent that they are both difficult to classify without making up a term such as mythic realism. We have here a new breed of children's fiction that could not have been predicted back in the mid-1980s. Whether its roots lie in the fiction of the preeminent children's author, Virginia Hamilton, and in the magical realism literary movement established in the twentieth century by Latin American writers, it is clearly an outgrowth of the New Realism that dominated children's literature in the 1960s and 1970s: realism with a playful edge.

Sutherland's prediction that the Newbery books of the late 1980s and 1990s would be unlikely to reflect trends in popular culture was also borne out, although we saw the trend itself move from formula romance to horror in the 1990s. Overall, the tone of children's and young adult fiction in the 1990s has been increasingly bleak, and while this is reflected in some of the Newbery winners from that time, it does not begin to approach the horror genre in popular culture. Still, one can't help but wonder if children's popular taste for horror and children's writers' preoccupation, at least from a literary standpoint, with death, abuse, and abandonment are merely coincidental in the waning years of the millennium.

Contrary to Sutherland's prediction, a nonfiction title did win the Newbery Medal for the first time in more than thirty years. The announcement that Russell Freedman's book *Lincoln: A Photobiography* had won the Newbery came not only as a pleasant surprise but also as a harbinger of change in both the look and the quality of children's nonfiction in the years to come. Freedman's recognition ushered in an era of nonfiction titles taken seriously as literature. This was evident in the Newbery committee's honor book choices in subsequent years, which still represented only a small sampling of the fine nonfiction available to children at the close of the century, much of it clearly influenced by *Lincoln*.

Among the Newbery winners of the past fifteen years we see a much greater diversity in genre, style, and narrative structure than we have ever seen in the past. For only the second time in Newbery history, a book of poetry was awarded when *Joyful Noise* by Paul Fleischman was selected. Beyond being a rarity in terms of genre (for the Newbery), it is unusual in that the poems are written for two voices to encourage choral reading, making this selection one of the most innovative—and daring—choices ever. *Out of the Dust* by Karen Hesse is a novel told in a series of spare free-verse poems, arranged chronologically, written in a style quite unlike any other published work for children.

Sharon Creech's *Walk Two Moons* successfully uses a complex narrative structure involving flashbacks and a story within a story. *The View from Saturday* by E. L. Konigsburg includes four short stories held together by a fifth narrative strand that ties them all together into a satisfying, cohesive whole. The inventive nature of *Maniac Magee* and *Holes*, which both blend fantasy and reality, has already been mentioned; in addition *Holes* uses a parallel plot structure, similar in complexity to *Walk Two Moons*. In what will quite likely be the most enduring Newbery Medal winner since *A Wrinkle in Time*, another science fiction title, *The Giver*, is the first committee selection to have an open ending allowing for more than one interpretation, a feature unsettling to many children and adults. Interestingly, Lowry was awarded the Newbery twice in a four-year period—for *Number the Stars* in 1990 and for *The Giver* in 1994—and the two books couldn't differ more from each other.

While these books show a great diversity of style and structure, they lack ethnic diversity in their authorship, a charge that is frequently leveled at the Newbery committee in these years of concern for multicultural literature. We must keep in mind, however, that the committee cannot award books that do not exist. The lack of ethnic diversity in the titles selected is more a reflection of what does—and doesn't—get published than it is of shortcomings on the part of the Newbery committee itself. Indeed, when one takes the honor books into consideration, specifically the titles written by Christopher Paul Curtis, Virginia Hamilton, Patricia C. McKissack, Walter Dean Myers, and Laurence Yep, one finds that 10 percent of Newbery selections were written by people of color, compared with 2 percent of the average number of overall titles during these years. It's clear that the field at large is hungry for more literary diversity: in 2000 there was a standing ovation at the press conference where it was announced that the Newbery Award was going to African-American author Christopher Paul Curtis for *Bud, Not Buddy*. Curtis was the first author of color to win the award since 1976.

Common themes and features will no doubt emerge as we begin to look at the titles individually in chronological order. *Sarah, Plain and Tall* by Patricia MacLachlan was a choice that was met with widespread approval at the time it was announced. A mere fifty-eight pages long, the book is at first glance notable for its accessibility to younger as well as to reluctant readers. The strength of this spare narrative lies in the sense of longing that comes through the voice of its young protagonist, Anna, who lives with her father and younger brother, Caleb, on the prairie some time in the late nineteenth century. They are anxiously awaiting Sarah, their father's mail-order bride, who the children hope will take the place of the mother they never really knew. Almost as soon as she arrives, the children begin to fear that she will leave them. They can see that Sarah herself is longing for something: her home by the sea back in Maine. When considered as a work of historical fiction, *Sarah, Plain and Tall* may strike readers as both idealized and nostalgic. But to expect the book to provide a realistic look at the hard lives of pioneer women is to miss the point. The story itself is more a lyrical exploration of two deeply felt desires: that of a child for a mother and of a woman for a home, both interconnected and subtly played out in the everyday interactions among the characters.

Sid Fleischman's *The Whipping Boy* offers another period piece of sorts, set in a hazy past of feudal kingdoms when bad guys were bad, good guys were good, and nasty little princes were always capable of reform. The hallmarks of this episodic novel are Fleischman's rollicking plot and biting wit. As he plays with old devices—the spoiled prince, the bumbling kidnappers, and mistaken identity—he lets readers know that he is playing with them. In many ways *The Whipping Boy* is a good old-fashioned children's novel in the best sense of the term. Ironically, this very fact makes it stand out as a Newbery Award winner—they just don't make children's books like they used to.

Nor do they make biographies like they used to. In his afterward to *Lincoln: A Photobiography,* Russell Freedman observes that Abraham Lincoln is the most written about figure in American history, both for children and adults. This makes the task of biographer all the more challenging: what can be said about Lincoln that hasn't been said before? Freedman's approach is original for two reasons. His use of documentary photographs do more than merely illustrate his text—they elucidate—and his intent in writing a biography for children is clearly to show the human side of Lincoln, the man behind the legend. These two approaches become perfectly harmonious here, as the photographs continually serve to show reality, whether it be the dead bodies of soldiers sprawled on a Civil War battlefield or the growing signs of strain on Lincoln's face in a series of photographs taken from 1861 to 1864. Thus the birth of the photobiography.

When Paul Fleischman won the Newbery Medal for *Joyful Noise: Poems for Two Voices,* he made Newbery history for a simple reason. His father, Sid Fleischman, had won the award just two years earlier, making them the first father and son medalists. He also made Newbery history for a complicated reason. As mentioned earlier, *Joyful Noise* stands as perhaps the most unusual book to have ever been awarded, certainly a risky choice on the part of the selection committee. It's daring not just because the book is a collection of poems, or because these poems are about insects, or even because they are specifically written for two voices; it's daring because the book must be read aloud in order for it to be fully understood as a work of art. In effect, it is the first work of oral literature to win the award.

Like *Sarah, Plain and Tall* and *The Whipping Boy,* Lois Lowry's *Number the Stars* is a relatively easy-to-read historical novel. Unlike the other two, however, it is set in a clearly defined time and place—Copenhagen, Denmark, in the midst of World War II. Annemarie Johansen and her family get caught up in the Danish Resistance Movement after the Nazi occupation begins to threaten the lives of their family friends, the Rosens. Told through the innocent eyes of a ten-year-old girl, *Number the Stars* provides a gripping story for young readers, with details of time and place subtly woven into the narrative for necessary context. Throughout, Lowry skillfully uses metaphors and familiar literary allusions that can be easily understood and even discovered independently by inexperienced readers. Perhaps above all other Newbery winners of its time, *Number the Stars* offers the strongest combination of accessibility, child appeal, and literary depth—a feat that should not be taken lightly.

When Jerry Spinelli's *Maniac Magee* came bursting onto the literary scene, it was recognized, albeit slowly at first, for being quite unlike any other children's book ever published. Spinelli succeeded in creating a mythic hero for today's children in the character of young Jeffrey Magee, nicknamed "Maniac" by the neighborhood kids. An orphan who lives largely on his own in the streets, Maniac quickly achieves legendary status for abilities that can be only fully appreciated by a child: he excels at every sport, he can outwit—and more importantly outrun—all his enemies and, most amazingly, he can untie any knot. Maniac also has the ability to travel back and forth between the east side and west side of town (divided, not coincidentally, by Homer Street) and to be accepted by both black and white kids, although somewhat grudgingly. Spinelli may fall short in a simplistic portrayal of race relations that sometimes borders on the stereotypical, but in the end *Maniac Magee* offers a good example of a flawed book that's much more interesting than a perfect one. Like its namesake, *Maniac Magee* has heart.

Where would children's literature be without its heart-wrenching dog stories? *Shiloh* by Phyllis Reynolds Naylor is the first in a successful trilogy of novels about a contemporary rural boy who secretly hides a mistreated hunting dog from the abusive neighbor who owns it. Marty's growing sense of guilt about his own continual lying comes into conflict with his concern and compassion for the dog. Oddly enough, in its tone *Shiloh* feels more like a historical novel than *Sarah, Plain and Tall* or *The Midwife's Apprentice*; its modern references are frequently jarring. The difficult moral choices that Marty faces, however, are timeless.

Grief and loss are the central focus of Cynthia Rylant's short novel *Missing May*. By age twelve, Summer has already suffered more loss than most folks do in a lifetime. She was orphaned as a young child and passed from relative to relative until she was finally taken in by her Uncle Ob and Aunt May. But after Aunt May dies, Uncle Ob sinks into a depression so deep that Summer feels she has lost him, too. Her attempts to raise her uncle's spirits fail miserably; only a false hope that he will be able to contact May through a spiritualist in a neighboring county keeps Uncle Ob going. Rylant's quirky, original characters and lyrical style give this otherwise depressing story its power. More than anything else, *Missing May* seems to be a product of its time, an era in which many novels for children and young adults featured children in relentlessly sad situations, abandoned by adults, forging ahead on their own.

Lois Lowry's *The Giver* is clearly the masterpiece of this era, not only within the small group of Newbery winners but within the much wider of field of late-twentieth century children's literature in general. From the beginning, readers are so closely aligned with the point of view of the book's twelve-year-old protagonist, Jonas, that they are as shocked as he is to learn that the futuristic utopia in which he lives is not all it's cracked up to be. When Jonas receives his life "assignment" and is apprenticed to the Giver, who cares for all of his society's cultural memory, he experiences both pain and pleasure for the first time, two feelings that had been obliterated in the sterile utopia in which he had been raised. Within this context, Lowry raises some deep philosophical and ethical concepts for young readers to think about: what happens when a society strives to make the entire world a safe place? Would such a world even be desirable? The author provides no answers. Even the book's ending is open to interpretation, challenging readers to make up their own minds. As soon as it was published, *The Giver* became both a critical and a popular success. It has not been without its detractors, however, as some adults find the book disturbing. Not surprisingly, these adults are generally the very ones who firmly believe that the world can be made completely safe, at least for children.

Walk Two Moons, a fine serio-comic novel by Sharon Creech, has also proved to be a critical and popular success. On a cross-country car trip to find her absent mother, thirteen-year-old Sal entertains her eccentric grandparents with a story about her best friend, Phoebe. Until the very end of her story, neither Sal nor her readers realize that she is actually revealing much more about herself and what she knows about her mother's disappearance. The parallel plot structure is surprisingly accessible to children due to Creech's meticulous crafting of this story within a story, and her strong characterization of Sal, Gram, and Gramps is especially memorable.

The main character of *The Midwife's Apprentice* by Karen Cushman is a nameless orphan girl derisively called Dung Beetle by the folks in the small medieval English town in which she lives. After hiring herself out to a midwife in exchange for room and board, Beetle eventually establishes her own identity and finds the strength to stand proudly on her own two feet. In spite of the seriousness of her circumstances and the earthy details of the hard lives led by working people in the Middle Ages, Cushman's concise, pithy novel is filled with humor, particularly in clever turns of phrase.

Like *Walk Two Moons*, E. L. Konigsburg's *View from Saturday* successfully employs a more complex structure than we typically see in books for children. Four sixth graders, who call themselves the Souls, all seem to be unlikely choices for Epiphany Middle School's Academic Bowl team coached by Mrs. Olinski; however, each of the four has a story to tell that reveals exactly how they are interconnected and why each one is a perfect teammate. Indeed the novel's structure echoes the connections among the students and their teacher, while Konigsburg's wry commentary throughout brings the story about as close to social satire as children's books ever get.

Out of the Dust by Karen Hesse is one of the most distinctive selections ever made by a Newbery committee. Few books for children have ever made such a dramatic use of setting, which in this case is rural Oklahoma during 1934 and 1935, the height of the Dustbowl. Fourteen-year-old Billie Jo's first-person account of their day-to-day struggles is told through a series of short free-verse poems, each one offering insight into raw human emotions. Although each poem stands on its own as a starkly beautiful piece of writing, the true power of *Out of the Dust* comes in the cumulative effect as the poems are read, one after another, and Billie Jo's story unfolds.

It seems only fitting that the last book to win the Newbery Medal in the 1900s would turn out to be one of the best. In fact, *Holes* combines the outstanding qualities of some of its immediate predecessors: it has the child appeal and accessibility of *Number the Stars*, the structural complexity of *Walk Two Moons*, the over-the-top humor of *The Whipping Boy*, the wry social commentary of *The View from Saturday*, the mythic proportions of *Maniac Magee*, and the intellectual depth of *The Giver*. Yet it is a complete original. The intricately plotted story follows the fate of Stanley Yelnats, wrongly accused of a crime and sent to juvenile work camp where he is assigned to dig a hole each day, five feet wide and five feet deep. "It builds character," he is told by the people in charge. Stanley, however, begins to suspect that he and his fellow prisoners are actually being forced to dig for another purpose—they're looking for something. How Stanley's present-day story intertwines with his own family's past, a parallel plot to which readers alone are privy, is humorously intriguing and emotionally satisfying. Ultimately *Holes* deals with two very child-centered concerns: justice and loyalty. It is far too early to make any predictions about the place of this novel in the context of children's literature. Less than a year after its publication, however, it seems destined for greatness.

Like *Holes*, Christopher Paul Curtis's *Bud, Not Buddy* brings some much-needed humor to the field of contemporary children's literature. And like *Holes*, Curtis blends humor with some serious social issues as ten-year-old Bud Caldwell journeys through Depression-era Michigan in search of the father he's never known. Bud's charming, hyperbolic first-person narrative adds levity to what might otherwise be a somber tale. Here we have an abandoned child, an orphan, with a happy-go-lucky attitude that stems from both innocence and experience. Bud is a streetwise kid who keeps an ever-growing list of rules to live by, based on some of the blows he's been dealt. No one is going to pull a fast one on Bud. But, in spite of his wordliness, Bud is still childlike, willing to place his trust in strangers who just want to make his journey a little bit easier.

Looking at the selections of the past fifteen years as a whole, two features in particular stand out. The first is that children's books in general, as reflected in the Newbery Medal winners, seem to have truly come of age by the end of the twentieth century. Not only has the quality of writing steadily improved over time, they have become structurally more complex and imaginative. Children's authors are not just being allowed to take more inventive approaches to their writing, they are consistently being awarded for it.

But in the midst of all this creativity, one can't help but notice the second outstanding feature in children's books at the end of the millennium, equally evident in Newbery Medal winners and children's books in general: the vast majority deal with children who have been abandoned by their parents or even by society at large. While orphans have always played a significant role in the children's literature of the past hundred years, in earlier times they struggled to find a home, a family, and a happy ending. In our more recent literature, however, we see more and more child characters bypassing adults completely as they strive for self-reliance and opt for independence. Since we cannot overlook the fact that children's books are created, critiqued, and awarded by adults, one can only wonder what message we're giving to children through books. Are we telling them that we adults have made such a mess of things we are giving up completely and passing the torch directly to the children? That children, once seen as our hope for the future, are now being seen as our hope for the present as well? Are we finding the strength to tell our children the truth by admitting that as adults we may have failed them? Only time will tell. For now, we can only hope that the outlook for the twenty-first century is not as bleak as it appears to be in children's books.

The Caldecott Medal 1986

The Polar Express

written and illustrated by
Chris Van Allsburg

published by
Houghton Mifflin, 1985

Horn Book Review

Just when it seemed that all possible variations on Christmas motifs had been explored, Chris Van Allsburg has created a haunting, original fantasy, sparkling with the essence of childlike wonder yet overlaid with the enigmatic intensity that has become his hallmark. Full-color illustrations accompany an economical narrative, his best writing to date, in recounting the adventures of a boy who, one Christmas Eve, boards the mysterious Polar Express, which materializes after the townfolk have fallen asleep. Bearing a full complement of children, the special train rushes through snow-shrouded landscapes to the North Pole, "a huge city standing alone at the top of the world, filled with factories where every Christmas toy was made." There, in the city's center, he is selected by Santa Claus to receive the first gift of Christmas. Although he could choose any of the myriad delights surrounding him, he asks only for one silver bell from a reindeer's harness. The wish granted, Santa departs on his traditional journey, and the children board the train for their return home. At that crucial moment the boy discovers that the bell has slipped through a hole in his bathrobe pocket, leaving him without the evidence to convince his more skeptical friends that Santa Claus does exist. But, on Christmas Day, the boy finds the bell under the tree and discovers its peculiar properties: only children— or adults who still believe—can hear its silver sounds. As in *The Wreck of the Zephyr* (Houghton), Van Allsburg uses reminiscence as a narrative form; it is a particularly effective device in this story, for it makes the implicit theme, found in the concluding sentences, logical and allows the necessary breadth for the sophistication of the art. The illustrations, like the text, show further development in his ability to work within the constraints of the picture-book format. As always, the forms are sculptured, the perspectives as dazzling as they are audacious, the colors rich and elegant, the use of light and shadow masterful. The landscapes are dreams made real, larger than life, awe-inspiring but never frightening—like images conjured up by the warm firelight on a cold winter's night. What is most exciting, however, is the interpretation of the characters: Santa Claus is a magnificent figure rooted in myth, rather than in the clichés of Madison Avenue; the elves, too, are folkloric beings, not diminutive, coy servants; and the children, each lovingly depicted as an individual, are charming because they convey universal emotions—not because they are falsely cherubic. Text and pictures are absolutely essential to one another; together they convey an inner vision which is splendid yet accessible to child audiences. An outstanding example of the picture-story genre, this book is one which proves that excellence and popularity are not mutually exclusive elements. It does not compromise artistic integrity, yet it reaches out to children—and to those who remain children at heart.—*Mary M. Burns*

Booklist Review

There's always been an element of mystery in Van Allsburg's books, and this one is no exception. Here, a young boy awaiting Santa's sleigh on Christmas Eve is instead summoned aboard the Polar Express, a larger-than-life train bound for the North Pole. Upon arrival, the boy sees "a huge city standing alone at the top of the world, filled with factories where every Christmas toy was made." The occasion for the visit, the boy learns, is that Santa will pick one child out of the train-load of youngsters to receive the first gift of Christmas. The narrator is the one picked, and he wishes, not for something from Santa's bag, but for one silver bell from Santa's sleigh. St. Nick obliges, and the boy soon returns home. There he finds that the bell makes "the most beautiful sound my sister and I had ever heard," but no adult is able to hear it. In fact, as years pass, it remains audible only to the narrator: "the bell still rings for me as it does for all who truly believe." The story unfolds alongside deep-toned, double-page paintings as full of mystery as the story itself. Darkened colors, soft edges, and the glow of illuminated snow flurries create a dreamlike adventure that is haunting even as it entertains. An imaginative, engrossing tale of Christmas magic.—*Denise M. Wilms*

1986 Caldecott Acceptance Speech

Chris Van Allsburg

The first book I remember reading is probably the same book many people my age recall as their first. It was profusely illustrated and re-counted the adventures and conflicts of its three protagonists, Dick, Jane, and Spot. Actually, the lives of this trio were not all that interest-ing. A young reader's reward for struggling through those syllables at the bottom of the page was to discover that Spot got a bath. Not exactly an exciting revelation. Especially since you'd already seen Spot getting his bath in the picture at the top of the page.

The Dick, Jane, and Spot primers have gone to that bookshelf in the sky. I have, in some ways, a tender feeling toward them, so I think it's for the best. Their modern incarnation would be too painful to look at. Dick and Jane would have had their names changed to Jason and Jennifer. Faithful Spot would be transformed into an Afghan hound, and the syllables at the bottom of the page would reveal that the chil-dren were watching MTV.

In third grade my class paid its first visit to the school library as pro-spective book borrowers. It was on this occasion that we learned about the fascinating Dewey decimal system. None of us really understood this principle of cataloging books, but we were inclined to favor it. Any system named Dewey was all right with us. We looked forward to hear-ing about the Huey and Louie decimal systems too.

The book I checked out on my first visit was the biography of Babe Ruth. I started reading it at school and continued reading it at home. I read till dinner and opened the book again after dessert, finally tak-ing it to bed with me. The story of Babe Ruth was an interesting one, but I don't think it was as compelling as that constant reading suggests. There was something else happening: I just simply did not know when to stop, or why. Having grown up with television, I was accustomed to watching something until it was finished. I assumed that as long as the book was there I should read it to the end. The idea of setting the book aside uncompleted just didn't occur to me.

This somewhat obsessive approach to reading manifested itself again—during the summer after third grade. My neighbor had a collec-tion of every Walt Disney comic book ever published. I took my little wagon to his house and hauled every issue back to my bedroom. For a solid week I did nothing but read about Pluto, Mickey, Donald, and Daisy. It was spooky. By the sixth day they'd become quite real to me and were turning up in my dreams. After I returned the comics I felt very lonely, as if a group of lively houseguests had left suddenly.

As years have passed my taste in literature has changed. I do, however, still have obsessive reading habits. I pore over every word on the cereal box at breakfast, often more than once. You can ask me anything about Shredded Wheat. I also spend more time in the bathroom than necessary, determined to keep up with my *New Yorker* subscription.

It seems strange now, considering my susceptibility to the power of the printed word, that I'd been reading for more than twenty years before I thought about writing. I had, by that time, staked out visual art as my form of self-expression. But my visual art was and is very narrative. I feel fortunate that I've become involved with books as another opportunity for artistic expression.

Over the years that have passed since my first book was published, a question I've been asked often is, "Where do your ideas come from?" I've given a variety of answers to this question, such as: I steal them from the neighborhood kids; I send away for them by mail order; and, they are beamed to me from outer space.

It's not really my intention to be rude or smart-alecky. The fact is, I don't know where my ideas come from. Each story I've written starts out as a vague idea that seems to be going nowhere, then suddenly materializes as a completed concept. It almost seems like a discovery, as if the story was always there. The few elements I start out with are actually dues. If I figure out what they mean, I can discover the story that's waiting.

When I began thinking about what became *The Polar Express*, I had a single image in mind: a young boy sees a train standing still in front of his house one night. The boy and I took a few different trips on that train, but we did not, in a figurative sense, go anywhere. Then I headed north, and I got the feeling that this time I'd picked the right direction, because the train kept rolling all the way to the North Pole. At that point, the story seemed literally to present itself. Who lives at the North Pole? Santa. When would the perfect time for a visit be? Christmas Eve. What happens on Christmas Eve at the North Pole? Undoubtedly a ceremony of some kind, a ceremony requiring a child, delivered by a train that would have to be named the Polar Express.

These story elements are, of course, merely events. A good story uses the description of events to reveal some kind of moral or psychological premise. I am not aware, as I develop a story, what the premise is. When I started *The Polar Express*, I thought I was writing about a train trip, but the story was actually about faith and the desire to believe in something. It's an intriguing process. I know if I'd set out with the goal of writing about that, I'd still be holding a pencil over a blank sheet of paper.

Fortunately, or perhaps I should say necessarily, that premise is consistent with my own feelings, especially when it comes to accepting fantastic propositions like Santa Claus. Santa is our culture's only mythic figure, truly believed in by a large segment of the population. It's a fact that most of the true believers are under eight years old, and that's a pity. The rationality we all embrace as adults makes believing in the fantastic difficult if not impossible. Lucky are the children who know there is a jolly fat man in a red suit who pilots a flying sleigh. We should envy them. And we should envy the people who are so certain Martians will land in their backyard that they keep a loaded Polaroid camera by the back door. The inclination to believe in the fantastic may strike some as a failure in logic or gullibility, but it's really a gift. A world that might have Bigfoot and the Loch Ness monster is clearly superior to one that definitely does not.

I don't mean to give the impression that my own sense of what is possible is not shaped by rational, analytical thought. As much as I'd like to meet the tooth fairy on an evening walk, I don't really believe it can happen.

When I was seven or eight, on the night before Easter, my mother accidentally dropped a basket of candy outside my bedroom door. I understood what the sound was and what it meant. I heard my mother, in a loud whisper, trying unsuccessfully to keep the cats from batting jelly beans across the wooden floor. It might have been the case that the Easter Bunny had already become an iffy proposition for me. In any event, this was just the moment the maturing skeptic in me was waiting for. I gained the truth, but I paid a heavy price for it. The Easter Bunny died that night.

The application of logical or analytical thought may be the enemy of belief in the fantastic, but it is not, for me, a liability in its illustration. When I conceived of the North Pole in *The Polar Express*, it was logic that insisted it be a vast collection of factories. I don't see this as a whim of mine or even as an act of imagination. How could it look any other way, given the volume of toys produced there every year?

I do not find that illustrating a story has the same quality of discovery as writing it. As I consider a story I see it quite clearly.

Illustrating is simply a matter of drawing something I've already experienced in my mind's eye. Because I see the story unfold as if it were on film, the challenge is deciding precisely which moment should be illustrated and from which point of view.

There are disadvantages to seeing the images so clearly. The actual execution can seem redundant. And the finished work is always disappointing because my imagination exceeds the limits of my skills.

A fantasy of mine is to be tempted by the devil with a miraculous machine, a machine that could be hooked up to my brain and instantly produce finished art from the images in my mind. I'm sure it's the devil who'd have such a device, because it would devour the artistic soul, or half of it anyway. Conceiving of something is only part of the creative process. Giving life to the conception is the other half. The struggle to master a medium, whether it's words, notes, paint, or marble, is the heroic part of making art. Still, if any of you run into the devil and he's got his machine, give him my name. I would, at least, like to get a demonstration.

An award does not change the quality of a book. I'm acutely aware of deficiencies in all of my work. I sometimes think I'd like to do everything I've ever done over and get it right. But I know that a few years after I'd want to do everything over a third time.

This award carries with it a kind of wisdom for someone like me. It suggests that the success of art is not dependent on its nearness to perfection but its power to communicate. Things can be right without being perfect.

Though this is the second Caldecott Medal I've received, believe me, it is no less meaningful than the first. Being awarded the Caldecott is an experience to which one cannot become jaded. I am certain of this and stand ready to endure any efforts to prove otherwise.

I would like to thank these people at Houghton Mifflin for their support, encouragement, and, occasionally, commiseration. My editor, Walter Lorraine, and Peggy Hogan, Sue Sherman, and Donna Baxter.

I would also like to take this opportunity to thank the people here tonight who have committed themselves to getting children and books together. I know that if it weren't for your efforts my readers would be not only small in size but in number too.

And finally I'd like to thank Mae Benne and the other members of the Caldecott Committee for this great honor. I accept it as both praise and encouragement.

Chris Van Allsburg

David Macaulay

Chris Van Allsburg

In 1982 when Chris Van Allsburg won his first Caldecott Medal for *Jumanji* (Houghton), David Macaulay composed the following biographical sketch. Not only is Chris's art consistent, so is his life. Since his success has changed so little of that life, we are reprinting the biography, with one or two factual changes, for those who have not had a chance to see it.

When Chris won the Caldecott Medal, I heard about it first from his wife, Lisa. That wasn't surprising. As long as we've been friends, Chris has never actually announced any of his triumphs. The information either seeps out inadvertently during a conversation, or it comes directly, with great pride and enthusiasm, from Lisa. Chris's modesty is genuine, and it should not be confused with a lack of confidence. He knows he's good; we've all told him he's good; and more important, he knows why he's good. But there is an inevitable distrust of praise, especially when it comes so quickly.

There are certain mundane requirements of every biographical sketch, including age, place of birth, siblings, and amusing quirks. I will dispose of these as quickly as possible. They are: between thirty-four and thirty-seven, Michigan, one (female)—and a reluctance to fly. The last is bad news for Houghton Mifflin's promotional programs but good news for me because most people will never meet Chris and therefore will have little choice but to believe what I tell them.

Looking back over *The Garden of Abdul Gasazi*, *Jumanji*, and *Ben's Dream* (all Houghton), I think it is clear that houses big and small have been the main sets around and inside of which Chris's dramas unfold. Just as these houses are essential to his tales, so the Van Allsburg house is essential to mine. One fourteen is not an imposing edifice. At first glance it might even appear normal. Architecturally, it is just another American interpretation of a slightly Scandinavian-possibly-Bavarian woodman's cottage built just before 1920 by a neo-Victorian. In short, it is Carl Larsson's house bronzed.

Only gradually does one become aware of the house's true character and, more important, of the true characters of its inhabitants. There is a well-maintained 4-H sign by the front door. As far as I know, it is the only 4-H sign displayed so prominently on a house in Providence. This isn't surprising, considering the size of the city's farming population. At the other side of the front door is a bell which has been out of order for so long that even the most recent handwritten "knock" sign has abandoned the aging Scotch Tape for better things. This is an uncharacteristic detail, given Chris's concern for order, but it does display a sort of reassuring fallibility,

Inside the house a large stuffed raven and a smaller stuffed crow perch atop the glass-doored bookcase which houses the seldom warm television. The glassy-eyed corvus corax often sports a miniature Red Sox batting helmet indicative of Chris's interest in athletics and concern for the welfare of animals. On the mantel are two carved giraffes, a lithograph of a lion, and a bust of Dante. These are indicative of Chris's love of classical literature and admiration for exotic wild animals. Cecil, a Siamese cat of almost human persuasion, is the only living exotic animal residing at 114. Other shelves proudly display the growing collection of cast-metal Statues of Liberty and bulldogs indicative of Chris's patriotism and curious interest in pugnacious domestic animals.

Also on display are four pieces of Chris's sculpture. The first is a coffee cup falling off a cylindrical cabinet, as if nudged by some unseen elbow. The contents of the cup pour permanently over the rim because the cup, the coffee, and the cabinet are all made meticulously out of wood. In the dining room are three bronze cones. Each is caught at a particular moment of impact with an invisible missile, and each rests on a turned oak base inset with a marble top. The description of the impact is so convincing, you can almost hear it, not to mention feel the rush of the wind.

The largest room in the house is the recently completed absolutely-from-scratch-no-old-materials-used-authentic-late-1930s kitchen—complete with red-and-white checkered tile band above the counter and a raised four-seater booth. Second only to his fear of flying is Chris's fear that the first thing any new owner of the house would do is modernize the kitchen.

The second largest room in the house is upstairs, and it is the studio. It is the modest sky-lit space roughly seven by thirty feet in which Alan P. Mitz, Abdul G., Judy, Peter, and Ben, and—over Cecil's objections—Fritz first appeared on paper. The calm of the studio is gently reinforced either by the mellow sounds of 103 or the more classical sound of 89.5 on Chris's FM dial.

It is here on most days that Chris and Cecil can be found—Chris hunched over the drawing board, Cecil hanging by his front paws from a door frame. Occasionally, Cecil joins Chris at the drawing board. Although he rarely gives his impressions of a drawing, he has been known to leave his impressions on a drawing. In those instances the serenity of studio life is shattered. Cecil, having been temporarily and unexpectedly airborne, continues to watch from a distance, as his master and trainer attempts to remove, or at least blend, a combination of paw print and claw mark into the fragile surface of the drawing.

In no time all is forgotten and forgiven. Once again, particles of graphite or pastel ride the currents dancing in the beams of light which find their way past the shades on the skylights. After a particularly demanding and gratifying stretch of drawing, the sounds of the radio are often replaced by the sounds of live music. Chris is a self-taught musician of little promise who owns, among other instruments, a tenor and an alto recorder. In order to play both the lead line and the accompanying harmony he has learned to play the instruments simultaneously with his nose. It is an unusual and slightly unsettling sight.

When he's not in his studio, Chris is probably at school or asleep. Professor Van Allsburg teaches a number of classes in the illustration department at the Rhode Island School of Design. In addition to his rigorous drawing courses with their emphasis on careful observation and technical proficiency, he also offers a class called "Design Your Own Country." Students are required to produce a number of visual documents, including posters and postage stamps, which illustrate and in effect prove the existence of their own imagined countries. What the sneaky devil has done in the guise of play, is introduce students to the two main elements of illustration—elements so clearly visible in his own work. The first is the use of imagination—these countries must not only be created but also understood in some depth by their creators. The second is the development of technical skills without which the students would not be able to communicate and support their inventions.

Chris is a demanding teacher and is respected for it. The standards he sets for his students are high—but not as high as those he sets for himself. If Chris has a competitive streak, it is evident only in his determination to make each of his drawings better than the one that preceded it. It is perhaps his abhorrence of mediocrity that stands out above all his other virtues and quirks. His refusal to accept anything of inferior quality or of tainted integrity is as evident in his work as it is in all other aspects of his life, even including how much cheese one should expect when one orders a double cheeseburger. For Chris no detail is insignificant, no technical problem insurmountable, no challenge to the imagination too great. And no biographical sketch is entirely accurate.

The Newbery Medal 1986

Sarah, Plain and Tall

written by
Patricia MacLachlan

published by
Harper, 1985

Horn Book Review

With her wonderfully eccentric characters, her preoccupation with intergenerational affinities, and her calm, lucid prose, the author reached
a high point in the artlessly crafted *Unclaimed Treasures* (Harper). Now
she tells a much more simple, but no less subtle, story of a motherless
pioneer family living on the great prairie, which "reached out and
touched the places where the sky came down." Anna vividly recalls her
mother, who died just after her young brother Caleb was born; with
sadness and yearning she tells the questioning little boy about the con-
tented old days when their parents sang songs—"every-single-day." Then,
quite suddenly, mild, gentle Papa announces that he has advertised in
the newspapers for a wife; and all the way from the coast of Maine
comes a brisk response. Soon the lonely children, full of quiet hope,
await the arrival of Sarah; "I am plain and tall," she wrote to Papa, and
"tell them I sing." But Sarah—strong, versatile, and vibrant—turns out,
at first, to be ominously homesick. Some writers might have been
tempted to flesh out the story into a full-length novel, but the brief,
well-rounded tale has its own satisfying completeness.—*Ethel L. Heins*

Booklist Review

A near-perfect miniature novel that fulfills the ideal of different levels of
meaning for children and adults. Two children, motherless since the
younger one's birth, are waiting on the prairie for the arrival of their possible new stepmother, who has answered their father's newspaper adver-
tisement for a wife. Their loneliness and hope are tangibly detailed in
expectant preparations for her arrival, among them several letters, both

homely and funny, that are exchanged between the family and Sarah ("I will come by train. I will wear a yellow bonnet. I am plain and tall"). The simplicity of plot, style, and characterization is deceptive. Sarah proves not only plain and tall, but also kind and good, coming like water to three people thirsty for someone caring. Yet Sarah misses her Maine coast, and there are uncomfortable tensions between the children's well-meaning father and his strong-willed bride-to-be. The dialogue is natural, varied but always vivid, ranging from scenes of soft singing to a romp in the cow pond to a raging storm. When Sarah comes back from town, a trip that the children fear signals her permanent departure, the reader is as deeply moved to happiness as the family itself. "Soon there will be a wedding. Papa says that when the preacher asks if he will have Sarah for his wife he will answer, "Ayuh." Poignant but never sentimental, this is a worthy successor to Wilder's Little House books and a prime choice for reading aloud.—*Betsy Hearne*

1986 Newbery Acceptance Speech
Patricia MacLachlan

There should be words more eloquent than thank you, words that communicate the great satisfaction I feel that the Newbery Committee has chosen *Sarah, Plain and Tall* (Harper) for the Newbery Medal. One of my children informed me rather pointedly that there are close to a hundred words for snow in Eskimo, implying that I, too, ought to be able to find precise, meaningful words of my own. However, "thank you" seems just right for this book that is as plain and simple as "thank you." And because I have never forgotten my third-grade teacher's rule that every story must have a beginning, a middle, and an end—and I suppose a speech must follow the same rule—I would like to add my appreciation here for those people who have, in one way or another, had great influence on my beginnings as a writer.

Thank you, Craig Virden, for bringing out both the worst and the best in me and for knowing that both parts translate into words. Thank you, Jane Yolen, for luring me into the world of children's literature. Every writer should have a loving reader who has the courage to write both "I love this" and "Ugh" on the same page. Thank you, Natalie Babbitt, for offering bare-boned advice and honest and true friendship. When I asked Natalie what I should say today, she replied, "Say anything. Just don't natter on." That is both advice and friendship. A child reader offered the same wisdom when he wrote,

"Congratulations. I know you have to write a speech. Try, if you can, not to be boring." Last, thank you to my extended family at Harper & Row, particularly Charlotte Zolotow, who has in ways both wise and sly allowed and encouraged me to pull this story out into the light where I could see it well enough to write it.

I wanted to write a beautiful speech full of truths that would astonish you all, and I set about reading the writings of others, those who have won a medal and those who have not. After all, we are only a breath apart. The truths, I found, have all been told, spoken by thoughtful, articulate writers and lovers of children's literature. "Why is an idea always better in your head than on paper?" a small boy once asked me. Wise child. Edith Wharton, I told him, said the same thing when she wrote "I dream of an eagle, I give birth to a hummingbird." If that is the way of books, it is just as true of the writing of this speech, which is every bit as difficult to write as any book. With the fervent hope that there is not one thing wrong with a hummingbird, then, that is what you'll be—a hummingbird of a speech. It has also occurred to me that it would be unseemly to write a Newbery acceptance that is longer than the book for which the award is given.

My daughter, Emily, at age five said what is closest to what I feel now—children often do—when on the hottest of summer days she put on winter clothes to go out to play. "Why?" I asked her. "It's much too warm." "Because," she told me matter-of-factly, her hand on the door, "wearing these clothes makes me feel joyish." A child's truth. Wearing the clothes of the Newbery makes me feel joyish, too, though I'll admit the outfit is made up of layers, many of which are well worn, some new and unfamiliar, like gold lamé draped on a dime-store dummy. And although those who know me well know that I am uncomfortable talking about myself, except after sodium pentothal or several glasses of wine, I would like to tell you about the roots of this story, in the process of which you will probably know more about me than you care to know.

When I learned that I had won the Newbery, it was after lunch with friends, not my best time of day, even though my fortune cookie was the only one with a prophetic message. It said: "Your talents will soon be recognized." Honest it did. I will carry it with me always so that when I am in the middle of a book or a speech, where I am always convinced that I am tedious or dull or self-conscious, I will remember that once upon a time I was talented.

My best time of day as a writer—not as a parent—is between five-thirty and eight in the morning, when I make what at the time seem to me to be the most startling observations. The observations, mind you, that later as I write them become as common as the odd glass of water, the coffee dregs, the garbage of the day—those things, surprise or no surprise, that are what life and literature are made up of. The sunrise and I are close friends; we are well connected. Good word, connection, for if I feel connected to the sunrise, I am even more connected to childhood. Once when I was young, I had a dream that the sun did not rise because I had overslept. Ah, the wonderful self-centeredness that is allowed, that is necessary in childhood, suspicious in adulthood. Dare I admit that I have had the same dream as an adult? You bet I do. My daughter gave me permission when she exclaimed one day, "When are we grown up anyway?" When, indeed. E. L. Konigsburg, writing in *Celebrating Children's Books* (Lothrop), confesses to the same thing after describing a trip to New York after winning the Newbery: "But because I retain this ability to see myself as the center of the universe, I can write for children. And because the adult part of me can see how absolutely ridiculous I am when I am doing it, my writings are readable." I wonder if there really is that adult part of me, for every morning as the sun comes up I crash downstairs, first one up, to clamp myself against the kitchen sink and watch the sun come up over the hills. It does not seem ridiculous. It is serious business.

At the moment that Dudley Carlson of the Newbery committee told me of the award, I was articulate and adult—you can ask her. I was, however, at that same moment touched by a curious, childlike sense of immortality, much like one of my children who asked one day if I could please see to it that he be buried standing up, as if he might one day walk right out of the situation. When I said that I would probably die before him, he did not seem terribly perturbed. These thoughts of immortality surfaced later in the week when I was being interviewed. "What would you like written on your tombstone?" asked the interviewer. I leaned forward. "Do you mean I'm going to die?" I asked. I think I was kidding. Definitely the gold lamé part of the outfit. What I remember most, what fit best, was that as I spoke to Dudley and Liz Gordon and Charlotte Zolotow, our dog, Hilly, was nosing her dish around the floor, three hours ahead of time as always. My son Jamie was waiting for me to continue an absurd, ongoing, nineteen-year-old game of who can touch whom last, which has no rules except that I lose and laugh about it and find myself lurking behind doors like a fool. My husband, Bob, was there where he had always been, and there was a red-breasted nuthatch on the bird feeder. I knew that if I called our oldest son, John, he would burst into tears of excitement. I did, and he did. And so did joyous Emily. And I thank them all, even the nuthatch who has been at the feeder ever since, for reminding me that it is the sturdy shoes that happily endure; those ground-gripper truths that reassure us that with the champagne comes tuna noodle surprise for dinner. The old dog is fed or she makes your life miserable; the familiar bank teller hands you a congratulatory flower the next morning and tells you that you're overdrawn—evidence of life, both the magic and the muck of it. After all, the muse whispers to me, you were a full-blown adult, a wife, and a mother, long before you ever became a writer. Just what is the magic—the literature or the life from which it grows?

Sarah, Plain and Tall grew out of these same experiences, what my mother used to call the heroics of a common life. When Julius Lester praises children's literature as the "literature that gives full attention to the ordinary," he echoes my parents' belief that it is the daily grace and dignity with which we survive that children most need and wish to know about in books. My parents believed in the truths of literature, and it was my mother who urged me to "read a book and find out who you are," for there are those of us who read or write to slip happily into the characters of those we'd like to be. It is, I believe, our way of getting to know the good and bad of us, rehearsing to be more humane, "revising our lives in our books," as John Gardner wrote, "so that we won't have to make the same mistakes again." My father and I played out daily scenes in the cloaks of characters, engaging in extended plots that we changed as we wished. More rehearsal. It was a safe way to bump up against life, and exciting because my father always invited questions and disagreement. Our plots could make you cry, and I don't mean tears of joy. His enthusiasm—coupled with my mother's incredible tolerance for the eccentricities and subtleties of people, particularly children—meant that I could risk being a rascal. And I was, like the horse Jack in Sarah, Plain and Tall. It is the essence of my parents' acceptance reflected in the character of Anna and Caleb's father when he complains that Jack was feisty in town. " 'Rascal,' murmured Papa, smiling, because no matter what Jack did Papa loved him."

My mother told me early on about the real Sarah, who came from the coast of Maine to the prairie to become a wife and mother to a close family member. My mother remembered her fondly. "Is that real?" demanded a schoolchild. "Just what are the facts?" This is the question most asked by children, I suppose because part of childhood is concerned with sorting out the facts from the fiction, both truths of life.

Recently in Pittsburgh I was confronted by some heretofore unknown facts. While reading some children's comments, I saw the following. Question: What is the Newbery Medal? Answer: It is for telling the best joke. It looks like a tomato. It is a tomato. Question: Who is Patricia MacLachlan? Answer: She is famous because she had a baby on the Brooklyn Bridge.

I, too, am still trying to sort out facts for myself, though with little luck. "I've noticed," said a friend recently, "that you don't pay much attention to facts. They are not," she added, "of great importance to you." I confess to this. Facts are like an oil painting which begins with a figure and soon succumbs to layers of paint so that the original is lost underneath. Facts are, for me, close to what the writer Harriet Doerr describes as memories in *Stones for Ibarra* (Viking), when she writes that "memories are like corks left out of bottles. They swell. They no longer fit." I will believe anything, fact or fiction, if it's written or told well, as Jane Yolen will tell you. She called me once to read a passage she was writing about a dragon giving birth, laying its eggs in the sand. "Tell me if this works for you," she said. After she read I was incredulous. "I didn't know dragons laid eggs," I said. "I thought they had live young." There was silence. "Patty," she said, "dragons are imaginary." Oh. "It works," I muttered.

So the fact of Sarah was there for years, though the book began, as books often do, when the past stepped on the heels of the present; or backward, when something now tapped something then. Two of my children began to prepare to leave home for college, first one, then the other. But before they left, my parents took us on a trip west to the prairie, where they and I had been born. It was a gift for all of us, for the children to see a land they had never seen, to know family they had never met, to stand on the vast North Dakota farm where my father had been born in a sod house and, as Anna observes, "the prairie reached out and touched the places where the sky came down. " Maya Angelou said recently that when Thomas Wolfe said you can't go home again, he was right. But he was also wrong, for you can't really ever leave either. It was a startling connection from the past to open the door of the granary, the only building still standing, and find a gopher filling his cheeks with grain.

But mostly it was an important and poignant connection for my mother who was, because of Alzheimer's disease, beginning to lose her memory. How splendid if memories swell like corks out of a bottle! How cruel when they diminish and disappear. First there is no more present. Then there is no past. At last there are no more words. "Words, words, words," complained a frustrated young writer in a letter to me. "Is that all writers have?" Yes and no. Sarah speaks for me and my mother, for whom there are few words left, when she writes in the book: "My brother William is a fisherman, and he tells me that when he is in the middle of a fogbound sea the water is a color for which there is no name." This is my favorite sentence in the book, and I know why. It makes an attempt to say what I have always thought and only been able to say in Sarah's voice: that words are limiting, an odd thing for a writer to say. There is an entire world, complex and layered and full, behind each word or between words, that is often present but not spoken. And it is often what is left unsaid that shapes and empowers a moment, an experience, a book. Or a life. Actors know this. Musicians know it, too.

When I began *Sarah*, I wished for several things and was granted "something unexpected." Most of all I wished to write my mother's story with spaces, like the prairie, with silences that could say what words could not. I began the story as a picture book, and it is clear to me that I wanted to wrap the land and the people as tightly as I could and hand this small piece of my mother's past to her in a package as perfect as Anna's sea stone, as Sarah's sea. But books, like children, grow and change, borrowing bits and pieces of the lives of others to help make them who and what they are. And in the end we are all there, my mother, my father, my husband, my children, and me. We gave my mother better than a piece of her past. We gave her the same that Anna and Caleb and Sarah and Jacob received—a family.

One day when my mother still had words in her, we went for a drive in the country. We talked. Suddenly my mother reached out to touch my arm. "Now who are you?" she asked. "I am your daughter," I said. "Ah," she said, leaning back and smiling, "then isn't it nice that I like you."

Now I hope you can see why I am enormously pleased and honored to accept this award for this book. Thank you.

Patricia MacLachlan
Natalie Babbitt

No one, not even those who know her well, will ever say that Patty MacLachlan can be read like a book. But if Patty were a book, one that it was my happy and difficult task to review, the project might, with all of a reviewer's syntax in full cry, go at least as far as this:

Photo credit: Paul Abdoo

PATRICIA MacLACHLAN. By Philo and Madonna Pritzkau. With annotations by Robert MacLachlan. Volume II. Unpaged. Leeds, Massachusetts: 1986. No price possible. All ages.

Patricia MacLachlan

Right at the start, a confession must be made: this reviewer hasn't read volume 1. Still, each work in a series ought to stand by itself as a satisfactory story, and that is certainly the case here. Also, once one is familiar with volume 2, it isn't hard to imagine the nature of the content of that first volume, which opens in Wyoming and brings the heroine up to the time when she begins her career as a writer. The earliest part of this continuing biography must have been as full of humor and good sense as the present volume.

The setting for this second book is Massachusetts, where the heroine moves comfortably back and forth between her home in Leeds and a second house on Cape Cod, juggling her various roles as wife, mother, and writer with grace but, thank goodness, without any annoying symptoms of "Super-Momism." Occasionally she steps out on gigs to places as various, and as remote from New England, as Ohio and her home state of Wyoming, though some are as nearby as New Hampshire and Rhode Island. On these gigs she meets and laughs it up with other writers and is relaxed and effective with workshop students and library colleagues alike. She reads her own work aloud very badly, rushing through it in an embarrassed sort of way, but there is something endearing about this that makes it impossible not to respond to her. Indeed, those few in the book who are her friends are enviable people.

It's a full life we find on these pages, with enough of the ordinary to allow the reader to identify with the heroine but enough of the extraordinary to demonstrate her very special nature, a nature not easy to describe. Putting the volume aside, the reader still hears the sound of laughter—rueful laughter sometimes, even occasionally self-deprecatory, but always sharp and to the point, always free and warm and intelligent. But—and this is important—though the laughter lingers, it would be a mistake to say that Patricia MacLachlan is only a work of humor.

The book is far more than that. Humor is woven into all its parts, but there is gentleness, too, revealed primarily in excerpts from her work as a writer. And there is great thoughtfulness—ruminations on connections and interconnections, the probing of webs new and ancient, woven by generations of family. The heroine can see how, when one strand is touched, another distant one will quiver. And these ruminations and probings are by no means always lighthearted. There is irony in them and a healthy suspicion of sentimentality. If you want a book that sidesteps, glosses over, moves with a mincing step through its plot development, you had better look elsewhere. But if you demand a story that is honest, human, and evocative, you will find it here.

At the close of this volume, where the heroine is awarded a great prize for her work as a writer, the reader is filled with delight and satisfaction and can see clearly the logic and even the inevitability of such a climax.

Volume 3 is already in progress. There is every reason to expect that it will be as accomplished, engrossing, and full of measured optimism as the one just published. Patricia MacLachlan is a rare story. May there be many, many volumes.

A Hypothetical Dilemma

Robert MacLachlan

It is Saturday. I am sitting in the family room, thinking. The family room was once the woodshed of this two-hundred-year-old farmhouse. It is now pine paneled and carpeted, but one of its four doors opens to the original three-holer, still intact under the vacuum cleaner, boxes of outgrown toys, and other accumulations of family living.

In the same room Patty and our son Jamie are playing football: real football, vigorous football. She shoves him and grabs the ball. Jamie can make a shrill whistle noise with his voice. "I hate your whistle," Patty yells. "I hate your rules, too. You cheat when I'm ahead." She shoves the football into his chest and backs his six-foot frame onto the couch, where they both collapse. Jamie is breathless with laughter.

Because this house is a saltbox, the upstairs bathroom has a slanty ceiling and a short wall. There is a bookcase built into this wall, right over the radiator. The bookcase is always full to overflowing. Usually the magazines end up on the floor. Back issues of the *Horn Book Magazine* have been in the bathroom for years. From time to time I read them, so I know that sometimes a spouse is asked to write about the Newbery Medal winner. Now I am sitting in the family room, wondering how I will be able to convey the true essence of this lady football player, whose stories, after twenty readings, can still make me laugh. Will I say that I cannot read the first chapter of *Sarah* and keep dry eyes? Maybe I should start a file folder of ideas in case I am asked. I get a pad.

Friends, I write. Patty seems to have friends everywhere. A dozen of them appeared with lots of champagne barely four hours after the Newbery announcement. I remember her fortieth birthday party. There were nearly sixty people there, all Patty's close friends, yet most of the guests knew only a handful of the others. I guess that's diversity. In the process of researching an article on Patty, a reporter—who is also a friend—interviewed a number of people around the country. "Everyone seems to love you. Don't you have any enemies?" she asked plaintively. No enemies that I know of, I think to myself. Everyone truly seems to love her.

The house, I write next. Patty is an only child. She was not domestic when I met her, not much more so after we married. "There's no connection," I think she will say, "between domesticity and being an only child." Some days she sounds as though being an only child is a character deficiency. Patty admires a spare, orderly house. We have bare pine floors with scatter rugs—some braided, some hooked, a few Oriental. There are no curtains in the windows except in the bathroom. She's always complaining that we have too much furniture and not enough bookcases. Both complaints have merit. Maintaining a dusty, old house, however, has not been a high priority. That our house has more fireplaces than closets does not help matters much, nor does the fact that we are a family of collectors. Patty's closest friends love her casual attitude about order. After all, it is reassuring to know someone who will make you feel good about your housekeeping. Why not put dirty pans in the oven when someone's coming? They'll keep just as well there as they will in the sink. Visual order, not conceptual order, is Patty's priority.

When we were engaged, she once wrote down in a small blue notebook the names of my favorite dishes so that she could make them after we were married. The list was short, but she has not, to my recollection, made tapioca pudding during these twenty-four years. Otherwise, she has become an excellent cook. Our first son, John, is wonderfully quixotic and fiercely independent, traits which he showed at a very early age. I think Patty decided to imprint him on home cooking, like Lorenz's goslings, so that he would come home during college vacations. She need not have worried. Both John and Jamie do come home eagerly, with friends, and Patty's cooking is what they all rave about.

Music, I write down. Patty studied the piano during most of her childhood and, for a year or two, the cello as well. Her mother once told me that keeping Patty's skirt at a respectable level was what she remembered most about the cello playing. Patty said only that the cello fell apart after a while, so they took it back to the school, and she focused on the piano. Her teacher had three pianos, and he used to let Patty decide which one she wanted to play. Most often she would choose the grand, with the mirror behind the keyboard. She would sometimes become distracted by the image of her own hands, lose track of the music, and wander a bit. The laissez-faire approach was quite helpful years later when, during a solo recital, she forgot the music in the middle of a Bach piece. "I just made something up until I got to a place I remembered."

Patty's voice is sometimes heard around the house—a clear mezzo-soprano, usually singing à la Jo Anne Worley a loud "Bored!" Our house has a central chimney, and all the rooms flow around it. Her announcement is heard everywhere. Jamie, before his voice changed, would always send back a gurgling falsetto echo "Bo-o-o-red." And we all are familiar with "Dona Nobis Pacem," which we have been known to sing on the beach after dark.

When I was thirty-seven, Patty bought me a viola for Christmas. I am a pianist, and I had never played another instrument except a glock-enspiel in the Brown University band. But I had once said that I liked the viola and that if I were ever to play another instrument, the viola might be nice to learn. That was reason enough for her to buy one. I bought her a cello for her next birthday, and now we are the bottom half of a string quartet. The quartet is currently on sabbatical leave, since our second violinist has moved away. I suspect we'll find another fiddle player before too long, but I know Patty will probably practice alone three or four months before she'll play with anyone new. "I'm not competitive," she keeps saying. But she is, most often with herself.

Space. Space and spaces recur in Patty's writing. They seem important to her in several ways. Finding a writing space in our house that has no boundaries is a constant chore for her. Sometimes she types at the kitchen table or on the coffee table in the family room. But most often she writes in our bedroom, looking out at the meadow and the woods. The black-and-white television is usually on. "It helps me think," she says.

She was born in Wyoming on the high plains, and she is almost constantly rapturous in open country. Open country nurtures and inspires her. I think it really unfetters her imagination. She loves the ocean, too, for the same reason. Newfoundland is one of her favorite places, where bleak moors end at the edge of the sea, dropping suddenly over cliffs to the water. She loves birds, an acquired vice since she married into birding. But birds of the open spaces—particularly hawks—and sea birds are her favorites.

People. They are the core of Patty's life—not writing, not success. Family has always come first. When the children were younger, Patty booked her speaking engagements with the caveat "unless someone's home sick." And she stuck to it. After having two boys we decided to have a third child, and, as in a good plot, the baby was a girl. Emily is now in high school. She is spirited, clear-eyed, and funny. Many of her cogent observations of the world manage to end up in print, often almost verbatim.

Patty's parents are both transplanted from the plains, and all her relatives live west of the Mississippi. For an only child whose nearest kin is half a continent away, the nuclear family has special meaning. My family, which is larger and nearer, has adopted her. But nonetheless, these days, with her parents elderly and her mother not well, that nucleus is now tenuous, and there is a poignancy for all of us in her being an only child.

We've lived in Leeds, a small village in western Massachusetts, for over twenty years, and we are finally no longer new people. Neighbors have our house key. We swap dog and child care. Patty knows and likes the post office workers and the clerks in the grocery store. These people all have families and histories and wonderful idiosyncracies. They enrich her world, as I'm sure she enriches theirs. She is astonished that they relish and savor her current success. She is even astonished that they have noticed it.

She's such a mixture, this lady. It's hard to put her into words. Will I be able to give a fair picture of her? Will I leave out anything important? Maybe if I am asked by the *Horn Book Magazine* to write an article, I'll decline. I'll say it's an impossible assignment. Besides, an article isn't necessary. Patty really describes herself, briefly but with exquisite accuracy, in the words Sarah writes to Jacob when she agrees to come for a month's visit. Sarah adds a postscript to that letter, for the children. "Tell them I sing was all it said."

The Caldecott Medal 1987

Hey, Al

written by
Arthur Yorinks

illustrated by
Richard Egielski

published by
Farrar, Straus and Giroux, 1986

Booklist Review

Yorinks and Egielski come back to a familiar topic—dissatisfaction with life and what to do about it. In this case, it's Eddie the dog who wants more out of life. Eddie lives with easygoing Al, a janitor, in a one-room flat on the Upper West Side. The opportunity for change comes in the form of a huge bird who sticks his beak in the bathroom window and offers to get them out of town. Al is reluctant, but Eddie is insistent, so off they go to a lush, bird-inhabited island where all they have to do is swim and sip tropical drinks. But as the book so eloquently puts it, "Ripe fruit soon spoils." Soon, they find themselves turning into birds just like the rest of the island's inhabitants. A hasty and dangerous escape finally lands them back home, where Al and Eddie realize that "Paradise lost is sometimes Heaven found." Much of the story's bittersweet humor will be best appreciated by adults reading the story aloud, but there is plenty for children to like here, too. First and foremost is the book's outstanding artwork. The apartment scenes have a theatrical look, as though a fourth wall had been eliminated to allow the viewing of a stage set. The browns and tans of Al and Eddie's everyday life contrast beautifully with the enchanting colors found in paradise, and the island's wide assortment of birds (penguins, flamingos, roosters, dodos) will elicit more than a few oohs and aahs. The author and artist succeed again with a book that has something for everyone.—*Ilene Cooper*

1987 Caldecott Acceptance Speech
Richard Egielski

Let me start by saying how very honored I am to receive the Caldecott Medal. I feel honored not just because of the prestige and praise that come with this award but also because now my name will always be linked with Randolph Caldecott's.

Soon after Kay Vandergrift called to tell me the good news, I pulled a copy of a previous Caldecott winner off my bookshelf to stare at the medal that would soon be added to the jacket of *Hey, Al*. Believe me, it looked great.

Seeing that embossed image of John Gilpin on his runaway horse prompted me to take a fresh look at *The Diverting History of John Gilpin*, Caldecott's interpretation of William Cowper's poem. It's true that Caldecott didn't collaborate with Cowper himself, the way I do with Arthur Yorinks, but it still pleases me that the image on the medal comes from a collaborative work.

The double-page spread from John Gilpin that inspired the image on the Caldecott Medal has long been a favorite of mine, as well as an influence on my illustrations. I always get a laugh and a thrill from that picture of Gilpin, the sedate linen draper, clutching the mane of his frenzied horse for dear life. Both hat and wig are gone—they blew off on the previous spread—and two stone jugs of liquor dangle from Gilpin's belt as he bolts across the pages, scattering a flock of geese, pursued by dogs, and provoking a wide variety of responses from the aroused bystanders. An astonishing scene! The picture draws you close and fills your eyes with a panoramic view that rivals anything I've seen in CinemaScope.

But it's not just isolated images that make Caldecott a great picture-book artist. This particular spread is the payoff for the smaller scenes he uses to build to this point. Like an enticing melody, each sequence of pictures ebbs and flows. His pictures are never static; they're always moving, always enhancing and enlivening the text.

In *Hey, Al*, I tried to use what I learned from Caldecott to smoothly and alluringly move the story along from the monochromatic, one-room apartment to the brightly colored Bird Island and back again. I consulted both wordless spreads showing John Gilpin on his runaway horse before I created my own spreads for *Hey, Al*. And I tried to build a visual crescendo climaxing in my wordless spread, which shows Al and Eddie dangling from a tree, dumbstruck by the multitude of birds surrounding them. I wanted the lush panoramas of Bird Island to fill the eyes of my viewers and draw them into the pictures the same way Caldecott draws me in.

These pictures of Bird Island would never have come into existence if it weren't for the wonderful story that Arthur Yorinks wrote. It must be a very difficult task to write a true picture-book text, a text that succinctly tells its tale and still has the power to inspire a series of exciting images.

That's exactly what Arthur's text for *Hey, Al* did for me. It allowed my imagination to run free and create the sequence of pictures that turned his story into a picture book.

So, first and foremost, I want to thank Arthur Yorinks for writing *Hey, Al.*

You might say that Arthur and I got together because of a teacher I had during my senior year in art school. That year, Maurice Sendak's course in children's book illustration was offered at my school for the first time. Up until then, I had been drifting towards a career as a magazine illustrator. But when Maurice began revealing the mysteries of the picture-book form, I was immediately and irreversibly hooked. I had finally found a discipline that answered all my creative needs.

About a year after graduation, I went back to school to visit Maurice. On the way up in the elevator, someone tapped me on the shoulder and asked if my name was Richard. He told me that his name was Arthur Yorinks and that he was a writer. He said Maurice had been telling him about an illustrator who'd been his student the previous year, someone who would be perfect for Arthur's stories. But unfortunately Maurice couldn't remember my last name. So he told Arthur what I looked like, and said my first name was Richard. Arthur didn't think this information would be of much use in a city the size of New York. But we finally did meet that day, on our way up to visit Maurice, and soon after we began working together.

So thank you, Maurice Sendak, for introducing me to the art of picture books, for helping Arthur and me to find each other, and for the quality of your work, which is a continuing inspiration.

I would also like to thank my colleagues at Farrar, Straus and Giroux; my editor, Michael di Capua, for his help and encouragement; my designer, Cynthia Krupat, for the idea of using endpapers in two different colors; my wife, Denise, for her love; and the 1987 Caldecott Committee for giving this year's Caldecott Medal to *Hey, Al.*

Richard Egielski
Arthur Yorinks

Richard Egielski

On a rainy Monday last January, my telephone rang. I answered it and heard the distinctive crackle of long distance. "Hello, this is Kay Vandergrift of the Caldecott committee. We've been trying to reach Richard Egielski and seem to have the wrong number. Do you have his phone number?" Or words to that effect. It didn't take much brain power to figure out the meaning of this request. It was with immense pleasure that I relayed Richard's phone number, and it is with the same joy that I celebrate his award with this brief essay.

Richard Egielski, born in 1952 in Queens, New York, is the son of a police officer, the second of three Egielski children. His growing-up was not unusual, though for a children's book illustrator it was conspicuously devoid of children's books. Comic books, *Mad* magazine, and Max Fleischer cartoons supplanted picture books, and later on James Bond novels and Tolkien took the place of *Charlotte's Web* (Harper) and *The Wind in the Willows*.

Certainly, Richard drew as a child and enjoyed the feel of pens and paper, crayons and paint. But what led him to enter the High School of Art and Design in Manhattan, and then to take art more seriously, was a simple desire to escape the rigors of parochial school. In high school his interest in magazine illustration took root. At Pratt, and later at the Parsons School of Design, his path toward commercial art seemed set.

But destiny intervened. Taking a class with Maurice Sendak at Parsons altered Richard's outlook drastically. All at once, he discovered picture books and the artistic possibilities of book illustration.

I can't stress enough the importance of that class to Richard and, indirectly, to me as well. It led Richard to children's books, and it led me to Richard. It was through Maurice Sendak that we accidentally met; and it was through Michael di Capua, our editor, that we were given the opportunity to publish *Sid and Sol* (Farrar), our first book together.

I remember those early days of collaboration on *Sid and Sol*. Once, Richard came to my apartment, ready to show me how he had worked out his visualization of my story. He opened a small sketchbook, and on one page there were tiny boxes, thirty-two of them. In each box was a squiggle.

"Here it is," he said. "What do you think?" What I thought was that this man was crazy. I see squiggles; he sees a picture book. Indeed he did. To my amazement, the rhythm, the pacing, the interplay of words and pictures were all there. And I quickly learned not only Richard's squiggle language but his secret—he's a born picture-book artist, a natural.

He responds to a text the way a great singer does to a song. He gives it shape and color and breadth. If there is something wrong with the text, this flaw is reflected in his pictures (and then we try to fix both). If there is something right about the text, this also shows in his pictures. It shows in the inventiveness and absolute conviction of his images, which never violate the words but always expand them, direct them, move them along.

Can there be a better depiction of a man who has just lost his head than Richard's fourth picture in *It Happened in Pinsk* (Farrar)? No. Knife in one hand, roll in the other; no eyes, no face, no head; and still we know that Irv Irving is confused and asking himself, "What's going on?" Perfect.

Or how do you show the passage of time in the confines of a single, unchanged set, such as the apartment in *Hey, Al* (Farrar)? Pile unread newspapers at the front door. Simple, ingenious; again perfect. Or how do you dramatize the immenseness of Sol, the biggest giant in the world? Place illustrations on facing pages, each focusing on one of his boots as they tower over a skyscraper and a human pyramid.

Just a few more examples of Richard's extraordinary eye and unpredictable imagination: the recurrent "fish clouds" in *Louis the Fish* (Farrar), and Louis, as a salmon, sleeping peacefully in his pajamas; the poignant bedtime ending to Gelett Burgess's *The Little Father* (Farrar); and in *Hey, Al* the spread where all the birds turn their backs on Al's and Eddie's cries for help. I could go on and on.

It is especially gratifying that the Caldecott Medal should go to Richard Egielski in this fiftieth anniversary year, for in all of his work he lovingly invokes the spirit of Randolph Caldecott. Like Caldecott's, Richard's pictures are dedicated, not to themselves as separate images, but to their job of forming, along with the text, what is known as a picture book.

It has now been over ten years since Richard and I began creating books together. A decade has passed, and my respect for Richard as an artist continues to grow. It is a joy to work with him, just as it is a pleasure for my wife and me to spend time with him and his wonderful wife, Denise, discussing dog biscuits and couch fabrics, Hopper and Winslow Homer.

Richard met Denise at Parsons when they were students—it's obviously a great place for meeting—and this unique year also marks their tenth wedding anniversary. Kay and committee, what wisdom!

The Newbery Medal 1987

The Whipping Boy

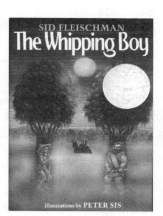

written by
Sid Fleischman

illustrated by
Peter Sis

published by
Greenwillow, 1986

Horn Book Review

Forsaking the American tall-tale humor and the elaborate plotting of his other novels, the author has written another kind of broadly comic tale and characteristically seasoned it with trickery, villainy, and hairsbreadth escapes. In the manner of Joan Aiken and Lloyd Alexander, he sets the story in an undefined time and place. It tells of a king's son—a lazy, arrogant mischief-maker dubbed Prince Brat—and of Jemmy, a rat-catcher's orphaned son, snatched from the city's sewers to serve in the palace as the royal whipping boy. Furious with Jemmy for silently enduring his brutal punishment, the prince behaves ever more scandalously, and he stubbornly remains illiterate while the stoic whipping boy learns to read and write. But Prince Brat is actually bored with his life of self-indulgence; determined to run away, he forces Jemmy to accompany him. Almost immediately, they fall afoul of two notorious outlaws—Hold-Your-Nose Billy, a burly, bushy-haired villain who smells "like a ton of garlic," and Cutwater, a scrawny character "with hollow cheeks and a nose like a meat cleaver." Realizing that they have captured the prince, the men decide to send a ransom note to the king. But only Jemmy can write; so the clever boy soon convinces the cutthroats that he is the royal scion and that the witless prince is only an ignorant servant boy. When one of the men goes off to deliver the note, Jemmy breaks loose and, with the prince always at his heels, leads the other rogue in a frenzied chase. Before the riotous adventure is played out, the two boys are rescued by a dancing bear. Sid Fleischman once remarked that his books are improvisations, and the new story rings changes on the theme of *The Prince and the Pauper*. It is populated with some time-honored stock characters of low comedy and peppered with nimble-witted repartee; but like much of the author's writing, beneath the surface entertainment the story also speaks of courage, friendship, and trust. The pen drawings have an appropriate air of droll exaggeration.—*Ethel L. Heins*

Booklist Review

A fabricator of tall tales about McBroom and his wonderful farm, and of zesty early frontier extravaganzas (Chancy and the Grand Rascal and Humbug Mountain), Fleischman now tries his hand at a story that has all the trappings of a fairy tale. Jemmy, an orphan plucked from the streets, is the designated whipping boy for all the bad things that spoiled Prince Brat does, such as refusing to learn to read and write and removing the wigs from the assembled court nobles. When Prince Brat decides to run away because he is bored, he takes Jemmy with him, but the boys' roles are reversed when they encounter the villains Cutwater and Hold-Your-Nose-Billy. After a climactic pursuit through rat-infested city sewers, the boys escape, and it is a chastened prince who escorts his former whipping boy back to the castle. There is no indication of locale, but the tale, accompanied by stippled, rustic-looking illustrations, has a Dickensian flavor. There's plenty of fast action for the adventure lover, and although no magic is used, readers will find the happy ending eminently satisfying.—*Mary Lathrope*

1987 Newbery Acceptance Speech
Sid Fleischman

At almost exactly nine o'clock on a crisp blue Monday morning in January momentous news was on its way to me. The phone rang. I was in the shower. When I stepped out, my wife, Betty, said, "You had a call from Chicago." And I said, "I don't know anyone in Chicago."

Betty handed me the name and phone number. Trev Jones? I shook my head, not yet recognizing it as the Trevelyn Jones of *School Library Journal*. "She wanted to know how long it takes you to shower."

I thought the question, coming from a stranger, a bit impertinent. I wandered downstairs to my office, returned the call, and heard a voice as bubbly as champagne ring out the news. A book I had struggled with for almost ten years had won the Newbery Medal.

I don't happen to believe in levitation, unless it's done with mirrors, but for the next few days I had to load my pockets with ballast. The Newbery Medal is an enchantment. It's bliss. It should happen to everyone.

And it set up a Pavlovian reaction. Every time I take a shower I expect the phone to ring.

Your timing, I must tell you, was impeccable. I had been deeply immersed for a number of months in a complex and difficult piece of work, finishing it up the Saturday before. Had the call come a week earlier, I can almost see myself turning to my wife to say, "That's all I need—one more interruption."

Chinese wisdom tells us that a long journey begins with the first step. My journey to this room tonight began with a misstep. For a writer I started out in the wrong direction. Instead of reading the classics, or even the Hardy Boys, I spent my adolescent years practicing card tricks. I intended to turn myself into a magician.

It never occurred to me to become a writer. First, my fingers got tired. And I had never seen a live author. They seemed as remote and mysterious and invisible as phantoms. I subscribed to the childhood folklore that all authors are dead. Or ought to be.

My years in magic were a happy detour, and perhaps not a misstep after all. The crystal ball doesn't exist that could have foretold that I would become a writer of children's books. But it's easy to glance back at the conditions and accidentals that made it possible.

My father unwittingly laid the groundwork. Like most Europeans, he had a zest for storytelling. With his natural sense of timing and eye for detail, he could make a trip to the barbershop sound Homeric. And although no Chesterton, he left me with a single piece of fatherly advice that allowed me to pursue a career of my own quirky choice. "Stay away from doctors," he warned. "They make you sick."

So there was no pressure on me to become a doctor. He had the same scorn for lawyers, sparing me a career in torts and contracts.

Like Jemmy in *The Whipping Boy*, I was a free spirit, left free to roam the streets of San Diego—they were safe then—and dream my boyish dreams. Thurston, not Thackeray. Houdini, not Hemingway.

My search for secrets led me straight to the public libraries. I'd make a beeline to the shelves where the magic books sat. I hopped streetcars to the outlying branches. I'd take the nickel ferry across the bay to Coronado to check the shelves there. I was dimly aware that there were other books in the stacks, but in those days I had tunnel vision. I taught myself sleight of hand out of library books.

In short order I became the boy pest of the Western world. If you have ever had an aspiring magician in the family, you will know what I am talking about. My mother and two sisters were wonderfully indulgent, but I could see them blanch as I approached with a deck of cards in my hands and the line on my lips: "Here. Take a card."

I became fairly adept, and soon I was creating new tricks. I can see now, in that random activity, that I was becoming a writer. I just didn't know it.

I needed to put my bafflers on paper. I sat down at the family typewriter, the old Remington with the faded, tenderized blue ribbon, and began rattling away. The pages stacked up. I had a short book. In literary style, it was on a par with the instructions you get with a digital clock. But it was published. I was nineteen.

The day those printed and bound volumes landed on our doorstep, and I saw my name on the cover, I was bedazzled. My aspirations took a tentative shift. What were all those other books in the library?

I wondered if I could write stories. But how was it done? Were there books on it? I moved to another part of the library. Behold! I had been through this before, and I knew exactly how to proceed. But now, perhaps, just maybe, I could become a self-taught writer.

And as a writer, I am almost entirely a product of the free public library system. I'd like to take this opportunity to express my gratitude.

My turning from adult to children's books was the result of a chance remark. My daughter Jane came home waving a slip of paper that Leo Politi, on a visit to the children's room of the Santa Monica Public Library, had been kind enough to autograph. We crowded around to look at it, and my wife, quite innocently, remarked, "But you know, Daddy writes books, too."

It was Jane's answer that did it. "Yes," she said. "But no one reads his books."

Never underestimate a father scorned. Some months later a stretch of free time opened up for me, and I decided to write a novel for the amusement of my three children. I put them in the story, of course, and read them each chapter as it came hot out of the typewriter. It was fun. At the time it seemed to be only family fun. But it proved to be much more.

I had written comedy lines before, but until I sat down to *Mr. Mysterious and Company* I had never done any sustained humorous writing. And with the publication of the novel by the Atlantic Monthly

Press, I wandered into the field of children's books. It was as if I had found myself—and I didn't know I had been lost.

I would like to pay homage to my first editor, the beloved Emilie McLeod, who became a pal through the years.

Soon I was asked to speak at schools and libraries. Like Leo Politi, I found myself signing slips of paper in a Santa Monica library. I looked up, and there in line stood my younger daughter, Anne, age seven, with a slip of paper in her hand. She wanted my autograph, too. I knew I had arrived.

I've had a glorious time writing for children. And unlike adults, they write back. Quite often their letters start out, "Dear Sid." It delights me that they regard me as a friend. They send handmade birthday cards. Around Valentine's Day we are ankle deep in glitter. Their letters abound with unconscious humor. A ten-year-old girl in Tennessee wrote, "My interests are reading, artifacts, and cosmetics." Another, from Wichita: "When did you start writing? When are you going to stop writing?" But almost always they ask, "Where do you get your ideas?"

It's not an easy question to handle. I recall a letter from a boy in Michigan who made a list and then added, "Please answer these questions to the best of your ability."

To the best of my ability, then. The problem for the writer is not in finding ideas. They are as common as weeds. What to do with the idea that touches you and excites the imagination—that's the writer's problem.

I stumbled across the catapulting idea for *The Whipping Boy* while researching historical materials for another project. I checked the dictionary. "A boy," it confirmed, "educated with a prince and punished in his stead."

My literary pulse began to pound. The common phrase as historical fact. What an outrageous practice, I thought. Here was a story I wanted to write, and with two main characters already provided, I'd make quick work of it.

It was as if history had set a trap in its pages, waiting for me to step into it.

After about eighteen months, I was still trying to get to the bottom of page five. More than once I thought of Fred Allen's imperishable line, "I can't understand why a person will take a year or two to write a novel when he can easily buy one for a few dollars."

I shelved the project. It wasn't yet a story, for I don't plot in advance. It doesn't worry me that I don't know where I'm going. But I know I'll know it when I get there. Writing for me, like life itself, is a daily improvisation. Who knows what surprises lurk in the typewriter! It may seem highly eccentric, but I have read that Tennessee Williams worked that way. Both Jill Paton Walsh and the late Ellen Raskin told me this was their writing method, and I'm certain there are others. And while it may appear to be a death-defying high wire act, it is not as risky as it seems. In all the years I have been writing, I have lost only two or three books. And I probably would have abandoned them anyway.

But I was losing *The Whipping Boy*. I recall hearing Eudora Welty in a television interview say that, "Each story teaches me how to write it, but not how to write the next one."

From time to time I'd take *The Whipping Boy* off the shelf and give it one more chance. During these years Clyde Bulla was a sustaining force. We live at opposite edges of the vastness of Los Angeles, and we often meet at a midway point for lunch. I must have sounded like a broken phonograph record as the waitress carried off the menus. "Clyde, I've definitely abandoned *The Whipping Boy*. This time I mean it."

And Clyde, a veteran of so many books, would fix me with those kind, compassionate eyes and give his head the barest shake. "But I like *The Whipping Boy*," he'd protest. "It just needs to simmer a while longer. You'll get it."

In the end, Clyde was right. I got it.

Looking back, it's easy to see what it was that froze my imagination. My original concept for the story was wrong. Wrong, at least, for me. I saw *The Whipping Boy* as a picture-book story.

A picture book must have the gift of simplicity. Simplicity is the most demanding and elusive of disciplines. Not long ago, my son, Paul, who has a Newbery Honor Book himself, said with characteristic whimsy, "I can't seem to write a sentence without four dependent clauses."

Writing as sparely as I could, it nevertheless took me the first five pages to open up the relationship between Jemmy and Prince Brat. That left only a few pages to spin a tale. Impossible!

I'd make cuts one day—mortal wounds—and restore them the next. I shunted aside the temptation to let the story run. I had a fixed idea that this was a picture book, and that was that.

I can't say it was a work in progress through those years—there was no progress. It was more a scornful presence sitting on the shelf, taunting me from time to time. A writer learns a mulish perseverance early on, but this was becoming folly. I had abandoned ideas before. Why not this one?

Every time my thoughts strayed back to Jemmy, that innocent caught up in a demented, institutionalized injustice, I simmered. And I had an affection for Prince Brat, as much a victim of his station in life as Jemmy. Both were being denied their childhoods: the prince by a smothering excess of privilege, Jemmy by none at all. I couldn't walk away from them.

I don't keep a journal, so I don't know the exact date. But it must have been on a January morning in 1985 that I again took the few manuscript pages off the shelf and read them over. In films, amnesiacs conveniently get hit by a taxi and regain their senses. Nothing as dramatic as that occurred. But something clouted me on the head. I looked up and said to myself: "Gaw. It's not a picture book."

Once I took the shackles off, the story erupted. Scenes, incidents, and characters came tumbling out of a liberated imagination. Within a few months I had it all on paper. Susan Hirschman, that gem of an editor, accepted it overnight. Peter Sis delivered his exquisite illustrations. Ava Weiss conceived the beautiful book design. And here I stand.

I feel the joyful presence of three old friends, Don Freeman, Ezra Jack Keats, and Paul Hirschman, who would have taken a cheering delight in tonight's celebration.

I'm grateful to my wife, Betty, who never doubted. I'd like to give my children, Jane, Paul, and Anne, a public hug and a kiss for starting their father off in the right direction.

I'm certain that every author who has preceded me to this dais has gone thumbing through the thesaurus looking for other ways to say "thank you." I have never had any luck in the thesaurus. But I, too, went searching for a word with bells and whistles on it. Again, *Roget* let me down. "Thanks! Many thanks! Gramercy!" The best of the lot seems to be "much obliged," but somehow that doesn't quite fill the bill.

So imagine the bells and whistles. Thanks, Susan, and my friends at Greenwillow and Morrow. Thanks, Clyde. Thanks, Pearl and Honey. Thanks to each of you in the American Library Association. And, gramercy, thanks to the Newbery committee for putting your gold seal on *The Whipping Boy*.

Sid Fleischman

Paul Fleischman

The scene was repeated all through my growing-up. I'd be dimly aware that my father had been typing. His study door would open and close.

My mother would call my two sisters and me, the whole family gathering in the living room, my father always at the table in the corner. Everyone got comfortable. The phone was entreated not to ring. A brief recap of the story was given. Then he read aloud the chapter he'd just finished.

Sid Fleischman

"The sun came up hot and clear," he might begin, "as if it had been cut out of a prairie fire with a pair of scissors."

Or, "Sometime during the night Cut-Eye Higgins left Hangtown for parts unknown."

Or, "At first light, Captain Harpe was up and shouting. 'Rise up gents! To the oars, my lazy mud turtles!'"

Or, "It was a week before we got out the next issue of *The Humbug Mountain Hoorah*. First we had to dig up the petrified man."

We were transported at once to the Old Post Road, to the decks of an Ohio River raft, to Hangtown or Matamoros. Part yarn-spinning session, vaudeville act, history lesson, and magic show, these readings transmitted, aside from their stories, so much of what I associate with my father.

First and foremost, we imbibed his love of language. We grew up knowing that words felt good in the ears and on the tongue, that they were as much fun to play with as toys. How could we help it, following the adventures of characters whose names were such fun to say: Pitch-pine Billy, Micajah Jones, Jingo, Hawg Pewitt, Billy Bombay, not to mention the McBroom family's children, Willjillhesterchesterpeterpollytimtommarylarryandlittleclarinda. Characters whose speech made you wish you'd been born a century earlier if only so that you, too, could shout, "By the eternal!" or "Hoolah-haw!" or "Hackle me bones!" or "Don't that bang all!"

His description was equally colorful. I feel safe in claiming that you won't find a single cliché in all my father's books. What you will find is lots of rich, visual imagery. A character wasn't simply thin. He was thin enough to take a bath in a shotgun barrel or to fall through a stovepipe without getting sooty. We never had trouble imagining the scene my father was reading. It takes a lot longer to write this way—especially when, after a long career, you're faced with your tenth or eleventh skinny character to describe. With more than thirty children's books behind him now, he still, somehow, managed to fill *The Whipping Boy* (Greenwillow) with plenty of fresh imagery.

I said that these readings were part history lesson. Weeks before my father actually began writing, stacks of research books would be brought from the library, piling up on the piano and eventually making their way into his study. I remember as a child being fascinated flipping through the notebook in which he kept his research. There were sections on food, clothing, language, prices of things, and various other subjects, filled with his penciled notes. I was hooked and years later would find myself filling similar notebooks of my own.

Despite his books' historical accuracy, listening to them read aloud was not at all like attending a classroom lecture. Here was history brought to life, the history that rarely gets into textbooks: gold miners sending their clothes all the way to China to be laundered, sailors' fear of ghostlike "dredgies," Gypsy signs and lingo, goose pulls. The dusty corners and vivid details of history have always attracted my father. Walking into his study when he was out, I would find myself wanting to read all those strange-sounding books on his shelves: *Thirty-Three Years among Our Wild Indians, Hawkers & Walkers in Early America, Extraordinary Popular Delusions,* and the *Madness of Crowds.* A few years back we gleefully joined in combing the used bookstores in search of all four volumes of Henry Mayhew's *London Labour and the London Poor,* a book he eventually drew on for *The Whipping Boy.*

In grammar school my father became interested in magic, learned the tricks of the trade—inventing quite a few along the way, the subject of his first published book—and after high school, during vaudeville's last days, toured the country with Mr. Arthur Bull's Francisco Spook Show. This experience came out in his books, several of which involve magic or adventuresome journeys or both. I suspect that his stage experience influenced his writing methods as well. He's an improviser and likes to keep himself as interested and in the dark about what's going to happen next as his readers. When he sits down at the typewriter in his silent study, he might as well be a comic stepping on stage in a noisy nightclub, trying to get a read on his audience, always thinking on his feet.

His reading aloud, likewise, partook of the stage. We four were his New Haven. He could tell from our reactions if a scene had worked or if it needed work. Our opinions were asked for. I remember being proud when my suggestion that Mr. Mysterious and his family get lost turned up in the following chapter. My younger sister, a little jealous, had less success with her proposal that their family piano ought to burn down.

These readings were live literature. Live like an old-time radio show, with the attendant tingle of excitement and the necessity of imagining the action. It's perhaps not surprising that we're all fans of "A Prairie Home Companion" and of the British radio game show "My Word." Or that I went on to write two books of poems designed to be performed aloud by two readers.

My father's specialty in magic is sleight of hand. No birthday party was complete without a few tricks; likewise, these days, no school visit when my father, reenacting his past, takes his act on the road each spring and fall. This style of magic is reflected in his writing. When he gave up being a professional magician, he became instead a prestidigitator of words, palming plot elements, making villains vanish, producing solutions out of thin air. He knows how to keep an audience guessing, how to create suspense, how to keep readers reading. A sleight-of-hand artist must be skilled at misdirection, keeping his audience's eyes away from the real action. My father is a master at doing the same with words, stealthily slipping in a clue, unnoticed by the reader, that will reappear in the book's climax, just as he used to miraculously pull nickels and dimes out of our ears.

His adult characters are also sleight-of-hand men of a sort. Mr. Mysterious, Uncle Will, Praiseworthy, Mr. Peacock-Hemlock-Jones are all tall, strong men. They rely, however, on their cleverness. They're quick with their wits, magicians at manipulating a villain through his vices. Though Praiseworthy throws a notable punch at one point, these figures are advertisements for the superiority of brains to brawn.

As much as his use of language and history and clever plotting, it's those irresistibly appealing adult characters, I suspect, that explain why his books are nearly all still in print and that the letters from children continue to pour in. How wonderful to imagine yourself out adventuring—but with an Uncle Will to watch over you. Someone who respects you yet protects you as well. Someone brave, big-hearted, never discouraged, whose mere presence reassures you that everything will work out. With so many children growing up away from their fathers these days, it's no wonder that the warmth and security offered by these figures has a strong appeal. My sisters and I were lucky. Sitting in the living room, ruminating on the chapter just read, we knew we had exactly such a figure—for a father.

The Caldecott Medal 1988

Owl Moon

written by
Jane Yolen

illustrated by
John Schoenherr

published by
Philomel, 1987

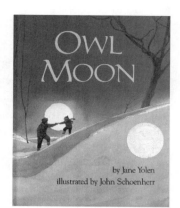

OWL MOON

by Jane Yolen
illustrated by John Schoenherr

Horn Book Review

The story of a child's nighttime walk with her father in search of a great horned owl unfolds against a backdrop of extraordinarily handsome illustrations. Well-wrapped against the cold, the two leave their farm, stepping high over the drifted snow, and wait, listening breathlessly in the shadowy woods for an answer to Pa's call, "Whoo-whoo-who-who-who-whooooooo." The moonwashed, double-page-spread snows-capes capture the brooding silence of the night and the chill expectancy of father and child. Rough barked and gnarled trees lean under their burden of snow and are a striking setting for the hushed moment when the great owl lifts itself from a nearby tree and is caught, yellow-eyed, in the glare of Pa's flashlight. The delineation of the owl's barred feathers, white bib, and curved talons will satisfy the sharp-eyed birder, but, more than that, the huge bird is imbued with a looming presence and mystery which transcends the description of his appearance in the text. It is splendid to find Schoenherr, known for his pictures in *Rascal, Gentle Ben* (both Dutton), and *Julie of the Wolves* (Harper), turning his hand to illustrations in a book which blends a quiet and reflective text with powerful and boldly conceived watercolor paintings.—*Ethel R. Twichell*

Booklist Review

An exquisite mood piece, *Owl Moon* is a poetic story of a winter-wrapped little girl and her father's owling adventure. The elusive magic and gentle shivery excitement that accompany the twosome are felt by the reader. The late-night walks are steeped in family tradition, no words are exchanged, but the companionship of the elusive quest speaks volumes. "When you go owling / you don't need words / or warm / or anything but hope. That's what Pa says." The integrity of Yolen's pleasure in writing about her subject is evident, and Schoenherr, also an owling enthusiast, captures the stark blue-black majesty of the nighttime forest in his powerful and evocative watercolor illustrations. Excellent for one-on-one or readaloud groups.—*Phillis Wilson*

1988 Caldecott Acceptance Speech
John Schoenherr

Receiving this medal is an honor I never expected. When I graduated from Pratt Institute thirty years ago, my intention was to be a painter of wildlife. The first book I illustrated was assigned to me because the first illustrator chosen was too busy. I love books, and making pictures is my life, but book illustration was an interruption in my chosen course. However, it was relatively pleasant. I was still drawing animals, and it helped pay the mortgage. Food and clothing were supplied by a great many other commercial assignments. That first book was *Rascal* (Dutton), and it was followed by a number of books by Miska Miles, *Julie of the Wolves* (Harper), *Gentle Ben* (Dutton), and the perennially reappearing *Dune* (Putnam).

I gradually learned, however, that my most satisfactory work was based on intuitive discovery, usually while painting and usually at the last minute. This approach is not accepted gracefully by most publishers. They require sketches, done on schedule, and finished work which relates directly to the sketches—also done on schedule. I was discovering that my best ideas usually happen in hindsight and on their own schedule.

Some forty interruptions later, I found the compromises of illustration too limiting and devoted myself fully to creating my own images, painted in my own manner and done on my own schedule. My idyllic reclusiveness lasted almost seven years and produced more satisfaction and reward than any other period.

Then Pat Gauch, an old friend and a fine author, became an editor. She knew of my crankiness, irascibility, and general bad temper when interrupted and rather tentatively asked me to read a new manuscript—something by Jane Yolen about a father and child going owling. I agreed. For return postage Pat would be mollified, and, with luck, I would be left alone for another seven years.

By my second reading of the spare text I was hooked.

Ironically, my own inclination was toward the exotic. Since I was twelve, I had spent as much time as possible away from New York City. I had spent years backpacking, spelunking, rock-climbing, and living wild from New York to Wyoming. I had studied animals in the field from Alaska to Iran and from the Everglades to the Rockies. All this book required was for me to walk out of my studio into my own woods. There was no excuse to go somewhere more interesting. The trees, fields, buildings, walls, and snow are all within a few minutes' walk of where I had lived in western New Jersey for over twenty years. A father and his six-year-old daughter came over and graciously spent a Sunday afternoon walking through the woods with me. I didn't even have to pick them up. They came by themselves.

I've done many illustrations in odd techniques, often using rare and hard to find materials. This book called for ordinary pen and water-color on paper. A phone call brought a quire of d'Arches to my door. I had the rest of the materials in my studio.

Owls were often around our woods, and I had twenty years worth of drawings and photographs. The story was quiet, and the winter woods were barren. That may have created a problem. But my wife reminded me of all the small animals that show up in odd corners in the woods. I knew them well already, and the deer literally come to my studio windows to keep the ivy and shrubs under control.

I was capable of going to any number of fascinating places in the world, but in taking on *Owl Moon* (Philomel), I could not come up with any valid reason for doing so.

Jane's story had a different appeal. I remembered the thrill of shar-ing those special experiences in the woods with my own children Jennifer and Ian. Jane's heroine was hardy and eager for experience. The situation was eminently believable and completely lacked saccharine sentimentality. Jane had expressed my own attitudes toward the wild.

I know the feelings of meeting a wild animal on its own ground. I've been face to face with field mice and Kodiak bears, bull moose and wild geese, wild boar and mountain goats, and, of course, owls. Large or small, I feel awe and wonder and respect. They are all presences and personalities, alien and largely unfathomable, but worth acceptance and contemplation for what they are. This is what I've found worth try-ing to express in my work. I was glad to discover I was not alone.

Even though I am alone in receiving this award, I would not be here without the inspiration and labor of many dedicated people.

My deepest thanks go first to Jane Yolen. Without her sensitivity and skill and artistry there would have been no book. We had never met until long after the book was published, although we had already shared experiences in spirit.

Then, Patricia Lee Gauch, who had the perspicacity to buy *Owl Moon* and the courage to ask me to illustrate it.

Next, Nanette Stevenson, art director and designer at Philomel and Putnam. She caught my more outrageous gaffs, let my minor lapses stand, and still designed a beautiful book, even though I took twice as long as expected to finish it.

My wife, Judy, has been my best friend for twenty-eight years. She has put up with windstorms, snowstorms, caves, deserts, swamps, mountains, and outdoor plumbing. She has stood fast when threatened by moose, bison, wild boar, and bugs. She has put up with my long working hours, my need for solitude, and my lack of interest in normal social activities. We are still best friends.

I'm thankful to my children for providing an audience for so many books and for being such forthright critics, even though they were usually right. I'm also thankful they have finally grown up.

My granddaughter Nyssa gets my thanks for simply being the joy that she is and inspiring me to do just one more book.

And, finally, the Caldecott committee has my deepest gratitude for this great honor, even though it has made me much more aware of every shortcoming in my pictures.

On the night after being notified of the award, I was leaving my studio under a full moon. Two owls were calling to each other from the trees. I listened for some time and silently thanked them for being, and for being there.

John Schoenherr
Patricia Lee Gauch

The first time I came to the Schoenherr farm, I was accompanied by twelve teenagers, one of them Ian Schoenherr, John Schoenherr's son. It was spring, and the mandate of the day for the students, a creative writing class I taught at a small private high school located not far from the Schoenherr farm, was to "see what you see."

It was an exercise meant to wake the young people up to the world around them, and even as John was greeting the class from the side porch of his 1865 farmhouse, the teenagers had scattered, checking curious piles of wood, lying on their stomachs to see a dandelion from a ground-eye view.

My mandate to them has seemed prophetic to me as I look back on that first visit to the Schoenherr farm, because I know now that this ability to see and then to capture in an illustration or painting not only what is obvious in the world around us but also what is silent and sometimes hidden is so clearly a mark of John's work.

John Schoenherr

Certainly this is so in *Owl Moon* (Philomel). Using luminous night-time colors and perspectives that sweep the winter countryside, John creates a woodland world that lets us glimpse not only the special relationship between the father and child but also the secret woodland world that coexists with the world we know is there—the fox crouching unseen behind the old stone wall, the mouse hiding in the log, the raccoon listening in the knot of a giant tree.

John has been fascinated with the details and wonders of the natural world for a lifetime. His farm in rural Locktown, New Jersey, is set back off a gravel road, and trails lead from the two-story stone and clapboard house through acres of mostly oak woods surrounding it. One morning a telephone conversation between Philomel art director Nanette Stevenson and John was interrupted with an announcement that six deer were feeding right outside his window. Even his barn studio is set back at the end of the gravel driveway in a stand of trees. Always, I am struck with the quiet of this place.

Certainly as spelunker, rock climber, and hiker, John has pursued distant wilderness as well. In search of animals he will photograph and eventually paint he has traveled as far as the Iranian hills and Alaska and as near as Utah, Wyoming, Montana, and California. Ironically, however, John grew up in a city a long way from any wilderness. In the Sunnyside section of Queens, even in the winter, there were the sounds of car horns honking and kids shouting. Sidewalks banked noisy streets, and buildings rose around his one-family brick town house.

Indeed, it is safe to say that John discovered drawing before he discovered any wilderness. The son of a Hungarian mother and German father, he spoke only German in an ethnically mixed neighborhood until he was three, when he "made the unsettling discovery" that no one in his neighborhood could understand a word he said. To communicate he claims that he "grabbed up a pencil and drew." Attending school and reading comic books, he quickly learned to speak English, but he never stopped drawing.

In fact, the young John drew on any available surface, the margins of school notebooks, scrap paper, the backs of magazines. He was eight years old when he was given a set of watercolors by his parents, early supporters of their son's obvious talent, and soon after he was given oils. At thirteen he was already taking the subway into Manhattan alone to attend Saturday classes at the Art Students League, where he studied etching and lithography under artist Will Barnett.

It was during this same time that John's curiosity about his natural world began to emerge. He began relentless trips to the American Museum of Natural History, where he was entranced by the panoramic windows of wild animal life, and to the Bronx and Central Park zoos, where he watched and endlessly sketched the animals. Always, it was the nuances and details of the animals—large and small—that attracted him. He could not learn and see enough.

We talked about animals at the Schoenherr kitchen table recently. An oval oak table that fits neatly into a sunny bay window full of plants, it is a gathering place for friends and family who stop in at any time to talk and share ideas. John has an extraordinary reservoir of information from little known facts about the monument at Stonehenge to the comparative dental structures of the woolly mammoth and the mastodon.

"What exactly are animals to you?" I asked him.

"Animals are life forms," he said as his granddaughter Nyssa, a frequent visitor, pushed a train of toy mice across the table top in front of him. "Animals are equal to us. I don't like mice in the cupboards, but animals in their own place, wild and not to be exploited."

Reading, observing, John became an assiduous student growing up in Queens. He read Jules Verne and Howard Pyle and became fascinated with the old masters, Van Eyck, Rembrandt, Michelangelo, Vermeer, particularly their use of light. He also admired the work of Krazy Kat cartoonist George Herriman and, in time, was attracted to the work of photographers Ansel Adams and Edward Weston—intrigued with their strong design and again their use of light.

All of Schoenherr's childhood heroes were not artists. Among his heroes were scientists as well, and he attended Stuyvesant High School believing he might become a biologist. He recalls a decisive moment in high school; when told to dissect a frog, he realized he would rather draw or paint live animals than dissect dead ones. When he graduated from Stuyvesant, he went to Pratt Institute in Brooklyn to study art.

In the next twenty-five years John would illustrate forty hardcover books, among them such classics as Sterling North's *Rascal* (Dutton), Jean Craighead George's *Julie of the Wolves* (Harper), and Frank Herbert's *Dune* (Putnam). Retiring from book illustration seven years ago, he devoted himself full time to painting the large, dramatic paintings, sometimes two and a half by four feet, of bears, geese, and mountain goats that have become his mark.

Having faced Kodiak bears in Alaska and wild boar in Iran and having ridden over desert terrain in Utah to photograph Monument Valley, he found that *Owl Moon*, nonetheless, posed unusual challenges. It was the first children's book that he would illustrate in full color without color separation. Discovering what medium to use took thought. When he finally decided that the wash effect of watercolor would best enhance the shadowed winter woodlands, he could no longer get the soft English watercolor paper he wanted. Another Schoenherr detail: since linen underwear is no longer commonly made, linen rags are no longer available to create the soft watercolor paper. Finally he decided "cold-dressed d'Arches" would do, and discovering "the perfect pen" he began.

Clipping Jane Yolen's text to the side of his easel, he read and reread it. He credits an early sketch of the scene where the father and girl trek single file across the top of the page as the one that gave him the tone and style for the book. His wife of twenty-eight years, Judy, suggested the hidden animals.

Finally, he began painting in earnest. Deciding to paint large, twenty-two by thirty inches, since that was a size most comfortable to him, he came daily to his studio, usually after lunch and would remain, sometimes painting until two or three in the morning. After three months *Owl Moon* was finished.

I live only twenty miles from John, and he brought the finished illustrations to my home. My husband, Ron, my son John, and I sat in the "everything" room, so called because it is where everything important happens in our family from eating to celebrating, and John took the paintings out of their individual wrappings. Did he watch my face to see how I felt as he laid each of the paintings out, one by one? I hope so, because my pleasure must have been unmistakable. No one spoke for several minutes. I remembered. "If you go owling you have to be quiet and make your own heat." It is the same when one shares in exquisite art.

There has been a real respect for life in the making of this book, the initial respect by Jane for the relationship of child to parent and human being to the natural world, the inherent respect John felt for Jane's words and for the same natural world. Maybe *Owl Moon* comes as a relief to people, because for the length of a book, it slows the world down, allowing us to be a part of an experience of the most quiet sort, reminding us that the natural world in all its wonder is still there if we, like John Schoenherr, can only "see what we see."

The Newbery Medal 1988

Lincoln
A Photobiography

written by
Russell Freedman

published by
Clarion Books, 1987

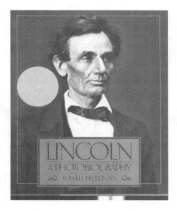

Horn Book Review

In some respects the title of this finely rendered account is misleading;
the handsome photographs illuminate the text, but the book is far more
than a photographic account. Used generously but judiciously, the pictures have been selected from the archival collections of several
libraries, museums, and historical societies. There are numerous photographs and drawings of Lincoln, political friends and foes, family members, and notable documents and the expected scenes of presidential
events, the Civil War, the assassination, and funeral processions. The
compact and cohesive narrative is a chronological examination of the
times and the life, personal characteristics, and career of Lincoln, with
a major portion of the book devoted to the shifting political complexities engendered by slavery in the 1840s and 1850s and the dismal
events of the resulting war in the divided nation. Freedman's intent is
to move beyond the simple folk hero to the human dimensions of the
Lincoln so much admired today and so strongly criticized in his own
time. The author represents Abraham Lincoln as somewhat enigmatic
and as a man of contrasts; he is humble but ambitious and even wealthy,
humorous but melancholy, unpolished in manner but highly intelligent.
Above all, he is seen as a man of great integrity, gradually acquiring a
willingness to speak out against slavery, deeply pained by the human
loss and suffering of the war, chagrined at the delays and reluctance of
his generals, and ever steadfast in his commitment to a united country.
The author draws on Lincoln's own words throughout the book and
appends a sampler of quotations from speeches and letters, a listing of
monuments and museums, and a selective list of popular and scholarly
books about Lincoln.—*Margaret A. Bush*

Booklist Review

Loved, revered, idealized, "more books have been written about Abraham Lincoln than any other American." In a calm, unemotional style Freedman seeks to dispense with the romanticized folk-hero imagery and misconceptions; for example, he notes that the long "freeze" exposure photography process of the time, which resulted in stiff and formal poses, never did justice to the real Lincoln. The author points out that while Lincoln was witty and talkative in company he rarely betrayed his inner feelings and was never fully understood by even his closest friends. Freedman traces Lincoln's early years and study of law and comments on his fierce ambition to rise above his log-cabin origins. The harsh emotional pain, melancholy, and depression endured by Lincoln and his wife Mary throughout their lives are also made clear. The antidote Lincoln so frequently used—his wit and rollicking humor—is seen in sharp contrast, making the accomplishments of this complex man all the more awe-inspiring. Following the account of the presidential/war years and assassination, Freedman includes a sampler of quotations from Lincoln's writings and speeches and a listing of historic sites. This eminently well-researched photo biography is outstanding; the man, his times, and his contemporaries are compellingly portrayed.—*Phillis Wilson*

1988 Newbery Acceptance Speech

Russell Freedman

Let me begin with a story. Not long ago, at an altitude of thirty-nine thousand feet over Omaha, I was chatting with a fellow passenger when she asked, "By the way, what kind of work do you do?"

"I'm a writer," I told her. "I write nonfiction books for children."

She looked at me quizzically, as Alice must have looked at the Mad Hatter, and said, "Nonfiction books for children? What a strange way to make a living."

She was absolutely right. To be "strange," the *Oxford English Dictionary* assures us, is to excite wonder or astonishment, as in "Many straunge and wonderfull sightes were scene this present yere in the skie." Strange implies wonderful, and it is truly wonderful to celebrate the strangeness of my craft at this gathering tonight.

I'm grateful to the members of this year's Newbery committee for honoring my book and for recognizing that a work of nonfiction can be worthy of this award. When I learned of their decision, I was thrilled. And I was astonished, as, I am sure, were many others who didn't expect a nonfiction book to win a Newbery Medal. The last time it happened was in 1956—thirty-two years ago. Of the sixty-seven Newbery winners to date, only six, including my own book, have been nonfiction.

Strangely, the book that launched these awards in 1922 was a work of nonfiction—*The Story of Mankind* (Liveright) by Hendrik Willem Van Loon. I still have my own boyhood copy, a special school edition that I read when I was ten or eleven years old. I remember where I read it— curled up on the maroon chesterfield that dominated our San Francisco living room. I spent several foggy summer days on that sofa, absorbed in *The Story of Mankind*. The title is revealing. It was a history book, to be sure, unmistakably a book of nonfiction, yet I read it that summer not to fulfill an assignment or write a report, but because I wanted to. I read it for pleasure, for the thrill of discovery. I think it was the first book that gave me a sense of history as a living thing, and it kept me turning the pages as though I were reading a gripping novel. It wasn't "just like a story"—it was a story.

Since *The Story of Mankind*, every nonfiction winner of the Newbery Medal has been a biography—the story of a life: *Invincible Louisa* (Little) by Cornelia Meigs in 1934; *Daniel Boone* (Viking) by James Daugherty in 1940; *Amos Fortune, Free Man* (Dutton) by Elizabeth Yates in 1951; *Carry On, Mr. Bowditch* (Houghton) by Jean Lee Latham in 1956; and this year, my own *Lincoln* (Clarion/ Houghton).

Along with the medal winners, there have been a number of nonfiction honor books through the years, including two previous biographies of Lincoln: *Abraham Lincoln's World* (Scribner) by Genevieve Foster in 1945, and *Abraham Lincoln, Friend of the People* (Follett) by Clara Ingram Judson in 1951. And, of course *Abraham Lincoln* (Doubleday) by Ingri and Edgar D'Aulaire was a Caldecott Medal winner in 1940 and remains a favorite today. So it seems that if you want to win a prize, Lincoln is a good subject.

And yet the fact remains that until recently, nonfiction books received a disproportionately small and meager share of the awards and prizes designed to honor the best literary work for children. While nonfiction has never been completely ignored, for a long time it was brushed off and pushed aside, as though factual books were socially inferior to the upper crust stuff we call literature. Upstairs, imaginative fiction dwelled grandly in the House of Literature. Downstairs, hard-working, utilitarian nonfiction lived prosaically in the servants' quarters. If a nonfiction book were talented and ambitious enough, it could rise above its station. But for the most part, children's nonfiction was kept in its place.

Milton Meltzer, who has written many fine nonfiction books for children, discussed this state of affairs twelve years ago, in February 1976, in his influential *Horn Book* article titled "Where Do All the Prizes Go? The Case for Nonfiction." "Librarians, teachers, reviewers—," he wrote, "the three groups who usually administer the awards or serve as judges—seem confident that only fiction can be considered literature." Meltzer's article was widely discussed, and it caused waves. The year it appeared, for example, a new category—nonfiction—was added to the Boston Globe-Horn Book Awards.

Why is it that factual books for children have had to struggle for the right to be taken seriously as literature? Surely there have been works of nonfiction during the past thirty-two years that were worthy of a Newbery Medal. Certainly no acceptable definition of literature can be so narrow as to exclude books based on fact. Good writing comes in many guises. Isaak Walton's *Compleat Angler,* a book about fishing, has been recognized as a literary classic for over 300 years. Emerson and Thoreau, founding fathers of American literature, were primarily writers of nonfiction. *Out of Africa* (Crown), *Anne Frank: The Diary of a Young Girl* (Doubleday), *Silent Spring* (Houghton) —they're all powerful works of nonfiction.

John McPhee has been highly praised for his adult nonfiction. He calls serious nonfiction "The Literature of Fact," which is the title of a writing course he has given at Princeton. Like others, McPhee emphasizes the fundamental role of the nonfiction writer as a storyteller—a storyteller who takes an oath to tell the truth. "Whatever you're writing," he says, "your motive is always to tell a good story while you're sitting around the cave, in front of the fire, before going out to club another mastodon. We keep finding new ways of doing this."

My father was a great storyteller. The problem was, we never knew for sure whether the stories he told were fiction or nonfiction. He was also a dedicated bookman. In fact, my parents met in a bookshop. She was a sales clerk, and he was a sales representative for Macmillan. They held their first conversation over a stack of bestsellers, and before they knew it, they were married. I had the good fortune to grow up in a house filled with books and book talk.

As a young man, I worked as a journalist and later a television publicity writer before discovering my true vocation. One day I happened to read a newspaper article about a sixteen-year-old boy who was blind; he had invented a Braille typewriter. That seemed remarkable, but as I read on, I learned something even more amazing: the Braille system itself, as used today all over the world, was invented by another sixteen-year-old boy who was blind, Louis Braille. That newspaper article inspired my first book, a collection of biographies called *Teenagers Who Made History* (Holiday).

I hadn't expected to become a writer of nonfiction books for children, but there I was. I had wandered into the field by chance, and I felt right at home. I couldn't wait to get started on my next book. As Sid Fleischman said in his acceptance speech last year, "It was as if I had found myself—and I didn't even know I had been lost."

That was during the early sixties. Since then, children's nonfiction has changed significantly in form and content. Consider biography. Until recently, children's biographies tended to be heavily fictionalized, dressed up with imaginary scenes and manufactured dialogue—as in "'Drink your tea, Eleanor,' said Franklin." There's an old tradition for this. In the United States, fictionalized biography has been a publishing staple ever since the Reverend Mason Locke Weems made up the cherry tree anecdote and inserted it into his *Life of George Washington*. The fifth edition of Weems' biography appeared in 1806; there we find the earliest known version of little George's immortal confession: "Father, I cannot tell a lie."

The whimsies of Parson Weems influenced generations of biographers. Fictionalization was justified on the grounds that it made history palatable to young readers, that it heightened interest and helped clarify complex issues. Along with fictionalization, children's biographies were characterized by a reverential tone, reflecting the educational values of the time. The purpose of biography was to bring the good news, to paint a life that was exemplary. Controversy and criticism were avoided; important historical figures were portrayed as idealized stereotypes; schools and school books presented a sanitized, sugar-coated version of history. For example, in the D'Aulaires' Caldecott-winning account of Lincoln's life, there is no mention that Lincoln was assassinated. As the book ends, the president sits down in his rocking chair to enjoy a well-earned rest.

Children's biographies have come a long way from the old days. That was inevitable, given the social and educational trends of the sixties and seventies that affected all forms of children's literature in so many different ways. The hero worship of the past has given way to a more realistic approach, which recognizes the warts and weaknesses that humanize the great. And fictionalization has become a naughty word. Many current biographies for children adhere as closely to documented evidence as any scholarly work. And the best of them manage to do so without becoming tedious or abstract or any less exciting than the most imaginative fictionalization.

Today's youngsters seem to prefer the facts. Isn't it more encouraging for a young reader to know that others, even the great figures of history, have shared the doubts and fears a child feels, than to be confronted with a paragon? Jean Fritz has done more than anyone to change the ground rules of children's biography. "'Children don't need a perfect picture,' she says. 'They need to see what human nature is, that history is made of the same stuff as our lives.'"

I grew up during the cherry-tree era of children's biography. Recently I looked again at a Lincoln biography I read as a boy; it contains my favorite example of invented dialogue. Abe is eleven years old in this scene, and his father is bawling him out: "'Books!' said his father. 'Always books! What is all this studying going to do for you? What do you think you are going to be?' 'Why,' said Abe, 'I'm going to be President.'"

I read that book as an elementary school student in San Francisco. Apparently the lessons of Lincoln's virtues were lost on me, for I was always being summoned to the principal's office. From the school corridor I would enter a small waiting room, and from there a door with a frosted glass pane led into Mrs. Koeppe's inner sanctum.

I would sit on the wooden bench in that waiting room—waiting for the ghostly form of Mrs. Koeppe to appear behind the frosted glass as she rose to open the door and say, "Come in, Russell." On the waiting room wall hung a pendulum clock, tick-tick-ticking off the seconds as I waited. And looking down at me from an adjacent wall was the bearded visage of Abraham Lincoln. George Washington may have been the father of our country, but Lincoln was the one who always knew when I was in trouble.

His picture reminded me that in America a boy could travel from a log cabin to the White House. Or rather, a good boy could. And from what I had read, young Abe was definitely a good boy. He was never late to school, and he always kept his clothes clean. As a young man working in a general store, he was so honest that he walked, or maybe ran, miles through drifting snow to return two cents change to a forgetful customer. Honest Abe—always fair in games and work, always kind to man and beast. That's the Lincoln I grew up with, a first cousin to Goody Two-shoes. It's worth mentioning that *The History of Goody Two-shoes* was published by John Newbery in 1765.

If there was a man behind the Lincoln myth, I knew little about him. It wasn't until years later that a passing remark in a piece by Mary McCarthy ignited my interest in Lincoln. Mary McCarthy, hardly a sentimentalist, said that she was fascinated by Lincoln's intellect and melancholy. Melancholy? That was my first inkling that a complex and paradoxical man—a believable human being—was concealed behind the layers of historical make-up. After that, Lincoln intrigued me, and when Clarion Books suggested that I write a presidential biography, Lincoln was my first and immediate choice.

One of the great joys of writing nonfiction for youngsters is the opportunity to explore almost any subject that excites your interest. I picked Lincoln as a subject because I felt I could offer a fresh perspective for today's generation of young readers, but mostly I picked him because I wanted to satisfy my own itch to know.

Approaching a biography of Lincoln is daunting. There have been more books written about him than any other American—thousands of titles covering every imaginable aspect of his life and career. Luckily, a friend told me about the Abraham Lincoln Bookshop in Chicago, so I made a beeline to that shop. I introduced myself to Daniel Weinberg, the proprietor, and told him what I was planning to do. Dan Weinberg saved me. He helped me chart my course through the Lincoln literature and decide which books to focus on. If it weren't for him, I'd probably still be researching Lincoln. My book wouldn't be finished today.

Along with my reading, I had a chance to enjoy the pleasures of eyewitness research. I visited Lincoln's log-cabin birthplace in Kentucky, his boyhood home in Indiana, and the reconstructed village of New Salem, Illinois, where he lived as a young man. I went to Springfield, with its wealth of Lincoln historical sites, and to Washington, D. C., for a firsthand look at Ford's Theatre and the rooming house across the street where the assassinated president died.

There's something magic about being able to lay your eyes on the real thing—something you can't get from your reading alone. As I sat at my desk in New York City and described Lincoln's arrival in New Salem at the age of twenty-two, I could picture the scene in my mind's eye, because I had walked down those same dusty lanes, where cattle still graze behind split-rail fences and geese flap about underfoot. When I wrote about Lincoln's morning walk from his house to his law office in downtown Springfield, I knew the route because I had walked it myself.

I'll never forget my visit to the Illinois State Historical Library in Springfield. One afternoon while I was working there, Tom Schwartz, the curator of the Lincoln Collection, came over and asked, "How would you like to see the vault?" I followed him through narrow aisles past crammed library shelves to an impressive bank vault. He twirled the big combination lock, swung open the heavy door, and invited me to step inside. It was cool and still in there, with temperature and humidity precisely regulated. Tom began to show me original documents written in Lincoln's own hand—a letter to his wife, a draft of a speech, scraps of paper with doodles and notes scrawled during long-ago trials in country courthouses. Each document had been treated with a special preservative that removed all traces of acid from the paper. Tom Schwartz pointed to one of Lincoln's courtroom notes and told me, "This will last a thousand years."

I didn't actually learn anything new in that vault or see anything that wasn't available in facsimile. And yet looking at those original documents, I could feel Lincoln's presence as never before, almost as though he had reached out to shake hands.

The more I learned about him, the more I came to appreciate his subtleties and complexities. The man himself turned out to be vastly more interesting than the myth. Of course, I was never able to understand him completely. I doubt if it's possible to understand anyone fully, and Lincoln was harder to figure out than most people, "the most secretive-reticent-shut-mouthed man that ever lived," according to his law partner, William Herndon, who knew him as well as anyone. That's something I wanted to get across to my readers—a sense of the mysteries of personality, the fascinating inconsistencies of character.

I was never tempted to write an idealized, hero-worshiping account. A knowledge of Lincoln's weaknesses throws his strengths, and his greatness, into sharper relief. And it certainly wasn't necessary to embellish the events of his life with imaginary scenes and dialogue. Lincoln didn't need a speech writer in his own time, and he doesn't need one now.

One of the beauties of his speeches was their eloquent brevity. He agonized over his speeches, revising and cutting and polishing until the moment he mounted the podium. He couldn't stand folks who were longwinded. Referring to one such person, Lincoln said, "That . . . [man] can compress the most words in the fewest ideas of anyone I ever knew."

He loved to tell the story about the lazy preacher who was notorious for his long-winded sermons. When asked how so lazy a man could write such long sermons, one of his deacons replied, "Oh! he gets to writing and is too lazy to stop."

I tried to keep that in mind as I was writing this speech.

I've been asked, "How long did it take to write your Lincoln biography?" Well, Lincoln was my thirty-fourth book, so let's say it took thirty-three books to write it. And it took the help and support of a great many people.

It took the help of Vernon Ives, an original founder of Holiday House, who gave me the encouragement I needed to finish my first book and who published that book in 1961; and the help of Marjorie Jones, my first editor at Holiday House, who treated me gently while I was struggling to learn my craft.

I've been associated with Holiday House for so long that I'm indebted to just about everyone there—to Barbara Walsh, the managing editor, and David Rogers, the art director; to John and Kate Briggs, who have made me part of their family; and to Margery Cuyler, an inspired editor and dear friend who has never stopped pushing and prodding me to do better.

I'm grateful to Ann Troy, my editor at Clarion Books, who put her magic touch on *Lincoln*—as I knew she would; to Carol Goldenberg and Sylvia Frezzolini, who designed the book and thereby graced it; to Marjorie Naughton, whose enthusiasm and skill helped make this evening happen; and to Jim Giblin, a staunch friend and ally long before he became my publisher. Lincoln said, "The better part of one's life consists in his friendships." The children's book field has given me some truly wonderful friends, and this is a perfect moment to thank them all.

Finally I want to thank each of you in the American Library Association. You're the people who set the standards for children's books and put those books into the hands of readers. As you know, Lincoln valued books and librarians. Speaking before the Springfield Library Association on February 22, 1860, he said: "Writing, the art of communicating thoughts to the mind through the eye, is the great invention of the world . . . enabling us to converse with the dead, the absent, and the unborn, at all distances of time and space."

The poet John Keats once said: "A life of any worth is a continual allegory." Maybe that's why I started with a book of biographical sketches and after some byways, was drawn back to biography, to Lincoln. Perhaps, after all, it is that sense of worth, that allegorical illumination, that both fiction and nonfiction are after. And I take your support to be the recognition of that secret yearning in us all.

Russell Freedman
Frank J. Dempsey

Russell Freedman

The term Renaissance Man has been overworked in recent decades, but how else would you describe someone who has written books about famous teenagers, poisonous snakes, the Boy Scouts, farm animals, Jules Verne, killer fish, Indian chiefs, immigrant children, and Abraham Lincoln? Since some of these things weren't around during the Renaissance, perhaps Twenty-first Century Man would better describe Russell Freedman.

Over the past thirty years Russell has written at least one book a year and has built up a solid reputation among teachers, librarians, and the reading public for his craftsmanship, reliability, and intellectual integrity. One book a year—unless you're Robert Ludlum—won't permit you to live too flamboyantly on the Upper West Side of Manhattan, so Russell has frequently augmented his hardcover productions with articles for such estimable publications as *Columbia Encyclopedia, Merit Students Encyclopedia, The Book of Knowledge,* and, on many occasions, pieces for that splendid magazine for children, *Cricket.* He also conducted writing workshops at the New School for Social Research in New York City from 1969 to 1986, and more than one of his students went on to be a published writer in his or her own right. Before moving uptown, he lived from 1958 to 1967 in appropriately cramped quarters in Greenwich Village, as suits struggling young writers—although he never described himself, and probably didn't perceive himself, in terms of that romantic cliché.

Russell Freedman was born, one of two children, to Irene and Louis Freedman in 1929 in San Francisco. It would be tempting to digress and review the absorbing life of Freedman père (neé Garbowitz), one of fourteen children, who grew up in New York City, joined the U.S. army at age fourteen in World War I—to accomplish this, he shed

Garbowitz for the name of his best friend, Freedman—married an American girl, and spent twenty years of his life as the manager of the West Coast sales office for Macmillan Publishing Company. But that is another whole story which needs to be told itself someday. Perhaps Russell will tell it.

Considering that Russell grew up in a strictly urban—albeit Western —milieu, his later penchant for tusks, fangs, and the Great Plains is a bit puzzling. His only early exposure to animals, he tells us, was represented by a cat named Sally and a dog named Spot, and whatever birds and squirrels were willing to tolerate the yearlong chills and fogs of San Francisco's Richmond District. His "bookish inclination"—as Benjamin Franklin would have dubbed it—was heavily augmented, no doubt, by the fact that Louis Freedman had filled the house with books. One title in particular Russell recalls with affection: Ernest Thompson Seton's *Wild Animals I Have Known*, published in 1898, a collection of gentle sketches about creatures far more tractable and cuddly than Russell's menagerie of biters and scratchers. John Steinbeck, William Saroyan, and John Masefield all dined at the Freedman house, "and they all had leg of lamb," Russell remembers, "since that was the one thing my mother trusted herself to cook. Whenever she came home from the butcher with a leg of lamb, I knew another author was coming for dinner."

If anything of particular significance happened during Russell's school days, first in San Francisco and later in Connecticut, he's not telling, and the great adventure of later going to college at the University of California in Berkeley was tranquil compared to later years of that tortured campus. As with most little boys, Russell at first wanted to be a fireman, then a policeman, and then, of course, a writer. Uncle Sam wanted him to be a soldier.

In that unequal controversy, Russell was clearly the loser and ended up spending from 1951 to 1953 in Korea, some of it in combat status, with the Second Infantry Division. After that early police action ended, the pen replaced the bayonet, and he got his first real job as a reporter and editor for the Associated Press. "That was where I really learned to write," Russell reminisces. No more Chaucer, no more Sheridan, no more Brontë. His life changed from "Great Classics of English Literature" to "The Front Page." But, good job that it was, it was still in San Francisco, even in those days still considered something of a backwash by the Fourth Estate in the East. Russell wanted to be a part of the New York establishment and took a job with the J. Walter Thompson Advertising Agency, where he spent the next thirty-six months writing television publicity for such popular slices of Americana as "Kraft Television Theatre," "Father Knows Best," and "The Real McCoys." Russell says of that period: "Many people thought I had one of the most glamorous jobs in the world, but I didn't think so. I wanted to write about people and things that I cared about."

The catalyst that was to launch this career into reality was a story Russell read in *The New York Times* concerning a sixteen-year-old blind boy who had invented a Braille typewriter. Then, as he read further, he found out the Braille system itself was also invented by a sixteen-year-old. The youth of these men particularly impressed Russell, and he reasoned there must be other true and fascinating stories about people in this same age group who had an impact upon their worlds. There were indeed, and this realization was the genesis of Russell's first hardcover book, *Teenagers Who Made History* (Holiday), a remarkably durable title that remained in print for nearly twenty years. "I never expected or planned to become a writer of non-fiction for young people," Russell remarked recently, "but I certainly have no regrets." The book was followed by *2000 Years of Space Travel, Jules Verne,* and *Scouting with Baden-Powell* (all Holiday), *Thomas Alva Edison* (Study-Master)—and then came the animals.

The first of the animal books, which were to total twenty-three before he turned elsewhere, appeared in 1969, *How Animals Learn* (Holiday). It was also about this time that Russell decided to make what would be a major shift in the format of his books: using striking, informative photographs, rather than drawings to illustrate his texts. This approach, which he still follows, proved popular and successful, and he began to develop a well-deserved reputation among book buyers for a consistently informative and entertaining style. This format also led to countless hours of research in photo archives the country over to locate just the right picture. The plaudits were heard early on, with starred reviews in *Booklist* and elsewhere. The last animal book, *Sharks* (Holiday), surfaced in 1985, when Russell decided to return to the human comedy for future productions. "But I may write some more animal books," he recently cautioned.

Right away a built-in restriction asserted itself regarding the use of photographs. Wishing to continue the heavy and successful emphasis on photography in his books, he was necessarily limited to people and events occurring after the 1840s, the decade photography was invented. This problem turned out to be not-at-all insurmountable.

Further motivation was provided, if not needed, by Street Kids: 1864–1977, an outstanding photography exhibit at the New York Historical Society featuring wonderful photos of New York City's children in the nineteenth century. "I was deeply moved and impressed by this show," Russell remarked later, "and by the poignant expressions on the faces of these children, most of whom had never had their picture taken before." This experience led directly to Immigrant Kids (Dutton). Reviews, as usual, were very good, but sales were modest.

But sales were not a problem with the next book. Children of the Wild West (Clarion/Houghton), which resulted in Russell being awarded the prestigious Western Heritage Award from the National Cowboy Hall of Fame for the outstanding juvenile book that year on a Western theme. The award ceremony, as it always is, was held in Oklahoma City, and he reported to me in rather awed tones, "I sat on the dais next to Kirk Douglas and Burl Ives!"

Since he had treated cowboys, there obviously should be equal time for Indians, and, sure enough, Indian Chiefs (Holiday) came out the following year. Because he wanted to give fair and equal attention to all six of the native American leaders he was describing, Russell said that this book was the hardest one he had attempted to date.

Then came Lincoln: A Photobiography (Clarion/Houghton). I grudgingly admit that I was one of the mistaken Jeremiahs who predicted, "Another book on Lincoln? It is not needed and won't sell"— so much for calamitous prophets. Even before the Newbery announcement, his colleagues were saying "what a wonderful book," "his best yet," and other such encomiums. From the handsome cover and binding all the way to the back cover photos of Lincoln with McClellan at Antietam, the book is a class act.

I was privileged to be in Springfield, Illinois, with Russell while he was doing research on the Lincoln book. His enthusiasm for his subject was unbridled. Yes, we had to go through the Lincoln house carefully; yes, we had to visit New Salem and spend several hours trudging its streets; yes, we had to spend time at the old train station and go to the Lincoln-Herndon Law Offices. His fervor rose in inverse proportion to my own fatigue.

As we finally emerged from the old Lincoln home at Eighth and Jackson Streets, we saw two boys, one black, one white, playing boisterously and naturally, as boys do, near the corner. They were obviously best friends and paid great attention to what the other was saying or doing. Then they strolled off, their arms encircling each other's shoulders. "He would have liked that," Russell smiled at me. I think Lincoln would also have been pleased to have such a gifted and caring biographer.

The Caldecott Medal 1989

Song and Dance Man

written by
Karen Ackerman

illustrated by
Stephen Gammell

published by
Knopf, 1988

Horn Book Review

It is not hard to coax Grandpa up to the attic and persuade him to perform his old vaudeville routines. A former song and dance man,
Grandpa can still set his feet to tapping, recall the favorite old songs,
and chortle over ancient jokes before his three delighted grandchildren.
They love his magic tricks and applaud his grand finale, complete with
top hat and gold-headed cane. After refolding his striped vest and wrapping his tap shoes in what he calls a shammy cloth, Grandpa clambers
downstairs with the children for the most glorious of hugs. Finally,
with a beautifully depicted look of pride, mixed with sadness and longing, Grandpa pauses at the foot of the attic stairs as the children "wonder how much he really misses that time on the vaudeville stage, when
he was a song and dance man." The quiet, almost understated text,
related from the children's point of view, is brought to warm and affectionate life by the superb artistry of the illustrator. As Grandpa taps
and twirls across the pages, we, too, are drawn to the genial old gen-
tleman who can still "strut his stuff." The drawings of the mop-haired,
somewhat scruffy children and a baggy-trousered Grandpa convey their
loving relationship and allow readers to share a special and even transcendent family moment.—*Ethel R. Twichell*

Booklist Review

In this affectionate story, three children follow their grandfather up to
the attic where he pulls out his old bowler hat, gold-tipped cane, and

most importantly, his tap shoes. Grandpa once danced on the vaude-ville stage, and as he glides across the floor, the children can see what it was like to be song and dance man. As the enthralled children watch, Grandpa sings, pulls a silver dollar from one child's hair, and tells jokes. For a grand finale, he performs a tap dance that had him leap-ing in the air, the children's applause ringing in his ears. Gammell cap-tures all the story's inherent joie de vivre with color pencil renderings that fairly leap off the pages. Bespectacled, enthusiastic Grandpa clearly exudes the message that you're only as old as you feel but the children respond—as will readers—to the nostalgia of the moment. Grandpa says he wouldn't trade a million good old days for those he spends with his grandchildren, but the way he glances up the attic stairs gives a hint of the depth of his feelings. Utterly original.—*Ilene Cooper*

Stephen Gammell
Anne Schwartz

Stephen Gammell

My relationship with Stephen Gammell takes place over the phone, through the mail, and across a desk only occasion-ally. I'm familiar with only the profes-sional part of a very private person, someone who seems tough to know at all. Of course I can make a good guess that, for example, he'd prefer dropping in unannounced and sharing some sim-ple conversation and a couple of beers to lunch at a fancy restaurant. Why do I assume this? Because of the way Stephen worked on *Song and Dance Man* (Knopf), and even because of the kind of work he produced—down-to-earth, spontaneous, warm, energetic, seriously playful.

So I will write about what I know: how Stephen worked on illus-trating the book. His first letter (January 1987) was short and to the point:

> Okay, Okay—uncross your toes. I'll do it! *Song and Dance Man.*
> Call me, and we'll go over those ugly, sordid details of money,
> size, deadline, etc.

Everything got off to an unusually smooth start. A contract was negotiated with lightning speed and amazing ease. Stephen, Denise Cronin—Knopf's art director—and I chose a trim size for the book. But then Stephen asked for revision of the manuscript. I loved, as it was, this exuberant, poignant story about a grandpa who re-creates his old, still dear-to-his-heart vaudeville act for an audience of curious grandchildren up in his attic. But at that point Grandpa's performance consisted almost exclusively of singing and dancing, and Stephen wanted more to draw, more bits of stage business. I felt his unique, visual perspective on the material was valid. Nervously and with all the editorial tact I could muster, I passed his thoughts on to author Karen Ackerman, not knowing how she would react. Fortunately, Karen responded with enthusiasm, taking Stephen's general comments and making them her own. She added a couple of wonderfully visual episodes that resulted in some of Stephen's best illustrations: Grandpa rolling the bowler hat down his arm and later pulling the seemingly endless red handkerchief from his pocket.

The next written communication from Stephen, in September, accompanied a characteristically thin package. Instead of a complete dummy with text and loose drawings in place to show us his intent for the finished book, he sent an art-free, text-only dummy, along with just seven sketches. Six were of Grandpa alone, and one was of the grandchildren arriving. Later, Stephen explained that he only does a preliminary drawing in order to "see on paper something I already see in my head, or to resolve a question I may have about a particular scene." He also sent some notes.

> Well, here's what I've done so far. The general spirit and color and technique are pretty much what you see. I do like Grandpa with glasses; however, he takes them off for the show . . . How about rain? The weather isn't integral to the story anyway, and all we want is something to make the attic more cozy . . . . Off to Bismarck, North Dakota, to talk with the librarians and prairie dogs.

In the sketch that would later be refined to become cover art, Grandpa was without glasses. But somewhere in the process Stephen must have decided Grandpa needed his glasses on. And in the sketch of the opening scene, Stephen showed the grandchildren coming over through a rainstorm. No rain appeared anywhere in the final book. Stephen decided to jump right into things and begin in Grandpa's house—effectively shifting the focus of the story from the children to Grandpa himself.

Our comments were extremely minimal; we were pleased with what we saw. Denise did the major design work and sent Stephen a type-dummy based on his own divisions of the text. Two months later we received the package of finished art, along with a note:

> I have no dedication. I would like someone to talk with me before (or during) the writing of the flap copy, so it doesn't end up being the same old thing. I'd like to have it eliminated (my part) altogether. Well, I hope you like the art. I did my best (I'd like to think anyway).

We liked the art. We loved the art. I let Stephen know in a letter that also requested some biographical information for publicity purposes. He didn't want to fill out our standard author's questionnaire. Instead, he wrote this note, attaching the photo we'd requested: "I was born in Des Moines, Iowa. Live and work in St. Paul. . . . *Song and Dance Man* drawings were done with colored pencils. I like chocolate chip cookies and milk, Laurel and Hardy movies, and slippers. . . . (Is this what you want?)"

Well, we managed fine. The flap copy was written, including Stephen's bio for the back—much more mundane than the information he'd supplied. Some time in February of 1988 mechanicals were sent to the printer in Singapore. We got a first set of proofs off to Stephen in April, and he sent us a warm response:

> I just want to say how pleased I am about how the book looks. I think they are truly beautiful reproductions. The way they bleed off the page, and the nice choice of type face and placement make for a very attractive book. I am very happy with it. And I don't think the printing is too dark or too heavy. Perhaps they are as compared to the originals, but I like the look of it. Leave it? Please? Yes, I agree that the title should be in some color or colors. So, I thank you for your part in making a book of mine look so good!

The long wait for finished copies was hard on veteran Gammell: "*Song and Dance Man* off-press yet? Am anxious."

But, at last, in September, books! He wrote:

> The books arrived at my studio yesterday. I love *Song and Dance Man*, and hope that it's promoted well. . . . It's one of my better books, and it deserves a long life . . . for Karen's sake, all grandpas everywhere, and kids who have them.

And that's all there was to it, easy-as-pie for us at Knopf. As far as I was concerned, *Song and Dance Man* was the first book I'd worked on that had illustrated itself. There was almost no planning, no back-and-forth, not even any substantial input on Denise's and my parts. Stephen just sat down, drew his best pictures, and sent them in. No wonder his art feels so absolutely fresh, explodes with such energy, seems so free and easy. There is no trace of the effort that surely, secretly, went into their making.

Early on, right after Karen Ackerman had seen one of the preliminary sketches of Grandpa, she wrote a few prophetic words:

> I'm so pleased with Stephen's initial artwork—it's difficult for me to describe the feeling of contentment I have. Grandpa even looks a bit like my father, for whom the book was written. I've got a feeling this one will be a winner for us all!

The Newbery Medal 1989

Joyful Noise

written by
Paul Fleischman

illustrated by
Eric Beddows

published by
Harper/Zolotow, 1988

JOYFUL
NOISE

Poems for Two Voices

PAUL FLEISCHMAN
illustrated by Eric Beddows

Horn Book Review

Every so often a book is published which demands accolades. This marvelous, lyrical evocation of the insect world belongs in that category. Scored for two voices, "one taking the left-hand part, the other taking the right-hand part," it is a companion volume to *I Am Phoenix* (Harper/Zolotow), but, unlike many such complementary works, stands on its own merits, equaling—perhaps even surpassing—its predecessor. The subjects, ranging from grasshoppers to butterflies, represent familiar insect classifications. Each is personified according to its particular habitat and notable habits so that the poems flow from the nature of the subjects: symbolism and emotion are thus logical derivatives rather than artificial impositions. Consequently, there is variety in tone, mood, and theme, making the collection one which can be used selectively with younger children but with broad appeal for intermediate and older audiences, including adults. "Water Boatmen," for example, with the insistent refrain "Stroke" punctuating short, straightforward, descriptive lines could be used for voice choirs in the early grades; in contrast, "Mayflies," with its references to "birthday / and dying day, I this particle of time I this single sip of living," needs a more sophisticated audience. Similar demands are made by the humor of "Book Lice," chronicling the romance between two insects with differing literary tastes, and "Honeybees," contrasting the worker's with the queen's perspective. In these latter two poems Fleischman has achieved an effect similar to that used in opera in which voices blend in a duet, yet each part has a different message to convey. The imagery throughout the volume is as remarkable as the technique: memorable but never intrusive, again because the words seem exactly right for the particular voice. There are fourteen poems in the handsomely designed volume, with stylish endpapers and wonderfully interpretive black-and-white illustrations. Each selection is a gem, polished perfection. If Paul Fleischman never wrote another book, his reputation would remain secure with this one.—*Mary M. Burns*

Booklist Review

Similar in style and format to the author's *I Am Phoenix* (*Booklist* 82:530 D 185), a book of poetry concerning birds, this collection of poems for two voices explores the lives of insects. Designed to be read aloud, the phrases of the poems are spaced vertically on the page in two columns, one for each reader. The voices sometimes alternate, sometimes speak in chorus, and sometimes echo each other. Fleischman steps imaginatively inside each insect and in fine, free verse gives that creature's own point of view on its unique qualities, life cycle, and habits. Beddows, who illustrated the earlier book under the name Ken Nutt, uses lively pencil drawings that are well composed, precise, and witty. While the book may need introduction to children, it could be used successfully for offbeat choral readings in the classroom or auditorium.—*Carolyn Phelan*

1989 Newbery Acceptance Speech
Paul Fleischman

My father was in the shower when his Newbery call came. I was in a dentist's chair. Apparently genes do indeed rule our lives. The receptionist told me to call home before leaving. When I did, my two-year-old, Dana, answered, then his older brother Seth took the phone and spoke the words "New baby." I paused. I was not aware that my wife and I were planning to have a third child. "You're kidding," I said. Then Becky got on and made a minor adjustment in pronunciation. "You're kidding," I said, and said again, and again. And occasionally still say.

Within a few hours of that call I began receiving suggestions for a Newbery speech that would match, in necktie-and-handkerchief fashion, a book of two-voiced poems about insects. Turn the amplifier to the "Echo" setting! Release a swarm of cicadas into the room! Sign the Temptations to sing behind you, repeating key phrases from your speech! My own first impulse was to begin by quoting, at great length and in learned fashion, from Aristotle's *Poetics*, Robert Graves' *The*

White Goddess, and various other works I hope to read someday. Discarding that notion, I've decided instead to draw from an anonymous author, a man who gave me a ride when I was hitchhiking fifteen years ago in the Berkshires. He was dressed entirely in white, a color, he explained, that would have a calming effect on people in the event of a calamity. This seemed a less-than-glowing recommendation of his driving habits. Later, however, talking about music, he gave me my epigraph for tonight's talk. "Some people understand the flute," he said. "Some people understand the violin. Some people understand the saxophone. But everybody understands the drum."

Fireflies flickering, gleaming glowing. 1-2-3 1-2-3, 1-2 1-2.

Of Joyful Noise's many tributaries, music was the widest. I began taking piano lessons from Miss Dixon when I was seven years old. Ironically, my mind never mastered eighth notes and quarter notes and the rest of the code for conveying rhythm. My heart, however, lusted after the small plaster busts of the great composers which she presented to worthy students, and so I listened to how she played a piece and duplicated it. I often played duets with her and with a close family friend who had two pianos.

Upon graduating from elementary school, I determined to put away childish things, specifically piano lessons. In eleventh grade, however, I rediscovered classical music. It began with Scheherazade. Then Brahms' Fourth Symphony. The Firebird. Then one day my father brought home from the library the score of Tchaikovsky's Romeo and Juliet, which we followed with our fingers while the music flew by. I was entranced by the visual beauty of a score, and by all that simultaneous activity, so carefully worked out by the composer. Writing books held no exotic appeal for me. But writing music, filling those twenty-five staves with all manner of intricate goings-on, precisely timing entrances and exits, whispering secrets with the double bass while the listener's ear was fixed on the woodwinds—there was a notion that kept me awake nights. At a time when future writers are usually devouring books, I was racing though the newly appeared record collection in the Santa Monica, California, public library. Schubert! Chopin! Beethoven! Brahms! I felt like the first miner to hit the gold fields.

Like writing, Los Angeles held little lure. Following the laws of the physics of adolescence, having grown up in the southwestern corner of the country, I desired to move as far as possible in a northeasterly direction. After two years of college, I rode a bicycle up the coast to Vancouver, took the train across Canada, and settled down in the woods of New Hampshire. One town away, in Henniker, was a college that sponsored a recorder consort. Though I'd brought along no winter coat, no gloves, no scarf, and no long underwear, I had prudently packed my alto recorder, an instrument I'd taken up a few years before. I sat down and learned my quarter notes and eighth notes. I joined the group, the first I'd ever played in—and found myself back in the gold fields.

Purcell! Morley! Loeillet! Telemann! This time, however, I was making the music. This new role effected a revelation. Playing a piece of music, I discovered, gave far more pleasure than merely listening to it. And playing music with other people was infinitely more enjoyable than playing alone. It was glorious fun, and at its best gave a rapture I've never found elsewhere. The seed for *Joyful Noise* was planted.

Or, rather, one of the seeds. In the 1930s an Austrian composer, Ernst Toch, had written a work entitled Geographical Fugue. It was composed in the strict style of a fugue, but was meant not to be played, but rather spoken by a chorus. "Trinidad," begin the tenors, "and the big Mississippi and the town Honolulu and the Lake Titicaca . . ." followed by the altos, then the sopranos, then the basses. It was a brilliant idea. Back in high school, a friend of mine had heard the piece. As a project for a class on the Bible as literature, he'd written his own Biblical Fugue, scored for four solo voices and making use of the Bible's rich store of proper names. I was one of the speakers who performed it.

That was in the twelfth grade, when I was writing what seemed to me to be poetry. By coincidence—an uncanny one, since I only recently heard Geographical Fugue for the first time—I had in my notebook an Ernst Toch-like line, a line I didn't know what to do with. It was "Cyprus, Sicily, Corsica, Crete." The next year, for a college music class, I composed my own multi-voiced piece. It was written for three voices and called Fruit Milange. The title was all too apt. It began with "Cyprus, Sicily, Corsica, Crete," then wandered on through "Merrill Lynch Pierce Fenner and Smith," Asian geography, heavenly bodies, bicycles, berries, and sundry other matters.

After some exposure to real musicians, I realized that I belonged to a different flock. I also decided that I wasn't meant to teach history, my main subject in college. Writing, however, seemed a possibility and on the brink of graduation, needing to earn a living, it was time to reach for the possible.

It turned out to be the perfect choice. I could continue to scavenge among American history—I was an inveterate trash can searcher as a child, combing the alleys of Santa Monica. I could still loiter in libraries and used bookstores, hunting information on silhouette cutting, binnacle boys, yellow fever, wigmaking, or serendipitously stumbling on something I wasn't looking for, something that might lead to a future book.

Similarly, I found that I could make use of my musical interests. Writing prose had much in common with writing music. From Berlioz and Britten and company, as much from Twain and Gogol and Dylan Thomas, I learned to seek a form with a pleasing shape, to build in both unity and contrast, to love both entrances and the cadence of closings. Every chapter, every paragraph, every sentence, I discovered, has an arc to it, like a musical phrase. Every word has both a meaning and a music.

I write only a page or so a day. After several books it dawned on me that this was because I was writing prose that scanned, something that makes for slow progress. "The weathervanes of Boston were pointed north—the frigates, the angels, the cocks, the cows—and so, below, was Mr. Baggot." This first sentence in *Saturnalia*, the novel that occupied me last year, has three parts, each of which contains four beats. You could say it, and all my prose, is written in 4/4 time—though I never let the meter become so obvious as to attract attention. I work out my books in detail before starting, so that most of my writing time is devoted not to sense but to sound: to rhythm, to the rhyme of "so" and "below," then the pivot to the alliteration with "Baggot." This might sound like hard labor to some. Eight hours of this generally leaves me refreshed, not exhausted. The time passes quickly. I'm playing in the vast sandbox of the English language.

Writing, for me, is in fact very close to play. As a child, a demonstration of how to string flowers in a chain came as an epiphany. I moved on to building with driftwood at the beach. At Berkeley I made pine needle houses. In New Hampshire, waiting to catch a ride at the bottom of my road, I used sticks, weeds, cans, whatever was at hand, searching for a way to connect them. Play is usually viewed as among those childish things one does well to put away. I've always remembered flipping through my mother's copy of *Minute Sketches of Great Composers*. Each page featured a grim-faced portrait, a brief text, and a motto such as "The Chopin of the North." It was the entry on the Scarlattis, Alessandro and Domenico that fascinated me. Seeming to point out the terrible wages of play, their motto read "Serious Father, Frivolous Son."

Here was my shameful destiny prefigured! A leather-skinned beach bum building driftwood sculptures, peddling painted rocks for drinks in bars, telling all who would listen that my father was the famous author of children's books! In actuality, frivolity, improvisation, experimentation—play led me to this august gathering tonight. What can you make out of a handful of sticks? How can you connect a half-dozen characters? It's much the same problem, and the same joy: the joy involved in joining both post to lintel and hero to villain, in rummaging for supplies at the beach or among books, in watching a wall go up or a paragraph. The joy found in making has begotten all my books.

After six of those books had been written, I took another look at Fruit Milange and wondered if it might be possible to do a multivoiced book for children. Birds attracted me as a subject. They'd been my clock hands and calendar in New Hampshire. I would write a suite, beginning with the finches' exultation at dawn and ending with the calling of the owls at night. Here was a chance to cast aside sense—or at least plot and character development—and devote myself almost solely to sound. "Berries everywhere, there's berries everywhere" from Fruit Melange became "Sparrows everywhere, there's sparrows everywhere." The pieces came quickly and easily. I was in paradise, as close to writing music as I'll ever get. I'd no idea whether such a book would be published; all I knew was that I'd never had so much fun writing one.

The book was published, as *I Am Phoenix*. I'd no idea what response it would get. One of the first reviews to come in could be summarized with the three words "Shred this book." When I visited schools, however, I found that a reading of a single poem removed the book's arcane aura and that even the poorest readers wanted to step up and join me. Performing poetry, of course, is old, not new, as old as Homer, the revered father of rap music. Meter, rhyme, alliteration—they're all forms of repetition, something children don't need to be taught to appreciate, having been tutored in the womb by their mothers' heartbeats, followed by graduate work in the rocking chair. Performing poetry brings out those repetitions more forcefully than silent reading. As Donald Hall has said, "Poetry begins in the mouth."

Shortly before *I Am Phoenix* came out I thought of doing another such collection, but quickly dismissed the idea. Sequels were for Nancy Drew and Rocky. Instead of moving backward, I would move ahead. I would write a different sort of multivoiced book, one with not just two voices, but eleven. This became the picture book *Rondo in C*, published last fall, a book with a roomful of narrators, each of whom gives his or her associations evoked by a single piece of music played at a piano recital. Miss Dixon, I hope, would approve.

The idea of more two-voiced poems, however, wouldn't leave my head. Though I'd spent many hours watching birds, I was led to insects as a subject through books, and serendipity. When I'd taken the train across Canada, I'd run out of reading material in Manitoba—it's a big country. In the Winnipeg train station I'd bought a book called *Beyond Your Doorstep*, by Hal Borland. In it he mentioned his marvelous fellow nature writer Edwin Way Teale. I read several of his books, and many years later, when I happened to notice "Teale" on the spine of a volume in a used book store, it jumped out at me. The book was *The Strange Lives of Familiar Insects*. Others are touched by destiny at birth or in battle or on mountaintops; with me, the scene always takes place in used bookstores.

At the time, I was at work on a novel. As a dessert-like reward for finishing it, I promised myself at least a try at another two-voiced book, on insects. Unfortunately, that novel struck a rock and sank in chapter 4. I certainly wasn't raised to eat dessert before finishing a meal, but what else was I to do? Trying to drive from my mind my broken pact, I started on the poem I'd been itching to write, a requiem for the insects slain by the first frost of fall. But when I put pencil to paper, nothing worked out. Perhaps this was due to the fact that I was using the first lines of the requiem mass in Latin, not their English translation. Or perhaps it was a sign from above. I tried the moth's fevered serenade to the porch light. Again, unlike with *I Am Phoenix*, the words wouldn't come, wouldn't fit, wouldn't rhyme. If this account were rendered as a gothic novel, a storm would be bearing down at this point, the wind shrieking "Finish your novel," the rain striking the windows with a sound remarkably like "No sequels."

I took the hint. I abandoned the book. I'd never failed to finish one book before, much less two in a row. I'm grateful I didn't know at the time how many abandoned books I would shortly claim to my credit. After snatching up the nuggets in my own gold field, the pickings were suddenly scarcer. To avoid repeating myself, I had to tiptoe around all my previous books as well as those on the horizon. Perhaps after eight years of writing it was time to lie fallow, to soak up the rain.

Unaware that I was supposed to be lying fallow, I kept myself frantically busy. Various chimerical projects dazzled me, then disappeared. I tinkered with the requiem and the serenade over a period of months. Eventually I got them right, but only after such toil that it seemed clear to me I wasn't meant to continue. I labored to salvage my novel, without success. More months passed. I kept opening my file, taking out "Requiem" and "The Moth's Serenade," reading them, and putting them back. But like a cricket in the house, they kept chirping to me. They were polished now. I forgot their difficult deliveries and grew fond of them. I couldn't let them go to waste—it would be like throwing good food away. Fall came, a time when I often start a book. Desperate to prove to myself that I could finish one, I set to work, and with much less struggle, wrote the other twelve poems. It was like building a house because you happened to have a nice pair of doors on hand.

Insects might seem an unpromising choice of subject to some. The creed "Nothing human is alien to me" would seem to exclude the doings of arthropods. I've never found them impossibly foreign, dating from the day, years ago, when I went to retrieve an open gallon of paint and found a wasp, completely enveloped in white, laboring to swim to the side of the can. I don't believe I'll be guilty of anthropomorphism if I allege that the wasp was struggling to live. I happened to be in the midst of a depression at that time. I found no barrier to identifying with the wasp.

Or with any of the other creatures in the book. Though some were chosen purely for their musical possibilities, most struck me as metaphors for myself. Like A. E. Housman, who could tell a line of true poetry by the bristling of his skin, I search for something—an object, a character, an historical happening, an insect—that produces a similar effect because it embodies my current circumstances. Like the self-absorbed shoemaker's apprentice in *Graven Images,* I see signs and symbols everywhere. But I write fiction, not autobiography. Just as a snowflake forms around a speck of dust, I build a story for children around that metaphorical center, a story in which my own situation is transformed past recognition. For my loyalty, once I've found my idea is fixed entirely on the snowflake, on the facts of a digger wasp's life, not my own. Sometimes, as with a dream, even I don't understand how the book is related to me, the knowledge often arriving years later, like light traveling from the stars.

If insects seemed a strange choice of subject, two voices must seem an even stranger method. This method itself attracted me as a metaphor as much as a form. We all have more than one voice within us. A writer lives off these multiple voices. I recall an interview with John Nichols, who said there were close to 200 characters in his novel *The Milagro Beanfield War*—and that every one of them was him. The composer Robert Schumann gave names to his three dominant voices: stormy Florestan, sweet-voiced Eusebius, and the introspective Raro. I think of my own as Eros and Thanatos, characters who inhabit us all. The former writes my comedies of courtship, my fast movements; the latter loves sculptures and silhouettes, lifeless images of the living, and writes all my darker pieces. Both are always present. Both demand their due. I feel that my best books are those they've both had a hand in, the books that embrace both spring and fall. In *Joyful Noise*, which makes a circuit of the seasons, their authorship is clear. As it is, I notice in retrospect, in that first impelling pair of poems, a love song and a requiem.

A book for two voices requires two readers. Reading it is a social, not a solitary, pastime. All through my years at home it was my parents' habit after dinner to retire to the living room to play a game or two, games my sisters and I often joined. As with geologic eras, those years could be divided into concentration and rummy, early cribbage, chess, double solitaire, late cribbage, and so on. For a time, my mother copied out the cryptogram from the *Saturday Review* and raced my father in decoding it. I'm sure that those thousands of evenings, that education in the pleasures of being with others, in the joys to be found in joint amusements impossible alone, led in large part to my two-voiced books. One hand can't produce a clap, or play a game of checkers. Two can. Synergy! The television, I might add, was in a different room and seldom seemed to be on. A family watching TV together isn't engaged in a cooperative activity; they're each playing solitaire.

When I speak of this, people tell me about the entertainments of their own youth. One friend described a small cigar factory in which the workers sang together while they rolled the tobacco leaves, entertaining themselves and the people in the neighborhood, who would gather around the open doorway to listen. The sight of anyone doing something, producing something, seems to fascinate us. Think of people watching sports or construction projects. The doer acts, putting his stamp, large or small, on the world. To be the doer oneself, to sing instead of merely listening from the doorway, is an empowering experience. For me, to do one's doing with others, to be one of several hands producing a clap, multiplies the magic.

I grew up without brothers, in a neighborhood full of girls. Perhaps this explains the lure that groups—small and nondenominational—have had for me. Like many of the children who use your libraries, I also grew up apart from extended family and without a strong sense of membership in a religion, ethnic group, or community. I wanted to be part of something larger than myself—the very thing that previous generations, builders of the suburbs and the nuclear family, had struggled to be free of. In college I discovered the Greek myths. Like a newborn duck imprinting on its mother, I decided that the Greeks were my group. I would learn by heart their history and their legends. Their gods would be mine. I would be one of them, and indeed, motifs from those myths appear in many of my books.

There were, however, very few ancient Greeks around to associate with. I needed a more tangible group, the sort that met on Wednesday nights. I found it, at last, in the recorder consort. Here were the pleasures of doing, of making, of playing, engaged in with six or eight others. The joys of joining voices, from soprano to bass, of connecting people, of building music—that monument to synergy.

Porch light, hear my plight! I drink your light like nectar Dream of you by day, gaze in your eyes all night! Porch light! Bright paradise!

I've tried to put those same joys, that same excitement, interplay, spontaneity, partnership into my books of verbal duets.

You've now heard my partial answer to the question "Where did you get the idea for *Joyful Noise*?" Most books probably boast such long lineages. I've actually left out quite a lot: contradancing, bagel-baking, the a capella group Sweet Honey in the Rock, municipal bands, my shortwave radio, our family printing press—they were all involved, too. But I wanted to leave time to thank my cherished editor, Charlotte Zolotow, a lover of flowers as I am of the birds and insects who visit them. To use the title of one of her own books, some things go together. I'll always be grateful that she took a chance on *I Am Phoenix* and *Joyful Noise*. And my hope is not only that the books will give you and your readers the combined pleasures of poetry, double solitaire, house-building, and performing a Morley madrigal. I would like to think as well that this Newbery Medal will lead writers and publishers both to "follow their bliss," in Joseph Campbell's phrase, rather than simply the market in deciding what to write and publish. It was bliss, not *Writer's Digest* or *Publishers Weekly* that led to *Joyful Noise*. Conventional wisdom (i.e., "Anthropod poetry never goes paperback") gives us only conventional books.

I would also like to thank Charlotte's colleague, Laura Geringer, for her editorial help, and Ken Nutt (who goes also by Eric Beddows) who provided the captivating artwork for both the two-voiced books. He's a fine artist who deserves his adjective.

Both last and first, my gratitude to the members of the Newbery committee. When the British biologist J. B. S. Haldane was asked for his conception of God, he replied "He's inordinately fond of beetles." The same, apparently, can be said of this year's Newbery committee. Thank you. You understand the drum.

Paul Fleischman
Sid Fleischman

Our kids didn't get hand-me-down clothes. They got hand-me-down typewriters. My old Olympia, resettled on Paul's bedroom desk, sat largely silent while Paul was away at college. When he returned for the Christmas holidays in 1977, I could hear the machine rattling away again.

Paul Fleischman

Late one afternoon, he ambled downstairs and casually tossed a few typewritten pages on the couch. "I've written a story," he said, "if you'd like to read it."

Here was a situation of some delicacy. Amateur scripts generally remind you of someone trying to play on an untuned piano. Would he feel I'd be disappointed in him if the story was no good?

Not to worry.

I read the pages with growing amazement. This was not a story written with the telltale creaks and groans of the beginner. It was a skilled handling of a difficult subject, the uncanny relationship between a boy and an apple tree planted in celebration of his birth. It was a bravura performance.

I looked up with a rush of paternal pride. "It's wonderful!" And then, "Paul, have you been writing stories in secret?"

No. He hadn't.

Paul's gift for writing surfaced in early childhood. But sculpting a story demands an additional set of skills. Long after *The Birthday Tree* (Harper) was accepted by the first editor to whom it was submitted, Charlotte Zolotow, I remained somewhat mystified. Without the usual apprenticeship, how had Paul learned to stage-manage his scenes, to fine-tune the story tensions, to bring his characters to life?

It slowly dawned on me that he'd had an apprenticeship after all. I simply hadn't noticed it. There have always been writers and editors in and out of the house, talking story. We forget that kids are listening. Paul was a lightning-quick study. I believe he could have defined denouement before he was nine—and spelled it, too. At the dinner table I'd often ask the kids for help with some balky story problem, and ideas would bubble up. As Paul was later to write in a July/August 1987 *Horn Book* article, "I remember being proud when my suggestion that Mr. Mysterious and his family get lost turned up in the following chapter."

You can tell what was turning over in his mind from the whimsical little booklets he'd hand-craft for my birthdays. Almost all focus on the theme of the working writer. From *Misery and Happiness* (copyright, it says, 1964), illustrated by his sisters Jane and Anne:

> "Happiness is having a good illustrator."
> "Misery is not knowing if you should trust I before E except after C."
> "Happiness is capturing the villain on the last page."
> "Misery is having to autograph books with a blister on your finger."
> "Happiness is a phone that unplugs."

When *The Birthday Tree* was published to extraordinary reviews, those who didn't know Paul very well, or at all, assumed that I was tutoring him through his pages. Far from it. Only once did I take him aside to show the power of cutting a word to sharpen a sentence, a sentence to sharpen a paragraph. For the rest I have been a happy spectator. He has a sense of privacy about his writing, and when his forthcoming novel, *Saturnalia*, was a work in progress, he would reveal nothing but the title.

Our middle child, Paul was born in Monterey, California, and grew up here in Santa Monica. He was a whiz at school who was almost never seen doing any homework. We later discovered that he was tossing it off on the school bus. Music has been a constant in his life. When he'd cut school, it was to sequester himself at the public library and listen to Brahms or baroque or chamber music. Returning home these days, he heads for the piano in the living room. He celebrated the Newbery Medal by buying a piano for his Pacific Grove home.

He's an autodidact, who taught himself to play the recorder and had a brief fling with a rented saxophone. With characteristic consideration, he'd practice in the basement to spare us the foghorn blarings and bleatings.

Paul has a sharp-shooting sense of humor. You have to listen closely, for he is soft-spoken, and his wit is apt to come out in muttered asides. Over the telephone he was reporting on his son Seth. "He's beginning to talk a lot." And then the aside: "I think it's early Serbo-Croatian."

The moment of truth for a writer is his second book. Paul picked up a mechanical pencil, his writing instrument of choice, and forged ahead on a novel about a boy, born mute, who becomes separated from his mother during a storm and must fend for himself.

In *The Half-a-Moon Inn* (Harper), the earlier foreshadowings are confirmed—the freshness of imagination, the gift for imagery ("the stars . . . sleepwalking across the sky"), and the haunting sense of fantasy in the midst of life. Miss Grackle, the villainous proprietor of a country inn, peels back the eyelids of her sleeping guests to read their dreams.

Mr. Cyrus Snype in *Coming-and-Going Men* (Harper/Zolotow) is an itinerant cutter of silhouettes in vengeful and cunning pursuit of a human form who casts no shadow—the Devil. In his Newbery honor book, *Graven Images* (Harper), Paul wrote of New England villagers whispering their secrets into the ear of a binnacle boy, the carved and lacquered figure off a death ship, unaware that they are being watched by a girl who can read lips.

In a television interview Isaac Bashevis Singer said that an author needs an address. It may seem unlikely that a writer who grew up on the sunny beaches of southern California should find a literary address in New England, where Paul has set so many of his tales. I choose to think that there's more to this than the two years he lived in Bradford, New Hampshire. I regard it as a prodigal's return after more than three centuries; on his mother's side Paul has ancestors who debarked about twenty minutes after the Mayflower. The family scandal is that the kids are descendants of Mary Parsons of Northampton, Massachusetts, who was ahead of her times—she was tried as a witch years before Salem. She got off on a technicality. She wasn't a witch; but she was uppity.

Paul plans his books in detail and writes in a small hand in spiral-bound notebooks. He doesn't cross out; he erases as he goes along, so that his early drafts are swept away like bread crumbs.

A few years ago Paul and his wife, Becky, a registered nurse, bought their own home among the pines in Pacific Grove on Monterey Bay. The increase in their family can be followed in Paul's book dedications. The recently published picture book, *Rondo in C* (Harper/Zolotow), says "For Dana, con amore." Dana is two. *Joyful Noise* (Harper/Zolotow), now ablaze with the gold seal of the Newbery Medal, is for four-year-old Seth, "our porch light." Multurn in parvo.

An award of this magnitude becomes a family event. His wife, his mother, his sisters, and his aunts—all feel a shared glow. And me? "Happiness is getting an award for a book you didn't write."

The Caldecott Medal 1990

Lon Po Po

written and illustrated by
Ed Young

published by
Philomel, 1989

Horn Book Review

By dividing the illustrations into three and sometimes four longitudinal sections, Young has given his fine retelling the look of old Chinese decorative panels. What is in the panels is quite another matter; a wolf, long of tooth and mean intent, inveigles his way into a house by pretending to be the grandmother of three little girls who have been left alone. The power of the wolf's threatening presence bursts out of the narrow panels as a fearsome eye peering through the narrow doorway slit or a huge shadow leaping across the wall. The three little girls ask the formulaic questions about grandmother's furry feet, sharp claws, and deep voice, but, unlike the European Red Riding Hood, the girls aren't taken in for long. Taking matters into their own hands, they dispatch the wolf quite handily with a trick of their own. The slightly blurred illustrations are subdued in color but seem to throb with the mystery and terror of the wolf and the round-eyed fright of the children. Although the placement of the text on colored backgrounds is sometimes a disadvantage, the wonderfully fine illustrations more than compensate.—*Ethel R. Twichell*

Booklist Review

In this Red-Riding Hood variant from China three children stay home while their mother goes to visit Grandmother. Warning them to latch the door at sunset, the mother walks away, little guessing that a cunning wolf observes her departure. Disguised as an old woman, the wicked wolf knocks, claims to be the children's "po po" (grandmother), and gets the younger children to open the door, though Shang, the eldest, is suspicious. Blowing out the candle, the wolf embraces the children and proposes sleep. Once in bed, Shang stretches out and, feeling a furry tail, exclaims, "Po Po, Po Po, your foot has a bush on it." The

104

wolf smoothly replies, "Po Po has brought hemp strings to weave you a basket." However, when Shang relights the candle, she catches a glimpse of the hairy creature before he quickly blows it out again. Tricking the wolf by appealing to his greed, the three children climb the ginkgo tree outside the door, lure him into a basket on a rope, raise him high, and drop the rope, dashing the creature to the ground. With the wolf dead, the children latch the door, sleep peacefully, and, on the next day, tell their mother of their adventure.

Not for the faint-hearted, *Lon Po Po* (Grandmother Wolf), is a tale of menacing danger and courage. The similarities to Red Riding Hood are many: a visit to grandmother, a mother's warning disregarded, a villain-ous wolf who dresses as Granny, a series of questions the heroine poses to the wolf, and, of course, a happy ending. On the other hand, there is no woodcutter conveniently strolling by the door. In this version, the children must rely on their wits to save themselves. They triumph, yet even after the wolf's death, a threatening aura of evil remains.

The sense of foreboding arises from the illustrations more than the text. Dark, lupine shapes are subtly woven through every piece of art-work. The opening scene that shows mother waving goodbye as her children stand at the cabin door is portrayed against a brooding back-drop that is recognizably the elongated head of the wolf. When the frightened children gaze down between the branches at the beast, the angle of the tree trunk and limb form a shadowy but unmistakable wolf's open jaw, jagged teeth at the ready, just as they begin to hope that he is dead. Even the ending holds little triumph or comfort; the last scene is no cozy reunion but a double-page spread showing their house surrounded and all but engulfed by dim enigmatic forms—the inscrutable forces of nature and our fears—with, again, the wolf's body forming an integral part of the landscape.

Young creates a series of powerful illustrations in pastels and water-colors. Contrasting broad areas of subtly shaded darkness with incan-descent candle- and moonlit scenes, he underscores the innocence of the children and the malevolence of the wolf. The separation of some of the spreads into three or four vertical panels, as in Chinese screen or panel paintings, recalls the story's roots as well as the artist's own. His com-mand of page composition and his sensitive use of color give the book a visual force that matches the strength of the story and stands as one of the illustrator's best efforts. The dust-jacket illustration, featuring a white-eyed wolf staring over his shoulder against a mottled Chinese red background, foreshadows the emotional power within.

Recalling an Indian prayer to the spirit of a deer before releasing the arrow to kill it. Young dedicates the book "To all the wolves of the world for lending their good name as a tangible symbol for our darkness." The simple blue-and-peach pastel sketch that accompanies this tribute involves the viewer in a Gestalt shift: the bent figure is that of grandmother and wolf. Is Young saying that evil is within us all, or in our perception of the world? In this compelling book, he offers much to ponder.—*Carolyn Phelan*

1990 Caldecott Acceptance Speech
Ed Young

Winter has always been an introspective season for me. Emerging from that period and the wake of the Year of the Snake, one would expect the shedding of old life to begin anew with the Year of the Horse. But I had been wrapped up instead in a birth—the hatching of my first film, *Sadako and the Thousand Paper Cranes*, a story about the courage and hope of a young Japanese girl inflicted with leukemia as a result of radiation from the Hiroshima bomb. The drawings—over 230 of them, fifteen times as many as in any book in my experience—were due by the end of January and were so overwhelming for me that I had little time to pay serious attention to anything else, let alone astrology.

And what had my youngest child, *Lon Po Po* (Philomel), been up to? After all, it had been brought up properly and had already flown the coop. As a parent of forty-one books, I no longer can keep track of the years and titles of earlier creations except to trust that they are alive and faring well in the world.

So in the ninth month of incubation, when *Sadako* was beginning to stir, any interruption was considered an intrusion. That was when the phone rang. It was a call from Chicago with what sounded like a New Year's Eve party in the background. It seems *Lon Po Po*, that youngest child, had won the Caldecott Medal. I was asked if I would appear with it on the *Today* show the following morning.

For me, it was a choice between Randolph Caldecott and Sadako Sasaki! I believe few mothers in their right mind would consider giving up the urgency of the moment of birth for a 7:45 A.M. television interview in New York City, especially when the weatherman was forecasting hazardous driving conditions. And when I heard that the Newbery Medalist, Lois Lowry, was actually flying down from Boston for those few minutes, I thought, "has the world indeed gone mad?" But I was willing to give the matter further consideration. By the end of that day, after a lengthy phone interview with National Public Radio, I returned to *Sadako* only to find the process had come to a halt. Randolph took over from then on.

Reaching into my own childhood, I remember playing every role; I drew everything that happened to cross my mind: airplanes, people, a tall ship that my father was very proud of, a hunter and a bird dog that came out of my head—I have always been happiest doing my own thing. I still see my mother's bewilderment at how badly I was faring in school, however. I remember one year my brother tutored me in math, but it was like pulling up one sock only to have the other sock fall down. If it wasn't math, it was something else.

Sometimes I played alone for hours without a toy or prop in an empty room. During that time, my imagination reigned supreme; I could be anyone or anything I wished to be, most usually a solitary hero for a worthy cause. Sometimes I fancied myself a magician like Walt Disney. Though I never voiced my question, I must have wondered, "why all the fuss about getting good grades in school?" It was a miracle indeed and certainly nothing short of the grace of heaven that with all my daydreaming I actually made it through school in my first nineteen years of life.

My guardian angel brought me to the United States and favored me with a scholarship to study architecture at the University of Illinois. My father, who was the dean of engineering at St. John's University in Shanghai and a senior partner in a construction company, had hoped that my artistic talent would develop along the lines of his trade. It took me three years to discover that architecture wasn't all visual designs and pretty drawings. In 1953, just for fun, I entered and won a badge contest for the homecoming football game at the university. Such a small thing, but it gave me courage to pursue my career as an artist. A *Saturday Evening Post* article about a noteworthy professional school in Los Angeles caught my eye. In 1954, my first Year of the Horse in the United States, I took an eight-week summer session at the Art Center School in Los Angeles before enrolling as a freshman once again to study advertising design and illustration. The best of me was greatly challenged when Korean War veterans returned, with their experience and incentive, to win the scholarships I had hoped to secure. Competing for the scholarships and developing my portfolio turned out to be preparation for the discipline of a lifetime even though I never received any school aid at the Art Center. It also fed the fire of the budding artist in me—to prove myself as worthy as any that ever lived. I wanted to take on the world!

That brought me to New York City upon graduation. Though I worked in advertising doing illustrations, I continued to take classes at Pratt Institute in graphic arts and industrial design. With my architectural training, I drew pictures of old, majestic New York buildings ready to be demolished, the subway, the streets, a cemetery—anything that caught my eye.

Meanwhile, I began my study of tai chi chuan, a Chinese meditative movement of relaxation and balance that kindled my interest in the sound and rhythms of people and animals. I spent many lunch hours in Central Park sketching people, animals, and birds in motion. In 1961, when my advertising career came to a close, this training had unwittingly prepared me for the world of children's picture books.

I knew nothing of publishing when I was told to make an appointment with a certain Ursula Nordstrom at Harper & Row on Park Avenue. In reaction to my experience in the world of advertising, where I had been asked to wear a tie and jacket, I was dressed in my now usual black turtleneck sweater. I carried my stack of animal drawings done on paper napkins and scrap paper in a brown shopping bag. The guard at the Harper door pointed me to the rear freight elevator, thinking that I was a delivery man, and the receptionist was equally reluctant to show me into Ms. Nordstrom's office. In spite of all this, Ursula went over my drawings patiently and pulled out a manuscript from her bottom-drawer for me to read. It was as if manuscripts grew on trees! My response after my first reading, however, was, "No animals of mine talk. I don't do that sort of stuff." But she said, "Take it home and think the matter over. If by next week you still feel the same way, you may return it without further explanation."

I finally decided I would do it, because I was curious to see something of mine through from drawing to the finished print; it was to be my first and last book. *The Mean Mouse and Other Mean Stories* by Janice Udry won an American Institute of Graphic Arts award in 1963. A book agent, Elizabeth Armstrong, took notice and talked me into working with her. Even so, I still insisted that I was a serious artist who worked in children's books only temporarily for a living.

In 1965, the Year of the Horse for the second time in my United States years, my tai chi chuan teacher, a sixty-year-old master of five formidable Chinese arts, had shown me by his work that being a fine artist is not just having raw talents and cleverness. I needed to give all of my life to study the principle of the spirit that gives life—in Chinese it is called sheng chito—to all beings.

For better or worse, as a foreigner brought up on Chinese legends and books, I was unaware of most classical children's literature and book awards in the West. Even a Caldecott Honor award for *The Emperor and the Kite* (Philomel) by Jane Yolen in 1968 did not change my life sizably except that I settled back to study and to play some more. By then I was no longer fully satisfied to examine or copy life from the outside of beings. I wanted to enter into life forms and to play out the story from its own center. So, again, I found myself in that empty room of my childhood. Only now the room was myself.

Nineteen seventy-eight, the Year of the Horse for the third time since I had come to this country, found me working on *White Wave* (Crowell), Diane Wolkstein's moon-goddess story from China. Because Diane is a friend, I wanted the book to fit her vision, and I involved her as author in the bookmaking process more than I had any author in any previous book. This involvement was expanded to editors, art directors, and salespeople for their input. In the end, it was more rewarding than any other book had been up to that time. Yet, it was still Ed Young largely studying and experiencing a story within the confines of someone else's cultural perspective, be it Chinese, Persian, Thai, or Indian. It wasn't until *Foolish Rabbit's Big Mistake* (Putnam), a *jataka* "Chicken-Little" tale, that I came to a new place in my work. In that book I broke the Indian miniature format in favor of the power of the bigger images and brighter colors in Rafe Martin's dramatic telling of this tale.

What I didn't realize was that all the invisible threads of everyone and everything of the past, present, and future—not only my own but that of those around me—were being drawn together all the while. This realization showed me in no uncertain terms that I am far from an isolated artist sitting in my remote studio doing my own little thing. For almost three decades I have been given to find ways to play out storytelling in picture books. Although I had intended to remain unseen, my offspring—my books—have since become public servants for almost a whole generation.

But if *Lon Po Po* is the fruit of the tree, and I the branch that produced the fruit, where, then, I ask myself, is the tree? What is, in turn, the earth that nourished the tree, the air and rain and the sun that strengthened the earth? The collaboration of many is what makes this one remarkable fruit. All the hundreds of heroes and ideals are the rays of my sun. Those happy childhood days in my father's house, a true haven for friends and relatives in wartime China, are the ground of my earth. My world of associates—neighbors, students, fellow artists past and present, friends, and above all my teachers, my wife and family—is the source of my air and water.

Lon Po Po is but one fruit among many, and I am but one twig in the orchard, and this is only one season in time immemorial. Still, it is one precious moment. It is our opportunity to celebrate the wisdom of our belonging to something greater, of facing our adversities as a chance for growth, and of giving hope and beauty to our future.

In this Year of the Horse, my fourth in this great country, my wish of being a magician has come true. *Sadako and the Thousand Paper Cranes* is finally born with no deficiencies, in spite of the interruption, and *Lon Po Po* remains, in your hands and the hands of all readers who pick it up, the fruit of one season that promises another. Strange but true—after twenty-eight years it still feels like my first and last book.

Ed Young

Patricia Lee Gauch

Ed Young

I met Ed Young before I ever worked with him. I had been visiting Putnam on another matter and saw a large, colorful book on the corner of the art director's desk. *Foolish Rabbit's Big Mistake* (Putnam), it was called, and when I opened it, I felt as if I were being confronted by story as I never had before. This amazing rabbit did not obey any boundaries—emotional, visual, or dramatic. Beginning with the jacket, I met a rabbit that leapt across the pages in ways I had never seen before in a book. Created with bold pastel images that fairly exploded on the page, it demanded my emotional participation. I felt as if I were experiencing some frontier of the mind, and perhaps the soul. What a discovery! I had met a book—no ordinary book—and an artist as well.

I know now that I had ventured into the strange and amazing terrain of Ed Young's mind; it is a terrain that seems to push at all traditional boundaries. This is both true and not true, only one of the many paradoxes of Ed Young.

Ed was born in Tientsin, China, and brought up in Shanghai, but he lived in a world within a world. The city of Shanghai even today is a city of contrasts. Built at the delta of the Yangtze River, port to, ocean liners as well as junks, it was, particularly before World War II, a bustling cosmopolitan city where both Westerners and Chinese lived and worked, where wealth existed among many, yet where Chinese peasants struggled at the edges of the city scrambling for some of the crumbs from the flourishing international community.

The Young family, however, was part of yet another world in Shanghai: a missionary world associated with St. John's University, an Episcopal institution founded by an American, where Ed's father, Q. L. Young, was dean of engineering. Educated in the United States and China, a Renaissance man of no mean proportions who could recite Shakespeare as well as design and build his own home, he and his wife, Tang Yuen, and their family lived near the city limits of Shanghai. It was a place where the doors were always open to friends of all nationalities as well as to neighbors and extended family members. Understandably, it was a place rich in ideas and conversation with a distinctly international tone.

This was the world within a world in which Ed grew up, one of five children, influenced by this amazingly versatile father and an equally artistic mother. It was a good home, a kind of fortress against the frequently tumultuous, war-torn days of the 1940s and 1950s in China. For Ed, however, there was yet one more world to inhabit. The world of his imagination teemed with images. Influenced by his mother, encouraged by his father, he began to sketch these images from the time he was a very young child.

As his father had before him, Ed at the age of twenty came to the United States on a student visa to study. At first he studied architecture at the University of Illinois, but eventually he applied to the Art Center School in Los Angeles, from which he graduated in 1957. From there, "with twenty-five dollars in [his] pocket," he went to New York to find a position, hopefully in editorial, perhaps at a magazine. What he found was a job at an advertising company where he worked until 1961, when he met the grande dame of editors, Ursula Nordstrom, and discovered children's books. He has since published over forty books for ten publishers, garnering awards from both design and literary associations.

Ed has become well known for his work in Eastern forms, but, ironically, he actually began to discover his Chinese roots after studying and working in the United States. Nor was it the first culture with which he became familiar. As an architectural student, he encountered Japanese art through Western architects such as Frank Lloyd Wright who admired the Eastern forms. Early in his illustrating career he was fascinated by Persian art; this is reflected in books such as *The Girl Who Loved the Wind* (Crowell) by Jane Yolen. In *The Bird from the Sea* (Crowell) by Karol Weiss his work suggests Indian miniatures, another form that interested him. It was after beginning his study of Tai Chi Chuan in the mid-1960s that he began to study and understand Chinese culture and art; this is reflected in books such as *The Emperor and the Kite* (Philomel) by Jane Yolen, where he uses an ancient Chinese paper-cutting technique. He was fascinated by panel art, discovering it in many cultures: medieval Christian and Middle-Eastern art as well as Japanese and Chinese. In *Yeh-Shen: A Cinderella Story from China* (Philomel) by Ai-Ling Louie, he embraces this form.

Brought up in a home that did not recognize the usual cultural and artistic boundaries, it is perhaps natural that Ed finds art forms in all aspects of life; in all places; indeed in all times, past and present. Yet he believes himself to be conservative. His primary obligation is to understand the principle of a law, whether it is understanding the discipline of an art form or a tradition. Once the law or discipline—or boundary—is understood clearly, only then can it be expanded upon. Thus, Ed can "break" boundaries, "break" new ground, because he inherently respects the boundary or ground. This is true of media as well as subject and form.

Even today Ed's journeys are still inward as well as outward. In discussing his path to children's literature, Ed discusses the "artist" in himself. But he does not mean the person that the observer sees; he is talking about the delicate internal voice that he believes directs his work. It is a creative spirit that he believes exists in every person. Though the artist in him is bold in vision, a pioneer in idea, it is somewhat shy in the light of the outside world; it does not like to be jostled, squeezed, compelled, or overdirected. The artist requires a free and airy environment that allows it to "speak," respectfully allows it to speak: a studio with the right light; the right arrangement of materials (and understandably there is almost no material that does not contain possibilities for Ed Young, whether it be gift wrapping paper, tissue paper, or brown paper, as well as more predictable materials); a publisher that allows for and respects the vagaries of the artist; an art director who is willing to listen to the artist's voice, no matter if the voice is faint in the beginning. No matter if the artist takes several paths on its way to idea.

The boundary between Young and the artist is almost indiscernible. Even as his outer world has expanded, his journey has always been inward; its expression, outward.

It is perhaps Ed's inward journey that has so engaged the reader in *Lon Po Po: A Red-Riding Hood Story from China* (Philomel). Readers have always been allowed to consider this old tale, in whatever form or language they have found it, as if they were observers sitting before a dais where the story is being drawn slowly across the stage. But Ed Young's work does not allow a three-sided stage. With proper respect for the wolf, to whom he makes apologies in his dedication, he explores light and darkness, evil and goodness, fear and courage by inviting the reader up onto the stage to share in these conflicts. In turning the pages of *Lon Po Po*, the reader is asked to stand a breath away from the wolf, so close that the shadow is at his or her fingertips. The reader is asked to sense the leaves in the ginkgo tree in illusory fashion, like lights after darkness in our own eyes; and then to look up into the tree, into the very eyes of the children who have turned the tables on the irascible wolf, who themselves have become hunters instead of hunted. The Chinese panels, drawn from ancient Chinese and Middle-Eastern traditions, work breathlessly, tightening the tension as the wolf is pulled up the tree—once, twice, and a last time, when the girls drop the rope and the basket. Not enough that you feel suspense, Young seems to say in his powerful art; not enough that you feel fear: you must cross both boundaries into the center, into knowing fully who you are. It is important, he seems to say, that you know that you hold the rope and that you can pull it or you can fling it, if the power comes from inside you.

When he was working on *Cats Are Cats* (Philomel), the anthology of poetry collected by Nancy Larrick, Ed Young came into the Philomel office with his drawings on brown paper. Yes, the same sort used in bags one finds at grocery markets. To his using brown paper instead of some more traditional material, his editors said, "Why not?" That is the answer the artist in Ed Young needs to hear. "Why not?" He is not a man who forgets or fails to respect the terrain he has traveled; he is a man who needs to range, always further, into new color, into new media, materials, design, story. He is a man who, like the small ships that plied the harbor in Shanghai where he grew up, needs to catch the wind and to sail with it.

Number the Stars

written by
Lois Lowry

published by
Houghton Mifflin, 1989

Horn Book Review

The setting is Copenhagen in 1943; Denmark, now under the domination of Hitler's Third Reich, is faced with the "relocation" of its Jewish citizenry. The Danes rally around their neighbors, eventually smuggling nearly the entire Jewish population of Denmark to Sweden—and safety. The heroism of these ordinary folk is commemorated in a noteworthy novel, scaled to the comprehension of elementary school readers without sacrificing elements of style. Lois Lowry belongs to the select group that has mastered the art of writing for this audience, perhaps because she has never quite forgotten what it is like to be teetering on the brink of adolescence. In this re-creation of times past, the protagonist is ten-year-old Annemarie Johansen, who, with her best friend, Ellen Rosen, remembers life before the war when there were no food shortages or Nazi soldiers standing on every corner and her older sister was still alive. In contrast, Annemarie's five-year-old sister serves as an effective foil, heightening tension with the unpredictability typical of her age. Then the Rosens learn of their imminent danger from the Nazis, and the Johansen family, through resistance contacts, hastily conspire to help them escape. The elder Rosens are spirited away while Ellen joins the Johansens as their daughter, something which the Nazis are reluctantly forced to accept. Annemarie is not only entrusted with details of the operation but must also exhibit remarkable courage in demonstrating friendship and concern for her neighbors' welfare. The appended author's note details the historical incidents upon which Lowry bases her plot. By employing the limited omniscient third-person perspective, she draws the reader into the intensity of the situation as a child of Annemarie's age might perceive it. The message is so closely woven into the carefully honed narrative that the whole work is seamless, compelling, and memorable—impossible to put down; difficult to forget.—*Mary M. Burns*

Booklist Review

Denmark is occupied by Germany, and when best friends Annemarie Johansen and Ellen Rosen are confronted by a pair of patrolling soldiers, they find the experience unnerving. More frightening, however, is news that Jews are being rounded up. The Rosens flee, quickly and silently, leaving Ellen in the care of the Johansen family, who shield her when the Nazis raid the Johansen apartment in the middle of the night. Afterward, Annemarie's mother moves the children to her childhood home, where Sweden can be seen in the distance and where Annemarie's uncle carries on his fishing business. The rural seaside is far from tranquil, however, for German soldiers patrol here as well. Unbeknownst to Annemarie, Uncle Henrik is involved in smuggling Jews out of Denmark; arrangements have been made for Ellen to be reunited with her parents and for the Rosens to be transported to Sweden. Lowry tells her story well, fashioning a tense climax and following the narrative with a lengthy author's note that fills readers in on the sometimes-surprising truths behind the story's fictional events. While the novel has an absorbing plot, its real strength lies in its evocation of deep friendship between two girls and of a caring family who make a profoundly moral choice to protect others during wartime. Permeated with clear elements of popular appeal as well as rich substance, this novel will also be an ideal support for classroom units on World War II.—*Denise Wilms*

1990 Newbery Acceptance Speech
Lois Lowry

For years, I have carried in my wallet, stuck in there among the frequent flyer cards and the MasterCard carbons and the cash register slips from the supermarket, two little wrinkled slips of paper which are fortunes from Chinese fortune cookies. Like everyone else, I've gotten countless fortunes from Chinese fortune cookies, and like everyone else, I tend to throw them away. Let's face it: fortune cookie fortunes are generally boring. They need better writers—and editors—in Chinese fortune cookie factories.

But I've saved these two because I have wanted each of them to come true.

And now they both have, both on the same night.

One says: "You will be famous in a far-out profession."

And the other: "You will attend a party where strange customs prevail."

No, I don't really think that this is a far-out profession. I'm aware that other people do. Let me describe for you the most recent evidence of that.

It has become customary for winners of this award to describe the circumstances in which they were notified that they had won the Newbery Medal. It's a little, I think, like the old come-as-you-are party, when the hosts phone with the invitation and hope to catch people in their nightclothes or bathing suits. And so we all know that Sid Fleischman was in the shower—a nude Newbery winner! The committee must have loved it. And Paul Fleischman was at the dentist—not as good as nude, but horizontal and probably in pain—it's a close second.

I myself spend a normal amount of time in the shower, and lately, a greater-than-normal amount of time at the dentist; but I wasn't doing either of those things when the Newbery committee called me. I was sitting at my desk, fully clothed and completely vertical, writing, the way I am almost every day of my life.

Maybe the committee was aware that "sitting at my desk, writing" was not going to make an amusing anecdote for an acceptance speech. Maybe that's why, when they called, they asked if I would be willing to get on a plane that afternoon and fly to New York in order to appear on the *Today* show the following morning. This was January, remember. This was Boston. Outside, there were snowflakes beginning to fall. A lot of snowflakes. Anyone in his right mind would have looked out of the window and said, "This is January; this is Boston; it is snowing outside; and you want me to get on a plane? What are you, crazy?"

But when they call and tell you that you have won the Newbery Medal, you instantly turn into a person who is no longer in his right mind. And so I said, "Of course." I packed a small suitcase and went to Logan Airport that afternoon and boarded the 4:30 P.M. Pan Am shuttle to New York, a flight that takes one hour.

Seven hours later, at 11:30 P.M., I was still on the same plane, but now it was sitting, buried in snow, on an abandoned airstrip in upstate New York, where it had to land after circling and circling and finally running low on fuel.

A certain grim camaraderie springs up among strangers who are stranded on an abandoned airstrip. Tales of woe are exchanged. We all felt genuinely concerned for the lady who had left her children with a baby sitter and promised the baby sitter, who had another commitment, that she would be home by seven o'clock. We chuckled ruefully with the man who was missing his son's Cub Scout banquet.

But I think that if a vote had been taken—maybe with an applause meter, the way they used to do it on the old "Queen for a Day" show— I would have won, for the saddest tale. The Woman Who Is Supposed to Be on the *Today* Show at Dawn: that was me. I was seated in the first row of the plane, but even the folks way in the back, in what used to be the smoking section—they were murmuring, back there, about me, and occasionally standing up and peering, just to get a glimpse of the Woman Who Is Supposed to Be on the *Today* Show.

I finally reached my hotel in New York at 2:00 a.m., and the *Today* show car picked me up, as promised, at 6:30 in the morning. I had planned, the day before, before leaving Boston, to be charming and witty on the *Today* show. By now, though, I was simply hoping to be awake on the *Today* show.

And so I sat there, in the waiting room, along with Ed Young—who lives in New York, lucky man—and I drank coffee. And more coffee, and more coffee.

Also in the waiting room, scheduled to be interviewed that morning as well, were a Catholic priest who writes sexy novels and a very thin French actress who had just been nominated for an Academy Award. I noticed little cards thumbtacked on a small bulletin board describing the scheduled interviews. "Andrew Greeley," one card said; that was the Catholic priest. "Isabelle Adjani," said another; that was the actress. And then there was one remaining little white card that said simply, "2 KIDS BOOKS PEOPLE."

After a while someone came into the room and glanced at those cards. Then he glanced at those of us sitting there. "The space shuttle's going off and we have to show it live," he said, "so we're going to drop one interview." He looked at Andrew Greeley, who was chatting with Gene Shalit as if they were old pals. And he looked at Isabelle Adjani, who didn't bother looking back because she was looking into a mirror, pinching her own cheeks, and murmuring, "I feel pale today." And finally, he looked at Ed Young and me. He looked back at the cards, to see who we were. 2 KIDS BOOKS PEOPLE: that's who we were.

Then he took the thumbtack out of that card, and removed us from the bulletin board.

Maybe this is a far-out profession, after all. It sure felt like it that morning.

Some of you may have seen Ed and me on the *Today* show, so I will explain that they did tape an interview, and they showed it later to the other time zones. That included, I think, all time zones in which I have no living relatives or friends. Ed looked very charming, and I looked very sleepy. When Deborah Norville asked me, "Your friend—the one whose story this book was based on—did you call her last night to tell her it had won the Newbery Medal?" I scowled at her and said testily; "How on earth could I do that? I was circling La Guardia."

I called my friend Annelise the next day. She is here tonight. And it is time for me to tell you a little about her, and her people, and the book that I wrote to honor them.

During the same years that I was a child growing up in a small Pennsylvania town—the years of World War II—Annelise was a child growing up in Copenhagen. I didn't know her then, of course. My entire knowledge of cultural geography in those years came from the books by Lucy Fitch Perkins. I probably thought that all children in foreign countries were twins. I read about the Belgian Twins, and the Scottish Twins, and the Dutch Twins, and if there were Danish Twins in that series—I no longer remember—then I read about the Danish Twins as well.

Certainly as I became older, I read about the roles of various nations during that war, and I read about the Danish people and how they saved their Jewish population.

But when Annelise and I became friends, some twenty years ago, when she was living in the United States, it never occurred to me to ask her about what I thought of in some vague way as "history." I asked her, instead, as I ask all my friends (and an occasional startled stranger on an airplane), about her childhood. And Annelise (a good storyteller, like all Danes) told me a lot of details of her growing-up years, so I began to know about her family, their home in Copenhagen, her school days, the clothes she wore, the games she played with friends. I feel, still, as if I know her mother's little garden as well as I do my own.

Our talk wasn't always light-hearted talk of gardens and games, but it was always personal memories. We had each, when we were young, lost a greatly loved older sister. We talked a lot about that, Annelise and I;

and about the effect on an entire family when the oldest child dies too soon, too young.

Two years ago, in the spring of 1988, Annelise and I took a vacation together. Always, before, our times together had been interrupted by jobs or friends or children. But now we stayed, just the two of us, for a week in a little guest house in Bermuda, and it was the first time, for an extended, uninterrupted period, we talked and talked and talked.

This time, for the first time, talking of the past, I became truly aware of the way her childhood had been colored by war. Not just colored by the concept of war in a broad and abstract sense, the way my own childhood had been; but war through the perceptions of a child in a conquered country: humorous perceptions, sometimes; frightened ones, occasionally; uncomprehending, often.

For the first time—why did it take me so long? —I really understood that historic events and day-to-day life are not separate things.

We all know that the events that happened under the regime of the Third Reich were the most huge and horrible events in the history of mankind.

But when I asked Annelise to describe her childhood then, she didn't describe anything huge and horrible. She said things like: "I remember being cold." And: "I remember wearing mittens to bed."

Those were exactly the kinds of things—the small, almost inconsequential details of a child's life, from day to day, that I realized, quite suddenly, would tell a larger story.

I would be a terrible newspaper reporter because I can't write well about huge events. They use the verb cover in newsrooms. They send reporters out to "cover" things. But if they sent me out to "cover" some catastrophe, I would stand there watching while flood water carried away houses, and flames spurted into the sky, and buildings toppled, and victims were extricated by the hundreds. I would watch it all, and I would see it all. But I would write about a broken lunch box lying shattered in a puddle.

As a writer, I find that I can only cover the small and the ordinary— the mittens on a shivering child—and hope that they evoke the larger events. The huge and horrible are beyond my powers.

This is, of course, not the only way of doing things. But I think it is a valid and effective way. Let me read you a poem, "Musée des Beaux Arts," one of my favorites, by Auden, one of my favorite poets. He wrote here about Brueghel's painting called The Fall of Icarus, which hangs in the Musée des Beaux Arts (the Museum of Fine Arts) in Brussels.

> About suffering they were never wrong,
> The Old Masters: how well they understood
> Its human position; how it takes place
> While someone else is eating or opening a window or just walk-
>   ing dully along:
> How, when the aged are reverently, passionately waiting
> For the miraculous birth, there always must be
> Children who did not specially want it to happen, skating
> On a pond at the edge of the wood: They never forgot
> That even the dreadful martyrdom must run its course
> Anyhow in a corner, some untidy spot
> Where the dogs go on with their doggy life and the torturer's
>   horse
> Scratches its innocent behind on a tree.
> In Brueghel's Icarus, for instance: how everything turns away
> Quite leisurely from the disaster; the ploughman may
> Have heard the splash, the forsaken cry,
> But for him it was not an important failure; the sun shone
> As it had to on the white legs disappearing into the green
> Water; and the expensive delicate ship that must have seen
> Something amazing, a boy falling out of the sky,
> Had somewhere to get to and sailed calmly on.

I don't think this poem—which tells of children on a pond, skating, not noticing that a horrifying thing is happening in the sky—is a poem about human indifference. It's about human incomprehension, and our inability to integrate into our daily consciousness the fact that something terrible is happening. We hear a splash, or a cry—but we don't understand its importance. We continue to plough our field, or sail our ship calmly on. We eat, we open a window, we walk dully along. The dog yawns; the horse scratches its behind; the sun shines on the legs disappearing into the green water. And the child skates on a pond at the edge of a wood.

The Danish people were the only entire nation of people in the world who heard the splash and the cry and did not, in 1943—in the poet's words—turn away quite leisurely from the disaster.

But because that was a huge event, I couldn't "cover" it. I could only write about the child who skates on the pond at the edge of events. The day-to-day life of a child in that place, at that time.

My friend Annelise gave me the glimpses I needed of that child. She told me what a little girl would have worn to school, and how she would have carried her schoolbooks in a stiff leather knapsack.

I put those things into the book.

She told me what the family dog, in a Danish family, would have been named. I put the dog in, and gave him that name.

And she corrected me when I had written apple pie into the manuscript. "Haven't you ever heard the phrase, 'as American as apple pie'?" she asked me. And so the apple pie—which the Danes would never have heard of—turned into applesauce (a much less satisfying dessert, in my opinion, but a more realistic one) in the final revision.

She introduced me to a woman in Copenhagen named Kirsten Krogh, an older woman who was a young bride at the time of the German occupation. It was Kirsten Krogh—who with her husband had been involved in the Resistance movement—who told me what novel a young mother would have read, and loved, during those years. It surprised me. *Gone with the Wind?* An American novel about a feisty Southerner named Scarlett who pushed and shoved her way around Atlanta as it burned?

But I shouldn't have been surprised, because it connected with something else that Kirsten Krogh told me. When I asked her what was the worst single thing she remembered from those years, she thought about her answer for a long time. Then she said: "the powerlessness."

Of course they loved Scarlett O'Hara. I put *Gone with the Wind* in the book, too.

And it was Kirsten Krogh who told me what flowers would be in bloom along the Danish coast in autumn, and, in telling me, reminded me that flowers continue to bloom in terrible times, and that children still play with kittens.

I put in the flowers, and a kitten.

In Denmark I collected countless details to add to those that Annelise and Kirsten told me of their own lives during the war years. In Copenhagen I saw a pair of shoes made from fish skin. It was true, of course, that during the occupation the Danes couldn't import anything, so there was no leather for shoes. And surely it was a marvel of ingenuity that they figured out how to make shoes from the skin of fish.

But when I saw the shoes, i didn't think about the economic consequences of war. I couldn't even marvel at the craftsmanship or the cleverness—because I was living, by then, completely in the consciousness of a little girl: a little girl who wouldn't know—or care—about imports or economics. All I could think was what that child would think, on being given such a pair of shoes: Oh, they're so ugly.

And I put the ugly shoes, and the child's reaction, into the book.

When I asked Annelise to describe, through the eyes of her own childhood, the German soldiers themselves, she said: "I remember the high shiny boots."

As all writers do, I had to sift and sort through the details and select what to use. There were some that I had to discard, though I didn't want to. The image of wearing mittens to bed was one of those that eventually I had to let go. The events about which I wrote took place entirely in October; it simply wasn't mitten weather yet. But I would ask you all tonight, sitting here as we are in great comfort and luxury, to remember that in the winter of 1943 a little girl wore mittens to bed because she was cold.

I certainly did use—and use and use—those high shiny boots. Annelise had mentioned them first; and then, when I pored over the old photographs, I saw them myself, again and again.

When I had delivered the completed manuscript to my editor, he called it to my attention. Walter Lorraine has been my editor—and friend—for seventeen books. I listen to what he says with great respect, and though we occasionally argue, he is almost always right.

This time he said that there were too many references in the book to the shiny boots. And I listened. I listened with respect. But I looked at the photographs again, and I tried to place myself within the visual awareness of a child. Sometimes we forget that their vantage point is lower than ours. They don't look into adult faces. Certainly a frightened child would not look into the faces of enemy soldiers. As Annelise did, the child would see—and notice, more than an adult—those terrifying boots. I asked Walter to give me a little time to make that decision, and he agreed.

That fall, the fall of 1988, when this book had been written and was still in the late stages of editing, I was sent by my British publisher on a tour of Australia and New Zealand. I had just seen the first preliminary design for the cover of *Number the Stars* (Houghton), the first time I had seen the art director's (Sue Sherman's) plan to use that beautiful gold necklace, with the Star of David, embossed against the haunting face of the young girl.

When I was in Brisbane, Australia, I met a woman, slightly younger than I, who was wearing an identical necklace. It is not an unusual necklace; indeed, its simplicity is what makes it so beautiful. But when

I saw it around her neck, I described the book, and its cover, to the woman. And she told me her story. I think she would not mind my retelling it, to you.

She was born in Holland, to a Jewish mother and a Christian father. That mixed parentage made her a potential victim, of course, of the Nazis. So her parents had created a hiding place under the floorboards of their Amsterdam apartment—a place to hide a tiny child, if the moment should come when it was needed.

As we know, those terrible moments did come; they came all too often. When the Nazis banged on the door of that Amsterdam apartment, as they did on the door of the Copenhagen apartment in my book, this little girl, no more than a toddler, was quickly lifted into the hiding place. She huddled there and watched through a crack in the boards while they took her mother away.

She told me that she wears the necklace in memory of the mother she never saw again.

I asked her, as we sat talking, if she remembered any of it.

She said that the memory was very vague, because she had been so very young. There was only one thing, she told me, that she recalled clearly from that day when she had peeked out through a crack in the floor.

She said: "I remember the high shiny boots."

So when I went back to the United States, back to Walter, I asked him to leave the boots there in the book—every reference—again and again and again. I decided that if any reviewers should call attention to the overuse of that image—none ever has—I would simply tell them that those high shiny boots had trampled on several million childhoods and I was sorry I hadn't had several million more pages on which to mention that.

Let us relax for a moment and go back to the fortune cookies. "You will attend a party where strange customs prevail."

This is certainly a very fine party. Is it a strange custom, the awarding of the Newbery Medal?

Here is a passage from another, earlier book of mine, a book called *All about Sam* (Houghton). "I really only wanted to talk to you for a minute," Anastasia explained, as she knelt beside him. "Sam," she said, "don't be disappointed if you don't win the prize. Prizes don't matter."

"Yeah, they do!" Sam told her. "Prize means best. I think King of Worms will be the best pet! I washed him. And I changed his dirt."

"But, Sam, every child thinks his pet is the best. And we don't really care what the judges think, do we? As long as we know King of Worms is the best, that's the important thing, isn't it?"

Sam shook his head. "No," he said. "The really important thing is to win the prize."

Sam, age three, who has entered a worm in a pet show at his local public library, does win a prize. So does every other child there. My own children, many years ago, entered their Newfoundland dog in the pet show at their public library, a pet show where each child, and each pet, won a prize. Our dog was designated Best Dressed Dog. He was wearing a paisley necktie.

As far as I'm concerned, the best kind of competition is the one where everyone wins. Which is not to say that I think I entered a worm in this contest. But I truly believe that when two people stand here and receive medals each year, it does represent a prize for every writer and every illustrator of children's books. When one thousand librarians gather to celebrate this occasion, it places a value on that far-out profession, the profession of KIDS BOOKS PEOPLE. I want to thank the Newbery committee as well as the publishers, editors, agents, writers, illustrators, librarians, and all the people here, not so much for honoring me and one particular book, but for the honor you bring to the entire realm of children's literature. It is not a strange custom at all, to remind the world that there is unending value to the work that we all do on behalf of children.

Now, in conclusion, I have a confession to make. I edited one of those fortune cookies. It doesn't say: "You will become famous in a far-out profession." It actually says: "You will become rich and famous in a far-out profession."

I didn't feel real comfortable with the word rich. But of course it does have a meaning beyond the mundane world of royalties. Let's endow it with that meaning tonight, and say that my Chinese fortune—the unedited version—really did come true; because I feel immensely rich here with all of you: rich with the affection and the support you have given me for a very long time, even before this party full of not-so-strange customs took place.

Lois Lowry
Shirley Haley-James

Pine logs snap and crackle in the fireplace of a cabin in the North Georgia mountains as four adults sit reading. There is no other noise.

It is a tradition that when it rains during their annual October weekend amid the fall foliage of the Appalachian foothills everyone reads on Saturday afternoon, undisturbed. One of the readers breaks the silence by giggling—at first a little, then a lot. A moment later she guffaws. This goes on until she looks up from her book to see six annoyed eyebrows questioning her. Saying, "You've got to hear this," she begins to read from *Anastasia Again!*

Lois Lowry

(Houghton). Now all four laugh, and three ask to hear more. The afternoon flies by as they all enjoy the remainder of the story. In books such as those in the Anastasia series, Lois Lowry takes people—the young and the not-so-young—out of themselves by tickling their funny bones.

Lowry takes readers into themselves as well. With "it was a long time ago," she begins her story set on Autumn Street. It is specific to a particular time and place, but it causes both young and more experienced readers to remember, and to reflect about the meaning of, their own "times of hollow places that ache with memory and with fear." Because they read about Autumn Street, both their self-understanding and their compassion for others grow.

But, most significantly, Lowry takes readers beyond themselves. In none of her books does she succeed in this to a greater extent than in *Number the Stars* (Houghton), a story in which she makes the abstract concepts of love, commitment, and courage visible and real. Through the decisions of Annemarie Johansen and her family, we are made to wonder, "Would I have it in me to do what they did to save others?" And we realize that, through this book, a new generation will be informed of a time in the history of the world that humankind dares not forget.

Books that ring as true as Lois Lowry's virtually always emerge from honest exploration of experience and from an inner ear finely tuned to what is going on both within and around the writer's life. There is integrity as well as consistency in who the writer is, what she studies, and what she writes. This is true in the case of Lowry's work. She can tickle funny bones with her books because she sees and appreciates the humorous and the ridiculous in the things she, and all of us, say and do. She can touch the pain in our lives because she has lived through her own and because she is not afraid either to relive it when that serves a purpose or to enter ours when she can be of help. She can write about the devastation of the Holocaust as well as about the courage and humility of people who risked their lives to save others, because her conscience requires that she speak of the unspeakable as well as honor that which is good.

Integrity and consistency also characterize her daily life and her relationships. I have heard her speak to parents, librarians, teachers, and children. Each time, she has tailored her presentation to fit the audience. I have watched her interact with family, friends, and strangers over a span of a dozen years, and, without exception, all have been treated straightforwardly, respectfully, and fairly. It's easy to understand why even people who have just met her feel that she is their friend—or at least that she would be, if they needed one.

Beneath the integrity and consistency that characterize Lowry's work and her daily life and relationships, there is a woman of strength who has worked for and achieved a peace with herself. She can speak of her goals and of her mistakes, of times she has been treated unfairly, and of what she feels proud of without self-pity and without smugness. She knows who she is. She works on polishing what she views as her rough edges.

On this bedrock Lois Lowry creates. She is a photographer whose pictures arrest the eye and compel the viewer. She is a nonfiction writer for adults who has published articles in numerous well-known magazines. She is an author of fiction for young adults and children whose legions of faithful readers finish her most recent book and begin anticipating the next. She is a booster of morale, an instiller of confidence, and a picker-upper of those around her when they are down. Beyond all of this, she tells funny stories, and she loves to laugh.

It is not just Lowry's writing skills that account for her ability to take readers out of themselves, into themselves, and beyond themselves. It is also the person she is and the way she has chosen to live her life. It is the sum of all her parts that could create such a sterling book as *Number the Stars*. And that is why we rejoice that it has received the prestigious Newbery Medal.

The Caldecott Medal 1991

Black and White

written and illustrated by
David Macaulay

published by
Houghton Mifflin, 1990

Horn Book Review

This picture book toys with the reader just as it experiments with the concept of time, simultaneity of events, and the question of one story impinging on another. The author-artist has created an addictive puzzler which can, like a Nintendo game, draw a susceptible audience into an endless exploration of the book's many possibilities. The story—or stories, depending upon one's perspective—comprises four sequences, each consistently placed in a particular quadrant of successive double-page spreads. Each is executed in a distinctive style—ranging from the impressionist quality of "Seeing Things" through the more precisely limned "Problem Parents" and "A Waiting Game" to the dissolving figure-ground images of "Udder Chaos." In the first, a boy observes the changing landscape from the window of a train; in "Problem Parents" two children are amazed by the antics of their usually staid mother and father after commuting from a long day at work; "A Waiting Game" records the endless boredom of standing on a train platform while listening to accounts of unexplained delays; "Udder Chaos" proves that Holstein cows, once released from pasture, are difficult to locate, which may be useful information if you're an escaped con—yes, the masked escapee from *Why the Chicken Crossed the Road* (Houghton) makes an appearance. One solution proposes that all the episodes are connected through the train motif; on the other hand, the author-artist states on the title page that "this book appears to contain a number of stories that do not necessarily occur at the same time." Perhaps there is no one explanation but rather a series of playful allusions and clever delusions which are meant to be enjoyed by the freewheeling and freespirited as an escape from the ordinary.—*Mary M. Burns*

Booklist Review

What's black and white and read all over? Macaulay's latest picture book. Though divided into four stories, which run consecutively, the book also dares its audience to see it "all over," as a whole, rather than left to right, top to bottom, and page by page. And though the very title may suggest a back-to-basics approach to bookmaking, the words black and white appear in white, green, and blue on the black background of the dust jacket and in scarlet on the title page, belying the words themselves and reminding readers that few things in life are just "black and white."

As the book begins, a rotund convict escapes his prison, and the following message appears: "WARNING: This book appears to contain a number of stories that do not necessarily occur at the same time. Then again, it may contain only one story. In any event, careful inspection of both words and pictures is recommended." Thereafter, each double-page spread divides into four rectangular frames in which four tales unfold. With few exceptions, the vignettes stay within their frames, though elements of the stories coincide. Each tale continues through the book, building to a climax on a page without frames or color. Then the colors return for a quick denouement.

Entitled "Seeing Things," the first tale, with watercolor illustrations reminiscent of Edward Ardizzone, tells of a boy's overnight train trip, his first trip alone. A mysterious old woman (the convict in disguise) shares his compartment for a while, then disembarks. Cows block the tracks until the engineer chases them off. An apparent snowstorm becomes a shower of torn newspaper as the train draws into a station where oddly dressed people stand singing. Falling asleep, the boy later awakens to see his parents meeting his train.

"Problem Parents," the second tale, in shaded sepia, black, and white, is a first-person account of a teenage girl who is sitting in the living room with her younger brother (who looks like the boy in the former tale, painted in a different style) when their parents arrive home from work in a frivolous, not to say batty, mood, wearing newsprint costumes over their clothes. As the narrator becomes increasingly uncomfortable with her parents' antics, the tone of the story becomes more frenzied, to great comic effect. Again, many visual details link up with the other stories; for instance, the convict (bearing a striking resemblance to the family dog) appears on their television screen, and the parents' costumes and singing point to happenings on the railway platform in the third tale.

The next story, "A Waiting Game," done in line drawings washed with chalk-box colors, unfolds at a railway station where the train is unaccountably delayed and the waiting passengers react improbably by folding their newspapers into paper hats and costumes and bursting happily into song. Intermittent announcements over the loudspeakers supply the only text, a droll counterpoint to the giddy action. The final frame shows the convict on the platform, contentedly waving good-bye to the train.

The fourth tale—and the most enigmatic—"Udder Chaos," concerns a herd of Holstein cows who wander off the farm and into a choir festival, across a railroad track, and finally, back home to be milked. While the narrator nonchalantly asserts that "the worst thing about Holstein cows is that if they ever get out of the field, they're almost impossible to find," the black-and-white garbed convict, hiding among the black-and-white cows, appears and disappears as the flat colors of the scenes involve readers in visual gestalt shifts.

Mental shifts as well occur throughout the book as elements of one story cross into another but refuse to be pinned down into a simple narrative sequence. The more one looks, however, the more one finds and the more one becomes intrigued with what is happening. Rather like a dream in its interconnectedness instead of a conventional picture book with a dear beginning, middle, and end, this work engages another side of the mind. It's a story; it's a puzzle; it's a game.

Like the escaped convict confidently romping through his illustrations, Macaulay refuses to be confined by the conventions of the picture book. Play is the wellspring of creativity, and Macaulay is playing with the form itself. Not everyone will appreciate that. However, for every child who's entertained by the individual parts (and irresistibly funny bits abound) but confused by the import of it all there'll be another who sees its daft playfulness and recognizes a kindred spirit.
—*Carolyn Phelan*

1991 Caldecott Acceptance Speech

David Macaulay

Even after all this time, it still amazes me that I am finally a bride. But, in the past few months, the euphoria which followed the announcement has been tempered by an increasing sense of responsibility. I feel obliged to say something tonight that matters, at least to me, and something which will, I hope, make a difference to you. Not an easy task, I assure you, in a world where so many people have something to say and where so little of it seems to make a difference.

But first, a warning: This presentation will appear to contain four little speeches that for obvious reasons cannot possibly be delivered or read at the same time by the same person. Then again, it may contain only one speech. In any event, you're on your own.

SEEING THINGS

For some time now, I have been encouraging people to ask themselves why things look the way they do. At the Rhode Island School of Design, I do it by teaching drawing and illustration. In my books, I do it by constructing buildings and brains and by explaining machines. I use pictures and words to emphasize the common sense behind the design of any object in an attempt to demystify an increasingly complex and detached world of skyscrapers and light switches and four-stroke engines and compact disc players. In *Black and White*, my intentions are the same, but the subject of this book is the book. It is designed to be viewed in its entirety, having its surface "read all over." It is a book of and about connections—between pictures and between words and pictures.

Seeing necessitates looking and thinking. When I teach drawing, I must constantly remind my students to distinguish between what they see and what they think they see. Thinking—at least the lazy, day-to-day kind of thinking—often gets in the way of the drawing process, which requires a stubborn curiosity about why things look the way they do. Nothing can be intelligently or intelligibly recorded on a piece of paper unless true seeing occurs: first on the part of the person making the picture, and then on the part of the person reading it.

I honestly think all of us would be better off if everyone took the time to draw, if for no other reason than the better we see, the more inevitable curiosity becomes. Lack of curiosity is the first step toward visual illiteracy—and by that I mean not really seeing what is going on around us. On one level, avoidance of informed looking and thinking results merely in inappropriate architecture, endless rows of neon signs, advertising agencies, political marketing consultants, Teenage Mutant Ninja Turtles, Barbie dolls, and Hallmark cards—in general, mediocrity. But on another, much deeper level, it threatens to turn us into isolated, insensitive, incapable, and ultimately helpless victims of a world of increasing complexity and decreasing humanity.

Let's say a dog walks across this platform during the evening's proceedings. At first, you can't believe your eyes. You look at the people on either side of you. They see it, too. There is indeed a dog walking across the stage. Not a bull, not a frog, but a dog. And you even notice that it is sort of small and black and white. But not so fast. If I pass out fifteen hundred pieces of paper and fifteen hundred pencils and ask you to draw the dog once it is out of sight, what would I get? Illustrators aside, probably a couple of generic dog pictures, twenty-five in-the-ballparks, two hundred and fifty you've-got-to-be-kiddings, and eleven hundred creatures that should be put down immediately.

In your defense, many of you would say, "But I can't draw a straight line." Well, there are two problems with that argument. First of all, the only straight line in the canine world is the invisible one between beast and hydrant. And second, drawing—and I'm not talking about making art here—has only as much to do with the marks you make as it does with the thought behind them. We are all able, with very little information, to recognize things with remarkable certainty. That dog needn't have been on the stage more than a fraction of a second for us to mentally record its presence. But look at your picture. You call that a dog? That mutant peanut on four sticks? All those years of dog watching without seeing.

Now, on a second piece of paper, I ask you to illustrate a dog fight. Think about it for a minute. What would you draw? Again, based on my teaching experience, the most common image would be that of two or three dogs doing a minuet. So there will be no mistaking the subjects, they are invariably frozen in position to reveal each tooth and claw. But while the cast of characters may be dogs, the subject of the illustration was dog fight. And a dog fight is anything but frozen. It is chaos, motion, noise, terror. So now the problem has become more complicated. Not only must we think more about our subject, but we must select from among the teeth and fur and fleas and vaccination tags that information which best tells the story. Simply recording all the pieces is not enough. Illustration is a process of selection of that which needs to be seen from all that can be seen.

Okay, you can put away your imaginary pencils now. The problem of not really seeing sounds inoffensive enough; after all, we can't be expected to see everything. But as soon as not seeing becomes a habit, we start accepting our visual environment without question. As technology becomes increasingly more complex, we are less and less able to actually see how things work. Switches and buttons are hidden behind plates. Just flip or push, but don't ask questions. Visual complacency rears its ugly head, and each time it does we humans lose a little ground.

Another major cause of our visual narcosis is that much-maligned, immensely powerful glowing box, overused and understocked, around which so much of daily life seems to revolve. Just look at the bulk of the programming we put up with on television. For years we have tried to compensate by purchasing programs from the British, who in turn feed their audiences *I Dream of Jeannie* and *The Monkees*. You see how international the problem of visual illiteracy has become. Stories presented on the news by tanned news personalities backed up with slick graphics and live footage often end up as the basis of made-for-television films. Sometimes, incidents invented for television films are imitated in real life and end up on the evening news.

When we hear news stories, we must remain attentive to both what is said and what is not. In picture making, that which is undrawn is referred to as "negative space," and it is essential to read both the positive and the negative spaces together to fully understand the image. Regarding the media, and particularly television—its priorities so carefully established and often brutally controlled by the cost of every minute—it is particularly important that we constantly consider what is not said. If truth and television have anything to do with each other, the truth will be found somewhere between what is presented and what is withheld.

Come to think of it, what is this speech, after all, but a word picture? In any speech, as in a drawing, we get details, and if we're lucky, we get an overall impression as well. But also, as in reading a drawing, we must pay equal attention to both what is said and what is left unspoken. Listening to speeches is never a more serious business than when we are choosing our leaders—the people to whom we entrust enormous power, we hope for our own good. We would like to believe that some intelligent, kinder, and gentler person has things under control and that each time we see and hear that person, we are reassured. It seems to me we choose leaders because they promise, not to lead, but instead to maintain some sort of deceptively reassuring status quo. The less they say, the more likely we are to elect them. In the visual world the danger of not seeing is taking things for granted, but in the political world complacency means being taken for granted.

While I am insisting that we remain curious—skeptical, even—I am not promoting total suspicion. We shouldn't be learning to see just the negative, in spite of its increasing abundance, but both the good and the bad, and unlike network news we must vigilantly maintain our ability to distinguish one from the other.

PROBLEM PARENTS

They look innocent enough. But let me give you some facts. They brought us up—my sister, baby brother, the Cairn terrier, and me—in a kitchen in a house at the end of a row of identical brick houses in a neighborhood of identical blocks in Bolton, Lancashire, England. There was one other room on the first floor besides the kitchen, but that was kept permanently on alert for unexpected company. It was off-limits to us. Forbidden terrain! The other reason we spent so much time in the kitchen was heat. A coal stove kept the room warm during the typically cold and damp north-of-England winters. Pretending it was all a matter of coal rationing, they only lit the fire in the sitting room—notice it wasn't even called the living room—when company finally showed up. So there we were, trapped by our own instincts for survival: love of warmth on the one hand, fear of entering the sitting room on the other. The long and short of it is that I was forced to play in the same room, and often at the very same table, where after dinner on Sundays I was required to sit for hours until I'd chewed and swallowed the gristle that always seemed to end up in my roast beef.

(Where did they get those cows anyway? Some ritual peat bog burial site, most likely.)

We were captive, and they could do whatever they wanted with us. They introduced us to humor, jokes like "Why did the chicken cross the road?" and "What's black and white and read all over?" I thought they were pretty funny. I should have known I was in trouble. Wonder what I'm complaining about? Does it sound pretty cozy so far? Well, hold on to your hats. It gets worse.

Much worse. My parents made things. They still do, but now they have a basement and a sewing room and a house to themselves. But during the first ten years of my life, when they decided to make something, they made it in the kitchen. Oh, it sounds innocent enough. A little sewing, a little knitting, a little woodworking, you know, fairly inoffensive stuff. But it snuck up on us. And what's really frightening is that after a while it started to seem natural. We got used to seeing people make things. But I'm not just complaining about occasional saw-dust or hammering or balls of wool lying around. I'm talking about the P word. Process.

It was inescapable, insidious, and what's more, it was contagious. We didn't even know what was happening, but they did! And they just kept on doing it. Pretty soon we were all making things. We drew. We sewed. I specialized in blanket stitch and embroidered a bee on a hand-kerchief. They must have seen the damage they were doing, tinkering mercilessly with innocent young minds. But did they stop? No way! Next thing I knew my mother was cranking out pullovers with a new-fangled, hand-operated Swiss knitting machine, and my father was pro-ducing easels for the local elementary school. Process. Process. Process. My siblings and I were systematically and brutally denied mystification of process. We were blatantly encouraged to make things, to under-stand how things went together and how they came apart. Maybe we didn't know how everything was made, but we knew there was an order to it, and we knew there was a right way and a wrong way to do things. By the time we got out of that kitchen, we actually believed that cre-ativity and craftsmanship were desirable—even normal.

Sunday afternoons, after the gristle, were particularly brutal. Family outings. Picnics. Nature. Sites "of cultural significance."

The one good thing about living in a small house was that it forced us to play outside a lot. We had to get out of that kitchen even though we needed the heat. But it was too late for me. I was so maladjusted that when I did escape, I usually played alone. I pretended I was on horseback galloping around and snorting like an idiot through the woods at the bottom of our street, oblivious to any other reality. I actu-ally derived pleasure from the discovery of rodent skeletons, aban-doned gas masks from the war, strange rocks to collect and catalog, and even frog spawn to scoop up in a jar each spring and watch turn into frogs.

It just feels so good to finally be able to get this stuff off my chest with a few close friends.

No wonder my imagination grew. It never stood a chance. It was force fed! But I couldn't stay out forever. I mean, eventually I had to return to The Kitchen. I asked my mother to draw pictures for me; Cinderella running down the staircase became a favorite. Then I started building things—working contraptions out of cardboard, string, and packing tape (the kind you have to lick). My parents' campaign was relentless. Before bed each evening and on cold Saturday mornings in their bed, they read to us: the stories of Hans Christian Andersen and the Brothers Grimm, *The Water Babies, Alice in Wonderland* (without Tenniel), and *The Wind in the Willows* (with Shepard). But what did I know about illustration? I was given *Ned the Lonely Donkey*, and thought it was terrific, and *Robinson Crusoe*. Oh, sure, Crusoe looks like a story all right. But it's really all about making things out of leftovers. Clothes. Furniture. Process rears its ugly head once more.

I was hooked, and I'm sure they knew it. What kid could possibly comprehend the subtlety of their strategy, never mind combat it? It's hardly surprising, then, that when it came time to choose the book I would receive for collecting money to keep the Methodist Missionary Society in business, I chose *The Encyclopedia of Science for Boys and Girls,* which I thought was English but actually came from some place called Racine, Wisconsin. It was filled with pictures about natural history, astronomy, chemistry, meteorology, and so on, and so on. I was doomed: a terminal victim of curiosity. And they did it to me.

But the greatest cruelty of all is yet to be revealed. Brace yourselves. Not until I was almost ten did they think to bring a television into the kitchen. And when they finally came to their senses—black and white, of course—the best the BBC could come up with was an hour of children's programs each afternoon, and then they went off the air until the evening programs started: ballroom dancing from Blackpool, etc.

But enough complaining. Those were the fifties. These are the nineties, and, fortunately, things are different. More parents work, so kids are much less likely to have to confront this kind of deconstructivist environment. Central heating means a family doesn't have to be together in the same room at the same time. Kitchens are for defrosting and nuking food. Gristle is almost extinct, and that which remains is used in the manufacture of athletic shoes. Most things now get made in faraway factories, which is as it should be, and appear as if by magic, and in a truly terrific innovation most of them are offered in catalogs with toll-free numbers and twenty-four-hour operators standing by. With a wiggle of the finger, we can reach out and touch someone whether they like it or not—and probably while they're eating. Even company calls before it comes over, greatly reducing the element of surprise and eliminating the need for sitting rooms.

If things must get made in the home—and let's face it, there will always be a few reactionaries out there—it happens in the basement or out in the garage or in some specially set-aside room. And television, that marvel of electronic communication, offers an inexhaustible stream of imagination busters and intelligence debilitators. In short, it is now possible for almost any child to get through childhood without any knowledge whatsoever of the P word, and without suffering the slightest case of curiosity. Even kids with problem parents have a fifty-fifty chance of leading normal lives.

There's no question about it. We've come a long way from the path of curiosity and process in the past forty years. I just hope our children are smart enough to appreciate the progress.

A WAITING GAME

I have been making books now for almost nineteen years, and I have been honored twice with silver medals. Until this January, I had never received The Big One. On a couple of occasions during the past two decades, I actually found myself disappointed not to have won.

On one occasion in particular, although I can't remember which book would have been in contention, or mercifully, which book won, I was convinced I was going to take it. I tossed and turned all night waiting to hear. I even kept the phone plugged in. Nothing. Not a peep. A few days later, when I heard the victorious title, I couldn't believe it. That's when I decided to give up once and for all on committees.

Of course they didn't choose my book. How could they? Committees exist to perpetuate compromise, and compromise always results in mediocrity. How could the concepts of quality— "most distinguished picture book" —and compromise possibly coexist? The really bad stuff and the really good stuff never survive a committee, so naturally you end up with books that don't elicit strong emotions at either end of the scale. What higher praise, I sneered. I was despondent, of course, but at least I was vindicated in my defeat. Suddenly, I realized what a narrow escape those two honor medals had been. Phew! But somehow, no matter what I told myself, my dismissal of the process seemed slightly hollow, if not a tad self-serving.

This year I never gave the medal a thought. In fact, I had completely forgotten that it was time once again for a group of people, having read and reread hundreds of books in preparation for the final showdown, to meet somewhere in Chicago to select a book they could all agree on. My ignorance of and indifference to this event can be directly attributed to two things: first, I was, and still am, very much in the middle of another book. In fact, the middle is getting longer every day. And second, I had already accepted the fact that *Black and White*, while it pleased me, was just not the kind of book that any committee of sound, compromising mind could possibly agree on.

But then came the call. Not the one which sent half a million soldiers into Kuwait. Not the one rush-ordering eight million yards of yellow ribbon. But the one that said, "Mr. Macaulay. You won!" Well, isn't that always the way. Just when you finally come to understand the truth about someone or something, they turn around and do something so entirely inappropriate and uncharacteristic. Obviously I was forced to regroup, to suspend hostilities, to entertain the possibility of another point of view. To go out to lunch.

But that was my problem. What about the poor audience? What of their plight? While it is adults who give other adults Caldecott Awards, what must never be forgotten is the impact of this ritual on kids. That little foil seal has been put there to indicate something special. It denotes a book that will be opened with expectation and possibly even reverence.

The content, then, is crucial. Medal winners and honor books alike should be the books youngsters will aspire to as they learn to write and draw. As such they must rise above the plague of safe, superficial, and unfortunately often highly profitable books that descends upon the market annually. The seeds of visual complacency are unwittingly sown whenever one of these books is held up as the best.

The committee's choice this year goes far beyond making me the most difficult ego in the room at the moment. It tells readers, especially young ones, that it is essential to see, not merely to look; that words and pictures can support each other; that it isn't necessary to think in a straight line to make sense; and finally that risk can be rewarded.

Utter Chaos

The words utter chaos describe perfectly a seductive and often frustrating form of self-abuse called the creative process. The creative process, in turn, is that sequence of actions, erratic and unpredictable, by which the creative processor sets out to bring order and extract meaning from a conglomeration of parts and elements which are without order or connection.

Utter chaos also describes, with equal acuity, the state of mind of the aforementioned creative processor at various times during the shaping of the formless void and the distillation of primordial matter. But as painful and exhausting as the process gets, chaos is both the problem and an essential part of the solution. While uncertainty brings with it the chance for screaming failure, it also offers the possibility of exhilarating surprise. Accidents will inevitably happen, and the attentive creator will recognize them and promptly claim them as his own. The longer one can stretch out the process and still have it remain creative, the more likely the occurrence of useful accidents. Under these circumstances, procrastination can actually become a virtue. Involuntary procrastination, if such a condition can be said to exist, had a great deal to do with the creation of this year's medal winner. In fact, *Black and White* is perhaps best described as an example of visual Darwinism; it took almost as long to evolve as it did for monkeys to walk upright and run for office. Seven years of failed attempts. From books about journeys—specifically about travelers unaware of the effects of their journeys on the journeys of others. Paths that cross by chance. U-turns. Side streets. Dead ends. Next, a history of roads and cities becomes the complete guide to civilization—delusions of profundity. Then an alphabet journey book that fizzles before reaching the letter *F*.

The road along which my ideas travel is now littered with smoldering wrecks, vehicles with square wheels, locked rest rooms. It is not a public highway, but there are many toll booths and no exits. I must have picked up the Triple A guide to the Donner Pass by mistake. My creative excursion occasionally runs out of sustenance but not determination. At some point the road disappears into a long, dark tunnel. Finally, a glimmer of light—a chaotic cause-and-effect story ignited by a terrified chicken driven into the middle of the road by human gastronomic self-indulgence. And then two years later, four stories or maybe not, four journeys or maybe one. *Black and White* in full color. From utter confusion and disorder comes the illusion of utter confusion and disorder. Subversive publishing. Finally a rest stop owned and operated by the Association for Library Service to Children, part of the well-known American Library Association chain. I pull over to smell the roses. But can't stay for too long. I have a ship to build.

This has not been a speedy journey; therefore, the list of people whose advice and encouragement has brought me to this place is very long. As a humanitarian gesture and out of respect for Article 378 of the Geneva Convention, I will limit myself to the very top of the list. First and foremost, I wish to thank Walter "If You Believe in It, We'll Do It" Lorraine for nineteen years of helping to create and channel utter chaos. Ruth Macaulay for thirteen years of tolerating and critiquing it. Tom Sgouros, of the Rhode Island School of Design, for first showing me how to see it. And, of course, my mother and father for being such fabulous problem parents.

Rest assured, those of you who remain somewhat skeptical about the book in question, that my being awarded the 1991 Caldecott Medal will not encourage me to make more *Black and Whites* but rather to pursue the process from which it has emerged and of which it is simply one off-spring. For that encouragement I thank each and every member of the Caldecott committee. You took a chance, and you made a statement. And when committees start taking chances, we all have reason to hope.

David Macaulay: The Early Years

Chris Van Allsburg

David Macaulay

David Macaulay was born forty-four years ago in the English city of Burton on Trent, best known as the home of Bass Ale and Double Diamond Beer. For the first few years of his life he lived in a home that had a large sand-box in the backyard. This sandbox now looms in David's memory as a vast open pit that might have held ropes and ladders small children could use to pull themselves out.

When David was three, his family—which now included a "dreaded" younger sister—moved to Bolton, another Midlands indus-trial town. His two favorite books from this period both dealt with loneliness: *Robinson Crusoe* and *Ned the Lonely Donkey*. But he was not a lonely boy. He had a circle of friends that included Peter Smith, "who got beat up a lot," and Ian Hibbert, who helped him make forts using discarded funeral decorations from a nearby cemetery.

David also enlisted his father's help in his building projects. At age seven he received a Mechano Set—the English Erector Set—that was too advanced for him but that he was determined to use, anyway. Each evening, returning from work, Mr. Macaulay would find his young son waiting for him, ready to demolish the previous night's effort and build something new.

This constant industry showed up in other areas of David's life. Every Saturday for one year he visited the homes in his neighborhood of row houses to collect money for the Methodist Missionary Society.

One contributor was so impressed by the zeal of her young weekly visitor that she gave him money as a gift to be shared with his sister. David went directly to a toy, store, where he spent the entire sum on two cap guns and a deluxe double holster set.

He was proud of his fancy gun set. He was also proud of the professional-quality leather soccer ball he'd received on his ninth birthday. He kept it lubricated with neat's-foot oil and carried it with him to school. He didn't care much for soccer, though, so he usually turned the ball over to classmates while he pursued other interests.

One of these interests was penmanship. The hands that grew up to draw cathedrals and pyramids first distinguished themselves in 1956 by winning a national handwriting award. David still has the certificate acclaiming this achievement. He insists that giving up his soccer ball to study penmanship did not brand him a sissy in the eyes of his school chums. Good handwriting was held in very high esteem at Bolton Elementary.

David's father was an engineer whose specialty was keeping temperamental textile machinery running. In 1957, when David was not quite eleven, Mr. Macaulay accepted a job in New Jersey and made arrangements to bring the family across the Atlantic on the SS United States.

Before they left England, David's mother returned from a shopping trip with a very special package for her son. It held something he'd longed for but had not expected would be his for years to come. Once on the ocean liner David retreated to the Macaulay cabin, opened the package, and for the first time in his life put on long pants.

Most of the passage David spent in the ship's theater. At that point in his life he'd seen only six films, and in the five-day crossing he meant to make up for lost time. He had no intention, however, of missing the Manhattan skyline. When he'd been told the family was moving to America, the first thing that had come into his mind was a vision of huge buildings, with one taller than any other: the Empire State Building. But his first view of that landmark was a disappointment. From the deck of the ship, five or six miles out to sea, it looked rather small to him.

Being a new kid in school who talked funny was not especially traumatic. David, a train lover, found comfort in the railway tracks nearby that brought one-hundred-car freight trains of the Erie Lackawanna Railroad through the neighborhood. Standing in the middle of the tracks, looking toward Manhattan, he could see a familiar sight: the distant spire of the Empire State Building. It still looked rather small.

The first two years in America the Macaulays lived in Bloomfield, New Jersey, and then moved to Verona, New Jersey. Once again, David adapted quickly to his new surroundings and made new friends. He had his own tiny bedroom in this new house, large enough to hold only his bed and a small record player on which he played Dave Brubeck records.

In 1962 the Macaulays moved once again, to Cumberland, Rhode Island. David does not recall this move as being as simple for him as the earlier moves. This was partly because, at fifteen years of age, very little seemed simple. Like most teenagers, David sought some kind of identity, some way to distinguish himself among his peers. He sensed that good handwriting was not going to do the trick at his new school. But some other kind of handiwork might. David began doing pencil drawings of famous people, specializing in the Beatles. He would bring these to school and casually show them to classmates in the cafeteria or study hall. Upon graduation, the Cumberland High School year-book named him the best artist, recognition he finds trivial and insignificant compared to his National Handwriting Award.

David was not a "fast" or reckless youth. It is consistent perhaps that a boy who waited till he was ten to ride a bike would not bother to get a driver's license until he was nineteen. Neither of these late starts was a result of parental authority, just a lack of interest. Of course, this lack of interest in mobility can have dire consequences for teenage romance. At the age of seventeen, David was still pedaling his bike to his girl-friend's house and listening, hand in hand, to her older sister's Johnny Mathis records. In the living room. With her parents.

After graduation, David went on to the Rhode Island School of Design. He continued to live at home and call on girlfriends by foot or on his bicycle. He says living at home seemed fine to him at the time, but now realizes that certain social opportunities may have eluded him.

His enrollment at RISD had nothing to do with the art that had given him pleasure and made him famous throughout the halls of Cumberland High. David saw college as a place to learn a trade, not to have fun. He elected to study architecture, something with rigor and discipline. Fortunately, he discovered that rigor and discipline don't necessarily exclude fun. The design process was exciting and rewarding to him and an unexpected outlet for humor that made his architectural presentations favorites of his instructors and fellow students.

Oddly, this gift and enthusiasm for the design process were not accompanied by any ambition or desire to be an architect. He didn't think of the building of little cardboard houses as a stepping stone toward the fulfillment of a dream to build real houses. He simply liked to make little cardboard buildings and ponder the design implications of his decisions.

In his fifth year at the School of Design David was chosen for the European Honors Program and sent to study in Italy. It was an extraordinary experience for him, and not simply because of the stimulations of Rome. Aside from Boy Scout camp, it was his first time away from home.

The year abroad did nothing to help focus the soon-to-be college graduate. When he returned home, he took a job teaching art at a junior high school and continued to work part-time at a summer job he'd had earlier. This part-time job included design and drafting work for an interior decorator named Morris Nathanson. Morris sensed a restlessness in David that he had experienced in himself. There was something both men wanted to say as artists that couldn't find expression in the creation of restaurant interiors.

It was Morris who shared his enthusiasm for picture books with his young draftsman. David agreed that picture books had a unique combination of text, design, layout, and art. The two collaborated on a book, and though it was rejected by all the publishers who saw it, they were given encouragement.

David put together three books on his own, all fantasies with no special focus on architecture. These were rejected, too, but David was not deterred. He wrote a fourth fantasy about a boy, the son of a medieval stonecutter, who one night finds himself locked in a cathedral where the gargoyles his father has carved come to life.

David took this effort to Houghton Mifflin, where he'd sent some of his other stories. The editor there, Walter Lorraine, looked over the drawings and the story. He was not taken with the idea, but before David left, Mr. Lorraine said to him, "You know, I like the drawing of the cathedral. Maybe you could just do a book about that."

The Newbery Medal 1991

Maniac Magee

written by
Jerry Spinelli

published by
Little, Brown, 1990

Horn Book Review

Part saint, part legend, part homeless boy, Jeffrey—better known as Maniac—Magee is almost always on the run. Appearing in the town of Two Mills apparently out of nowhere, he is scoffed for his under-nourished, ragged appearance. Until, that is, he slips into a high-school football practice and stuns the team with his remarkable interception. Even more impressive is his rescue of a boy from the back yard of the dreaded Finsterwald house and his ability to run, where others only walk, on a single track of the railroad. A Black family in the East End of town takes Maniac in, but he leaves, for their sakes, when the racist word fishbelly is scrawled on their house. Then, an elderly man named Grayson befriends him but soon dies, leaving Maniac alone once more. At odds now with both sides of town, Maniac is adrift—sleeping with the buffaloes at the zoo or in abandoned cars and eating whatever he can find, but always bringing a new direction to those he encounters. The author brightens the story with exaggeration, humor, and melo-drama, but avoids the feverish hilarity of his earlier books. Despite Maniac's accomplishments and the author's clear message for racial harmony, the book avoids mawkishness through, the good-natured characterization of people of both races and by, the vigor and clamor of their speech and actions. The book becomes, in the end, a kind of twentieth-century morality play, with Maniac a larger-than-life leader and his rag-tag companions promising, if not totally redeemed, disciples.—*Edith R. Twichell*

Booklist Review

Part tall tale and part contemporary realistic fiction, this unusual novel magically weaves timely issues of homelessness, racial prejudice, and illiteracy into a complicated story, rich in characters and details.

Orphaned at three, Jeffrey Lionel Magee, after eight unhappy years with relatives, one day takes off running. A year later (so the story goes), he ends up 200 miles away in Two Mills, a highly segregated community.

Each of the book's three sections is set in one of Maniac's temporary homes. The white boy's first home is with the Beales, a loving black family in the East End; his second is with Grayson, a lonely former minor league ballplayer, in the band shell in the city zoo; and the third is with the McNabs, a white, West End family of tough, neglected boys.

A deep sense of story permeates this multiveined novel: Maniac runs (accomplishing fantastic athletic and superhero-type feats—bringing about both his folk hero image and nickname, "Maniac") and reads, although he never attends school. He changes others people's lives with books, either by reading from or by teaching the printed word. For instance, he entices Grayson to tell him baseball stories and later teaches the man to read. Furthermore, Maniac educates white families about black ones and black families about white ones, proving through his own actions the shared humanity of both groups.

As he jogs readers into analyzing what makes a home, Spinelli, in his best book to date, creates a provocative slice of life, showing graphically (and sometimes humorously) the pitfalls that face the homeless. Although this demands much concentration on the part of the reader, it is a unique effort, an energetic piece of writing that bursts with creativity, enthusiasm, and hope for the future; in short, it's a celebration of life. Good readers will thoroughly enjoy this, and teachers looking for interesting novels will find plumbing its depths rewarding.—*Deborah Abbott*

1991 Newbery Acceptance Speech
Jerry Spinelli

The middle and the end of this talk have changed a few times as I have thought about it these past months, but the beginning has always been the same:

To the members of the Newbery committee, I can only say that while my "thank you" may end with this speech, my gratitude never will. You have given me something I could never give myself. It is the most wonderful gift. It has done everything from bring back old playmates to raise the eyebrows of my dry cleaner, who had previously thought me just another overcoat. I was talking to Maniac today, and he told me to tell you that he feels he now has fourteen new moms and a dad. He says you're family. I feel the same way.

To my editor John Keller I have been grateful for about ten years now. John took a chance on an unpublished author and brought into print *Space Station Seventh Grade*. Several years ago I called John and told him I had an idea for a story about a boy who has no home, no family, and doesn't go to school. I asked him if I could get away with such a thing. He didn't hesitate. "Sure," he said, "why not?" Thank you again, John, for taking yet another chance.

Also at Little, Brown I want to thank copy-editor Betty Powers. The gentleness of her suggestions belies the sharpness of her vision. And Chris Paul, who designed the book and whose suggestion it was that the cover show simply a boy running. And photographic artist Carol Palmer, who made the simply perfect picture.

And thank you to the best support group an author could have: Betsy Groban and Anne Quirk and Linda Magram and Stephanie Owens Lurie. The committee have come here from all over. Little, Brown came from Boston. The others came on the train with me:

My wife and fellow author, Eileen, who says yes or no to every chapter, whose judgment I trust more than my own, and who creates the world in which I write. When the committee gave it to me, they gave it to us.

My mother and father, who have come from farther than Norristown, Pennsylvania, to be here tonight.

And our agent Ray Lincoln and husband Jerry, the best of friends. They were thrilled to learn that *Maniac Magee* was dedicated to them, and this was long before the night of January 13, 1991 . . . .

I was doing what all respectable Pennsylvanians were doing at 12:30 A.M., a half-hour after midnight: I was sleeping. How was I to know that the telephone's ring originated in Chicago, where it was "only" 11:30?

Have you ever gotten good news at 12:30 A.M.? Neither had I. So why was I hurrying? I was hurrying to stop that infernal phone from ringing in the middle of the night.

The phone is in the hallway. I leap up. I am in my underwear. In a flurry of modesty I blindly grope for my bathrobe. Am I afraid a stranger has entered the house and is peeping from the top of the stairs? Do I fear the caller will sense my indecency? I grab the robe. It is dark. I am groggy. I cannot find the sleeve holes. It is 12:30 A.M., and the phone is ringing.

Bathrobe in hand, I lurch into the hallway, flick on the light, dive for the phone, kill the ringing, gird myself for the bad news, pray everyone's alive.

"Hello?" I say.

The voice that responds is unfamiliar to me. A doctor? The voice tells me its name is Alice Naylor. It says something like, "We want you to know that we have been very careful not to let the facts get mixed up with the truth." It says the word "Newbery."

The rest is fuzzy.

I remember Eileen standing in the doorway. She tells me she thought she heard me say "metal"-m-e-T-a-l-and was wondering who might have gotten hit on the head with a metal something.

I remember Alice Naylor saying she was standing amid a hotel room full of committee members, all awaiting my witty reactions. I'm afraid I disappointed them. I am not at my best in my underwear in the hallway in the middle of the night.

I'm not even sure I had the presence of mind to say thank you to Alice Naylor. I certainly have since, several times, and I may yet once more, perhaps some Sunday night by phone, say, oh, around 12:30 A.M.

We say goodbye. We hang up. The screaming begins.

Sean staggers bleary-eyed from his room and croaks, "What happened?"

"We won the Newbery!" we sing.

He smiles sleepily—"Oh . . . congratulations"—and goes back to bed. Ben never wakes up.

We go downstairs. We talk, pace, giggle, drink Poland Spring water. At 4 A.M. we go back to bed. We sleep straight through to 4:15. At 7 A.M. we give up, go out to the Vale-Rio diner, have breakfast. I order French toast. I never get bacon. I get bacon. We come back home. We sleep till noon.

And now again the phone starts ringing. This time there is no stopping it.

Not long ago a kid in a group I was speaking to raised his hand and said, "Where do you get all that stuff?"

I looked out into a library full of cross-legged floor-sitters, their eyes wide, mouths agape, all wondering the same thing, their classmate having put his finger on their second most pressing question (the first being, of course, "How much money do you make?"). I pointed to them all, and I smiled and I said, "You. You're where I get all that stuff."

The expressions didn't change. They weren't buying it.

"Look," I said, "What do you think I do, make up all this stuff? I get it from you. I get it from the me that used to be you. From my own kids, your age-mates. For my first two books, I didn't even have to look outside my own house."

And I told them how I found *Space Station Seventh Grade* early one morning in my lunch bag, my fried chicken having been reduced to bones by one or more of the six sleeping angels upstairs. I told them that the warfare between Megamouth and El Grosso in *Who Put That Hair in My Toothbrush?* was nothing compared to the real battles between Molly and Jeffrey in my own house.

I pointed to them again. "You're the funny ones. You're the fascinating ones. You're the elusive and inspiring and promising and heroic and maddening ones. Don't you know that?"

I looked over the faces. No, for the most part, they did not know. And just as well. How regrettable if they did know, and thereby ceased to be themselves.

The obvious prompting of her teacher notwithstanding, how could anyone but an unself-conscious sixth-grader have written this:

Dear Mr. Spinelli,

I am very sorry that I was playing Tic-Tac-Toe while you were talking. I know that I had no right to it. I should have listened to you. It was positively mean and rude of me and my friend to play Tic-Tac-Toe right under your nose. I regret it terribly and I seriously would understand if you hated me. I liked your talk and your books anyhow. If you do come back to Chatham, even after the rudeness of my friend and me, I hope that you get treated more kindly than this. Like I said before, I am really very, very sorry that I played Tic-Tac-Toe instead of listening to you. Please do not unlike the school because of our terrible rudeness. With all our heart we are sorry.

Most sincerely,
Katie Rose Loftus

Where do I get this stuff?

I get it from Brooke Jacobs, who wrote, "When you came to our school, I thought I'd see a big, tall man in a suit looking rich. When I saw you, I got very relaxed."

I get it from the young lady who wrote, "I will not say I totally enjoyed your talk, because that would be untrue . . . . Mr. Spinelli, you are a great writer. However, you, in my eyes, do need to work on your group speaking skills."

I get it from Niki Hollie, who wrote to me recently from Schuylkill Elementary, just a few blocks from my house: "I think no matter if people are black, white or green, there is no difference in the way they get treated. It's the inside not the outside."

I get it from my old friend, who at the age of nine months was left nameless on the doorstep of a judge of the court of common pleas, a red cloth badge of the Sacred Heart pinned to his blanket. He was taken to a Catholic orphanage and there acquired the three names he answers to today: those of a judge, a nun, and a saint.

He spent his first seventeen years in this institution, called a "home," and was thus known as a "homie." Prospective foster parents were called "friends." They would come to audition the orphans on Saturdays. A childhood of Saturdays passed, and the sisters' call went out to others, never him: "Hurry up now, your friend is waiting."

Around the age of seven or eight, my friend found himself among a busload of fellow homies streaming and chattering toward a swimming pool. There was a turnstile—only one child admitted at a time. When my friend's turn came, a brawny hand clamped the metal pipe and held it still. It would not move. And my friend, who until then had known merely that he was black, discovered now that it made a difference.

He does not know if the running began that day. He recalls only that he ran everywhere he went. He ran the three miles to Tony and Pete's Hoagie Hut, because if you were a homie, your hoagie from Tony and Pete's was free. He made that trip two or three times a week. The farthest he ran was twelve miles—six out and six back—to Bristol, where the nearest movie theater was.

When he wasn't running to or from somewhere, he simply ran.

That was the first patch in the quiltwork that became *Maniac Magee*. There were many others.

There were the summer afternoons on the Elmwood Park basketball court, myself the only white skin among fifteen or twenty blacks. I remember a small, quiet feeling of gratitude, of pride, of admittance. There was no turnstile for me.

There was Skag Cottman. I was barely thirteen when he first became my baseball coach. He would pitch batting practice. Once to each player he would throw his special pitch. He called it the "stop ball." "It comes up to the plate all big and fat," he told us. "Then it stops and waits for you to swing, and then it goes on to the catcher's mitt." It was true. I know it was true because none of us ever did more than whiff at, or at best graze, the stop ball.

Several years later, a sophisticated seventeen-year-old, I dared him to throw me the old stop ball. He did. I creamed it, and for days thereafter hated myself for growing up.

There was the school in New York State several years ago. I had finished my talk in the library—not a tic-tac-toe player in sight—and a teacher came up and said he wanted to introduce me to a particular sixth-grade girl. He said there was something very interesting about her. Every day she carried her entire home library to school in a suitcase, because she could not bear to abandon her books to the crayons and sharp teeth of her siblings and pets at home. I met the girl and gave her my address and made her promise to write to me. She hasn't. I wish she would. I'm afraid she doesn't know that she became Amanda Beale in the book that won the Newbery.

And there was Dr. Winters, my mother's dentist. She would take me along to his office on East Main Street. My own teeth were still too new to need repair, but I was jealous and the dentist was kind, so he would lift me into the chair and tilt it back and, with mirror and probe, pretend to examine me. To this day I can feel his sure and sturdy fingers in my mouth. Cavities and an awareness that Dr. Winters was black arrived at about the same time, but by then we had moved. And now it is far too late to tell him that he became Amanda's mother: Maniac "especially loved the warm brown of Mrs. Beale's thumb, as it appeared from under the creamy white icing that she allowed him to lick away when she was frosting his favorite cake."

Maniac Magee is, to my way of thinking, both the kid we all once were and the kids we now look after. He is us and ours, was and is. And insofar as he has no address, everywhere is home; insofar as he belongs to no one, everyone is free to claim him.

Where do I get this stuff?

Let us recognize and celebrate the ones who really should be here tonight: the kids.

Let's agree to a joint custody. When my kids are in your school or library, they're yours. When your kids are reading my book or Avi's or David Macaulay's or another author's, they're ours.

And let us wish, let us urge this for them:

> That they seek their happiness not so much at the finish line, as in the running;

That they have the strength not to lift tremendous weights, but one fallen friend;

That they learn to fight their own battles with a never-ending string of temporary cease-fires;

Not that the occasion make them smile, but that their smile make the occasion;

That their bridges be built not over rivers, but over misunderstanding;

That their wealth be not in their banks, but in their hearts;

That they gain power not over others, but over themselves;

That they never fail to leave the stage before their applause is done;

That they bow not to little people with big titles, but to big people with little titles;

Not that they never know grief, but that they never know joy the moment after;

That their names be household words not throughout the land, but in their own households;

That their monuments be found not in public parks, but in the lives of those they've touched.

And to all of you, my wish is for a gladness such as you have given me.

Thank you.

Jerry Spinelli
John Keller

Photo credit: M/ Elaine Adams

Jerry Spinelli

There are two emblematic stories about Jerry Spinelli that I'd like to relate. The first took place one evening in the early days of Jerry and Eileen's marriage when, to put it succinctly, money was tight. Jerry turned on the television to watch the local Philadelphia educational channel conduct its annual fundraiser. The various items one could bid on for the benefit of a presumed higher standard of television viewing flashed on the screen. Jerry paid indifferent attention. Then, in the midst of expensive meals at the best local restaurants and costly facials at chic beauty salons, came an item that caught Jerry's attention: a night of dinner and conversation with George Plimpton. Now there was something worth winning! George Plimpton was a writer who not only wrote graceful, evocative prose but who also enjoyed considerable commercial success. Jerry turned to Eileen and said something to the effect that such an evening would be a wonderful experience. Perhaps George Plimpton might say something inspiring, let loose some kernel of information that might help a man who more than anything wanted to write fiction and find an audience for that writing.

Eileen heard the longing in her husband's voice. She believed in Jerry's talent. Without missing a beat she went to the desk, checked the balance in the savings account, took a very deep breath, and called the station to bid much more money than they could afford for an evening that she hoped would be inspirational, educational, and fun.

Sometimes the gods listen. Jerry and Eileen won the bid, and several weeks later they were whisked off in a private limousine to spend an evening with the urbane and loquacious Mr. Plimpton.

For many years, Jerry worked for a technical publisher. The work there, I understand from Jerry, was nothing to get excited about, but it kept the family clothed and fed and it allowed him to take lunch hours during which he could go off to a small private room and write. I had a hard time imagining anyone having the persistence to write one sort of thing for a living, write another sort of material during lunch hour, and then continue with that kind of writing at night after the working day was over. Nonetheless, it worked for Jerry, and I mentally applauded his perseverance. Then he told me that he was quitting the job and was going to spend all his time writing novels! Any editor who hears that news and does not shake in his boots for the author must have a heart of stone. We all know how difficult this business is for novelists who write for young people. They strive; they struggle; and, even when they succeed, the monetary rewards are usually less than generous. I think I said something about how tough such a life might be, but Jerry told me that he had thought about it long and hard and that he wanted to give it a try. What could I say? Let me put it this way: I thought he'd be back at the technical publisher before long.

I don't know the details of the evening with George Plimpton. I do know that Jerry never went back to the publisher, and I relate these anecdotes to share with you my view of Jerry Spinelli. He is a man who shines forth with the desire to be a writer, a man whose great drive is to share his vision of the world with his readers. As he creates the honest and accurate worlds reflected in so many of the passages of his novels, he is also a man whose enthusiasm for what he does is infectious for those who have the privilege and enjoyment of working with him.

And what passages they are! I first came upon Jerry's work sometime in 1981 when a manuscript by a writer I'd never heard of from an agent I didn't know landed on my desk. The title was promising enough: *Space Ship Seventh Grade*. The subsequent decision to change it to *Space Station Seventh Grade* (Little) occupies several ongoing chapters in the Spinelli-Keller correspondence that might be called "I see what you're trying to tell me, but . . ." When I began to read, I liked the first chapter's conversational, unpretentious tone. It wasn't, however, until I got to the fourth chapter, "Hair," that I knew I had happened upon a writer who was special. When I read that chapter, in which Jason Herkimer tells about his ambivalent feelings about the onset of puberty and the absence or presence of pubic hair as noted in the boys' shower room after gym class, I broke into a big grin and thought, Exactly!

For that, I believe, is Jerry's greatest strength. He gets it right. He gets the details right. I had never heard of a butterscotch Krimpet before I read *Maniac Magee* (Little)—had you? He gets it right about the ways boys both look forward to growing into manhood and regret leaving childhood behind. He gets it right about the fury brothers and sisters can inspire in one another as they live within a family that truly wants to function well. He gets it right about girls like Marceline McAllister who from an early age refuse to conform to the stereotypes that boys want to believe about them. He gets it right about prejudice and unconditional love, and he gets it right about the magic every young person carries with him or her—a magic that shines forth if anyone takes the time to listen and observe.

Jerry has listened and observed, and, in language that is never self-consciously literary, he illuminates that rough magic children carry around with them. He allows us to see it and savor it, too. This honest observation has not always endeared Jerry's work to adult readers. Jerry shows children who haven't had the edges of their personalities sanded into a smoothness that will enable them to glide more easily through life. The characters in a Jerry Spinelli novel are apt to spit on the street, pop ants in a popcorn popper, put a hair on somebody else's toothbrush, and, yes, even go to a dump and hit a rat as hard and as far as possible. His characters are also capable of gestures of great generosity and courage. I believe that Maniac Magee is the best realized of this quintessential Jerry Spinelli character. He is a boy who doesn't yet know where he belongs in the great scheme of things. He roams from the darkness of his troubles, but he runs toward the light he sees shining forth from the decent people he encounters on his picaresque journey. Children, I am willing to wager, will understand at once what Maniac Magee is all about and accept him immediately as one of their own. They'll put him in that pantheon of beloved characters who become sacred (points of reference when, years later, they talk about the books that meant something to them as they took that difficult, wonderful, and exciting trip through childhood.

As I said, I don't know what Jerry, Eileen, and George Plimpton talked about on that night long ago. I don't know whether Mr. Plimpton said anything terribly important to the aspiring novelist who had won his company in an auction. I do know, however, that for whatever reason Jerry Spinelli was determined to become a writer whose books would find an audience and have an impact. He has clung to that vision of himself, and through times of good reviews and bad, good sales and not-so-good, he has practiced his craft. I, for one, am thankful for his persistence, his drive, and his talent, and I know in my bones that the young people who read his novels are, too.

The Caldecott Medal 1992

Tuesday

written and illustrated by
David Wiesner

published by
Clarion Books, 1991

Horn Book Review

A surreal, almost wordless picture book shows the mysterious levitation of lily pads and frogs from a pond one Tuesday at dusk. The frogs soar around town until they fall to the ground at sunrise. Large, detailed watercolors use dramatic points of view and lighting effects and often show a humorous range of expressions. There is a forecast of further surprises to come on following Tuesdays.—*Lolly Robinson*

Booklist Review

While technically not a wordless picture book, this has no text other than occasional markers of time, "Tuesday evening around eight" or "11:21 P.M.," to guide viewers through one remarkable night and suggest what happens one week later. On the first night, frogs rise from their ponds on lily pads that magically float like flying carpets. Leaving their country home, the frogs fly into town, where they peek through windows, enter a house to watch television, and terrorize a dog. At dawn the magic ends, and the frogs hop back home, leaving wet lily pads in the streets to puzzle the townsfolk and the police. The following Tuesday at dusk, pigs rise into the air, like helium balloons. Then the book ends, leaving viewers to imagine the magic and mayhem to follow. As in *Free Fall* (BKL Je 1 81), Wiesner offers a fantasy watercolor journey accomplished with soft-edged realism. Studded with bits of humor, the narrative artwork tells a simple, pleasant story with a consistency and authenticity—that make the fantasy convincing. While this trip may not take children far, its open-ended conclusion invites them to carry on the fantasy, allowing for unexpected magic in everyday, modern settings.—*Carolyn Phelan*

1992 Caldecott Acceptance Speech
David Wiesner

Bufo Marinus, the Australian Cane Toad, secretes a toxic substance when it is attacked. This substance is lethal to nearly all predators, including dogs and other large animals, and it can have an incapacitating effect on humans.

In the early 1970s, some adventurous young Australians discovered an interesting use for the cane toad. After the toad is boiled down into a broth or a resin, it can be ingested as a liquid or smoked as a powder. The toxin, Bufotenine, produces a hallucinogenic reaction in the user. To this day it is a criminal offense to smoke a cane toad in Australia.

I'm often asked where I got the idea for *Tuesday*. The question is usually accompanied by a suggestion or two. Did I have a pet frog while growing up? Do I live near a swamp? Do I have a "thing" for frogs? I have discovered only recently that an awful lot of people have a special affinity for frogs. My favorite comment, though, was a rhetorical question from Laurence Yep, who gave me a funny look and asked if I had been importing cane toads.

The truth is that the imagination needs no outside stimulus. To watch children at play is to see the mind in all its uninhibited glory. Growing up in New Jersey, my friends and I recreated our world daily. The neighborhood would become anything from the far reaches of the universe to a prehistoric jungle. To believe that giant pterodactyls were swooping down on us required only a small leap of faith.

Dinosaurs were an important part of my world as a child. Just as the caves of Lascaux, France, are full of images of the animals hunted by prehistoric man, so my room was full of drawings of the dinosaurs I hunted in my backyard. In an attempt to make them more real and alive, I drew them over and over again.

I had many books about dinosaurs. My favorite books were the ones that had the best pictures, and the pictures I liked best were in a *World Book Encyclopedia* supplement about the evolution of the earth. It wasn't until many years later that I realized the pictures were by the artist Charles Knight, the man who first visualized what dinosaurs looked like, and on whose work all subsequent dinosaur renderings were based.

The dinosaurs were executed in exacting detail, with solid musculature, and the animals had a real presence. Thinking about it now, I'm aware it probably wasn't the greatest printing job, but back then the washed-out quality of the black-and-white reproductions created a real sense of atmosphere for me. I thought they were photographs. Even after I should have known better, I thought they just might be photographs.

The realization that the pictures were painted by an actual person was a revelation. The reality I perceived in those scenes was totally captivating. At the time, I couldn't imagine being able to paint so convincingly. But now, as I work, I'm continually trying to recapture for myself that total belief in the world I'm creating on paper.

As I moved on from dinosaurs, I discovered other imagery that exerted a powerful hold on me. In the stacks of the Bound Brook, New Jersey, Public Library, I would sit and pore over the Time-Life books on the history of art. I was drawn immediately to the Renaissance artists, Durer, for one, and Michelangelo, and da Vinci, before they were Ninja Turtles. The Mona Lisa is a compelling portrait, but it's the landscape she sits in front of that I found fascinating. It's a wonderfully alien-looking place, more like Mars than Italy. Hieronymus Bosch made a deep impression on me too, and the landscapes of Pieter Brueghel the Elder fascinated me even more. Your eye can wander in and out of his paintings, from the extreme foreground to the distant horizon with incredible clarity and detail. I was also intrigued by the surrealists, Magritte, de Chirico, Dali, who depicted the dream world with an unsettling precision.

Every painting seemed to be a scene in a story, like a frame in a film. I longed to be able to switch on a projector that would show me what happened before and after the image that was captured on the canvas.

And of course I went on trying to put my own reality down on paper, not always with welcome results. When I was in the fourth grade, we'd find a short assignment on the blackboard every morning that we were supposed to work on until the bell rang to start class. This was called "A.M. work," and we did it on paper that was about six by nine inches and sort of an ochre color. It was cheap paper, but it had a nice bit of tooth to it and was great for drawing. One morning I looked up from a scene I was creating to find our teacher, Miss Klingibel, standing next to me. She was not amused. She took my picture and wrote an angry note home to my mother: "David would rather be drawing than doing his A.M. work." In my opinion, that was the most astute comment she made all year.

I went on to study at the Rhode Island School of Design. I was finally in a place where everyone would rather be drawing than doing A.M. work.

During my freshman year, my roommate, Michael Hays, casually described to me a book that would become a catalyst for many of my own visual ideas. He had seen this book in the rare books collection in the Hunt Library at Carnegie-Mellon University. It was an allegorical novel for adults about good and evil, life and death, and spirituality. And it had no words. The story was told in a series of about 130 woodcuts.

I couldn't get the idea of this book out of my head. A year and a half later, I visited Mike in Pittsburgh. I arrived in the evening and the first thing the next morning we were at the library.

The book is called *Mad Man's Drum*, and is by Lynd Ward, whose book *The Biggest Bear* won the 1953 Caldecott Medal. Sitting in the artificial air of the library's climate-controlled rare book room, I read that book in amazement. Each turn of the page opened a door in my mind a little wider.

Back at school I began to explore the possibilities of wordless storytelling in some of my assignments. It was in my senior degree project that I had the chance to investigate the form more fully. I created a forty-page wordless book based on Fritz Leiber's short story "Gonna Roll the Bones." I began to understand the process by which a story is distilled and the essential information presented in visual terms.

When I graduated and began working as an illustrator, my goal was eventually to publish a wordless picture book of my own. I was very fortunate to make a connection with Dorothy Briley, who believed in the vision I had and let me bring it to fruition in an uncompromised form. *Free Fall* was the culmination of many ideas about an impressionistic kind of storytelling that I had been forming since art school.

There were many other possibilities I wanted to explore. I longed to do a book that was wildly humorous, almost slapstick. When I talked about this, people who knew my work found it a little hard to believe. I was offered a number of manuscripts to illustrate, but none of them seemed to fit the particular mood and tone I had in mind. I knew that I would have to make up my own story someday.

That "someday" turned out to be *Tuesday*.

So what was the inspiration for the book?

My first professional job, which I got while I was a senior at RISD, was the March 1979 cover for *Cricket* magazine. So when I was asked to do the March 1989 cover for *Cricket*, I was very pleased—two *Cricket* covers exactly ten years apart would make nice "bookends" for my first decade in children's books.

Another reason why I was happy to accept this job from *Cricket* is that their instructions for a cover are the perfect assignment: "Do anything you want to do." They let me know, as food for thought, that because this was the March issue, there would be stories about St. Patrick's Day and about frogs—the link there being green, I think.

St. Patrick's Day didn't strike a chord—but frogs, they had potential. I got out my sketchbook and some old *National Geographics* for reference. Frogs were great fun to draw—soft, round, lumpy, and really goofy-looking. But what could I do with them?

I drew one on a lily pad. That shape . . . the round blob with the saucerlike bottom . . . suddenly, old movies were running through my head: *Forbidden Planet* and *The Day the Earth Stood Still.* Together the frog and lily pad looked like a fifties B-movie flying saucer! As I drew, I saw that the frogs and toads weren't actually flying. It was the lily pads that had the power of flight, like a carpet from *The Arabian Nights.*

For the *Cricket* cover I showed a group of frogs rising up out of a swamp, heading off to who knows what mischief. I liked the picture a lot, and I began to like the frogs and toads themselves. They had distinct personalities. They looked pretty silly, yet up in the air they clearly felt dignified, noble, and a bit smug. I wanted to know more about them. As I did when I looked at a painting as a child, I wondered what happened before and after this scene.

Now I could find out.

Appropriately, I was in midair when I finally got around to thinking seriously about "the frog book." I was sitting in an airplane, looking through my sketchbook, and I thought, "Okay, if I were a frog, and I had discovered I could fly, where would I go? What would I do?"

Images quickly began to appear to me, and for fear of losing them I hastily scribbled barely legible shapes onto the page: a startled man at a kitchen table; a terrified dog under attack; a room full of frogs bathed in the glow of a television. A chronology began to take shape, and within an hour I had worked out a complete layout, which remained essentially unchanged through to the finished book. Everything was there: the story, the use of the panels, the times of day, and the titles.

At least as often as people ask me where I came up with the idea for the book, they want to know, "Why Tuesday?" When I decided to punctuate the story with the times of the day, it became clear that the mysterious element had to do with the particular day of the week when these strange things happened. So I tried to decide what the funniest day of the week was. I immediately discounted the weekend; Saturday and Sunday had too many connotations, as did Friday. Monday was next to go, being the first day of the work week. That left Tuesday, Wednesday, and Thursday. But Wednesday's spelling had always bothered me, so it was out. Thursday was all right, but the more I said "T-u-e-s-day," the more I liked the ooze quality it had. It seemed to go with frogs.

A wordless book offers a different kind of an experience than one with text, for both the author and the reader. There is no author's voice telling the story. Each viewer reads the book in his or her own way. The reader is an integral part of the storytelling process. As a result, there are as many versions of what happened that Tuesday night as there are readers. For some, the dog in the story is rightfully defending his territory against amphibian invaders, and their sympathy lies with the dog when the frogs get the best of him. For others, the dog is a humorless bully who gets his come uppance. As the author of a wordless book, I don't have to concern myself about whether the reader's interpretation of each and every detail is the same as mine. My own view has no more (and no less) validity than that of any other viewer. Since my intent was for the book as a whole to make people laugh, all that matters is that the pictures are funny.

A series of individually funny pictures, however, does not necessarily add up to a successful story. The book was very carefully plotted, and details were developed in ways that move the story forward as logically as possible, from the full moon that rises slowly in the sky that first Tuesday night to the gibbous moon that appears a week later at the end. By placing my characters in the context of familiar reality, I hoped to entice readers to take that great leap of faith and believe that frogs, and perhaps pigs too, could fly—if the conditions were just right.

One result of winning the Caldecott Medal is the opportunity to travel and meet a wide variety of people who are interested in my book. Readers can be quite passionate about their perceptions. I've heard heated arguments over what *Tuesday* sounds like. Some people are sure it's a silent squadron of frogs gliding through a still summer night. Others are equally positive it's full of zooming cartoon sound effects accompanied by Wagner's "Ride of the Valkyries."

It has been great hearing children tell me how much they love "those frogs" and how funny they think the book is. One first grade class wrote their own book, *Wednesday*. In it, their school is subjected to some interesting revenge fantasies involving scissors and math papers.

I keep waiting for letters telling me how frightening *Tuesday* is. I'm waiting only because many people—and by people I mean adults—keep bringing up this possibility, whether I'm at a signing, a speaking engagement, or on the *Today* show. Fortunately, kids know funny when they see it. If after reading *Tuesday* one evening before bed they look out the window and see frogs flying by—well, we should all be so lucky.

I'm always delighted when teachers and librarians tell me about the ways they use wordless books. These books have become springboards for all kinds of writing, bookmaking, and even drama classes. Teachers of English as a Second Language tell me that wordless books are particularly useful in helping students express their thoughts in English. The students aren't inhibited by the burden of having to translate literally. That kind of interaction between books and children is very exciting. To know that my own pictures may be inspiring imaginations with the same wonder I felt as a child is a very satisfying feeling.

In 1989, when *Free Fall* was given an honor medal, I felt supported in my interest in the wordless format. By awarding *Tuesday* the 1992 Caldecott Medal, this year's committee has challenged the perception of the wordless book as a novelty. I thank all the committee members for the great honor of being included among the distinguished roster of medal winners. I hope Lynd Ward would have been pleased.

I would like to thank a few others who have played a part in my being here tonight.

My thanks to my family for a lifetime of encouragement and support.

To Tom Sgouros and David Macaulay, two unfailingly generous teachers.

To everyone at Clarion for making it such a fun place to publish books, and to Carol Goldenberg and Dinah Stevenson for good advice and great humor.

To Dorothy Briley, who was the first person to give me a chance to be an author. When I presented her with the pencil dummy of *Tuesday*, which was not the book she was expecting, I thank her for laughing.

To Dilys Evans, who has been with me every step of the way, always ready with biscuits and a pot of tea.

Finally, to my wife, Kim, who is a part of every book I do. Thank you for asking me to the Sadie Hawkins Dance.

Thank you all very much.

David Wiesner

By David Macaulay

David Wiesner

There are three things about David Wiesner which stand out in my mind. The first is his imagination. The second is his skill. The third is his reserve. Actually, there is a fourth—the speed with which number three disappears when the conversation turns to the process that employs numbers one and two. David's passion for making pictures—particularly pictures that tell stories—is clearly evident not only in his books but also in the enthusiasm and sincerity with which he animatedly describes their creation. Honored by his request to write the Caldecott Medal winner's profile for the *Horn Book,* I found myself playing amateur reporter. David and I chatted one Sunday afternoon in March as I scribbled away. While I had no idea how or even if it would all come together, I was nevertheless delighted at having the opportunity to get to know a little better one of my very best former students turned colleague. Whether or not the following is what he actually told me, it is definitely what I heard.

On Sunday, February 5, 1956, the population of Bridgewater, New Jersey, increased by one. Born to Julia and George Wiesner on that day was their fifth child and second son in ten years. In addition to populating their house, the elder Wiesners also imbued it with a nurturing atmosphere in which creative endeavor, while never forced, was always encouraged. This, at least, is how David remembers it. In fact, the cunning with which the minds of the unsuspecting Wiesner kids were shaped is perhaps best illustrated by the achievement-oriented wallpaper found on page thirteen of David's unpaginated and highly autobiographical book, *Hurricane* (Clarion). The stimulating pattern of rockets, magnifying glasses, elephant heads, ships in bottles, books, and, believe it or not, medals comes directly from the walls of the very room in which he played, slept, and dreamt for the first eleven years of his young life—the formative years. I never did find out what the rest of the wallpaper in the house looked like, but whatever it was, it seems to have worked. His eldest sister and his brother were both artistically inclined and generously passed down their used or unneeded art supplies, along with a fair amount of natural reinforcement. His second oldest sister trained in opera. Her artistic impact on David has yet to reveal itself.

While it might seem presumptuous, or at least premature, to suggest that David was destined to become an artist, his early years could not have been more appropriately spent. Even trips to the local paint and wallpaper store were filled with special pleasures. There, in a small section devoted to art supplies, David found himself scouring the shelves and opening the drawers, to see, touch, and ultimately sniff the various materials housed in this exotic treasury.

The first nonfamily member whose artistic impact David readily acknowledges was the goatee-toting, plaid-clad, coolest-of-artists—John Nagey. The granddaddy of television art teachers, Nagey took to the airwaves every Saturday morning, after the agricultural shows, and took over the imaginations of thousands of impressionable viewers, and young David and his similarly inclined siblings were among them. Introducing the ideas of a light source and simple perspective, Nagey made one drawing a week in which he transformed circles into form and straight lines into depth. In the brief fifteen-minute process he transported a ten-year-old New Jersey boy to new heights of ecstasy and ambition. Over the months and years that followed, David faithfully completed almost every sequential exercise in the accompanying workbooks, learning not only how to create illusion but also about the joys of drawing from direct observation. As his ideas and skill grew, so did his interest in storytelling through pictures—an interest fed both by comic books and repeated television showings of such classics as *King Kong*.

David's early artistic education was not just an indoor activity. In fact, whatever familial life did for young David's imagination, it was at least equaled, if not surpassed, by life outside. His Bridgewater neighborhood was one of those perfect places to grow up because it encouraged playing outside. First, there were people to play with. Like his house, but on a larger scale, the neighborhood was populated with kids of different ages. The older ones invented games for the younger ones, who in turn looked up to, idolized, and in time became the older ones. Second, there were many wonderful places to play. A network of lawns, trees, and shrubs linked the houses, while at the edge of the neighborhood there were woods and a brook. Armies could freely chase and stalk each other through the vegetation, but once they hit the sidewalks, the rules changed. Because these were the rivers, both feet had to be kept on the ground at all times. Fleeing the enemy was now much more problematic since only very small steps were allowed and you had to carry your stick—which was loaded—over your head to keep it dry.

As the neighborhood kids grew, their games became more sophisticated. In UFO, a favorite, a wire coat hanger was bent into a circle and attached to the open end of a plastic bag. Across the diameter of the circle another piece of wire supported a wad of burning fabric. As the bag filled with hot gas, the whole flimsy contraption lifted into the air and drifted dangerously away. The journeys of these do-it-yourself hot-air balloons sometimes covered two miles and were tracked by the walkie-talkie-bearing pyromaniacs, either on foot or by car.

Meanwhile, at home, the older Wiesner siblings were slowly moving on and, more importantly, out. David eventually occupied his own second-floor room, and into it came one of his prize possessions—a sturdy oak drafting table lugged home by Dad. Its very presence underscored the importance of the act of drawing and transformed a mere bedroom into a studio. Now, with a suitable environment, the young artist increased production. There is a price, however, for the extraordinary pleasures associated with the primarily solitary process of making art. Whether or not David's increasing artistic conviction grew in response to a pre-existing shyness, or whether it helped create it, is neither here nor there. The fact is that he was an extremely reticent youngster. It wasn't until high school that his self-esteem got a boost from his growing identity as class artist. Although this did nothing to seriously elevate his status, Wiesner, like all teenagers, was grateful for any identity.

By this time, David had become familiar with the images of such artists as da Vinci, Dali, De Chirico, Brueghel, and Dilrer—all available in the *Time-Life Books of Great Artists* and all contained within the Wiesner home. Fed by these artists' often fantastical landscapes, David's imagination touched everything before it was rendered. He realized that just by changing his point of view, the Derailleur gears on his bike or even the vacuum cleaner could become an amazing technological landscape—jumping-off places for invention and creativity. Nowhere is the power of point of view more clearly displayed, or more masterfully handled, than in *Tuesday* (Clarion). In addition to the creation of his own comics, which described the exploits of anti-hero "Slop the Wonder Pig," David and his high-school friends produced a live-action vampire film entitled *The Saga of Butchula*. This silent classic was accompanied by a taped musical soundtrack which was best played on a variable-speed tape recorder so that the music and the action could be kept more or less in sync. One of David's most "satisfying moments" came at the senior talent show where, during the film's screening, people laughed at the right times—to his relief and amazement.

It is hardly surprising that Bob Bernabe, the art teacher at Bridgewater Raritan High School, would be the first in a series of in-person teachers, as opposed to television or book folk, to influence and encourage young Wiesner. He was undoubtedly delighted just to get someone in his class looking for more than credits or a rest. In this case he got someone looking for much more. Motivation was never an issue, and Bernabe soon had his eager pupil working well beyond the assigned problems, exploring the possibilities of print making, photo silk screens, and watercolor. An important, out-of-school experience was a trip to the Museum of Modern Art in New York City. When young Wiesner first saw Guernica, he was bowled over by the power and size of the work—and Picasso's work finally began to make sense. On that same trip he also saw Dali's Persistence of Memory—only in this case he couldn't believe the smallness of a work he found so powerful.

For better or worse, high school; as those of us who have experienced it know, doesn't last forever, and there is always that nagging question of what comes next. For David, this question was answered while he was still a sophomore. Sometime in 1971 Mr. Bernabe's art class was visited by a college student who showed films he had made and with great humor talked about something called art school. For David the experience was both revealing and reassuring. "You mean there are places where I can go? You don't have to have a real job? Wow!" And in one fell swoop, the school's guidance counselor was off the hook. It would no longer be his or her responsibility to figure out what to do with this very shy, intensely curious, and passionately creative young man.

In September of 1974, David left New Jersey to study illustration at Rhode Island School of Design. He left behind a mountain of drawings but brought with him an imagination and level of commitment which those of us who had the pleasure of working with him quickly realized was exceptional. As a sophomore, he produced a ten-foot-long by forty-inch-high mural in response to a problem called "metamorphosis." In it orange slices turned into sailboats, which turned into fish. He recalls putting it up and hearing a deep, reassuring chuckle from his teacher, who was standing at the back of the room. The teacher went on to point out all the things which came naturally to David— such as choosing unique points of view, or pushing things up to the front of the picture to enliven the composition and reinforce the depth.

The metamorphosis that evolved on paper encouraged another, albeit slower, transformation from shy, retiring person to confident, retiring person. It also served as the genesis of a wordless book that would emerge some thirteen years later and win David his first Caldecott Honor Medal.

Also during his sophomore year, David began oil painting. Although he valiantly struggled with it, he never enjoyed it and eventually returned to watercolor. Under the tutelage of Professor Tom Sgouros, David found that his technical and conceptual skills continued to soar. The extent of Sgouros's influence and the importance of his contribution are best illustrated by the fact that it is to him that *Tuesday* is dedicated.

During his senior year, having been inspired by a Lynd Ward wordless picture book, David designed and began producing one of his own. Although he finished only two watercolors, he thoroughly explored the process, creating mounds of sketches. A department-wide problem called "series" resulted in another sequence of wordless images. In eight steps the image of King Kong on top of the Empire State Building gradually became Leonardo's famous study of human proportion. The simpler and more open-ended the problem was, the more inventive would be David's solution. He remembers students continually asking one professor questions about a problem he had assigned and thinking that each answer, while illuminating, was also a kind of restriction. The more ambiguous the problem, the more he liked it, and the better it served his inventive mind.

By June of 1978 we had done all we could for David Wiesner, so we graduated him. From Rhode Island he traveled to New York and began his career as a free-lance illustrator. In March of 1979, he was commissioned to do a cover for *Cricket* magazine. Three years later, he found himself working on his first jacket and interior art for a book called *The Man from the Sky* (Knopf) by someone named Avi. He has just been asked to create a new jacket for the book's reissue. This he agreed to do as long as the publisher promised not to use the original illustrations. David's standards have been growing along with his self-confidence.

In 1983 an apartment fire destroyed all his possessions, including work done up to that time. Also lost in the fire was the precious oak drafting table his father had retrieved. But it would take more than a fire to stop this smitten bookmaker; *The Loathsome Dragon* (Putnam), a story retold by David and his surgeon wife Kim Kahng, was published in 1987. Take a look at the watercolor landscapes it contains and tell me you don't see a little da Vinci in there. In 1988 came the Caldecott Honor Book *Free Fall* (Lothrop), a direct descendant of that ten-foot-long mural and either the second appearance of the loathsome dragon or a very close relative. In 1990, *Hurricane* blew into town. It is no coincidence that the names of the two young boys who play on the tree toppled by the storm are David and George—alias the brothers Wiesner—since the story is based on a real incident. And finally in 1991 came the glorious culmination of his efforts to date—which brings us back to *Tuesday*.

"So, why frogs?" I asked. In 1989, David was asked to create his second *Cricket* cover. When he asked what kind of an image they were looking for, they wisely suggested that he should do whatever he wanted. The only clue they offered was the theme of that particular issue: Frogs. And that, as usual, was all it took.

The Newbery Medal 1992

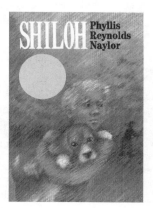

Shiloh

written by
Phyllis Reynolds Naylor

published by
Atheneum, 1991

Horn Book Review

The adventures of a boy and his dog almost always make an appealing story, but when the boy faces a very difficult decision and takes a giant step toward maturity, the story acquires depth and importance. How Marty Preston saves the beagle he names Shiloh by facing down a bullying adult and standing on principles he knows are right—in the face of laws that may be wrong—is just such a story. In a believable, rural voice, Marty narrates the reminiscence, which is accessible to third-grade readers but has enough substance to appeal to older children. There is plenty of potential for a class discussion on values and decision making as well as enough grit in the young hero to engage.
—*Elizabeth S. Watson*

Booklist Review

In the West Virginia hill country, folks mind each other's privacy and personal rights, a principle that is respected in 11-year-old Marty Preston's family and reinforced by a strict code of honor—no lying, cheating, or taking what isn't yours. When a beagle he names Shiloh follows him home, Marty painfully learns that right and wrong are not always black and white. Marty's dad realizes that the beagle is Judd Travers' new hunting dog and insists they return Shiloh to his rightful owner, even though they both know that Judd keeps his dogs chained and hungry to make them more eager hunters. Sure enough, Judd claims the dog and greets him with a hard kick to his scrawny sides. Marty worries about Shiloh being abused and makes plans to buy the dog . . . if Judd will sell him. Then Shiloh runs away again, and Marty secretly shelters the dog, beginning a chain of lies as he takes food and covers his tracks. Though troubled about deceiving his family, Marty reasons, "a lie don't seem a lie anymore when it's meant to save a dog."

The West Virginia dialect richly seasons the true-to-life dialogue. Even when the Prestons care for Shiloh after he is nearly killed by another dog, Mr. Preston insists Shiloh be returned to Judd if he recovers; however, Marty makes a deal with the malicious Judd to earn Shiloh for his own. Not until the final paragraph can readers relax—every turn of the plot confronts them with questions. Like Marty, readers gain understanding, though not acceptance, of Judd's tarnished character. Fueled by the love and trust of Shiloh, Marty displays a wisdom and strength beyond his years. Naylor offers a moving and powerful look at the best and the worst of human nature as well as the shades of gray that color most of life's dilemmas.—*Ellen Mandel*

1992 Newbery Acceptance Speech
Phyllis Reynolds Naylor

In the manic days that followed the phone call from Pat Scales, and the heady weeks thereafter, I have said to myself many times, on different occasions, "So this is what it's like to win the Newbery." I said it when a stranger called one morning, scarcely before my eyes were open, to ask if she could drop by with her manuscript; I said it when David Wiesner and I were warned, just before we went on TV together, that there could be "no long pauses in which to think"; I said it when a photographer asked me to climb up our box elder to pose, then took the ladder away; I said it every evening for three weeks when I carried all the bouquets I had received up into a spare bedroom, and retrieved them again the next morning, so that our cat—the one that ate the forty yards of Christmas ribbon—would not devour the leaves.

But now I stand before you in delight and wonder and say to myself, "No, this is what it's like to win the Newbery."

In those first stunned moments after the phone call, my mouth full of cereal, I began to wonder if I had imagined it. My husband was out jogging, and our two cats went on yawning and preening themselves on the rug, oblivious to the wild-eyed woman who stood with one hand over the telephone and the other over her stomach.

"If this is true," I finally told myself, "someone else will call." The phone did ring again—the *Today* show, asking me to come to New York that evening.

At some point Rex returned, and I remember telling him that I had twenty-four hours to lose thirty pounds, but those first few days are a fog of elation, sleeplessness, and the constant ringing of the phone.

Thank you, Pat, and all the other members of the Newbery committee, as well as the American Library Association. Thank you not only for loving Marty Preston and his dog as much as I do, but for not calling me in the middle of the night to tell me so.

And then, in typical Lanman fashion, there was Lucy's paw print along with Jon's signature. I may be the only author in the world whose acceptance letter was cosigned by a dog.

To properly begin my thank-yous, I should really start with my parents, who are no longer alive to hear them. Thank you, Mother and Dad, for reading aloud to us every night as far back as I can remember—Mother with her Midwestern accent, Dad in his Mississippi drawl.

Thank you for the drama in your voices as you recounted the adventures of Tom Sawyer and Becky Thatcher, of Huckleberry Finn and Jim, and Prince and the Pauper, the mad March Hare, Mother West Wind's children, the Bobbsey Twins, and the Israelites on their journey to the Promised Land. I was never interested in the authors; it was the story that was important.

Thank you, John Reynolds, for being younger, so that long after I felt I was too old to snuggle down beside you and Mother on the couch every evening, I could still sit at the dining room table doing my homework and laugh, with you, over Toad and his motor car.

Thanks to my sister, Norma, for teaching me to draw, so that I could illustrate my little books, even the one I wrote at age nine after Mother told me the facts of life, which I titled *Manual for Pregnant Women*, with illustrations by the author.

Thank you, Jean Karl, for your faith in me when you took my first book for Atheneum, *Witch's Sister*. Thank you even though my witch books seem to frighten some people who have never read them. Long ago, as a fledgling author, my aim was someday to write for Jean Karl. Since then I have written . . . and written . . . and written, and you allowed me to try even those books which we both knew would not be especially popular, because you realized I was saying something that just had to get out. Thank you for your ability to articulate so well what it is that keeps a manuscript from being its best.

Thank you, both Jon and Jean, for putting up with my confusion about time. For a woman who has a clock, sometimes two, in every room of the house including the basement, and almost as many calendars—who usually knows how she is going to spend every fifteen-minutes segment of her day—I cannot explain why I have such trou-

ble with time in my manuscripts, as shown by this comment in a letter from Jean Karl about my book *Alice in Rapture, Sort Of.*

At the start, one must assume that that first day is sometime during
at least the second week of vacation. The sleepover could be the Friday
of the second week of vacation. But that would make it near the end of
June already. Patrick's birthday then has to come during the third week
of vacation—are we getting into July? A week later the permanent has to
be in the 4th week of vacation—surely well into July. Yet on page 67 there
are still two months of vacation left, and on 82 it is still the middle of
July and a lot seems to have happened in between. On page 92 it is still
the middle of July. But then on 93 it is the first week of August . . .

One problem of mine is that I want to squeeze too much into a single lifetime. I don't seem to mind very much squandering a few dollars,
but if I waste sixty minutes, I know it is something I will never get
back. And then I have that troop of noisy characters in my head to con-
tend with, all nattering away, demanding a place in a book, and it's
enough to make my teeth rattle.

What shall I tell you about *Shiloh*? If it were my book, *The Keeper*,
receiving the award, I could tell you how it was adapted from a chapter
in my own life, and that would take up the rest of this talk. If it were
A String of Chances, I could tell you about my struggles with faith. If it
were *Send No Blessings*, I could talk of the numerous drafts it took to
work out Beth's problems with self-esteem.

But *Shiloh*—the first draft, that is—was written at breakneck speed.
It was as though I were obsessed with getting to the end of the story
and finding out just what happened between Marty and Judd Travers—
as though Marty himself were perched on the arm of my chair, telling
me the story in his own way.

As with most of my books, however, the roots of this one go deep.
In many of my other books, I deal with problems I wrestled with as a
child or teenager, but in the writing of *Shiloh*, I was dealing with discomfort that was still new.

Many of you already know the story behind it—how my husband
and I were visiting friends in West Virginia, and rose one morning for
a long walk in the little community known as Shiloh. How we had
passed the old grist mill and crossed the bridge, and just beyond the
school house, we found the hungry, trembling—and strangely silent—
dog that was eventually to become Shiloh in my book.

How it was so frightened and beaten down it kept slinking away
from us, but how finally, when I whistled, it inexplicably came bound-

ing over, leaping up to lick my cheek. How it followed us back to the house of our friends, and sat out all day in the rain, head on its paws, watching the door. How I agonized all the way back to Maryland that evening, until finally my husband said, "Well, Phyllis, are you going to have a nervous breakdown, or are you going to do something about it?" The something, of course, meant writing, which was a catharsis for me, but did nothing for the dog.

I want to thank Rex, at this point, for not putting me out of the car that day. I want to thank him for listening all these years to my dark nights of the soul, for his loving encouragement, and his intelligent criticism of every book manuscript I've ever written.

As for Shiloh, whatever saint looks out for strays must have had his eye on this one, because a few weeks into the story, a note from our friends said that they had encountered the dog again a few days after we left, brought it home, and named it Clover.

So why didn't I put my manuscript aside and say, "Fine. It's settled, then"? Because I got hooked on that dog, as Marty would say—whistling as though I meant something, then offering nothing. I felt I owed it more.

The second reason I couldn't let go of the story was that while we talked about the dog that day with our hosts, Frank and Trudy Madden, they had patiently explained that the animal sitting out in the yard was only one of many that owners abandon in those hills. And though they didn't say so, I knew Frank and Trudy were thinking that here I was, upsetting us all by focusing on this particular dog, ignoring what they had to deal with often. I wanted to write about how, once you become emotionally involved in a problem, all bets are off. Your perspective changes.

"Open up your eyes, Marty. Open your eyes!" his father tells him. "How many times have you walked to the school bus and seen a chained-up dog in somebody's yard? How many times you ever put your mind to whether or not it's happy, its ribs sticking out like handles at the sides? Suddenly you're face to face with a dog that pulls at your heart, and you all at once want to change things."

And so I went on with my story. I didn't want to add any more to the Maddens's burdens than I already had, so I did not ask them the research questions they might easily have answered. Instead I wrote letters to all the West Virginia agencies that could give me information, one of them the small post office in the town of Friendly, where I inquired about a postman's routine, the kind of vehicle he might drive, postal routes, and other facts I would need to portray Marty's father.

Imagine my chagrin when I got a letter back with the necessary information from Frank Madden. The harried postmistress simply turned my letter over to him and asked if he had the knowledge and time to "answer this lady's letter."

As the novel progressed, I discovered that it also dealt with justice. One reason that writing for children is satisfying is that they may, in reading your book, face a new idea for the first time. And when you consider that there can only be one "first item," you realize that the impact of that encounter may affect a child's thinking for the rest of his life.

If he sees the world as black and white, he may develop knee-jerk reactions to key words or slogans. If he determines that the end justifies the means, his ethics may tend to slip and slide. But if he sees that much of life is more complex than he thought, that each problem must be approached in its unique situation, and that he must base his actions not only upon his family's values, but upon his own innate sense of what is true and good, then he will get a taste of what being an adult really means.

From the absolutes of early childhood, through the growing awareness that there are exceptions, and on to the realization that much of life is, of necessity, compromise, the child—if he is to mature—must leave his comforting stereotypes behind him. When should he give in, and for what principles should he hold out?

While Marty eventually comes to the conclusion that Jesus would not want him to turn the beagle back over to Judd Travers, it does not solve his problem of deceit. Where is the dividing line between lawful duty and being true to one's conscience? Between loyalty to one's family and the love of a dog?

When I was a child, I first faced the problem of justice in the Old Testament. When the Ark of the Covenant was being moved, the Bible tells us, the oxen stumbled and it started to tip. Uzza reached out to steady it and was immediately struck dead. I was indignant. Never mind that God had commanded that no one touch it. Didn't anyone get points for using his head?

Apart from God's justice, however, my punishment, for all the contributions I had not made to the Humane Society, was a guilt that got heavier the more I wrote. What if Clover, who turned out to be female in real life, barked all night? What if she got in fights with other dogs? What if she killed the Maddens's cat?

And speaking of justice, what kind of justice was it that I was going to get a book out of all this, but my friends were stuck with the dog? Should I send them a check? Offer to pay Clover's medical bills? Change the dedication in the book to "Frank and Trudy Madden, with thanks and ten percent."

Gradually, however, as the book took shape, I remembered the love of our springer spaniel when we were growing up, and how there is nothing comparable to a dog that sits at your feet, follows you about, is prepared to be sad with you or rejoice with you, even give its life for you, all at a moment's notice. I decided finally that having a dog may be its own reward.

But my battles went on. At every turn, it seemed in the final chapters and in subsequent drafts, I found still another way that Judd might try to trick Marty, another way that Marty could win and yet lose at the same time. I had to discover, like him, that nothing is as simple as you guess—not right or wrong, not Judd Travers, not even Marty himself or the dog.

And so, the book was finished. If a mother-to-be has visions of producing the next president of the United States, that takes second place to her hope that the child is born healthy, with the proper number of fingers and toes. The same is true of a writer. If she occasionally daydreams about the Newbery, that is second compared to her earnest wish to see the book published at last, with all its paragraphs intact.

Up to this point, she knows where her manuscript is at all times: with the editor, the copy editor, the marketing people, the illustrator. . . . She can check and make sure it's still breathing. But suddenly, sooner than she thinks, it is out in the world on its own. It is trucking down a highway in Oklahoma toward towns she never heard of; it is being dangled upside down in a bookstore by a three-year-old with jelly on her fingers; it is cozying up to a boy with green-spiked hair.

She has sent it off to boarding school, and the most she can hope for is a report now and then from a reviewer, or even more wonderful, an honest letter from a child. But this time, with this book, the best news of all. I realize what an honor it is to be here with Avi and Russell Freedman, and I'm still trembly.

I would like to thank Maureen Hayes, my guardian angel at Atheneum, just for being herself, and for the wonderful friends I have made over the years as she's sent me on speaking tours to libraries around the country. Thank you, to those same librarian friends, for your many warm letters since the Newbery was announced. I may not be able to connect all your names and faces, but I remember the pieces of your lives you shared with me, as I shared mine with you, while we drove from city to city, school to school. As I said, it's the story, to me, that's important.

Thanks to Judy Wilson, of the Macmillan Children's Book Group, and all those people in its many departments who have assisted at the births of my books.

And finally, thanks to our two sons, Jeff and Michael Jeff, for realizing how important this award was to me when I telephoned you with the news; Mike, for your usual irreverence when you said, after listening to me babble on about it, "Mom, have you ever won this award before?" You both, along with your families, have added new dimensions to my books and my life.

A year ago, I was speaking to a school assembly where the children had been warned to be on their best behavior. They would not ask any embarrassing questions, the principal assured me, certainly not how much money I made, and definitely not my age, which always seems a little severe to me, because how else are they going to know? So during the question/answer session, they asked the usual: How many books had I written? Seventy. Had I ever won any awards? Some. Had I ever won the Newbery? No.

At this last answer, a small boy in the second row, to the horror of the teachers, rose up on his knees and crowed disdainfully, "Seventy books, and she's never won the Newbery?"

Well, now I have. And along with my marriage to Rex, the births of our sons, and the arrival of my word processor, it's about the nicest thing that ever happened to me. I thank you with all my heart.

Phyllis Reynolds Naylor

Rex Naylor

Photo credit: Katherine Lambert Photography

Phyllis Reynolds Naylor

A Bradford pear tree that we planted in celebration of one of our wedding anniversaries stands outside our kitchen window. Bursting with white blossoms in the spring and with a range of bright yellow, red, and green leaves in the fall, it is a special source of delight.

Our house, on a suburban street, is usually quiet inside. No music while Phyllis is writing. The television and radio are silent most of the time, anyway. All this changes when our sons come to visit with their wives and daughters; then we enjoy a house full of chatter, laughter, and music.

I'm reminded of something Phyllis has said at times during our marriage: "If we had only known, back when we first met, that we would have all these years of good health and happiness together, that we would have two healthy children and that they would grow up to lead satisfying, productive lives—how much worry it would have saved us!" Fortunate we have been, and for that we are more than grateful, knowing that life offers no previews, and that concern about children does not end with their graduation or marriage. But the comment demonstrates something I learned early about Phyllis. She longs for closure. She yearns to draw a warm, protective circle around those she loves most.

She needs much of her time alone, relatively uninterrupted, for writing. But if the material is lighter, she can take a clipboard with her to the hairdresser or on a train and write in the middle of a hubbub. I once left her in the lobby of a hotel while I returned our rented car and came back to find her standing beside our luggage cart, writing away on top of a suitcase, oblivious to the racket around her.

Not at all reclusive, she loves talking with many people, singly and in groups, and is moved or touched by them. She dislikes small talk but can sit down with strangers on a train and within minutes share some personal story of her own and draw out the same kind of response from them.

Events from her life as family member, neighbor, concerned citizen, and passing stranger feed into the writing, but usually indirectly. Life-affirming and positive, Phyllis has nevertheless used writing to work through all manner of vexing concerns about herself, her work, family, friends, and the lives of those who spring from the pages of the newspaper—not to mention the creatures of her thriving imagination. One of her fears is that she will die with characters still trapped inside her. Some of her vivid, detailed, and often hilarious dreams betray how easily she worries.

Phyllis organizes her waking hours like a railroad timetable. Give her a little free time, and she will plant another azalea, mend a shirt while indulging herself with a bit of wasteland television, send a gift, talk with other writers on the telephone, make peach preserves, walk two or three miles through the neighborhood, write a letter to a congressman, listen to music while she loads the washing machine, and so on. A constant struggle for her is how best to use her time for writing and still open herself to and make room for those who need her.

It's a cliché, but writing is as necessary for her as eating or sleeping. Her disposition is usually sunny; but a day or two without time to write, and it begins to cloud up. When the accompaniments of writing intrude—doing the painstaking research, studying contracts, reading proofs, keeping necessary records—she may get fretful and impatient. But she accepts criticism well and benefits from it. She has taught this family the value of focus and perseverance. A rejected manuscript or an unfavorable but fair review simply spurs her to greater effort.

When involved in a writing project, she goes straight for what serves her purposes and resists distraction by either worthy causes or irrelevant pastimes. She seems not to need play for its own sake. Her real play is in her work. She is always trying to "buy time" and will pay to have almost any chore taken off her hands so that she will have more time to write. But come December, pans will cover every available space in the kitchen while she bakes dozens of cookies from treasured recipes to send to friends and relatives. Meanwhile, the compact disc player will be going full blast with seasonal music, from spirituals to madrigals. Christmas, which she literally plans for all year, is a time for her to connect with family and old friends.

When Phyllis turned from her Methodist upbringing to the Unitarian church, her mother was dismayed at the prospect of her younger daughter's departure from traditional Christianity. But the family ties held firm. In a final cementing of those ties, Phyllis co-authored with her mother, then eighty-seven, *Maudie in the Middle* (Atheneum), a novel based on the latter's recollections of her childhood in the early 1900s. Lura Schield Reynolds died in 1991 at age ninety.

Crazy Love: An Autobiographical Account of Marriage and Madness (Morrow) tells about the most wrenching period of Phyllis's life—her eight years of marriage, starting at age eighteen, with a man who became a paranoid schizophrenic. Fifteen years went by before she could put this experience on paper. Their old phonograph record of Mozart's Requiem still sits in its wrapper, undisturbed; she will not listen to it, yet.

One corner of Phyllis's home office, where she spends the most time, has both walls covered with family photographs. She works hard at keeping the lines of communication open among family members. Favorite pastimes—apart from her writing—are almost any activity with the family, or going to the theater. Travel just to view scenery or historic landmarks is too passive for her. She enjoys travel more when it relates to a book she is working on, when she can interact with people, or when the whole family is involved.

Phyllis avoids most organized activities, regularly attending only the Children's Book Guild of Washington, D.C., and a weekly meeting with a small group of writers who critique one another's work. But she corresponds at length with many people—other writers; someone she met on Amtrak; individuals who have read one of her books and have written in desperation because their problems match those of one of her characters. She writes letters as a member of Amnesty International, which works worldwide to free prisoners of conscience.

After the Freedom of Information Act was passed, she wrote, out of curiosity, to find out whether the FBI had a file on her. She found that she had been investigated because she had written letters to two United States senators to protest the imprisonment of a Korean poet. The FBI, after searching five police jurisdictions and finding no arrest record, decided to close the case, concluding that "Naylor has demonstrated the nature of being a prolific letter writer."

Although I regularly read all Phyllis writes for publication, we often suspend being writer and reader to carry on in other ways the passionate friendship we began the day we met. Years ago, with carefully hoarded funds to spend, we flew to Barcelona, Rome, and Paris. Later we took our boys to London, then through England and Scotland by train. By contrast, then and now, we like to take a blanket and picnic in Rock Creek Park or at Hains Point on the Potomac, or disappear for a day or two to small towns on the ocean or Maryland's Eastern Shore, or drive to the Catoctin Mountain, or bicycle along the C&O Canal, or go apple picking.

Though she insists she is full of worries and fears—of riding in airplanes, for one—Phyllis loves to laugh. After the news of the Newbery award, editor Jon Lanman invited us to a celebratory luncheon with other friends at a quiet but elegant restaurant. In due time the attentive, dignified waiters wheeled in the tiered dessert cart and lifted its many offerings one at a time, describing each in some detail. In the pregnant silence that followed came a plaintive question from Phyllis: "Is that all?"

As I try to tell about this lovely, happy, remarkably productive woman I'm married to, words seem less than adequate. Sometimes when I'm reading what she writes underneath I hear passages of her favorite folk or classical music—lively yet haunting, moving between major and minor keys, happy and sad, "because that's life;" as she says.

Similarly, a poignant humor—rueful, yet undaunted—is a counter-point in her life and in much of her serious fiction. She captures this same spirit in two wry self-portraits cartooned on letters and notes to close friends. One is of a forlorn, waif-like person, balancing an apple on her head while arrows fly about her; the other is of an endearing but impetuous woman with a rose in her teeth, gamboling naked through the world.

The Caldecott Medal 1993

Mirette on the High Wire

written and illustrated by
Emily Arnold McCully

published by
Putnam, 1992

Horn Book Review

McCully has created an independent female protagonist—one with panache and a soupçon of something out of the ordinary. In a wonderfully exuberant picture book set in late nineteenth-century Paris, Mirette is the daughter of the hardworking widow Gateau. Madame Gateau runs a boarding house for the traveling players from all over the world who come to perform in the theaters and music halls of Paris. One evening, a handsome stranger who introduces himself as Bellini, a retired high-wire walker, asks for a room. Unlike the usual gregarious boarders, he keeps to himself, practicing his routines in the back courtyard—to the delight of Mirette, who is fascinated with his skill and longs to learn the art. Despite his refusal to become her mentor, she stubbornly proceeds to teach herself, thus inveigling him into acknowledging that she might have talent. Inadvertently, she learns that her friend, once an internationally famous daredevil, has retired because he had become fearful—a fatal emotion for one in his profession. How she salvages his self-respect and earns a place of her own in the limelight is the climactic moment in a well-conceived tale with the charm of an Offenbach score and the brilliance of a poster by Toulouse-Lautrec. McCully is thoroughly comfortable with the watercolor medium, exploiting its potential to achieve remarkable effects in creating interior and characters. A bravura performance.—*Mary M. Burns*

Booklist Review

McCully has created a picture book in a totally different vein than that of *Picnic* or *School*. Set 100 years ago at a boarding house in Paris, the story features Mirette, the owner's young daughter. One day the great high-wire walker Bellini arrives to stay, and in fascination Mirette observes him practicing his craft. Curious and committed, Mirette begins studying with Bellini and quickly learns the tricks of the trade. She also discovers, however, that her teacher is stricken with fear and no longer performs. In refusing to accept this, she spurs Bellini to stage a comeback above the streets of Paris. McCully delivers an exciting outcome, and her gutsy heroine and bright, impressionistic paintings provide a very satisfying reading experience.—*Kathryn Broderick*

1993 Caldecott Acceptance Speech
Emily Arnold McCully

The glow from this splendid honor has illuminated a certain continuity in my life and restored some lost fragments. Out of the misty past, for example, came an exuberant note of congratulation from a librarian who remembered being at camp with me in 1948. "Those counselors had heart failure when you used to hang from the rafters in the old barn," she recalled. I had forgotten entirely. But it fits. In fact, *Mirette on the High Wire*, for all it owes to fin de siècle Paris, is an intensely personal book. Of this I was not immediately conscious. Rather, I felt emotionally detached from the story—curiously detached. It took a friend to point out that I had rummaged in my own past for both matter and metaphor.

The wonderful reception accorded *Mirette* kept me thinking about the book long after I'd ordinarily have put it aside. There it was, forcing me to dwell not only on all the ways I might have made the pictures better, but also on the parts of myself I'd unwittingly invested. I see now that I was not so much detached as defended. The story and the artistic challenges it presented had forced me to step out on a wire, throw off my cloaks of irony, humor, and sketchiness and embrace Mirette's desire without reservation. For you to understand how perilous and finally how liberating it was, I will have to provide some history.

Most of my life I've subscribed to a rule that can be found in the Chinese book of wisdom *I Ching*: "Perseverance furthers." I absorbed it at an early age (although not from the *I Ching* and phrased more often at home as "That's not good enough yet"). At three I learned to read and began to draw. Observing that I drew what I could see, my mother decided to improve the impulse. She stood over me while I worked at accuracy with regards to ears, or the drape of a jacket, guided not by convention, but the actual thing. There was never a period of stick figures and happy suns for me, but instead the discipline of daily practice, the elusive goal, the pain of failure, and the end product. This wasn't a grim ordeal; I did it because I was fascinated and fulfilled. The complicated yet instinctive act seemed to use my whole being and link me with the external world. Drawing sharpens the eye and the hand and also the affections. It isn't possible to draw something without feeling it.

My mother did not draw; her authority lay in the realm of criticism. But that didn't squash my maverick tendencies. I started drawing grotesques, much encouraged by a traveling show of Leonardo's notebooks, and grim urban scenes inspired by my beloved Ashcan School. "Why can't you draw things people will like?" mother complained. But I persisted with "expressive faces" and male figures in action. I loved the rugged, the startling, the dynamic. I wrote stories about lone child heroes, then illustrated and bound them. My attachment to text was so great that nearly everything I drew was an illustration.

I have a photograph of my first grade class posing before a mural that depicts a countryside at Eastertime. It covers one whole wall and I conceived it all by myself. I turned out posters, scenery, illustrated reports, greeting cards, house portraits, and copies of Old Masters (which I peddled from a stand like lemonade). On Memorial Day, when the town celebrated with a parade and a fair, I drew dozens of "two-minute" portraits at twenty-five cents a head.

My father worked in radio and I had seen from the control room how stories were delivered by actors and sound effects simulated with props and voices. But still, alone in my room with my imagination, I surrendered to illusion and the broadcasts came vividly to life. I illustrated them, too, and learned the trick of dramatizing through suggestion.

My sister and I were active and resourceful children and we improvised all sorts of play and playthings. We also dared each other to climb a higher branch, go all the way to the roof, hand over hand up the cornerstones, leap off on a bet, and in general risk life and limb. Our mother, whose frustrated talents were for music and drama, compounded the pain of a failed marriage with endless domestic labor. My sister and I did a great deal of chopping and scrubbing and digging and we ate a few kidney stews. Our Sisyphean route was spiced with memories and phrases in French from Mother's student year abroad. We had the strong feeling that she was last truly happy in Paris, her unrealized promise forsaken there. It gave the place a potent, already bittersweet allure. A joke tristesse, we would have said.

Pretty soon, wanting to please adults as well as to satisfy the impossible standards I was starting to set for myself, I told everyone I was going to be an illustrator when I grew up. My mother was determined that my sister and I be independent and self-supporting. Commercial art was the answer, in my case—certainly not precarious Art. My father had wanted to be a playwright, but earned his living writing radio dramas. I was aware of the ambivalence behind his pride in his achievements. His work, calling for cleverness and style, drew me inexorably, but it depended on the sufferance of the network. For protection, I tried not to take myself too seriously, and I trusted criticism more than praise.

By adolescence, writing and drawing served different purposes. My drawing had been almost a performance, certainly very public. Writing was a solitary search for the comprehending narrative that would later hold up to the light. When I set out to earn a living my focus was still divided between commercial art assignments and closet fiction writing.

But how lucky I have been! In 1966 or so, Ellen Rudin, then an editor at Harper, noticed a poster I had done for an advertising campaign and asked if I'd like to illustrate a children's book. For a long time afterward, illustrating and writing remained separate. But over the last decade I've hearkened back to the time when I made up my own stories and illustrated them. This offered such safety that I found myself, without any experience to go on, creating large happy families. Emotional truthfulness became more important than representational art. Generous, astute people and luck had steered me into the only medium that unites the two halves of myself, the one who writes and the other who draws.

I've been in the children's book field for nearly thirty years. With the recent sweeping changes and big profits in the publishing industry, many books have been taken out of print before they could find an audience. I saw a few of my own dismissed with what seemed like undue haste, and in the months before I began *Mirette*, gravity was weighing heavily on me. If I were not to succumb to discouragement, I needed to soar above perseverance, somehow to recapture the free spirit, passion for life, defiance, and inexhaustible enthusiasm of a nine-year-old daredevil. The story of Mirette became both a metaphor for artistic transformation and an actual artistic leap for me.

First, there were the ingredients from my past—refigured memories of work, persistence, aspiration, Paris, an elusive and uneasy adult male whose artistry beckoned but posed dangers, as well. There was also nostalgia, the volatile ingredient that separates us from children and drives us to tell them stories. After having written about the childhood I never knew, it was time to deal obliquely with the one I had.

Next came collaboration—every published work is a joint effort. One doesn't step out on a wire without perceptive encouragement. *Mirette* began in an unprecedented way when the brilliant young editor Arthur Levine asked if I had any ideas for picture books that we might work on together. I submitted six or so and he liked them all, but was most struck by the one about the little girl and the high wire walker in Paris. Over lunch we determined that the man would have a failure of nerve and somehow be revived by the girl. Usually I write the text first and then square it with the editor, but Arthur made no such requirement so I went right to the dummy, doing text and pictures simultaneously. This was followed by color sketches. They were going to be very different from my loosely drawn pastorals to suggest Paris in the 1890s. I was entering a new realm that had already been thoroughly interpreted by my idols of painting. Rather than look at those paintings for guidance, I kept a book of Atget photographs open on my desk. I was also stirred by my recent emotional return to Paris after twenty years.

Mirette's characterization came about with the help of photographs of Colette as a child. Her little sailor dress and gravity of mien were inspiration enough, but they vibrate with portent. What happened to Colette when she grew up made for an undercurrent of excitement in my own little girl's life. Mirette is by forceful design a heroine like Colette. When I was young and aspiring it was a disadvantage to be female. Girls still needed encouragement to see themselves as actors, not acted upon. Mirette is intrepid in her quest for poise and equality on the wire.

I presented my sketches to Nanette Stevenson, Putnam's exceptional art director, and she saw at once that since my book was a period piece and the period post-Impressionist, it would benefit from a more painterly approach. "Why don't you try dropping your line," she suggested.

But I had never made illustrations without line! I had no idea how to proceed without line! And what an irony, to embark on a book about tightrope walkers without my own tightrope. Ahead lay weeks of despair and futile regret that I'd never been trained at art school. But perseverance does further, especially when risk is high. I kept trying to make pictures that were like paintings, asking more of my little watercolor set, certainly more of my brushes than ever before, adding pastel for the first time, then failing less and finally getting to a point where I was comfortable enough to go on with the book.

I should say that as an evolving illustrator, I always struggle. My technique never seems quite up to the job of reproducing the images that will carry a story. And even after multiple revisions, I want the picture to seem spontaneous, for nothing to be still. My wastebasket fills with false tries. I'm not drawing from life anymore and the stuff of my imagination emerges in spasms. But the result is fully felt; whatever I've managed to capture is still wriggling. I hope that authenticates it in a way that a knockout graphic might not. Furthering the narrative with emotional verisimilitude is not the same as painting a masterful picture.

As an author of children's books, I am the adult version of a child who learned about the world in libraries. That often illicit thrill may be forever denied children today, who know everything before they know anything. But children do still pay attention to books, even as the hardcore adult readership dwindles drastically.

The current boom in children's books will be a boomerang if access, diversity, and guidance are not given to all young readers. Many gorgeous and expensive books are being produced these days. As we all know, several hundred specialized bookstores have sprung up to sell these beautiful books to parents and grandparents. Many are set up like libraries, for comfortable browsing. They serve the affluent well. Poorer children end up at warehouse-like stores in malls, buying formulaic books. I am always overwhelmed by respect and gratitude for the many teachers and librarians who buy worthy books for their classes with their own money and line up to have them autographed. They are attempting to make readers out of all children, without bias. The cultural inequality between the affluent and the disadvantaged can sabotage our democracy. The problem is the same one posed by the public schools: as we grow old in this country we can expect to become dependent on succeeding generations who are impoverished intellectually as well as by the deficit unless we find a solution. The institution designed to serve everyone equally is, of course, the library. Libraries must be adequately funded and esteemed or our future is compromised.

Thank you Jane Botham and the Caldecott committee for commending *Mirette* and taking my books into your library havens for so many years. Thank you Elizabeth Diggs, a brilliant critic and champion, who sees my work before anyone else does. I am so grateful to Harriet Wasserman, who hoped I was writing a novel, but has given boundless support to everything else. Thank you Margaret Frith—my relationship with Putnam could not have been more gratifying and you were all extremely good to me even before things started to happen. I am ever indebted to Doreen Rappaport for generously sharing Arthur Levine. Arthur, Nanette Stevenson, Colleen Flis and all the designers, you know what this has meant. It's our book, and it was immensely satisfying to work on it with you.

Mirette on the High Wire changed everything for me. But since perseverance still furthers, I say, on to the next!

Emily Arnold McCully
Arthur Levine

Emily Arnold McCully

The key to understanding the work of Emily McCully is one word: drama. I imagine that those who know Emily may find that a strange assertion, because she herself is not outwardly, obviously "dramatic." In fact when I first met her, I was struck by how normal she seemed: Emily Arnold McCully—the woman who illustrated the first children's book to win a National Book Award! Someone of her stature might well have appeared at my office swathed in scarves, sporting oversize dangly earrings. Perhaps I expected her to have a poodle in one hand and a cigarette holder in another, which she would wave at the tall, silent chauffeur-type who would be carrying her portfolio. Instead she appeared—as she has every time that we've met since—by herself: a petite woman in softly tailored clothes, with a generous smile and a calm, self-possessed manner. True, her voice has a musical quality. And if you look closely, her eyes shine in the manner of a person about to play a joke on you. But I didn't find her intimidating until after we'd begun working together. And that is because Emily McCully reserves the lion's share of her "drama" for her work.

Of course, drama can take many forms. And through three decades of illustration, Emily has expressed just about all of them. Take, for instance, a typically understated picture in *That Mean Man* (Harper), by Liesei Moak Skorpen, showing the perfectly horrid man of the title and his scowling, needle-nosed wife sourly rocking in a rowboat, as piranhas frolic beneath the waves. The text reads simply, "They honeymooned at sea." But the energy of the picture comes from the delightfully exaggerated characters and the implication of their impending doom.

Even in benign or fantastical situations, such as the ones posed by Sylvia Plath's text for *The Bed Book* (Harper), Emily is capable of suggesting layers of story and underlying conflict. Typical, I think, is the picture illustrating the concept of a "Jet-Propelled Bed / for visiting Mars." Certainly, in this picture, you have your requisite night sky over a bucolic rural backyard. But driving the rocketing crib in question is a baby who looks as apprehensive as he is excited. Some nighttime toys tumble from the "rocket," and the baby's brother and sister wave good-bye enthusiastically from the window, clearly as thrilled by the prospect of getting rid of their little sibling as they are with the miraculous bed! What could be truer both to the fantasy text and to the real relationships and emotions of children?

For Emily McCully, drama can also emerge from the absurd. If you doubt this, open up *The Twenty-Elephant Restaurant* (Atheneum) by Russell Hoban and turn to the illustration of a line of impatient elephants waiting for a pay phone that is being hogged by a temperamental pachyderm in a chef's hat. Only a New Yorker who has waited for an occupied pay phone could appreciate the truly incendiary potential of such a situation—elephants or no elephants.

From 1966 to 1984 Emily brought this unique sensibility and skill exclusively to the illustration of other writers' texts. As a writer of adult fiction, she was nominated for an American Book Award—for the novel *A Craving*—but had never been the author of a picture book. Ironically, her first such venture eschewed words entirely: the exuberant *Picnic* (Harper), winner of the 1985 Christopher Award.

Picnic is an example of pure, unbridled action, deepened by characterization and emotional truthfulness. In the first few pages a family of mice sets out for a picnic, leaving behind their youngest child. What follows is a brilliantly worked out sequence that has the spontaneous feeling of improvisation. Without such a clear sense of plot and drama, I believe Emily could never have made a wordless picture book so perfectly clear to follow—and so much fun.

Four more books chronicled the adventures of the mouse family. Then picture-book readers began to experience the treat of Emily McCully the writer as well as the illustrator. Not surprisingly, these newer efforts occasionally brought her even closer to a "dramatic" base, notably her charming series of books about a theatrical family of bears.

In the latest of these, *Speak Up, Blanche!* (Harper), a stagestruck sheep becomes apprenticed to the bear family by a pushy stage-aunt. Blanche (the sheep) fails miserably at all things thespian—she is simply too shy—until she gets a chance to paint the scenery. And here she shines, expressing all the things as an artist that she could not do as an actress.

Emily McCully, it turns out, is more than comfortable with both disciplines. Recently I saw her act in an off-Broadway play. I was impressed with how good she was. But not surprised. She has after all done so many things well: co-authored a musical in college, published wonderful picture books and novels, raised two children, earned a master's degree—not necessarily in that order. But what fills me with admiration is not only that she's done these things but that she continues to push herself to explore, to risk.

There is a scene in *Mirette on the High Wire* (Putnam) in which Mirette, having learned the true identity of her mentor, Bellini, bursts into the room to confront him. It was the first piece of finished art Emily sent in, and I vividly remember opening up the package. I suspect most editors have a moment of held breath at this point in a project—when the early stages have been so thrilling, so promising, that you almost can't let yourself hope that the finished art will live up to that promise.

But when I opened, up the piece, there it was: all the characterization and drama that was so typically McCully. The innocent, breathless excitement of the young girl punctuated by the sweep of her dress, the flush of her cheeks; and the counterpoint of Bellini at the moment of his greatest despair at having to disappoint his pupil. All of it in a style that we had never seen Emily McCully produce!

Who could have guessed that she'd illustrate a story about courage and risk with a technique that for her took so much of both? But I've come to expect nothing less from this exceptional artist—this exceptional person—than gutsiness, skill, truthfulness. And drama.

The Newbery Medal 1993

Missing May

written and illustrated by
Cynthia Rylant

published by
Orchard Books, 1992

Horn Book Review

In this haunting first-person narrative, Cynthia Rylant gives substance
to the abstract concept of love which philosophers have so often attempted to define. Orphaned at six, raised by an elderly West Virginia
aunt and uncle with more devotion than money, Summer is twelve
years old when Aunt May dies. Although Summer's grief is profound,
it is Uncle Ob who seems unable to go on living without his beloved
companion; that is, until he decides that her presence still lingers
nearby and that somehow he can contact her. With the help of another
loner, Cletus Underwood, one of Summer's schoolmates, the two leave
the dilapidated trailer which is their home and journey to another
county in search of healing at the Spiritualist Church of Glen Meadows. But their quest seems doomed when they learn that the preacher
they hoped to meet had died several months earlier. Then, as if in
answer to Summer's silent prayers, on the return journey Ob chooses
life over mourning, freeing both of them from months of longing for
the impossible. The final scene is a triumphant catharsis as they find
consolation in their memories and in each other. Although the focus
is the time following May's death, Rylant skillfully interweaves scenes
from the past to re-create her personality so that the grief of the survivors is both comprehensible and compelling. The book explores internal rather than external changes—a focus which is exactly right for
its theme.—Mary M. Burns

Booklist Review

Death is no stranger to children's literature. The picture-book set
learns that birds and pets can die, while myriad titles for older children
show what it means to lose a parent or a friend. The best books about
death, however, don't just make readers weep; they offer insights into

the human condition at the very moment when the terror of being human is at its most profound. They ask the niggling questions, the ones that stay awake with you in the middle of the night. Why, for instance, with all life's troubles, do people choose to go on?

Some don't, of course, and 12-year-old Summer, in Cynthia Rylant's *Missing May*, is worried that her Uncle Ob may be one of those whose fingers are slipping off the precipice. Summer's never seen anyone love each other as much as Ob and his wife, May. That love spilled over onto her when Ob and May came from West Virginia, saw that the relatives in Ohio didn't really want or need a little girl whose mother had died, and decided that, despite their age and their rusty old trailer of a home, they had everything they needed to make a little girl happy. And they did.

May dies in the garden that she loved, and after the funeral, Ob goes out to the old car parked by the dog house and sits there. Eventually, he lugs his body back inside, but his heart's with May. As Summer puts it, since her death Ob has not done much but miss May and hurt.

Then, one day, Ob senses May's presence. When Summer asks exactly what it feels like, Ob replies, "She felt like she did when we was packing up to go to Ohio . . . half of May would want to go and half of her would want to stay here. Couldn't make up her blame mind." The sensation of being with May is enough to rev Ob up again. Perhaps he can get in touch with May's spirit, find someone who can reach out to her. "I need me an interpreter."

The first choice is Summer's sort-of friend, Cletus. Collector extraordinaire, Cletus, whose hobby is making up stories about the photos he cuts out of magazines, once had a near-death experience. Summer's not too fond of the embarrassment that is Cletus, but she's willing to be nice to the "after-life antennae" for Ob's sake. Though Cletus can't make contact, the trio's attempted visitation in the garden performs another function for Ob and Summer. Ob "finally drained his cup of praises to May," and the two of them grieve properly.

Now, Ob really does feel like it's over. Summer tries to hide from her eyes the sight of Ob's life force dissolving. Then comes another reprieve: Ob hears of Reverend Miriam Young, a spiritualist who can communicate with the dead. With great anticipation, Ob, Summer, and Cletus plan a trip, deciding to make an adventure of it. First, they will hear all the news from May; then, they will visit Charleston and see the capitol—a special treat for Cletus, who's never been anywhere "except the middle part of Raleigh County and the middle part of

Fayette County. Hard to be a Renaissance Man when you can't get your nose any further than that."

It's during this trip that Rylant shows her true mettle as a writer. Right along with Ob, the reader has been hoping—make that "expecting"—that Reverend Young will put everything right. But the reverend is recently deceased. In a small way, the reader's disappointment mirrors Ob's greater despair. Do we really want to go with this story? This isn't the way it was supposed to turn out, and, like Ob, we can't bear the consequences.

But, of course, we do continue. One reason is the sheer pleasure of Rylant's writing. The weight of her subject matter is wrapped in the lightness of her style. Death, pain, and grief are the topics at hand, but they're written about with humor, grit, and love. Rylant makes us aware of the possibilities of life, even in the midst of tragedy. There is a freshness here that feels like a cool breeze.

Then there is Rylant's eclectic cast of characters. Arthritic old Ob, who makes whirligigs that represent storms and lightning—metaphors for all the emotions he can't articulate. You don't meet people like him every day. Nor like Cletus, who's a storyteller even though his stories only concern the people in his photo collection. Nor like Summer, despairing because she knows what love is and can't stand losing it to the caprice of life.

We're in with these people too deep to put the story down. We just can't make ourselves leave them. In the end, when Ob makes a remarkable turnaround—literally, as he decides not to go home and die, but to take the children to the capitol anyway—Summer thinks she knows why: "Because he couldn't bear to say goodbye to me."

That is Rylant's stalwart message: people count, and what makes all this life business worthwhile is the caring. It can be painful. It can bruise. There's not even the guarantee that the story will turn out the way it should. But perhaps the reason more people don't let go is because someone they love is holding on tight.—*Ilene Cooper*

1993 Newbery Acceptance Speech
Cynthia Rylant

Dear Friends:

This is the biggest thank-you note I've ever had to write in my life. Believe it or not, I've never been much good with words when I've tried to express gratitude, and especially, love. It is as if my heart swells so big that it cuts off all the circulation to my brain, which shuts down just as I need to find a few good words. It is our spirits which understand love, not our minds, and our spirits, wisely, are never wordy. When you see that quiet owl swoop across your path in the woods at night, or those beautiful geese fly V-shaped over a dark lake in early morning, or your own little child lie soft and moist in innocent slumber, it is your spirit which leaves you mute at the sight of these things and which moves you to understand them only with your heart.

Thus it is hard for me now to find words because on this momentous occasion when I am required to give a grand speech, I have been rendered nearly speechless.

I need to issue thanks to people who have made my life so beautiful that I have been inspired to write beautiful stories.

The first will be my mother, who managed, I don't know how, to never belittle or condemn any opinion I ever held. And, believe me, I have held some wild opinions growing up. She loved me without judgment and patiently readjusted as I came home on holidays sometimes a vegetarian, sometimes not, sometimes a Christian, sometimes not, sometimes married, sometimes not. I had a baby when I was young and broke, and she rescued me from those times I was only steps away from the welfare office. And not once, though she has had countless opportunities, has she ever said to me, "I told you so."

I was raised in an atmosphere of forgiveness and this may be the finest gift God has given me on this earth. Knowing I would be forgiven by my mother, my family, if I ever failed at anything I tried gave me the courage to be a writer, the courage to place my work in the world for judgment, and the courage to keep on trying to say something important in my books.

I must thank my grandparents, who raised me for several years in Cool Ridge, West Virginia, until I was eight. There is no question in my mind that it was during those years that the writer in me was being born. And though I don't remember it, I am sure I had many conversations with the angels as I walked in those West Virginia mountains, and what they said to me I tried to remember and write down after I was grown. I don't think I am the only person who spoke to angels as a child. I think probably most of us did. And whether we grew into writers, or painters, or teachers, or librarians, we kept that light inside us that was the evidence of God, and when we loved books like *Charlotte's Web*, *The Runaway Bunny*, *Frog and Toad*, and even *The*

Stupids Step Out it was because of all that angel light that had fallen upon us as children.

My grandparents gave me a small, warm, quiet house. They gave me faith in breakfast every morning and supper every night. They gave me a garden rich with the smell of carrots and potatoes and beans. They gave me the sacrifice of all their work on my behalf, and from them I learned steadfastness.

I grew up reading comic books because there was no library in my town or in my school, and I did not enter a public library until I was in my twenties.

When I was twenty-three, just out of college and desperate for a job, I went to the Cabell County Public Library in Huntington, West Virginia, and asked for a job as a clerk. I was hired and I was assigned to the children's department.

Having grown up reading comic books and the Nancy Drew books my mother bought for me at the dimestore, I did not know there was any such thing as children's literature. I had majored in English in college and still I did not know this.

I spent only five months working in that children's room—I was, myself, growing my own baby who would be delivered in the oranges and reds of the fall. In those few months in that treasure chest of children's books, I discovered what I was.

I was a children's book writer.

I also learned many things about libraries those months that I have never forgotten. The most important thing I learned is that they are free. That any child from any kind of house in any kind of neighborhood in this whole vast country may walk into a building which has a room full of books meant just for him, and he may choose whichever ones he wants to read and he may take them home because they are free. And they are not free in a way which might diminish him, not in the way of secondhand clothes or Salvation Army Christmas toys.

They are free in the most democratic and humane way. Both a poor child and wealthy child are privileged with free libraries, and whenever they enter one, *Make Way for Ducklings* will be sitting there waiting for them both.

When I discovered I was a children's book writer, I began writing stories at home and mailing them to publishing houses in New York City. I was still living in West Virginia, had never met an author or illustrator, had only just found children's literature myself, and had not the foggiest idea how people became published. But I bought a copy of a book which listed publisher's addresses and I mailed my stories to New York anyway. Because that's what I was put here on earth to do in 1978.

And that year I received two more gifts from God.

One, the most important, was my son, whom I named Nathaniel after one of my favorite writers. And that spirit in me which had been a little too quiet was stirred by this young child and I found in this stirring my strong writer's voice. It sounded like this:

When I was young in the mountains, Grandfather came home in the evening covered with the black dust of a coal mine. Only his lips were clean and he used them to kiss the top of my head.

And it was this voice, this writing, which led to the second gift of that year: the acceptance of my first book for children and new meaning for my life.

Writers, especially new ones, need editors, and the newer the writer, the more desperate that need.

God gave me a third gift: he gave me Richard Jackson.

I am not sure I would have written more than a few books in my life had I not been blessed with Dick Jackson on my maiden voyage. It is hard to believe you are worth much as a writer when you first start out, and if there's no one there convincing you otherwise, no one there waiting in hopeful anticipation of your next work, then it is hard to keep writing. You can talk yourself out of it and go work in a bank instead.

Perhaps most people think editors are simply the ones who fix the cracks and crevices in a writer's book until it is fit to be published. I certainly thought that, before finding Dick.

But I know better now. I know what it is that editors need to give and must give to the new writers who feel small and ungifted in this big corporate machine called publishing.

Editors must give love, first and foremost. It is love which guides all our best work, which makes anything on this planet permanent. Without it, whatever is born, whether a child or a book, will be unable to shine.

Dick Jackson loved me. He has loved many writers and painters and his love for their talent and their struggle and their innocence has given the world beautiful books like *The Slave Dancer* and *Dog Song*, and this love has made us all better.

We have had God's angels among us, and though we no longer see some of them, they are with us still. James Marshall, Arnold Lobel, Dr.

Seuss, Margaret Wise Brown: they gave us art which lifted us and reminded us of the light from which we came and toward which we are returning. They worked, always, in love.

I have many friends here tonight, fellow writers, illustrators, editors, librarians. I have my most dear ones here, my best friend, Diane; my sweetheart, Dav; my son, Nate; and my mother, Lee, who make my life safe and who make it worth living.

Outside this room, we all have the stars. We have squirrels in the trees and whales sublime in the oceans. We have birds which will leave us in winter and which will return to us in spring. And flowers promising to do the same. We have wet rain, white snow, and always the sky. We have the universe.

I want to thank the Newbery committee of 1993, the American Library Association, all children's book sellers, all children's book publishers, all children's librarians. I am honored to have been a part of you this past decade, and I cannot wait to see all of the beautiful books which are waiting for us in the future. Which wait for the poor child and the wealthy child. And which will be given to them with love.

Thank you and God bless you all.

Cynthia Rylant
Diane Ward

Cynthia Rylant

I first met Cynthia Rylant in 1983 when, as a children's librarian, I invited her to come to speak to children in Monongalia County, West Virginia. At this time *When I Was Young in the Mountains* (Sutton) had just won the Caldecott Honor Award, and *Miss Maggie* (Sutton), her second book, had been published. I loved them both.

She and I were new at author visits, and I made the mistake of overloading the schedule in the hope of having as many children as possible meet her. It was a grueling two days, which she bore gracefully, giving everything she had to those children, but we both learned from the experience.

What came out of that first meeting was the beginning of a great friendship that has lasted more than a decade. Since we've never lived in the same town, initially we had to learn more about each other through letters. Even now it's one of our favorite ways of keeping in touch. We imagine ourselves years from now, sitting in our rocking chairs, reliving our lives through a trunkful of letters.

On future visits, we set up a more reasonable schedule and, at Cynthia's request, headed out to those wonderful country schools where the library was often a closet and the librarians were parent volunteers. In these sessions, children heard the story of a little girl who, like many of them, had grown up without much money, in a house without running water; she had never even been in a library until she went away to college. Her way of talking to these children was respectful, honest, and straight to the heart. She was "Cyndi" to them, not a famous author who stood apart, and she instilled in them the hope that someone with roots like theirs could become what they dreamed. She told them that there was a period in her life when she was made to feel ashamed of how she had grown up, that she heard the word hillbilly and knew that was not what she was. She let them know that it took her a long time to understand that the way she was raised was special; when she wrote *When I Was Young in the Mountains*, it was meant as a tribute to her grandparents, Elda and Ferrell Rylant, for the love they gave her. Children watched and listened, and I can only imagine what seeds of hope were planted in the minds and hearts of these children of Appalachia.

There is one child in particular that I think about every so often. Her name was Mindy, and she was six years old. She was a little wisp of a child with thick glasses and straggly blond hair. She came into my library as part of a class of behaviorally disturbed children. Although I tried speaking with her, Mindy never answered and only stared at me. Once when I touched her gently on the shoulder, she cringed. There was something riveting about this child.

The class made weekly visits to the library. One day I watched Mindy as she roamed around and finally settled down with a book she had chosen. Rarely had I ever seen her spend more than a few minutes with any book, but this day was different. The book she had was *When I Was Young in the Mountains*. She stared at the cover for a long time, and then slowly, page by page, she studied the pictures. When she got to the end, she closed the book, looked at the cover again, and started over. Years later, I still wonder what that gentle mountain family was saying to this child.

Because of the descriptions in Cynthia's books, I felt I already knew Cool Ridge, West Virginia, before I visited there with Cynthia. We went through the screened back porch and into Grandmama's kitchen to find the matriarch of this family. She greeted us warmly in that beautiful soft Appalachian voice and offered us cookies and milk. As we talked, I had the feeling that it didn't take her long to know what you were about and that nothing much got past Grandmama.

Cynthia and I left the house and went walking. Within minutes we were standing in front of Miss Maggie's house. It was so much like Thomas DiGrazia's drawings—Cynthia had sent him photographs—that I half expected Miss Maggie to walk out the door, though I knew that she had died a few years earlier. Miss Maggie had been told before she died that a book had been written about her. And there was her house—no black snakes, no starling, no tobacco-chewing Miss Maggie—just her one-room log house with its rickety front porch.

On another trip, traveling alone through the state, I decided I wanted to see Beaver, West Virginia, and detoured off the interstate a few miles to do so. *Waiting to Waltz: A Childhood* (Bradbury), Cynthia's collection of poems, remains to this day one of my favorites of her works. Its setting is Beaver, where she lived with her mom from the time she was eight until she went away to college.

Coming to it from the country, proud that I finally had sidewalks to walk and indoor plumbing. Little strip of street called Beaver: Hardware, Laundromat, market, post office, Kool-Kup, and Moon-Glo motel. Beaver Creek holding it all together, and me on the edge. Like the water, muddy and rolling. Growing in Beaver.

Beaver is still a little strip of street tucked into the mountains with houses a few blocks back on either side, and Beaver Creek and a railroad track running right through it. I can imagine her growing up in this town, protected by its familiarity and smallness, but also dreaming beyond, knowing there was more, but unsure of what it was and how to find it.

So who is this person whose dreams did carry her into the world, who illuminates the lives of the simple folk: Mae, the homeless woman in *Children of Christmas: Stories for the Season* (Orchard); Pete, a boy who is duped by an itinerant preacher in *A Fine White Dust* (Bradbury); and, of course, Ob, Summer, and Cletus in *Missing May* (Orchard).

She's a mother, raising a child, Nate, who is now fourteen years old. She loves movies and chocolate and staying home. She has a nesting instinct that is stronger than that of anyone I've ever met. Cynthia is constantly redecorating and shifting things around. She has the kind of home where you feel immediately at ease—comfortable furniture with lots of soft pillows, handmade quilts hanging on the walls, family pictures, shelves full of books, beautiful old furniture collected piece by piece, and stained glass everywhere catching the sunlight and casting rainbows on walls. It's the sort of place that invites you to curl up under a blanket and read a book or have a cup of tea. Cynthia does it all herself. I've never known her to even have someone help her clean house, can't imagine her tolerating that intrusion.

She's a private person who needs space for herself. Even when we visit, we give each other time to go off and read or simply be alone and then come together for tea and conversation, shopping trips, and meals out. She loves animals, and when you're sitting down having that cup of tea, Martha, a two-year-old seventy-pound yellow Lab, is trying to climb in your lap, and Leia, a nine-year-old Welsh Corgi, is bringing you her rawhide bone and wagging every inch of her body, vying for your attention, also. Two cats—Blueberry, a black-and-white feline of unknown weight, and Edward Velvetpaws—share this home. Edward belonged to an elderly woman who had to enter a retirement home and could not take her cat with her. Cynthia rescues bats caught in windows and takes injured squirrels to the vet. When she wrote *Every Living Thing* (Bradbury), it seemed to me the most natural book in the world.

She believes that people have a right to lead any lifestyle that suits them. The important thing is to live life and be kind in the process. She walks gently through life, sifting her experiences and creating stories from them, remembering friends and sending surprise packages of tea and bubble bath, or note cards and candy, and always a short note that brightens your day. I learned of her Newbery Medal by receiving a bouquet of flowers with a card saying, "*Missing May* won the Newbery. Lots of love and joy, Cyndi."

Ten years after our initial meeting, Cynthia still has the grace and humor that marked our first dinner together. That evening in 1983, we sat down to lasagna and salad with my three children at the table and the dog under it. When it came time for dessert, I discovered that our cat had helped herself to the pumpkin pie keeping cool on the back porch. Cynthia laughed and said that two thirds of it were fine. So we finished off the meal with cat-eaten pumpkin pie, none of us minding very much.

I believe that these qualities of grace and humor, along with the love she has for those of us who are doing the very best we can with what life has given us, are what make Cynthia and her writing so very special.

The Caldecott Medal 1994

Grandfather's Journey

written and illustrated by
Allen Say

published by
Houghton Mifflin, 1993

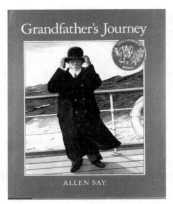

Horn Book Review

Returning to the picture-book biography format that worked so well in *El Chino* (Houghton), Allen Say tells the story of his own grandfather's travels throughout North America as a young man. Awed by sweeping deserts, oceans, and prairies, bewildered and excited by huge cities, and inspired by the racial diversity of the people he meets, he eventually goes back to Japan to marry his childhood sweetheart and bring her to the "New World." They settle in California and raise a daughter, but, unable to forget his homeland, he returns to Japan with his family when his child is nearly grown. It is there that the author himself is born, and although his grandfather speaks nostalgically of seeing California one more time, war interrupts. "Bombs fell from the sky and scattered our lives like leaves in a storm," writes Say. It remained for him to pursue his grandfather's dream. The author now lives in California, where he has raised his own family, returning to his native land from time to time. "The funny thing is, the moment I am in one country, I am homesick for the other. I think I know my grandfather now." The immigrant experience has rarely been so poignantly evoked as it is in this direct, lyrical narrative that is able to stir emotions through the sheer simplicity of its telling. The soft-toned watercolors have the feel of a family album. The illustrations sometimes resemble old-fashioned photographs depicting stiffly posed figures in formal dress and sometimes look like more modern informal snapshots. These are interspersed with panoramic landscapes of the Japanese countryside or the North American continent. They seem to be moments taken from a life, intensely personal and at the same time giving voice to and confirming an experience shared by countless others.—*Nancy Vasilakis*

Booklist Review: A Restless Journey

Say's stunning immigration story is a version of the American dream that includes adventure and discovery but no sense of arrival. He captures our restlessness, our homesickness, wherever we are. With the particulars of his own family story, he universalizes everyone's quest for home, and he finds not one place but many, connection and also discontent. The journey isn't a straight line, but more like a series of widening circles, full of surprising twists and loops.

As in the best children's books, the plain, understated words have the intensity of poetry. The watercolor paintings frame so much story and emotion that they break your heart. Looking at the people in this book is like turning the pages of a family photo album, the formal arrangements and stiff poses show love and distance, longing and mystery, beneath such elemental rites as marriage, leaving, and return.

The story starts off as cheery adventure. Say's grandfather leaves Japan as a young man on an astonishing journey to the New World. He explores all kinds of places and meets all kinds of people and never thinks of returning home. The huge cities "bewildered yet exerted him." He settles in California because he loves the light and the mountains and the lonely seacoast. He marries his childhood sweetheart from his village in Japan and brings her to the new country, and they have a child. But then as his daughter grows up (we see her posing stiffly with a blonde doll in a carriage), he begins to think about his own childhood and longs to go back. "He could not forget. Finally, when his daughter was nearly grown, he could wait no more. He took his family and returned to his homeland."

The village is as he remembered it, and he laughs with his old friends. But his American daughter doesn't fit in the traditional culture. She's an outsider in the Japanese village in her Western hat and purse, as awkward as her father was when he first left home. They move to a city in Japan; she marries, and her son, Allen Say, is born. His grandfather tells him many stories about California and longs to see it again. But the war comes described through the child's eyes ("Bombs fell from the sky and scattered our lives like leaves in a storm"): a single painting shows a group of refugees in a leveled city. Grandfather dies without seeing California again. But when the boy is nearly grown he leaves home and goes to see the place his grandfather had told him about, and he stays in the United States and has a daughter, just as his grandfather did.

But he says, "I can not still the longing in my heart." Like his grand-father, he has to return to Japan now and then. And as soon as he is in one country, he is "homesick for the other."

The pictures echo each other and connect the generations and their places. Say's grandfather in tie and cardigan staring out the window in San Francisco, remembering the mountains and rivers of home, is like a self-portrait of Allen Say today. The landscapes evoke a variety of styles: from the mountain photography of Ansel Adams to the Japanese pastoral and the romantic French Impressionists. The cover picture of the young traveler in his first too-large European clothes, clutching his bowler hat, has the sturdiness and poignancy of Chaplin. Allen Say has traveled and found riches everywhere. He captures what the Jewish American writer Irving Howe calls an "eager restlessness."

This book is a natural companion to Say's other autobiographical picture book, *Tree of Cranes* (1991), about his childhood in Japan and his mother remembering her childhood Christmas in California. Both are books to share across generations and in oral history projects with older students. Every child who's pored over strange old family pictures or heard stories of "back home" will relate to this, whether home was across the border or far across the sea or a midwestern farm. The story has special immediacy for immigrants, like me. It's also about all those who long for where they came from, even while they know they can't go home again.—*Hazel Rochman*

1994 Caldecott Acceptance Speech
Allen Say

I know that it's a tradition for the recipients of the Caldecott and Newbery Medals to talk about what they were doing when fate called. It always gives me pleasure to break traditions, and if that's rebellion I must be young at heart. Anyway, when I received my call, and when it became clear that the news wasn't some cruel prank or a grotesque mistake, I called Walter Lorraine, my editor. I asked him if I was the oldest person ever to receive the prize. "Oh, no," he denied emphatically. Then there was a pause. He was thinking. He couldn't think of anybody older.

But I am in good company. Freeman Dyson, the physicist, had this to say about being a late-blooming father:

> Life begins at fifty-five, the age at which I published my first book. So long as you have courage and a sense of humor, it is never too late to start life afresh. A book is in many ways like

a baby. While you are writing, it is curled up in your belly. You cannot get a clear view of it. As soon as it is born, it goes out into the world and develops a character of its own. Like a daughter coming home from school, it surprises you with unexpected flashes of wisdom.

A few days after the announcement, a librarian I know sent me a Caldecott fact sheet. I learned that the first award was given in 1938 and that I am its fifty-seventh recipient. It so happens that I am going to turn fifty-seven this August. And this honor is bestowed on the book that was published last year, which marked the fortieth anniversary of my coming to this country.

Then it gets stranger. When I was twelve, I attended a private middle school in a district in Tokyo called Shibuya. Just around the corner from the school, in an American housing compound called Washington Heights, there lived a twelve-year-old Lois Lowry whose father was General MacArthur's dentist. I like to think that we had seen each other in those days, two youngsters from very different backgrounds eyeing each other from the opposite sides of the track in my city. And tonight we've come to sit at the same table, to be honored with the highest awards in our respective crafts. And astonishingly, we've arrived here under the wings of the same editor. I thank my good fortune that I didn't aspire to be a novelist.

For me, this prize represents the icing on the great gifts I have received in my life: Noro Shinpei for master, my own apartment at age twelve, acceptance of my first children's book by Nina Ignatowicz, birth of my daughter, my association with Walter Lorraine.

But I would like to tell you about the most wondrous gift of all. I was not yet four when I received it, and the donor was a lordly personage whose face I cannot remember. The present was a magnificent ceremonial sword. I could barely put my small hands around the heavy scabbard; I unsheathed it halfway, to make sure it was real, then closed it with a satisfying click, and laid it carefully on the long cherry wood table in the dining room. Then I went to the bathroom, and when I returned, the sword was gone. I asked the maid, then my parents. They gave me a blank stare. In a frenzy I searched the house from top to bottom, and when I could not find it I threw a tantrum, accusing the grown-ups of hiding it. My mother finally understood and tried to comfort me. It was only a dream, she said.

I never entirely believed that it was a dream. Even today, fifty-some years later, the sword remains one of the most vivid objects I nearly possessed. And the incident marked the beginning of my lifelong confusion: I have a hard time separating my waking life from my dreams. Frequently, I am utterly lost in determining if a delicious pear I ate two days ago, or an interesting stranger I met three days ago, was real or a phantom.

While I was a student at Berkeley, I discovered the key to my dream life. It came in the form of a shiny silver coin, lying innocently on the ground. As I reached down toward it, another coin appeared, then another, and soon a fistful of them lay at my feet. That was when I knew I was dreaming. In real life, unclaimed or unearned money never presented itself to a poor student like me. Ever since then, when I see a cluster of coins, I know I can do anything my aching heart desires and not get arrested. My only fear then is of waking prematurely. So imagine my bewilderment when I spotted three coins on a sidewalk one time, reached down, and was stiff-armed by a panhandler. He was very real.

Back to square one.

My bewilderment deepened when I returned to Japan in 1982, to attend a grammar school reunion. *The Bicycle Man* had just been published, and carrying a stack of brand-new books I went back to the place where the story took place thirty-six years earlier. Mrs. Morita, the first-grade teacher, came to meet me at the train station. It was like one of those teary Japanese movies. Nineteen classmates came to the party, and we had to point one another out in the old school photographs someone had the sense to bring. I handed out copies of *The Bicycle Man* and the banquet suddenly died. No one remembered the incident. "That wonderful black American soldier, he rode the principal's bicycle, don't you remember?" I pleaded. They looked at me with embarrassment and incomprehension, even pity. Then they laughed and called me Urashima Taro, the fisherman of the ancient folktale who returns home after being away for four hundred years.

On the following day, some of my classmates took the day off and accompanied me to the street where I used to live. All the houses were standing, except mine. It had been demolished only a month before my return.

My homecoming wasn't turning out the way I had expected. Feeling a little woozy, I took the bullet train to Tokyo, to visit my prep school in the neighborhood where Lois and I had been children. Some of my old teachers were still there, and one of them presented me with a thirtieth anniversary school album. The slick book had pictures of anyone who had ever had anything to do with the school—teachers, parents, and caretakers. All except me. I had spent a fifth of my young life there and yet I did not exist in the school history.

I went back to Yokohama, the place of my birth. I had to find some evidence—any evidence—of my childhood. I knew that my first house, where I had been given the sword, had burned down during the war, but I was not prepared for the changes that awaited me.

The big goldfish hatchery next to my old house, where the carp pond in *Tree of Cranes* had been, was now replaced with rows of ugly concrete apartment buildings. The ancient fishing village from where my nanny had come was gone. The fine beach where our maid used to pick seaweed for the evening soup was gone. In fact, the entire seashore had been buried and a jumble of factories now stood over the playground of my memory. Like Urashima Taro, I had gone back to a world without a past. My childhood was entirely in my mind. A dream.

Feeling a sense of irretrievable loss and uncertainty, I came back to California. I was an advertising photographer at the time, and I think it was then that I began to lose interest in photography, a craft that relies entirely upon reality. It was like watching the dissolving of a sandcastle that had taken me twenty years to build. I began dabbling in commercial illustrations.

The malaise lasted four years. I was forty-nine, and I had a six-year-old daughter.

Then I got a call from Walter Lorraine. He asked me to illustrate a story by Dianne Snyder. Quite frankly, I didn't know who Walter was, other than that he was an editor and vice president. The world is full of vice presidents. In any case, I took on the assignment, with the idea that it was going to be my last children's book. *The Boy of the Three-Year Nap* came out in the spring of 1988, and a few months later, Walter called to congratulate me on winning the Boston Globe–Horn Book Award. I didn't know what it was. But I did work on another book. Looking back on it today, *A River Dream* seems like a pocket mirror of the state I was in at the time—weaving in and out of reality.

Once I decided to work full-time on children's books, I had a memorable dream. In it, I was walking with a friend in bright sunlight when I spotted a shiny dime in the gutter and, reaching down, I saw other coins scattered about. I picked up the dime, which was bent in the middle, and showed it to my friend. "Look, we're in a dream," I told him. "I know, but it doesn't matter," he replied. I tossed the dime back into the gutter and walked on.

The gutter needs no explanation. But why a bent dime? Well, you can't put a bent dime in a vending machine, not even a parking meter. It's useless. The coin had lost its meaning. And the friend is clearly the voice of my intuition, telling me that sleeping and waking are the two sides of the same continuum. "It doesn't matter," said the voice of wisdom.

This story gets even more interesting if I tell you that the friend in my dream was Walter Lorraine. What prompted him to call me that first time? I believe we are in the same dream.

I don't know how long the term multiculturalism has been around, but as I started to work in my new phase I suddenly came under the scrutiny of educators and book people. And caught up in the swelling wave of social awareness, I began to think of "building a bridge over the two disparate cultures that nourished me." A pompous, self-serving delusion. Mercifully, the lapse was brief. What drives me is far more elemental—and honest, I hope. I am trying to give shape to my dreams—the old business of making myths—the fundamental force of art. And so, *Grandfather's Journey* is essentially a dream book, for the life's journey is an endless dreaming of the places you have left behind and the places yet to be reached.

I am deeply honored to be a part of the milestone in Walter Lorraine's inestimable career. My heartfelt thanks to Nina Ignatowicz, who so long ago helped me find my voice in our adopted language. I thank everyone at Houghton Mifflin Company for assisting me in bringing this baby into the world. I thank all the librarians and teachers and reviewers who have made me a very proud father. And I am most grateful to the members of this year's Caldecott committee for acknowledging the beauty of this child who has already embarked on a journey of its own, displaying flashes of wisdom, which are quite surprising to the dreamer. Thank you, and sweet dreams.

My Father

Yuriko Say

I spend half of my life with my mother and the other half with my father. My father lives with a twenty-pound cat named Tofu. He calls me his favorite daughter. I am an only child.

My father's apartment is quite different from any other person's living space. Except for my room, there is no furniture. He doesn't like sofas or any comfortable chairs, so he has only a drawing table, a desk, and his bed. For three years he has resisted buying a stereo because he thinks it's ugly and will mess up his studio.

But Tofu has a scratching post and a cat bed, where he snores very loudly when he sleeps. He follows my father around the house until my father says, "Stop giving me the evil eye!" and gives him food. Tofu gets fed three times a day.

From my father's studio window, you can see a large part of San

Allen Say

Francisco. I like to watch the colors change in the bay when the sun is setting. All the walls are white, and framed posters of my father's last three books hang side by side. He spends a lot of time lying on the studio floor. That's how he thinks, he says. Then he does yoga. He has a big kitchen, and on top of the refrigerator is an old clock he winds every week for good luck. The last time the clock stopped, my father's car was towed and some other terrible things happened, so he has become very superstitious. When he goes out of town, he hires someone to feed Tofu and wind the clock so it won't stop.

The one thing he has plenty of is house rules. You have to take off your shoes when you come in. He won't allow anyone who wears a baseball cap into his house. He says only baseball players should wear baseball caps and only the catchers should wear them backward. Every time I go to stay at his house, he makes up a new rule. "House rule number 579, no television programs with laugh tracks!" he will say. But then he can never remember the numbers, so they change constantly.

The rule that he always enforces is the one that requires me to write a two-page essay anytime I want something. He didn't speak English until he was sixteen, and he had a hard time learning to write it, so he wants me to become a good writer at an early age. This ritual started when I asked him if I could have my ears pierced when I was nine. He said it was barbaric and told me I couldn't do it until I was thirty-five. But I kept asking him, and he finally said that if I wrote an essay and I could persuade him in writing why I wanted holes in my ears, maybe he would say okay. I wrote my first essay for my father, and after one month of writing and rewriting, he finally gave me his permission.

Proper etiquette is another thing my father insists on. I have to eat properly and speak correctly, or I get demerits. He went to a military academy when he first came to America, and his superiors gave him lots of demerits. But because he's never given me a demerit, I think it's just a threat. If I ever got sunburned, he says he would court-martial me because that is what they do in the army. He buys me a lot of sun block.

The first time he took me to a sushi bar, he said it was very rude to rub chopsticks together, and you never order more than one thing at a time. Just as he said that, a couple sat down next to us and rubbed their chopsticks together and ordered five or six different pieces of sushi. My father was very pleased. He is right most of the time.

When I began this profile, I started to think about all the things I remember about my father. After I put two thoughts on paper, I got stuck and couldn't think of anything more. I went to my father and asked him what I should write about. He thought for a moment and said, "If I were to die tomorrow, what would you remember about me?" I went downstairs and thought about what he said.

My earliest memories are the stories he used to tell me. When he read a book for me, he would always change the story, and we would laugh hysterically. But my favorites were the stories he made up himself and drew pictures about while he talked. I still have the drawings he did for me. And I remember the little storage room where he used to work. Until he moved to his new apartment, the little room was where he worked every day, as long as I can remember.

What I admire most about my father is that he always says exactly what he thinks. When I was seven years old, I dragged my father into a "Hello Kitty" store. After I had picked out the things I wanted, we walked up to the cash register. The lady at the register rang up the purchases, and just as she was about to put them in a bag, my father said, "I really wish this place would burn to the ground." The lady gave him a blank look. I was very embarrassed. But that's the way my father is. He'll say anything to anyone. I think a lot of people are afraid of my father because of his honesty. Some of my friends are afraid of him, and some of them think he is very funny. My father doesn't think he is funny. But he is, most of the time.

My father has given me many things, but I think the most important gift I have received from him is respect. Many adults treat young people in a special way. They never tell us certain things that they think are too "adult." My father tells me everything. I can ask him anything, and he will give me a straight answer. My father treats me as an adult, and he has been doing so for a long time. Perhaps this is because it's the only way he knows how to deal with anybody.

He is my favorite father.

The Newbery Medal 1994

The Giver

written by
Lois Lowry

published by
Houghton Mifflin, 1993

Horn Book Review

In a departure from her well-known and favorably regarded realistic works, Lois Lowry has written a fascinating, thoughtful science-fiction novel. The story takes place in a nameless community, at an unidentified future time. The life is utopian: there is no hunger, no disease, no pollution, no fear; old age is tenderly cared for; every child has concerned and attentive parents. Each aspect of life has a prescribed rule: one-year-olds—"Ones"—are Named and given to their chosen family; "Nines" get their first bicycles; Birth Mothers give birth to three children and then become Laborers; "family units" get two children, one male, one female. In Jonas's family, his father is a Nurturer, one who cares for the "newchildren" before they go to a family unit; his mother is in the Department of Justice; and he has a younger sister, Lily. But although their life seems perfect, the reader somehow becomes uneasily aware that all is not well. Young Jonas is eagerly awaiting his Ceremony of Twelve, the time when all the twelve-year-olds in the community receive their Assignments for their lifelong professions. He can guess that his playful, jolly friend Asher will work in Recreation, and that gentle Fiona will be Caretaker of the Old, but he is astonished to be selected to be trained to be the new Receiver of Memories, the most respected of the Elders. As he begins his training by the old Receiver, whom he calls the Giver, he discovers that the community is spared all memories of pain and grief, which are lodged in the mind of the Giver, and now transmitted to Jonas. He learns about war, starvation, neglect, misery, and despair. He learns, to his horror, the truth about the happy release given to old people and newchildren who do not thrive. But he learns also about toys that the community never experiences: they do not see color, or hear music, or know love. In a cliff-hanger ending which can be construed as allegory or reality, he asserts his new wisdom and knowledge. The story is skillfully written; the air of disquiet is delicately insinuated. And the theme of balancing the values of freedom and security is beautifully presented.—*Ann A. Flowers*

Booklist Review

Lowry once again turns in a new direction; this time to the future. Jonas lives in a world that many of us have longed for. There is no war, poverty, or family turmoil, and so no fear, no hardship, no everyday discontent, no long-term terror. Jonas lives with his father, who's a Nurturer at the childcare center; his mother, who works at the Department of Justice; and his sister, Lily, who is a Six. Jonas himself is soon to be a Twelve, an important age because each year at the annual Ceremony all the 12-years-olds in the community receive their life assignments from the Elders. Jonas is named to the most prestigious and unusual job in the community—the Receiver of Memory. There is only one Receiver, and when he grows old, he trains his successor. Jonas is both puzzled and frightened by his job, which requires him to receive all the memories of their world and the land that lies beyond their community, Elsewhere.

Like the falling of night, the story's mood changes almost imperceptibly. Readers lulled by the warmth and safety of the community will find themselves quite surprised as the darkness enfolds them. What the former Receiver, now the Giver, has to tell Jonas rocks the boy's sense of self and turns inside out the life he has known. At first, the Giver offers benign memories—of snow, sunshine, and color, things that existed before the community went to Sameness—and the boy grieves for what has been lost. But soon Jonas receives memories of pain and death, and then he is torn. Perhaps his community's decision to shelter the citizens from the world's sorrow has been correct. Yet by going to Sameness, the community has also eliminated all possibilities for choice and, finally, for happiness.

The simplicity and directness of Lowry's writing force readers to grapple with their own thoughts about this dichotomy; though it is clear what the "right" answer is (and, at times, the narrative lacks subtlety in insisting upon that answer), the allure of a life without pain will give even the least philosophical of readers something to ponder. Lowry forces the point for Jonas when he learns that baby Gabriel, whom the family had been raising, is to be Released. Jonas had always thought Release simply meant going Elsewhere, but now he knows the term's real meaning: the baby will be killed. So to save Gabriel, and with the Giver's help, Jonas decides to flee to Elsewhere. Lowry heightens the tension as Jonas and Gabriel dodge search parties and airplanes, face starvation, and become weaker seeking a better place.

Lowry's ending is the most unsatisfying element of the book. Jonas and Gabriel, freezing, starving, very near death, finally see the lights and hear the music of Elsewhere. But have they arrived? Or, as some (mainly adults, perhaps) will wonder—have the children died? With the book's tension level raised so high, readers will want closure, not ambiguity. Anti-Utopian novels have an enduring appeal. This one makes an especially good introduction to the genre because it doesn't load the dice by presenting the idea of a community structured around safety as totally negative. There's a distinctly appealing comfort in sameness that kids—especially junior high kids—will recognize. Yet the choice is clear. Sameness versus freedom, happiness at the risk of pain. Something to talk about.—*Ilene Cooper*

1994 Newbery Acceptance Speech
Lois Lowry

"How do you know where to start?" a child asked me once, in a schoolroom, where I'd been speaking to her class about the writing of books. I shrugged and smiled and told her that I just start wherever it feels right.

This evening it feels right to start by quoting a passage from *The Giver*, a scene set during the days in which the boy, Jonas, is beginning to look more deeply into the life that has been very superficial, beginning to see that his own past goes back further than he had ever known and has greater implications than he had ever suspected.

> . . . now he saw the familiar wide river beside the path differently. He saw all of the light and color and history it contained and carried in its slow-moving water; and he knew that there was an Elsewhere from which it came, and an Elsewhere to which it was going.

Every author is asked again and again the question we probably each have come to dread the most: HOW DID YOU GET THIS IDEA?

We give glib, quick answers because there are other hands raised, other kids in the audience waiting.

I'd like, tonight, to dispense with my usual flippancy and glibness and try to tell you the origins of this book. It is a little like Jonas looking into the river and realizing that it carries with it everything that has come from an Elsewhere. A spring, perhaps, at the beginning, bubbling up from the earth; then a trickle from a glacier; a mountain stream entering farther along; and each tributary bringing with it the collected bits and pieces from the past, from the distant, from the countless Elsewheres: all of it moving, mingled, in the current.

For me, the tributaries are memories, and I've selected only a few. I'll tell them to you chronologically. I have to go way back. I'm starting forty-six years ago.

In 1948, I am eleven years old. I have gone with my mother, sister, and brother to join my father, who has been in Tokyo for two years and will be there for several more.

We live there, in the center of that huge Japanese city, in a small American enclave with a very American name: Washington Heights. We live in an American-style house, with American neighbors, and our little community has its own movie theater, which shows American movies; and a small church, a tiny library, and an elementary school; and in many ways it is an odd replica of a United States village.

(In later, adult years I was to ask my mother why we had lived there instead of taking advantage of the opportunity to live within the Japanese community and to learn and experience a different way of life. But she seemed surprised by my question. She said that we lived where we did because it was comfortable. It was familiar. It was safe.)

At eleven years old I am not a particularly adventurous child, nor am I a rebellious one. But I have always been curious.

I have a bicycle. Again and again—countless times—without my parents' knowledge, I ride my bicycle out the back gate of the fence that surrounds our comfortable, familiar, safe American community. I ride down a hill because I am curious, and I enter, riding down that hill, an unfamiliar, slightly uncomfortable, perhaps even unsafe—though I never feel it to be—area of Tokyo that throbs with life.

It is a district called Shibuya. It is crowded with shops and people and theaters and street vendors and the day-to-day bustle of Japanese life.

I remember, still, after all these years, the smells: fish and fertilizer and charcoal; the sounds: music and shouting and the clatter of wooden shoes and wooden sticks and wooden wheels; and the colors: I remember the babies and toddlers dressed in bright pink and orange and red, most of all; but I remember, too, the dark blue uniforms of the schoolchildren: the strangers who are my own age.

I wander through Shibuya day after day during those years when I am eleven, twelve, and thirteen. I love the feel of it, the vigor and the garish brightness and the noise: all such a contrast to my own life.

But I never talk to anyone. I am not frightened of the people, who are so different from me, but I am shy. I watch the children shouting and playing around a school, and they are children my age, and they watch me in return; but we never speak to one another.

One afternoon I am standing on a street corner when a woman near me reaches out, touches my hair, and says something. I back away, startled, because my knowledge of the language is poor and I misunderstand her words. I think she has said "Kirai-des," meaning that she dislikes me; and I am embarrassed, and confused, wondering what I have done wrong: how I have disgraced myself.

Then, after a moment, I realize my mistake. She has said, actually, "Kirei-des." She has called me pretty. And I look for her, in the crowd, at least to smile, perhaps to say thank you if I can overcome my shyness enough to speak. But she is gone.

I remember this moment—this instant of communication gone awry—again and again over the years. Perhaps this is where the river starts.

In 1954 and 1955 I am a college freshman, living in a very small dormitory, actually a converted private home, with a group of perhaps fourteen other girls. We are very much alike. We wear the same sort of clothes: cashmere sweaters and plaid wool skirts, knee socks and loafers. We all smoke Marlboro cigarettes and we knit—usually argyle socks for our boyfriends—and play bridge. Sometimes we study; and we get good grades because we are all the cream of the crop, the valedictorians and class presidents from our high schools all over the United States.

One of the girls in our dorm is not like the rest of us. She doesn't wear our uniform. She wears blue jeans instead of skirts, and she doesn't curl her hair or knit or play bridge. She doesn't date or go to fraternity parties and dances.

She's a smart girl, a good student, a pleasant enough person, but she is different, somehow alien, and that makes us uncomfortable. We react with a kind of mindless cruelty. We don't tease or torment her, but we do something worse: we ignore her. We pretend that she doesn't exist. In a small house of fourteen young women, we make one invisible.

Somehow, by shutting her out, we make ourselves feel comfortable. Familiar. Safe.

I think of her now and then as the years pass. Those thoughts—fleeting, but profoundly remorseful—enter the current of the river.

In the summer of 1979, I am sent by a magazine I am working for to an island off the coast of Maine to write an article about a painter who lives there alone. I spend a good deal of time with this man, and we talk a lot about color. It is clear to me that although I am a highly visual person—a person who sees and appreciates form and composition and color—this man's capacity for seeing color goes far beyond mine.

I photograph him while I am there, and I keep a copy of his photograph for myself because there is something about his face—his eyes—which haunts me.

Later I hear that he has become blind.

I think about him—his name is Carl Nelson—from time to time. His photograph hangs over my desk. I wonder what it was like for him to lose the colors about which he was so impassioned.

I wish, in a whimsical way, that he could have somehow magically given me the capacity to see the way he did.

A little bubble begins, a little spurt, which will trickle into the river.

In 1989 I go to a small village in Germany to attend the wedding of one of my sons. In an ancient church, he marries his Margret in a ceremony conducted in a language I do not speak and cannot understand.

But one section of the service is in English. A woman stands in the balcony of that old stone church and sings the words from the Bible: "Where you go, I will go. Your people will be my people."

How small the world has become, I think, looking around the church at the many people who sit there wishing happiness to my son and his new wife, wishing it in their own language as I am wishing it in mine. We are all each other's people now, I find myself thinking.

Can you feel that this memory is a stream that is now entering the river?

Another fragment. My father, nearing ninety, is in a nursing home. My brother and I have hung family pictures on the walls of his room. During a visit, he and I are talking about the people in the pictures. One is my sister, my parents' first child, who died young of cancer. My father smiles, looking at her picture. "That's your sister," he says happily. "That's Helen."

Then he comments, a little puzzled, but not at all sad, "I can't remember exactly what happened to her."

We can forget pain, I thought. And it is comfortable to do so.

But I also wonder briefly: Is it safe to do that, to forget?

That uncertainty pours itself into the river of thought which will become the book.

1991. I am in an auditorium somewhere. I have spoken at length about my book, *Number the Stars*, which has been honored with the

1990 Newbery Medal. A woman raises her hand. When the turn for her question comes, she sighs very loudly, and says, "Why do we have to tell this Holocaust thing over and over? Is it really necessary?"

I answer her as well as I can, quoting, in fact, my German daughter-in-law, who has said to me, "No one knows better than we Germans that we must tell this again and again."

But I think about her question—and my answer—a great deal. Wouldn't it, I think, playing devil's advocate to myself, make for a more comfortable world to forget the Holocaust? And I remember once again how comfortable, familiar, and safe my parents had sought to make my childhood by shielding me from Elsewhere. But I remember, too, that my response had been to open the gate again and again. My instinct had been a child's attempt to see for myself what lay beyond the wall.

The thinking becomes another tributary into the river of thought that will create *The Giver*.

Here's another memory. I am sitting in a booth with my daughter in a little Beacon Hill pub where she and I often have lunch together. The television is on in the background, behind the bar, as it always is. She and I are talking. Suddenly I gesture to her. I say "Shhh" because I have heard a fragment of the news and I am startled, anxious, and want to hear the rest. Someone has walked into a fast-food place with an automatic weapon and randomly killed a number of people. My daughter stops talking and waits while I listen to the rest.

Then I relax. I say to her, in a relieved voice, "It's all right. It was in Oklahoma." (Or perhaps it was Alabama. Or Indiana.)

She stares at me in amazement that I have said such a hideous thing.

How comfortable I made myself feel for a moment, by reducing my own realm of caring to my own familiar neighborhood. How safe I deluded myself into feeling.

I think about that, and it becomes a torrent that enters the flow of a river turbulent by now, and clogged with memories and thoughts and ideas that begin to mesh and intertwine. The river begins to seek a place to spill over.

When Jonas meets the Giver for the first time, and tries to comprehend what lies before him, he says, in confusion, "I thought there was only us. I thought there was only now."

In beginning to write *The Giver*, I created, as I always do, in every book, a world that existed only in my imagination—the world of "only us, only now." I tried to make Jonas's world seem familiar, comfortable, and safe, and I tried to seduce the reader. I seduced myself along the way. It did feel good, that world. I got rid of all the things I fear and dislike: all the violence, prejudice, poverty, and injustice; and I even threw in good manners as a way of life because I liked the idea of it.

One child has pointed out, in a letter, that the people in Jonas's world didn't even have to do dishes.

It was very, very tempting to leave it at that.

But I've never been a writer of fairy tales. And if I've learned anything through that river of memories, it is that we can't live in a walled world, in an "only us, only now" world, where we are all the same and feel safe. We would have to sacrifice too much. The richness of color would disappear. Feelings for other humans would no longer be necessary. Choices would be obsolete.

And besides, I had ridden my bike Elsewhere as a child, and liked it there, but had never been brave enough to tell anyone about it. So it was time.

A letter that I've kept for a very long time is from a child who has read my book called *Anastasia Krupnik*. Her letter—she's a little girl named Paula from Louisville, Kentucky—says:

> I really like the book you wrote about Anastasia and her family because it made me laugh every time I read it. I especially liked when it said she didn't want to have a baby brother in the house because she had to clean up after him every time and change his diaper when her mother and father aren't home and she doesn't like to give him a bath and watch him all the time and put him to sleep every night while her mother goes to work . . .

Here's the fascinating thing: nothing that the child describes actually happens in the book. The child—as we all do—has brought her own life to a book. She has found a place, a place in the pages of a book, that shares her own frustrations and feelings.

And the same thing is happening—as I hoped it would happen—with *The Giver*.

Those of you who hoped that I would stand here tonight and reveal the "true" ending, the "right" interpretation of the ending, will be disappointed. There isn't one. There's a right one for each of us, and it depends on our own beliefs, our own hopes.

Let me tell you a few endings which are the right endings for a few children out of the many who have written to me.

From a sixth grader: "I think that when they were traveling they were traveling in a circle. When they came to 'Elsewhere' it was their old community, but they had accepted the memories and all the feelings that go along with it."

From another: "Jonas was kind of like Jesus because he took the pain for everyone else in the community so they wouldn't have to suffer. And, at the very end of the book, when Jonas and Gabe reached the place that they knew as Elsewhere, you described Elsewhere as if it were Heaven."

And one more: "A lot of people I know would hate that ending, but not me. I loved it. Mainly because I got to make the book happy. I decided they made it. They made it to the past. I decided the past was our world, and the future was their world. It was parallel worlds."

Finally, from one seventh-grade boy: "I was really surprised that they just died at the end. That was a bummer. You could of [sic] made them stay alive, I thought."

Very few find it a bummer. Most of the young readers who have written to me have perceived the magic of the circular journey. The truth that we go out and come back, and that what we come back to is changed, and so are we. Perhaps I have been traveling in a circle, too. Things come together and become complete.

Here is what I've come back to:

The daughter who was with me and looked at me in horror the day I fell victim to thinking we were "only us, only now" (and that what happened in Oklahoma, or Alabama, or Indiana didn't matter) was the first person to read the manuscript of *The Giver*.

The college classmate who was "different" lives, last I heard, very happily in New Jersey with another woman who shares her life. I can only hope that she has forgiven those of us who were young in a more frightened and less enlightened time.

My son, and Margret, his German wife—the one who reminded me how important it is to tell our stories again and again, painful though they often are—now have a little girl who will be the receiver of all of their memories. Their daughter had crossed the Atlantic three times before she was six months old. Presumably my granddaughter will never be fearful of Elsewhere.

Carl Nelson, the man who lost colors but not the memory of them, is the face on the cover of the book. He died in 1989 but left a vibrant legacy of paintings. One hangs now in my home.

And I am especially happy to stand here tonight on this platform with Allen Say because it truly brings my journey full circle. Allen was twelve years old when I was. He lived in Shibuya, that alien Elsewhere that I went to as a child on a bicycle. He was one of the Other, the Different, the dark-eyed children in blue school uniforms, and I was too timid then to do more than stand at the edge of their schoolyard, smile shyly, and wonder what their lives were like.

Now I can say to Allen what I wish I could have said then: "Watashi-no tomodachi desi." Greetings, my friend.

I have been asked whether the Newbery Medal is, actually, an odd sort of burden in terms of the greater responsibility one feels. Whether one is paralyzed by it, fearful of being able to live up to the standards it represents.

For me the opposite has been true. I think the 1990 Newbery freed me to risk failure.

Other people took that risk with me, of course. One was my editor, Walter Lorraine, who has never to my knowledge been afraid to take a chance. Walter cares more about what a book has to say than he does about whether he can turn it into a stuffed animal or a calendar or a movie.

The Newbery committee was gutsy, too. There would have been safer books. More comfortable books. More familiar books. They took a trip beyond the realm of sameness, with this one, and I think they should be very proud of that.

And all of you, as well. Let me say something to those of you here who do such dangerous work.

The man that I named the Giver passed along to the boy knowledge, history, memories, color, pain, laughter, love, and truth. Every time you place a book in the hands of a child, you do the same thing.

It is very risky.

But each time a child opens a book, he pushes open the gate that separates him from Elsewhere. It gives him choices. It gives him freedom.

Those are magnificent, wonderfully unsafe things.

I have been greatly honored by you now, two times. It is impossible to express my gratitude for that. Perhaps the only way, really, is to return to Boston, to my office, to my desk, and to go back to work in hopes that whatever I do next will justify the faith in me that this medal represents.

There are other rivers flowing.

Lois Lowry
Walter Lorraine

Lois Lowry

I first met Lois in a short story many years ago. As I recall, it was about a young girl who goes to the big city alone for the first time. She buys what she has been led to believe is a magic box. In a few simple but immensely effective passages, the reader learns that life is not as nice as it seems, that reality can disillusion the strongest faith. Yet an impression is left, whatever the harshness of reality, that it's good to believe in magic. The writing had many levels. Here obviously was a writer, but, more important, a writer who really had something to say.

At least that is how I interpreted the story. Other readers likely came away with different impressions. There is a quality in Lois's writing that encourages this. She invites each reader to bring his or her personal experience to the story. In one sense her writing becomes more complete with the reader's participation—a true Gestalt in which the whole is greater than the sum of its parts. Often provocative contradictions result, sometimes to the extent that the protagonist dies or lives happily ever, each reader being convinced of a different interpretation.

Lois's writing is always accessible to a very broad audience. Young readers can accept most complicated concepts as long as they do not need adult experience to understand them. A successful poet that I once knew used references to Greek mythology to make his points about love and hate. Such writing is accessible to those people who know Greek mythology. On the other hand, love and hate can be expressed without those Greeks. The references in Lois's work are simple to understand, yet she is able to organize them to express most important concepts whether the work is as humorous as *Anastasia Krupnik*—or as serious as *Autumn Street*.

I do confess my memory is faulty. Age and the stress of publishing have killed off too many brain cells. Lois may remember the story in a different way. She prides herself on her memory, but she is nice about it. I never remember her birthday. She always remembers mine. I trust she will forgive me if I've done her story any injustice.

Lois is a naturally forgiving person. I have never known her to be judgmental in any of our dealings. She accepts all people and attitudes as being necessary to life, and harbors no deep or hidden prejudices. I have never heard her badmouth a person. Whatever someone's action, or problems, she remains open and responsive. She sees reason and good in most human activity. For her, the glass is always half full. She listens, not superficially, as most of us do, but with attention. She makes you feel important, that she is involved and not merely a casual bystander. She truly hears what you have to say. Whatever the gripe or sad story, whether from a privileged ten-year-old or a poor aging vagrant, Lois listens.

Early in her career, when she lived in Maine, we exchanged voluminous correspondence. Or perhaps more accurately, Lois wrote many entertaining letters to my occasional lumbering note. There was a sound to those letters, a rhythm that made them comfortable to the eye and mind. All of her writing has that quality. There is a meter to the relationship of the words which makes it uniquely accessible. With many writers, it takes the reader, at least a clumsy reader like me, half a chapter or so before he becomes comfortable with the style. I'd say half a book for Conrad. With Lois one sentence draws you immediately into the world of the story. There is an instinctive feel for the way all those word sounds are woven into a rhythmic whole.

Lois has friends everywhere. Certainly I am her friend. But, perhaps more important, I feel that she is my friend. I can depend on her. She would be there to help if I needed her, whatever the issues involved, no questions asked. She has put up with some very silly attitudes and never judged me harshly for them. I'm sure that others who know Lois feel as I do.

Any exchange I have with Lois is exciting and stimulating. Afterward, my burdens seem less, and I have renewed energy for life and the world around me. Some people drain energy from society. I'm sure you know the type. Lois feeds energy in rather than taking it out. The world needs more like her. But please do not let me mislead you. With all of these virtues, Lois is far from a Pollyanna or yes man. She has strong opinions. We don't always agree. On occasion we argue. But we argue nicely, I think. She can poke fun as she did one time in her Newbery acceptance speech for *Number the Stars*, mentioning my alleged reference to the Nazi's boots. One of my favorite exchanges with Lois occurred some years back. We were in a particularly heated discussion when, for one of the few times I remember, she became somewhat impatient. She turned, looked me dead in the eye, and said firmly, "Lorraine, you live in a—comic book." I've thought about the profound substance of that seemingly simple comment often since that time.

Her first book, *A Summer to Die*, was given an award by the International Reading Association. I believe it was one of the very first awards that they sponsored. That year I attended their national convention with Lois. I was quite worried. How would a new author with little to no experience perform? My palms got sweaty when I thought of her giving an acceptance speech. How would she handle the pressure? How would she respond to a live audience? Of course, I nervously gave her all sorts of helpful hints and advice on what to say and how to say it. Editors, after all, are supposed to reassure authors. As always, Lois listened attentively, looked puzzled for a moment, and proceeded to pat me on the hand with a "there, there, don't worry, everything will turn out all right." And of course she was right. That day, I believe, Lois became more the editor and I the insecure fellow in dire need of guidance. It has been so ever since.

Years ago I overlapped with her on a speaking engagement in Moscow, Idaho. I had never heard of the place, but Lois graciously invited me to dinner at the home of a friend of hers. I think there must be at least one Lois Lowry friend in every nook and cranny of the United States. I should not leave out Australia, Germany—the list might be endless. In typical Lois Lowry fashion, she was on a boat in the Weddell Sea when this year's Newbery Award was decided. Can't you just see those penguins with a copy of *Anastasia Krupnik* under their flippers?

Lois is a risk taker and a just plain good guy in an often cynical world. She has always taken chances. *Rabble Starkey* and *Autumn Street* are powerful and individual statements. The Anastasia stories are very funny, but woven into that humor is far more worldly insight than is usual for such popular fiction. In an age of conformity Lois is a unique and important voice. She is an author who truly has something to say and is willing to risk saying it. Which is Lois's best book? Certainly *The Giver* is an exceptional book. Still, I am absolutely convinced that Lois's best book is yet to come. I am looking forward to it.

The Caldecott Medal 1995

Smoky Night

written by
Eve Bunting

illustrated by
David Diaz

published by
Harcourt, 1994

Horn Book Review

Daniel's mother explains that the rioting in the street outside their apartment "can happen when people get angry." The aberrant behavior of the people who are smashing windows, cars, and street lights and the looters who look angry and happy at the same time fascinate Daniel. When the smell of smoke wakens the two of them during the night, they flee to a shelter with other residents of their building. Daniel is frantic because he cannot locate his cat, Jasmine. Mrs. Kim's mean orange cat, who always fights with Jasmine, is missing, too. Daniel and his mother don't have too much to do with Mrs. Kim and do not shop at Kim's Market because "Mama says it's better if we buy from our own people." Eventually, a firefighter appears at the shelter with one cat under each arm, claiming to have discovered the cats "holding paws" under the stairs of the burning building. When the cats drink from the same dish, Daniel observes that the animals might not have previously liked each other because they didn't know each other. Silence follows Daniel's innocent comment, until his mother introduces herself to Mrs. Kim: "My name is Gena. Perhaps when things settle down you and your cat will come over and share a dish of milk with us." Clearly, the African-American woman's attempt to reach out to the Korean-American woman is a result of surviving the riots together and understanding the commonality of their lives. Although the CIP page mentions that these events took place during the recent Los Angeles riots, young readers may need some additional explanation, since the setting is not mentioned anywhere in the book. Diaz's bold artwork is a perfect match for the intensity of the story. Thick black lines border vibrant acrylic paintings that are reminiscent of Picasso's early work, especially in the composition of the characters' faces. Diaz's work also evokes images of the French impressionist Georges Rouault and of the early books of John Steptoe, both of whom used black to outline individual elements in their paintings. Diaz places these dynamic paintings on collages of real objects that, for the most part, reinforce the narrative action. For example, a painting of Daniel observing someone looting a dry cleaners is superimposed on a collage composed of wire hangers and clothes wrapped in clear plastic. Because each double-page spread is so carefully designed, because the pictorial elements work together harmoniously, the overall effect is that of urban energy, rather than cacophony. Both author and illustrator insist on a headlong confrontation with the issue of rapport between different races, and the result is a memorable, thought-provoking book.—*Ellen Fader*

Booklist Review

Bunting says she wrote this story after the Los Angeles riots made her wonder about what riots mean to the children who live through them. A boy and his cat look down from the window at people rioting in the streets below. His mother explains that rioting can happen when people get angry: "They want to smash and destroy. They don't care anymore what's right and wrong." The boy says that they look angry, but they look happy, too. He sees them looting Mrs. Kim's grocery store across the street; his mother never shopped there. That night, the apartment building burns, and everyone has to rush out to the shelter. The boy's cat is gone, and so is Mrs. Kim's cat, but a kind firefighter finds both animals; they were hiding together. Then Bunting overstates her message: maybe the people, like the cats, need to get to know each other, so the boy's mother and Mrs. Kim agree to visit. Diaz's art is powerful—pulsating and crowded; part street mural, part urban collage. In each double-page spread, the background is a photograph of found objects and debris in a variety of textures and jagged shapes. On the right-hand page is an acrylic painting like a view through a heavy window, with thick lines and bright neon colors showing a multicultural cast. In fine contrast, the story is told quietly from the child's point of view, safe with his mother despite the fear, reaching out to the neighborhood community within the chaos.—*Hazel Rochman*

1995 Caldecott Acceptance Speech
David Diaz

Superstition runs deep in certain publishing companies. For instance, the word *Caldecott* is taboo. If that word is mentioned with reference to a particular book, it might jinx it. I am so thankful to the people at Harcourt Brace for not uttering "that word" over *Smoky Night*! Because, early one morning this past February, something quite extraordinary happened in my life. I was honored as the recipient of the 1995 Caldecott Medal. Daily I am overwhelmed with joy and gratitude for this prestigious award. My son Jericho, who is twelve, said, "I have always heard of other families being famous, but I never thought it would happen to us!" But my five-year-old son, Ariel, wonders, "How come I didn't get a Caldecott? I draw better than Dad."

I recall 1966, sitting in my first-grade class and receiving a mimeographed work sheet. The class had just come in from squinting into the clear blue Florida sky, trying to pick out a wisp of vapor trail from one of the space launches at Cape Canaveral. On the mimeographed paper there were twelve squares and within each square a drawing. Underneath each drawing was a word that could be completed with a vowel. Near the center of the page were the letters N_SE and above them the profile of a nose. I filled in the blank with the vowel O and afterward drew lines to the nose that made a profile of a face. That was when I first realized I wanted to be a "drawer." I had no idea what an illustrator, designer, or art director was. What I knew was that I had found my gift, drawing pictures.

There were a few things in high school that propelled me toward a career in illustration. One was meeting Cecelia, my wife. After a year of sarcastic banter, we became close friends. The focus of my time in art class became seeing how much I could distract her from her weavings and batiks. But she taught me about color and how to see color. About the colors you can miss if you're not paying attention. Like the color of black licorice when you bite into it—a kind of greenish, brownish, yellow black. At the time, my work was dominated by grays and muted tones. Cecelia opened my eyes to vivid color, and I began to use it.

The second key thing was having a great art instructor, Sandra Tobe. She had a gift for motivating students, and she encouraged us to enter numerous competitions. She showed us that there were jobs out there doing artwork. Money for pictures! Through her I was introduced to Duane Hanson, the hyperrealist sculptor. I apprenticed with him for several years through high school and art school. While working for Duane, I was exposed to a lot of the superrealist movement through his personal collection. I was drawn to the movement, and my work—very tight realistic pieces—reflected it. I labored intensely, sixty to eighty hours, over a drawing six inches square. I drew tiny circles with a razor-sharp pencil to create a rich, gradual tonal quality almost like a photograph. Until, while working on an assignment at 3 a. m., I thought: "Why not just take a photograph? Think of all the time it would save." Determined to find another approach to drawing, I began to experiment with a variety of techniques. A turning point finally came when I saw the German expressionist show at the Guggenheim in 1980. I saw beautiful work that conveyed the emotion of the artists with immediate, direct line—bold, simple, loose brush strokes.

Another influence on my development as an artist was the work of William Steig. I found a copy of his book *Male and Female* in a used bookstore. I was immediately drawn in by the depth of characterization he conveyed in so few lines. I sought out other Steig books. As I became more acquainted with his drawings, I saw an evolution in his work that I recognized, as he moved from tightly rendered pieces toward a looser line.

In 1979 when I arrived in San Diego, I began to show my portfolio and to receive editorial assignments. Although the pay was low, these assignments allowed me a lot of room for experimentation. I had the freedom to work in a variety of mediums: oils, acrylics, pen and ink, watercolor, woodcuts, scratchboard—as many as I could find. Typically at the end of an assignment there would be some materials left over. I would take those and make a small piece as a "thank you" for the art director who had given me the job. I'd send it along with the completed work. The response to these pieces was very positive, and I realized I'd hit upon a very effective way of promoting my work. These personal gift pieces allowed me to find my own direction in drawing and to become comfortable with the way I drew naturally. And, of course, the ideas I worked out in these personal pieces found their way into the work I did for assignments.

These gift pieces eventually evolved into limited edition books that Cecelia and I collaborated in producing at the end of the year.

There is nothing like receiving a piece made by hand. Part of the ethic of the arts and crafts movement was the idea that as you were surrounded by pieces made by hand, your life would be enriched. Furniture, ceramics, textiles, and books all bore the mark of the craftsman's hand. These "touch of the hand" pieces were a format for my personal work and sometimes resulted in assignments specifically requesting a new style.

The distinction between work for assignments and personal work narrowed. In 1989 I began to experiment with a series of bold, loose, brush stroke faces. My goal was to create an image without hesitation, lifting the brush from the surface as few times as possible. I believed that once I hesitated with the brush stroke, I'd pause to question what I was doing rather than complete the piece in one stream of thought. I wanted to put down on paper exactly what I had imagined. I experimented with this style for about three years. In 1992 while visiting my brother in Brazil, I worked on a series of faces as we traveled down the Amazon River. That series was incorporated into our year-end book *Sweet Peas*. We combined the faces with text and with objects found and made. For example, we bound in one spread a latex glove, in another a postcard from the 1930s. One page was a piece of waxed paper. During that year Diane D'Andrade at Harcourt Brace contacted me to illustrate *Neighborhood Odes* by Gary Soto. I stopped by Harcourt's office to give her a copy of *Sweet Peas*. When she saw it she said, "I have a manuscript I haven't known who to assign to! Seeing what you've done here, I'd like you to take a look at it." Of course, that manuscript was *Smoky Night*. I saw its possibilities right away. Eve Bunting had taken a timely subject and had handled it in a truly sensitive and thoughtful way. I felt the book could have a positive effect and help erode barriers of prejudice and intolerance. And above all, it was a book that could be a part of the post-riot healing process.

I wanted to do *Smoky Night*. And I wanted the art to have the same dignity as the manuscript. Although I had done hundreds of faces and images in this style, I was challenged by the job of carrying out character continuity through the book. I wanted *Smoky Night* to achieve a balance between the text, the design, the painted illustrations, and the collaged backgrounds. I wanted each element to add to the book and to create a cohesive unit.

One important decision I made was to use the same color palette for all the characters in the story. I did this to avoid any indication of ethnic background, and to let their personalities speak for themselves.

I would like to thank the members of the Caldecott committee for selecting and awarding *Smoky Night* the Caldecott Medal.

I want to thank Eve Bunting for her wonderful manuscript.

At Harcourt Brace, I'd like to thank Rubin Pfeffer, who, when he had reviewed the f&gs for *Smoky Night*, called me to say, "*Smoky Night* is a book that raises the level of what a children's picture book can be"; Louise Howton, for the freedom to design and create *Smoky Night*; Diane D'Andrade, my editor, who had the vision and insight into my work to give me *Smoky Night* to illustrate.

William Steig, for pointing the way.

And most of all, my sweet wife, Cecelia, who always believed and knew what could be.

David Diaz

Cecelia Diaz

David Diaz

High school, eleventh grade, Miss Sullivan's ceramic class. He sits across from me. I'm intrigued by the goatee, the drawstring pants, the clogs, the waft of musk. He's private, soft-spoken, not a jock bone in his body. Angling for his attention, I set up a daily sarcasm session, but I only confuse him. He is sure that I really don't like him. But how else do you get an attractive man's attention when his girlfriend is sitting next to him? That is how we met.

Twelfth grade, senior art class. I'm working on a weaving. Even though he never works on his assignments in class, David manages to win an art scholarship. He leaves a note squeezed through the door handle of my car. It's a photograph he had taken of me with an excerpt from *The Little Prince*: "In one of the stars I shall be living. In one of them I shall be laughing. And so it will be as if all the stars were laughing, when you look at the sky at night . . . . You—only you—will have stars that can laugh!"

David must have known, even then, that I would notice him, that he would win my heart. Now that he has been honored as the 1995 Caldecott Medal winner for *Smoky Night* (Harcourt), he has been noticed by everyone. The day we found out about the award, elated beyond measure, I took him to the children's department of our local library to introduce him to the librarian and show him his place among the stars on the poster of Caldecott winners.

Where did this star come from? National papers describe him as "unknown." How did he do it?

It was a road of small beginnings. In January 1979, we packed our bags and moved from Florida to California. One of David's first jobs was at a Fotomat, in one of those little drive-up booths where you get your film processed. His first illustration job was for a weekly newspaper, the *San Diego Reader.* He received twenty-five dollars. We celebrated the event by taking his picture at the beach as he held up the paper, sporting a hairdo called the savage, a successor to the bowl, which had lasted a long time. We've since recorded his hairdos, in chronological order, at our yearly visit to the Del Mar State Fair. Piling into the photo booth, we sit for our portraits, four for a buck.

Back then we owned a yellow Maverick we called "the Banana." The beauty of this luxury automobile was in the starting procedure. One of us would open the hood and choke the carburetor with a pencil, while the other one would turn the ignition. We never parked in front of a client's office. We lived on peanut butter and honey, tortillas, rice and beans, and salsa. At dusk we would comb the neighborhood for fallen avocados or lemons. Those were the character-building years.

David's persistence in showing his portfolio resulted in numerous editorial and design projects—more than five thousand to date. As the list of clients grew, so did his desire for work outside of the local arena. By promoting his distinctive style through hand-assembled limited edition books, he eventually garnered national attention and many awards. But what really drives David is his love for his family. Art is not something he does; it is who he is. From the love notes or drawings he would leave on my car twenty-one years ago to the ring he designed and had made for me on Valentine's Day to the boxes he creates and paints to house Christmas gifts, he is artistic in all that he does.

The morning we received notice of the Caldecott Medal, we were asleep. I heard the answering machine go on, then a great commotion, a loud voice, and people clapping and cheering. I thought we had won the Publishers Clearing House Sweepstakes! When I played back the message, I yelled, "David, get out of bed! You won't believe this, but you just won the 1995 Caldecott Medal!" We jumped up and down the hallway till we woke up the kids.

Excited would be an understatement. But what David said to me I will never forget: "Cece, now I'm really going to take care of you." That is the sweet man I married: It is not for the glory (though he is basking in it) but because of his love for his family—me, Jericho, Atiel, and Gabrielle—that he enjoys this moment of fame. We love you, David; you will always be our star.

The Newbery Medal 1995

Walk Two Moons

written by
Sharon Creech

published by
HarperCollins, 1994

Horn Book Review

While traveling to Idaho with her eccentric grandparents to visit her mother, who left the year before and has never returned, thirteen-year-old Salamanca Hiddle tells them about her new friend, Phoebe Winterbottom, whose mother also left without explanation. Although occasionally contrived, the novel movingly portrays a young girl's struggle to resign herself to life without her mother.—*Ann E. Deifendeifer*

Booklist Review

Thirteen-year-old Sal Hiddle can't deal with all the upheaval in her life. Her mother, Sugar, is in Idaho, and although Sugar promised to return before the tulips bloomed, she hasn't come back. Instead, Mr. Hiddle has moved Sal from the farm she loves so much and has even taken up company with the unpleasantly named Mrs. Cadaver. Multilayered, the book tells the story of Sal's trip to Idaho with her grandparents; and as the car clatters along, Sal tells her grandparents the story of her friend Phoebe, who receives messages from a "lunatic" and who must cope with the disappearance of her mother. The novel is ambitious and successful on many fronts: the characters, even the adults, are fully realized; the story certainly keeps readers' interest; and the pacing is good throughout. But Creech's surprises—that Phoebe's mother has an illegitimate son and that Sugar is buried in Idaho, where she died after a bus accident—are obvious in the first case and contrived in the second. Sal knows her mother is dead; that Creech makes readers think otherwise seems a cheat, though one, it must be admitted, that may bother adults more than kids. Still, when Sal's on the road with her grandparents, spinning Phoebe's yarn and trying to untangle her own, this story sings.—*Ilene Cooper*

1995 Newbery Acceptance Speech

Sharon Creech

Most of you are probably familiar with the Newbery traditions: the secret choice, the phone call, the *Today* show summons, and the frenzy which follows. I have lived overseas for sixteen years and was not aware of these traditions. All I knew was that the Newbery Medal was the most honored of blessings.

On February 6, I was home alone in England and had been wrestling all morning with a manuscript. Feeling ornery and frustrated, I fled to our backyard to vent one of my muffled screams (muffled because I am a headmaster's wife and it isn't seemly for me to scream too loudly). In the midst of that scream, the phone rang.

A ringing phone in a headmaster's house often signals a crisis, and when it rings, I'm well trained: I grab pencil and paper, ready to record the name of the student with appendicitis or the name of the dormitory whose pipes have burst. That afternoon, I scribbled American Library Association and Newbery Med . . . The writing trails off there.

I still go weak when I think of that call coming so unexpectedly, jolting my world so intensely. My first reaction was disbelief, followed by overwhelming gratitude. I felt as if the eye of God had beamed down on me, and I'd better do everything I was told. In the days that followed, whenever the phone rang—and it rang constantly—I stared at it suspiciously, expecting that this caller would say, "Oops, sorry! We made a mistake. It wasn't your book . . ."

I had a lot of difficulty coming to grips with why I was receiving such good fortune, and why my book was receiving such an honor. I'll be honest: I never dreamed a dream this big.

When I first read articles referring to me as an "unknown," I was amused. It made me feel peculiar, as if I'd previously been invisible. But the articles were accurate: I was virtually unknown in the field of children's books in the States. An unknown has simple prayers: please let my books be published; please let readers know these books exist; please let me keep writing. What the Newbery does is answer all of these prayers. It calls attention not only to my books, but to other new books as well. It celebrates children's literature. What a grand thing this Newbery is!

Several days after the Newbery call, I returned to the manuscript I'd been working on that extraordinary day, and I reread this opening paragraph:

"Life is like a bowl of spaghetti . . ." That's what my grandmother used to say, and I'd imagine myself rummaging among twisted strands of pasta. But there was more to her saying: Life is like a bowl of spaghetti: every now and then you get a meatball. It seemed to me that the meatball was a tremendous bonus you might unearth in all those convoluted spaghetti turns of your life. It was something to look forward to, a reward for all that slogging through your pasta.

On February 6, I received news of one glorious meatball in my plate of spaghetti, and no one on this earth could be more grateful than I am to receive it tonight. Thank you.

I'm grateful to many people for the birth of *Walk Two Moons*, and some of these include:

My husband, children, and larger family, who provided inspiration for many of the characters in this book.

Five editors, each of whom left his or her mark, as they came and went during the three years it took to polish *Walk Two Moons*: in England, Marion Lloyd, Lynette Wilson, and Isabel Barratt; and in the States, David Gale and Nancy Siscoe.

I would also like to thank Bill Morris, Virginia Anagnos, Alicia Mikles, Lisa Desimini, George Nicholson, and everyone at HarperCollins who contributed to *Walk Two Moons* or who aided me these past months.

My agents, Carol Smith and Jonathan Dolger.

My gratitude also extends to that wild and crazy Highlights' group at Chautauqua in 1988, who convinced me that writing for children was a most worthy and noble pursuit.

As for the American Library Association and the Newbery committee, I don't know if I'll ever be able to convey to you how much this award means to me. With one phone call from Philadelphia to London on February 6, you dramatically altered my plate of spaghetti.

And now to writing and the evolution of this book . . . I have to begin on a serious note, because it was a serious jolt that led me to all these words.

In 1980, when my children and I had been in England for nine months, my father had a stroke. Although he lived for six more years, the stroke left him paralyzed and unable to speak. Think of all the words we wanted to say to him, and all the words he must have wanted to say to us. Think of all those words locked up for six years, because his mind could neither accept nor deliver words.

A month after he died in 1986, I started my first novel, and when I finished it, I wrote another, and another, and another. The words rushed out. The connection between my father's death and my flood of writing might be that I had been confronted with the dark wall of mortality—we don't have endless time to follow our dreams—but it might also be that I felt obligated to use the words that my father could not.

How does a book begin? Here I would like to tell you something that my mother related to me in a phone call last year. She'd awakened suddenly in the night, to a voice commanding her to dash something to the floor. She grabbed the nearest thing at hand—the television's remote control—which she dutifully dashed to the floor. But no, that did not satisfy the voice. Next she grabbed the lamp and dashed it to the floor. There. That was it. The voice was quiet.

"Mom—" I said. "Did the lamp break?"

"Yes," she said. "It did." She did not seem troubled by the broken lamp, nor did she wonder why it was a lamp that needed to be dashed to the floor in the first place. Instead, she seemed relieved that she had accommodated the voice.

This is similar to how I begin a book—with a voice commanding me to dash something not to the floor, but onto paper, and I dutifully snatch any words or characters which appear. Only after the book is completed can I begin to identify some of the seeds from which these seemingly arbitrary characters and situations come, but I am reluctant to dig too deeply, and to explain why, I need to tell you about the talcum powder.

I once owned a bottle of Chanel talcum powder which I used daily. Oddly, the contents never seemed to diminish. Would the container never be empty? Did it refill and replenish itself? It was a mystery which I enjoyed. But I also feared that someone would come along and explain exactly why it was that it never seemed to empty, just as someone once explained—to my horror—that dreams are merely little chemicals sloshing around randomly in your brain at night. The truth is: I don't want to know the explanations for the mysteries of dreams or of a replenishing bottle of talcum. Like Salamanca, who needs to believe a tree is singing or that the spirit of someone she loves inhabits that tree, it is the mystery I need. And although I can—and will—tell you some of the sources for *Walk Two Moons*, I hope to leave some of it a mystery—even to myself.

Four years ago, after I'd already written two very different versions of this book—versions which did not include Salamanca or the

Hiddles—I received this message in a fortune cookie at a Chinese restaurant in Surrey: "Don't judge a man until you've walked two moons in his moccasins." Beneath this saying was the note "American Indian proverb."

This seemed a curious thing to receive in a Chinese restaurant in England. At the time, I would have preferred a more traditional fortune—perhaps one like Patricia MacLachlan once received proclaiming, "Your talents will soon be recognized,"[1] or the one Lois Lowry received, forecasting that she would "become rich and famous in a far-out profession."[2] Still, I was intrigued by the American Indian proverb with its suggestion of a journey and the resonance of that single word moccasins.

My cousins maintain that one of our ancestors was an American Indian. As a child, I loved that notion, and often exaggerated it by telling people that I was a full-blooded Indian. I inhaled Indian myths, and among my favorites were those which involved stories of reincarnation. How magnificent and mysterious to be Estsanatlehi, the "woman who never dies. She grows from baby to mother to old woman and then turns into a baby again, and on and on she goes, living a thousand, thousand lives."[3] I wanted to be that Navajo woman. I wanted to live a thousand, thousand lives. I crept through the woods near our house, reenacting these myths, and wishing, wishing, for a pair of soft leather moccasins. (I admit—but without apology—that my view of the American Indians was a romantic one.)

I also climbed trees. I think I spent half my childhood up a tree, for I had somehow got it in my mind that Indians climbed trees. And there in those trees—oh! You could climb and climb, and you could reach a place where there was only you and the tree and the birds and the sky. It was a place where the sky was wide and something in you—which was larger than you—was alive. And maybe the appeal of trees also lay in the sense that they live a thousand, thousand lives, appearing to die each autumn, and then—miraculously—be reborn in all their glory each spring.

During the summer of my twelfth birthday, my family took a car trip from Ohio to Lewiston, Idaho. What a journey! What a country! What spectacular and unexpected sights reared up around each bend! Midway through this journey—and because it was my birthday, I can tell you the exact date, July 29, 1957—we stopped at an Indian reservation, and there I was able to choose a precious gift: a pair of leather moccasins.

On the final day of our outward-bound journey, we crested Lewiston Hill and stared down at the road which switchbacked all the long way down into Lewiston, nestled at the bottom alongside the Snake River. And all the way down that hill, I prayed, for I feared that we would never make it to our destination alive.

Those of you who have read *Walk Two Moons* will recognize similarities between Sal's journey and my own. The significance of my journey in 1957 is that I remember it not only as a literal and physical journey across America, but also as a metaphorical journey: it was a time when I was enriched and inspired by our vast country and all the various people who populate it. There was a larger, lush and complex world outside my own.

The proverb in my fortune cookie revived that trip for me and restored the girl who wanted to be an Indian. I don't see Salamanca as a Native American; I see her as an American, who, like me, has inherited several cultures, and who tries to sort out who she is by embracing the mystery of one strand of that heritage. Salamanca needs those stories of reincarnation; they give her hope.

The portion of the proverb which became the title appealed to me on another level as well. In *Walk Two Moons*, I saw an invitation, from characters to writer, and from writer to reader: come along and walk with us awhile, slip into our moccasins so that you might see what we think and feel, and so that you might understand why we do what we do, and so that you might glimpse the larger world outside your own. You could live a thousand, thousand lives! Every book implicitly offers this invitation, and every book offers a journey, whether it is a literal one, a metaphorical one, or both.

Mysteries appeared as I wrote—the singing tree, the marriage bed, the characters themselves. In the afternoons, when I reread what I'd written in the morning, I didn't have the vaguest idea how some of these things got on the page.

It is nearly three years since *Walk Two Moons* was completed, and now I look at it with a different eye. I can see that Salamanca is me and my daughter. I can see that Gramps and the good-man-father combine elements of all the good men in my family, and that Gram is what you might get if you took all the women in my family and rolled them into a ball. I'd better add that we are not perfect people. If you spent some time with us, you'd see that sometimes we drive each other crazy, and we would probably drive you crazy, too. As one of my brothers once said, referring to our annual family reunion at Chautauqua, "It's a zoo, but it feels good in the heart."

And I know where the singing tree came from. On our school campus, bordering the playing fields, is a magnificent bank of trees. Overhead, clouds drift across a wide expanse of sky. While I was writing *Walk Two Moons*, I'd often escape to this place, where, increasingly, I felt that my father was inhabiting those clouds. It was comforting to think that he was always nearby (for there are always clouds in an English sky); he was watching over me. One day I heard a magnificent birdsong coming from the top of a tree, and it seemed that the tree itself was singing. Instantly, I had the further sense that my father had leaped from the clouds to the tree.

A few years ago, when my youngest brother and I were sitting on the porch at Chautauqua Lake, I told him about this incident and asked him, "Do you ever have the feeling that Dad is—in the clouds—or in the trees?"

My brother glanced at the clouds and the trees. "Nope," he said. "Can't say that I do."

Ah well. Still: maybe the talcum powder, the clouds, and the singing tree which surfaces in *Walk Two Moons* are related, for they all represent beautiful mysteries, and they all offer hopes of life never-ending.

I can also, I think, retrace the evolution of Gram's spontaneous eruptions of joy ("huzza, huzza!"), though I do so with a bit of worry about the talcum powder—for I'd hate to empty all the mystery. But here's one speculation I can offer . . .

In my study are dozens of pictures of my family, so that everywhere I look, someone is looking back at me. On the bulletin board nearest my desk are two quotes and two of my favorite pictures; these things have something in common. In one photo, my son is standing on an alpine peak, silhouetted against the sky; in a similar one, my daughter is reclining on a different mountain peak. There they are at the top of the world, like me in my trees, where the sky is wide and something in them is alive. You should see the expression on my children's faces. Each has been caught in a moment of supreme joy, and there is something else, too, less definable. I think it might be hope.

One quote tacked nearby is from Ernie Pyle's Second World War correspondence. It reads simply: "The human spirit is just like a cork."[4] I love that line. The second quote is from an autobiographical essay my mother wrote in 1933. She was fifteen years old, it was the middle of the Depression, and her life was not an easy one. But she says, in the middle of this essay, "Whenever I feel especially happy I tap dance." And I love that line, too.

It is hard to picture my mother tapdancing, but I like to think that she has had many moments in her life when she felt so happy that she tap-danced, when her spirits rose like a cork bobbing to the surface. Perhaps Gram's "huzza, huzza" in *Walk Two Moons* grew out of those pictures on my wall, the notion of a spirit rising like a cork, and the image of my mother tapdancing.

When I was writing *Walk Two Moons*, the newspapers and the BBC were filled with images of war and disaster: of bombings, riots, floods, earthquakes, famine, torture. Every day my students stared into Pandora's box, filled with all the evils of the world. Every day there was something difficult to face. Maybe I wrote this book because my students and I, like Salamanca, had stared those horrors in the eye as best we could, and then needed, for a time, to clutch the hope that was down in the bottom of Pandora's box, and with that hope turn to the other box, the one with the mysteries and "smooth beautiful folds" inside. Salamanca and I need to face the evils, but we also need mystery and we need hope. Maybe you do, too.

When I read Salamanca's story now, with some distance, I hear such longing in her voice—for her mother, for her father, for the land— and I know that her longing is also my longing. I know this book was also written because I was living an ocean away, longing for my children, my larger family, and for my own country.

I'm going to close soon, before I empty all the talcum powder out of this book, but I'd like to give it just a few more brief shakes.

Recently I received another "meatball" in the mail. It was not a Newbery Medal sort of meatball. It was a packet of letters written by my father to my aunt during the Second World War, and they, too, are filled with longing—for his wife, for his first child (who was born while he was overseas), and for his country. The miracle of this gift! There is his voice; there are his words! The last line in each of his letters is identical. He says, "Write me often." Fifty years later, maybe that's also part of what I'm doing: writing him often.

The final letter in the stack was not written by him—it was from my mother, telling my aunt that she'd just heard from my father, and that he was on his way home from the war. My mother wrote, "I'm so tickled and happy that I can hardly work. I jumped and squealed for joy last night." Do you hear that cork rising? Do you think she tap-danced?

People have asked me how I feel now, four months after the Newbery call. I'm very emotional about it: I still feel overwhelming gratitude; I still have bouts of disbelief; and I still fear that someone is going to come along and take this meatball away.

Thank you for honoring this book and for making it possible for me to be in these moccasins tonight. If I could sprinkle some hopes over all of you, they would include these: I hope you each find a meatball in the spaghetti of your life; I hope your talcum powder never empties, that your spirit is like a cork, and that you all live a thousand, thousand lives.

And finally:

At the end of the Newbery call, K. T. Horning, the committee chairwoman, said, "We have one last thing we'd like to say to you." What she said is also the last thing I'd like to say to you tonight, and it is the last thing Salamanca Tree Hiddle says in *Walk Two Moons:* "Huzza, Huzza!"

NOTES

1. Patricia MacLachlan, "Newbery Acceptance Speech," *Top of the News* 42, no. 4 (summer 1986): 392.
2. Lois Lowry, "Newbery Acceptance Speech," *Journal of Youth Services in Libraries* 3, no. 4 (summer 1990): 281.
3. Sharon Creech, *Walk Two Moons* (New York: HarperCollins, 1994), 278.
4. David Nichols, ed., *Ernie's War: The Best of Ernie Pyle's World War II Dispatches* (New York: Simon & Schuster, 1986), 249.

Sharon Creech

Lyle D. Rigg

When Sharon and I met sixteen years ago, we were both transplanted Ohioans who had found our ways to Thorpe, Surrey, England. Sharon came to England via Washington, D.C., and I came via Boston and Brazil. I think it was a combination of our Buckeye roots and ice cubes that drew us together. We met on our first day in England, when Sharon borrowed some ice—that rare commodity

Sharon Creech

in Europe—from me. Three years later, we celebrated our wedding with a party on a riverboat floating down the Thames.

If Sharon were not such a skilled writer, we probably would never have met. The headmaster of TASIS England American School who hired me as his assistant headmaster also hired Sharon in the same year to teach English and to write for school publications.

Before receiving an offer of employment, however, Sharon had to convince the headmaster that she, a single parent with two young children, could handle the considerable demands of teaching in an international day/boarding school in the suburbs of London. Although I have never read Sharon's letter to that headmaster, I have heard that it was a masterpiece of persuasion and was instrumental in her being hired.

As a teacher of American and British literature to American and international teenagers, Sharon has shared her love both of literature and of writing. She'd open up Chaucer's world in *The Canterbury Tales* and then head off to Canterbury with her students so that they could make the pilgrimage themselves. She'd offer *Hamlet,* and then off they would all go to Stratford upon Avon. Sharon would be the first to admit that all TASIS teachers do this and that this is what she loves about the school. "Get them out into the world," Sharon says, echoing the school's founder. Not surprisingly (and just as the headmaster had warned), the demands of motherhood and a full-time teaching position left Sharon with little time for herself—let alone for her writing. Even less time was available after Sharon and I were married, and we moved to Switzerland, where I assumed the post of headmaster of the American School in Switzerland. Because of Sharon's support, hard work, many talents, and endless diplomacy, I have now "survived" thirteen years as a headmaster in Switzerland and England.

It is difficult to pinpoint exactly when it was that Sharon started to do less writing for the school and more for her own pleasure. She'd studied and written fiction and poetry in college and graduate school, but it wasn't until soon after our "chickabiddies," Rob and Karin, graduated from high school, and shortly after Sharon's father died, that she began to pour her energies into her own work.

I remember her writing poetry—lots of it—with such titles as "Strip Tease," "Victor, Victorious," "Sun on the Bottom," and "A Man on the Road." Much of her poetry shows the same combination of humor and poignancy that is also characteristic of her prose. I like this stanza, for instance, from "The Sun on the Bottom":

In first grade he brought home paintings black paintings with the sun on the bottom and the tree upside down at the top. "He's disturbed," the teacher said. "Oh," my neighbor said, "maybe there wasn't any yellow paint left and maybe it's upside down."

One day in 1988, a phone call came "out of the blue," notifying Sharon that her poem "Cleansing" had been awarded the Billee Murray Denny Poetry Award (sponsored by Lincoln College in Illinois) for that year. I think that this recognition of Sharon's creative talents was a turning point for her.

Meanwhile—somehow—in the midst of teaching, attending and hosting social events, keeping a household functioning, and allowing me to transfer the frustrations of many of my days to her, Sharon had also completed her first two novels, *The Recital* and *Absolutely Normal Chaos* (her first children's book). Shortly thereafter, she also wrote *Nickel Malley* and a play, *The Centre of the Universe*. Soon after securing an agent in London, she placed all of her books with British publishers, and her play was performed off-off-Broadway in a festival of new plays.

Sharon wouldn't like for me to suggest that this was all as easy as it might sound. She'd also spent two years writing an eight-hundred-page manuscript which sits on her closet shelf, and she received her fair share of rejections along the way. But the next book was *Walk Two Moons* (Harper), and as soon as I read it, I knew it was special.

In the midst of all the excitement generated by the Newbery Medal, I have to confess that I also have a few regrets. I regret that I wasn't with Sharon when the phone call from the Newbery committee came "out of the blue." I had just started a two-week trip to the States to interview prospective teachers for our school. I also regret that this added recognition of Sharon's talents as a writer probably means that she will not be able to return to the classroom on a regular basis. Our students will be losing a first-rate teacher.

There are also some things that I do not regret. I do not regret having some students now refer to me as "Mr. Creech" (Creech is Sharon's maiden name), and I do not regret attending functions where I am introduced as just the writer's husband. Sharon has certainly attended her share of functions where she has been referred to as just the headmaster's wife. I also do not regret attending events where Sharon has to give the after-dinner speech.

If I were asked to name the things that Sharon probably considers the "smooth beautiful folds" in her world, I would have to list our children, all her Creech family (even if and when they create "absolutely normal chaos"), reading, trees, summers at our cottage on Chautauqua Lake, theater, sunshine, bookstores, canoeing, naps, fish sandwiches at Grace's Restaurant in Mayville, New York, and, of course, her writing.

Although the writing of *Walk Two Moons* has already made a remarkable difference in our lives, as far as I'm concerned the most important piece of writing that Sharon has ever produced is the letter that she wrote to the headmaster back in 1979 convincing him to offer her a job in England.

Sharon's a wonderful "gooseberry." I'm fortunate that she has added "huzza, huzza" to my vocabulary and to my life.

Let me end with an anecdote from this past February. As I've mentioned, I was in the States when Sharon received the Newbery news, and I was still there a week later, on Valentine's Day. This always happens. I'm always in the U.S. by myself on Valentine's Day. But a few weeks earlier, I'd bought Sharon's present and hidden it in my sock drawer. On February 14th, I called her and told her where to look. When she opened it, she cried like a baby (or so she tells me). Here's what I had chosen (before the Newbery news): a miniature enamelled egg, with the phases of the moon depicted on it, and around the top were these words—"May all your dreams come true."

The Caldecott Medal 1996

Officer Buckle and Gloria

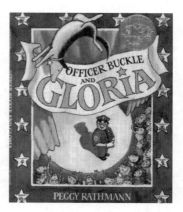

written and illustrated by
Peggy Rathmann

published by
Putnam, 1995

Horn Book Review

Officer Buckle is a fine safety officer; the problem is that when he addresses school assemblies, he is so boring that he puts all the students to sleep and his wise maxims are ignored. Until the advent of Gloria, that is—a beautiful and affectionate police dog who accompanies Officer Buckle on his school visits. When Officer Buckle says, "Sit!" Gloria sits. But when Officer Buckle turns his back on Gloria to address his audience, only the students see how Gloria acts out his hitherto deadly dull safety tips. The children are ecstatic at Gloria's slapstick antics, but Officer Buckle thinks it is because of his expressive voice. Letters pour into the station, thanking Officer Buckle and Gloria and asking them to come to other schools. Alas, Officer Buckle's burgeoning career is dimmed one day when he sees a film of himself and Gloria on the news; he realizes that Gloria is really the star of the show. Sadly, he refuses to visit any more schools, but Gloria's solo show proves to be a dud. So they return as a pair, with a new safety tip: "Always stick with your buddy!" Besides the beguiling story, the affable illustrations of the smiling Gloria, the accidental mayhem in the background, and the myriad safety tips—such as "always pull the toothpick out of your sandwich" and "never lick a stop sign in the winter"—add to the enjoyment. A glorious picture book.—*Ann A. Flowers*

Booklist Review

When rotund, good-natured Officer Buckle visits school assemblies to read off his sensible safety tips, the children listen, bored and polite, dozing off one by one. But when the new police dog, Gloria, stands behind him, secretly miming the dire consequences of acting imprudently, the children suddenly become attentive, laughing uproariously and applauding loudly. The good policeman is first gratified with the response, then deflated to learn that Gloria was stealing the show. Finally, he realizes that he and Gloria make a great team, and they take their show on the road again, adding a new message, "ALWAYS STICK WITH YOUR BUDDY!" Like Officer Buckle and Gloria, the deadpan humor of the text and slapstick wit of the illustrations make a terrific combination. Large, expressive line drawings illustrate the characters with finesse, and the Kool-Aid-bright washes add energy and pizzazz. Children will enjoy the many safety-tip notes tacked up on the endpapers and around the borders of the jacket front. Somehow, the familiar advice (like "Never leave a bar of soap where someone might step on it" or Never tilt your chair back on two legs") is more entertaining accompanied by little drawings of Gloria hamming it up.—*Carolyn Phelan*

1996 Caldecott Acceptance Speech

Peggy Rathmann

I have two embarrassing stories to share with you. The first is about why I started writing and illustrating. The second is about our family dog.

Ten summers ago, I was vacationing with my two nieces. The girls were three and five years old, and as far as I could tell, they didn't like me nearly enough.

One day, at the start of a family car trip, we were sorting ourselves into the front and back seats when both my nieces claimed a spot in the front seat next to another aunt. Now this other aunt cannot help that she is extremely attractive, intelligent, and pleasant to be around. I wanted to sit next to her, too. But there was only room for one, so the younger niece was sent howling to the back seat to sit with me. She glowered at me; I was the booby prize. We both felt deeply sorry for ourselves. I pulled out my sketchbook and began drawing a story that starred my niece and me as extremely attractive people with good personalities and high IQs. It worked.

Over the next two years the story grew into an illustrated epic. I gave a starring role to my other niece, too, so there would be no hard feelings. Because the girls never wanted books to end, I made my book endless: a whopping 150 pink-and-purple pages. It was two feet wide by three feet tall, and weighed at least twenty-five pounds. The book had everything—except a conflict and a plot.

When my nieces and I decided the book was perfect, I put on a gray wool suit and hauled my offering to a reputable publisher.

I explained to the editor that little children found my book irresistible. Alas, the editor did not.

Slumped in my moist wool suit, I contemplated the possibility that children could be attracted to something that wasn't publishable. I had produced a twenty-five pound Twinkie.

I retreated to my parents' house.

I needed to lie down.

My brother called to say he knew someone who knew someone who was published. I phoned this person, hoping he would recommend my book to his editor. Instead, he recommended a children's book writing and illustration class. My mother drove me to the class and took it with me.

On the first night, the teacher told us to write down the worst thing we knew about ourselves. We didn't have to show it to anybody. This embarrassing secret, the teacher advised us, could define both a character and a conflict.

People went home and never came back.

Those of us who returned denied having any embarrassing secrets.

Weeks went by, and the other students began submitting stories. I developed the overwhelming urge to swipe their ideas. Eventually, it occurred to me that this compulsion could be the embarrassing secret I'd been waiting for. I based my first book, *Ruby the Copycat* (Scholastic), on my secret shame, and a reputable publisher bought it.

Since then, all of my books have been based on embarrassing secrets. I am never at a loss for these. After a while, I found that I could use the family dog's embarrassing secrets as well.

In *Officer Buckle and Gloria* (Putnam), a school safety officer is upstaged by his canine partner.

Our family dog could jump twelve feet in the air and was a smart and attentive companion, but he did bad things behind our backs. He ate our wallets, and when he thought no one was watching, he licked our poached eggs. Once, when he was home alone, he plucked a diaper from the diaper pail and did a dirty diaper dance around the living room. When we returned, our dog, who ordinarily would have met us at the door, was conspicuously absent.

Now this dog had never been reprimanded for anything, so I can only assume that at some point during his celebration, our dog decided that he was guilty of bad judgment. I understand how he felt. It is how

Gloria the police dog felt the evening Officer Buckle saw her on the ten o'clock news jumping around behind his back. It is what I believe to be a central conflict of childhood: Just when you're having the time of your life, someone invariably gets hurt.

I wrote *Officer Buckle and Gloria* to fulfill an assignment in my writing class. The assignment was to write and illustrate a story which could not be understood by reading the text alone. I did it because the teacher told us to, but in the process, I discovered that this challenge was the very definition of a picture book. Officer Buckle was the words; Gloria was the pictures; and neither could entertain or enlighten without the other.

When Arthur Levine wanted this book for Putnam in 1991, it still needed a lot of work. Arthur, Nanette Stevenson, all the people in editorial and art, Margaret Frith, Cecilia Yung, my writers group, the guy at the copy place, four years, ten accident scenes later—well, sometimes it takes a village to make a book.

Back when I was collecting the 101 safety tips for the endpapers and the bulletin boards in this book, I offered my nieces, my nephew, and a dozen other young friends twenty-five dollars for any safety tip that made it past my editor. The response was very expensive. It pleases me that these children contributed to an award-winning book while still in elementary school.

I was with my parents the morning Julie Cummins called to say *Officer Buckle and Gloria* had won the Caldecott. My parents were eavesdropping outside my door. They thought I was being subpoenaed. I told them someone was trying to give me the Caldecott, but that I wasn't sure I was ready for it. My father said he was ready.

When my eight-year-old nephew, who earned a small fortune with his safety tips, was told of the award, he shook his head slowly, marveling, "And this is happening to us."

Yes, this is happening to us.

To my funny, big-hearted family with their overachieving dogs;

To Nanette Stevenson, whose friendship, hard work, and meticulous art direction made this book possible;

To Arthur Levine, who always believed in *Officer Buckle* even when I didn't;

To Barbara Bottner, my gifted teacher;

To Margaret Frith, Cecilia Yung, Donna Mark, and all the folks at Putnam who rolled up their sleeves and gave this book exactly what it needed;

To Marcia Wernick and Sheldon Fogelman, whose appreciation of storytelling through expressive drawing steadied my hand; and

To my husband and sweetheart, John Wick, who has heard all of my embarrassing secrets and knows I will never be at a loss for material.

I thank my lucky stars for the great, good humor of Julie Cummins and her amazing Caldecott committee. Bless all of you in the Association for Library Service to Children for bringing my book to children who will, I hope, someday share it with their children.

Aunt Peggy

Robin Rathmann-Noonan

My Aunt Peggy, Margaret Crosby Rathmann, was born on March 4, 1953, in St. Paul, Minnesota. Aunt Peggy is a very careful person. Not only is she careful for herself, she is careful for everyone else. She would be careful for you, too, if she knew you.

Peggy Rathmann

I remember when she was being careful about spiders. She had read a book about spiders, and after that, she carefully checked her spider book every time she saw a new one to make sure it wasn't poisonous. She also wanted us (my sister, A. J., and me) to be careful about sitting incorrectly on our knees. I think we didn't listen to her on that one. I know she has helped her neighbors in San Francisco to be careful about making sure that they are ready for earthquakes. I think that *Officer Buckle and Gloria* (Putnam) was her chance to help a lot of people to be careful, all at once.

My dad is Aunt Peggy's older brother. She has another brother and two sisters. Together they grew up in the suburbs of St. Paul. Aunt Peggy went to Falcon Heights Elementary School, Snail Lake Elementary, Edgewood Junior High, and Mounds View High.

When my dad was running for student council in ninth grade at Edgewood Junior High, Aunt Peggy was in the seventh grade at the same school. She created a bunch of beautiful campaign posters to put up in the halls of school. They worked! After the election was over, my dad went through the halls to retrieve the posters, but people had already taken them home as souvenirs. My dad was proud that he had a sister who could draw. He says that it was only Peggy who seemed unsure of the fact that her life would be in art. It was obvious to everyone else.

When Aunt Peggy graduated from the University of Minnesota, she thought she was going to be a psychologist. Then she thought she might be a doctor. Then she thought she might be a commercial artist, then a fine artist. Finally, she enrolled in the Otis Parson's School of Design in Los Angeles, where she learned to write and illustrate children's books.

I like Aunt Peggy's books because she always writes and draws about things in her life. *Ruby the Copycat* (Scholastic) is about a bad habit Aunt Peggy had of copying ideas from other people's stories. In *Bootsie Barker Bites* (Putnam), Bootsie's face is a self-portrait because Aunt Peggy was careful not to risk offending anyone else. *Goodnight, Gorilla* (Putnam) and *Officer Buckle and Gloria* are about Skippy, my grandma and grandpa's dog. Skippy used to play jokes and do funny things behind Grandpa's back, and that is exactly what the animals do in the stories.

Wherever she goes, Aunt Peggy carries a little watercolor set that fits in her hand. She is ready at any moment to paint what she sees. Out of all of Aunt Peggy's paintings, my favorites are the watercolors that she does for us. She paints portraits of my sister, A. J., my brother, Andy, and me that decorate our house. She even wrote her first book about A. J. and me.

Though Peggy looks like an adult and acts like an adult, she has a window into the world of children. With her words and pictures, she entertains us, teaches us, and cares for us. I have learned lots of things from my Aunt Peggy, but I think the most important thing is that you must do something you really enjoy. It may take you a long time to find it, but only settle for something that is right for you. I know Peggy is doing something that is right for her.

The Newbery Medal 1996

The Midwife's Apprentice

written by
Karen Cushman

published by
Clarion Books, 1995

Horn Book Review

In a sharply realistic novel of medieval England by the author of *Catherine, Called Birdy* (Clarion), a homeless, hungry orphan girl called Beetle is discovered trying to keep warm in a pile of dung by the village midwife. The midwife, Jane Sharp, takes Beetle in to work as a servant for little food, barely adequate shelter, and cutting words. To Beetle, however, it is a step upward. The midwife is far from compassionate, but she is, for her times, a good midwife. Beetle becomes interested in the work and watches Jane covertly as she goes about her business. Beetle also adopts a scraggly cat that she has saved from the village boys' cruel mistreatment, and she feeds it from her own inadequate meals. As Beetle grows and learns, she begins to gain some hard-won self-esteem, and renames herself Alyce. She becomes more accepted by the villagers and is sometimes asked for advice. On one occasion she employs her common sense and compassion to successfully manage a difficult delivery when Jane Sharp is called away. Jane is far from pleased; she wants no rivals and is angered when a woman in labor asks specifically for Alyce. But Alyce finds she knows less than she thought, and Jane must be called in to save the mother. Alyce, in despair and humiliation, takes her cat and runs away. She spends some time working at an inn, where she learns a good deal more about herself and the world. At last she admits to herself that what she wants most is to become a midwife, and she returns to Jane. The brisk and satisfying conclusion conveys the hope that the self-reliant and finally self-respecting Alyce will find her place in life. The graphic and convincing portrayals of medieval life and especially the villagers—given to superstition, casual cruelty, and duplicity—afford a fascinating view of a far distant time.—*Ann A. Flowers*

Booklist Review

Like Cushman's 1994 Newbery Honor Book, *Catherine, Called Birdy,* this novel is about a strong, young woman in medieval England who finds her own way home. Of course, it's a feminist story for the 1990s, but there's no anachronism. This is a world, like Chaucer's, that's neither sweet nor fair; it's rough, dangerous, primitive, and raucous. Cushman writes with a sharp simplicity and a pulsing beat. From the first page you're caught by the spirit of the homeless, nameless waif, somewhere around 12 years old, "unwashed, unnourished, unloved, and unlovely," trying to keep warm in a dung heap. She gets the village midwife, Jane Sharp, to take her in, befriends a cat, names herself Alyce, and learns something about delivering babies. When she fails, she runs away, but she picks herself up again and returns to work and independence. Only the episode about her caring for a homeless child seems contrived. The characters are drawn with zest and affection but no false reverence. The midwife is tough and greedy ("she did her job with energy and some skill, but without care, compassion, or joy"), her method somewhere between superstition, herbal lore, common sense, and bumbling; yet she's the one who finally helps Alyce to be brave. Kids will like this short, fast-paced narrative about a hero who discovers that she's not ugly or stupid or alone.—*Hazel Rochman*

1996 Newbery Acceptance Speech

Karen Cushman

Among a native Australian people, it is said, when the rice crop shows sign of failure, the women go into the rice field, bend down, and relate to it the history of its origins; the rice, now understanding why it is there, begins again to grow.

"Aha," I thought, as I read this passage, "such is the importance of stories. This is why I write."

I don't start a book by thinking of the listener or the reader; I just climb inside a story and write it over and over again until I know what it's about. Then I try to write as clearly and honestly as I can.

But when the book is finished and I hold it in my hands, I can see myself bending down to whisper it into the ear of a child. You are there, too—you writers, illustrators, booksellers, publishers, and librarians, all whispering away. And the child, now understanding, begins to grow. This is why I write—so children can begin to grow, to see beyond the edges of their own experience.

There are other reasons, also, why I write—not quite so philosophical and high-minded. I write because it's something I can do at home barefoot; because I can lie on my bed and read and call it work; because I am always making up stories in my head anyway and I might as well make a living from them; because I am 54 years old and I just figured out that I am not immortal. Like Jacqueline Woodson, I want to leave a sign of having been here. I have ideas, opinions, things to say, and I want to say them before I go. I want to take sides, to argue from my own passions and values and beliefs. I have questions I want to explore in an attempt to find with Herb Gardner "the subtle, sneaky important reason" I was born a human being and not a chair.

But maybe most of all I write because when I relax and trust myself, it feels so right to be a writer. Writing is my niche, my home, my place in the world, a place I finally found, like Alyce, the midwife's apprentice, found hers and Lucy Whipple finds hers in my next book.

And my place is full of words, of settings real and pretend, of people I have never met but know as well as I know myself, of events that never happened but have changed me in the imagining. This is why I write.

I write for the child I was and the child I still am. Like countless other lucky adults, I have much in common with children. We daydream, wonder, exaggerate, ask "what if?" and what we imagine sometimes is more true than what is. We like to play with squishy things—mud, clay, dough, words—and we make stuff out of them. We like kids, animals, rain puddles, and pizza, and dare to love silly things. We don't like brussel sprouts, the dentist, or books with great long passages of description, flashbacks, or dream sequences. We like happy endings—or at least, hope. And we love stories.

There is a Hasidic story (there is always a Hasidic story):

> Some followers go to their rabbi.
> "Rebbe," they ask, "what is heaven like?"
> "In heaven," answers the rabbi, "they sit at a table with all sorts of delicacies and good things. The only problem is their arms do not bend."
> "And what is hell like?"
> "In hell they sit at a table with all sorts of delicacies and good things. The only problem is, their arms do not bend."
> "Then, Rabbi, what is the difference between heaven and hell?"

"Ah, my children," said the rebbe, "in heaven they feed each other."

Writing for me is us feeding each other—writer and reader—54-year-old me and the young people who pick up my books. Me whispering in their ears and them talking back. They read and I am nourished, and my book becomes something richer and more profound than ever I hoped.

After *Catherine Called Birdy* was named a Newbery honor book last year, a number of interviewers remarked that I had come out of nowhere. I didn't. I always knew where I was. I just hadn't started whispering to the rice yet.

As a child I wrote constantly but never thought about growing up to be a writer.

I come from a working class Chicago-area family that loved me dearly but often didn't quite know what to make of me. I used to imagine I was the only child ever kidnapped *from* gypsies and sold to regular people. I didn't know writing was a job, something real people did with their lives, something like being a secretary, or a salesman, or a school crossing guard, like my Grandpa.

With school, writing became hard work—homework, assignments, term papers. Like many other students, I procrastinated, suffered, and counted words.

Besides, my greatest passion was not for writing but for reading: *Uncle Wiggily, Little Lulu* and *Donald Duck, The Story of Ferdinand, Rufus M., Homer Price* and *Caddie Woodlawn, Blue Willow* and *Strawberry Girl, The Bobbsey Twins, Kristin Lavransdatter, Microbe Hunters, Triumph over Pain, The Rise and Fall of the Third Reich, Mad Magazine.* We didn't own many books; in school I suffered through basal readers, but before long I discovered the library. Then chances were if I could reach it, I would read it.

Writers, I began to think, were people who had all the answers. I didn't have all the answers; I didn't even know all the questions. So I stopped writing, for a very long time, and for years endured the painful search for a place to belong. Some times were great, some empty and awful, but there was always something missing.

Finally, the day my daughter began filling out college applications, I sat down to write, for myself. I still didn't have the answers, but I began to know some of the questions: why? what for? what if? how would it be?

Writing was still hard work—hard to begin, hard to stop. But it also became a passion, and that made all the difference.

"To sum it all up," Ray Bradbury said, "if you want to write, if you want to create, you must be the most sublime fool that God ever turned out and sent rambling . . . I wish for you a wrestling match with your creative muse that will last a lifetime. I wish craziness and foolishness and madness upon you. May you live with hysteria, and out of it make fine stories . . . Which finally means, may you be in love every day for the next 20,000 days and out of that love, remake a world."

I read that, and I said "Yes." And out of my passion came *Catherine Called Birdy*, my first book. I wrote it despite my own doubts and the "don'ts" of others, because I needed to find out about things, about identity and responsibility, compassion and kindness and belonging, and being human in the world. How could I learn them if I didn't write about them?

Sometime during the process of writing *Catherine*, I thought of the title, *The Midwife's Apprentice*. I liked it. So I made a file. I wrote *The Midwife's Apprentice* on the tab. Inside I wrote on a slip of paper "Possible title-Midwife's Apprentice." And I filed it.

After I mailed *Catherine* off, I sat for hours looking at that file. I had a title. The research I had done for *Catherine* gave me a firm place to stand: I knew that village and those people so well. But I had no story, until finally I saw in the unrelieved darkness of a medieval dawn a homeless child sleeping on a dung heap, longing for a name, a full belly, and a place in the world. Although we were separated by geography, circumstances, and hundreds of years, I knew this girl and her longing for a place, her feelings of unworthiness, her fear of trying and failing, and her fragile confidence. The story poured out of me: the girl rising from her nest in the dung heap, the cat escaping from the bag, Alyce coming clean and shining from the river, the blossoms bursting forth on the trees, a celebration of rebirth and renewal as Alyce grew from waif to midwife's apprentice. Still Dinah Stevenson, my editor and often pipeline to reality, reminds me that I sent the manuscript to her with a note that said: "I don't know if this is a book or a writing exercise. What do you think?"

After we decided it was indeed a book, and it was written and published, I worried about Alyce the way I would the plain younger sister of a popular girl. *The Midwife's Apprentice* was quieter, more subtle than *Catherine*. Would anyone love Alyce as I did? Would anyone even find her among the thousands of books published each year? What about the many images of Alyce being born or the ways she is like the cat? The importance of her owning a name or her profound wounds and prosaic but effective tenacity? Would anyone notice or care? Would adults think her story too disturbing for children, and children think it too serious and dull? I took the risk and whispered the story of Alyce. And so many people have listened, noticed, and cared.

Children ask me who Alyce is—is she me or someone I know? Alyce is Alyce, a girl with no place in a world all about place, a girl who has to give birth to herself. And I am Alyce, who becomes truly alive only when she learns to smile and sing and tell stories to the cat. You are Alyce, if only in the way that all of us are, born cold and nameless, in search of a full belly and a place in this world. And Alyce is every child who is parentless, homeless, and hungry, who lives on the edges of our world, who is mocked or excluded for being different.

With the exception of this lovely noisy bunch of people down front here, I have in my life loved books more than anything. Writing is my way of honoring and sharing that.

"There's worms in apples and worms in radishes," says Arvella Whipple in my newest book. "The worm in the radish, he thinks the whole world is a radish." Those of us who read books know the whole world is not a radish. It is a crabbing boat in Chesapeake Bay, the walls of medieval Krakow, twenty-first century Zimbabwe, and the place where the wild things are. It is Narnia and Brooklyn and Gold Rush California. It is the glory of the whirligigs in May's garden, the lonely anger of Heidi's grandfather, the warmth of the wind blowing through the willows, and the terror of a Nazi death camp.

As children are what they eat and hear and experience, so too they are what they read. This is why I write what I do, about strong young women who in one way or another take responsibility for their own lives; about tolerance, thoughtfulness, and caring; about choosing what is life-affirming and generous; about the ways that people are the same and the ways they are different and how rich that makes us all.

Katherine Paterson, whose books both fiction and nonfiction have inspired me more than I can say, wrote, "It is not enough to simply teach children to read; we have to give them something worth reading. Something that will stretch their imaginations—something that will help them make sense of their own lives and encourage them to reach out to people whose lives are quite different from their own."

I remember an eight-year-old Karen, shy and dreamy and in love with books, running home from the library, flinging herself still in coat and woolen leggings onto the floor to read Lois Lenski's *Cotton in My Sack*. And I remember realizing with a pain in my heart that this book about sharecroppers in Arkansas was not a fairy tale, with trolls hiding under the bridge and a guaranteed "happily ever after." These were real people who had lives and dreams and troubles so real and so different from mine. I came back from the cotton fields of Arkansas to suburban Chicago a little different myself, a little changed.

"The goal of every storyteller," a Russian poet wrote, "consists of fostering in the child, at whatever cost, compassion and humanness, this miraculous ability of man to be disturbed by another being's misfortune, to feel joy about another being's happiness, to experience another's fate as your own."

Such is the importance of stories. This is why I write. And what can be more important in this world?

Although I write my books upstairs, alone except for an elderly cat with a gleaming patch of white in the dusty orange of her fur, I know that writing, like living, is a communal act. For helping me to this moment I would like to thank:

Dinah Stevenson and everyone at Clarion, the world's greatest publishers, for their genius, their faith, and their devotion;

Ginee Seo and the Harper Trophy folks for their enthusisam, support, and all those flowers;

James Levine, Dan, Arielle, and Melissa, for doing what agents do so well and with such goodwill;

Jack Hailey, my west coast agent, who generously shares his investigations, inspirations, and exuberant friendship;

Trina Schart Hyman for using her talent to make my girls live and breathe;

the Newbery committe for seeing what I was trying to do with Alyce and honoring it;

the Lipskis who were kings in Poland—especially my parents, Arthur and Loretta Lipski, for loving me and giving even when they didn't have;

Frances and Alvin Cushman, who have taught me the meaning of generosity, honesty, and humanity;

my daughter, Leah, who shows me every day how strong and independent yet gentle and compassionate a young woman can be;

and most of all, Philip, my husband, inspiration, love slave, and most ardent fan, who always believed I could do it; no matter what it was, he believed I could. So usually I did.

It was Philip who slept with the phone by his pillow on January 21 and so answered it at dawn. He handed it to me, whereupon I heard, sounding like the voice of God in a medieval mystery play, "Karen Cushman? This is Mary Beth Dunhouse from the American Library Association in San Antonio, Texas."

What does one say to that?

I said, "Yes." And it was the right response. Yes to writing without having all the answers, yes to Ray Bradbury and Alyce and the Newbery committee, yes to compassion and humanness, to being disturbed and feeling joy, to life and passion and love and remaking a world. God made people, says Elie Wiesel, because He loves stories. Such is the importance of stories.

Karen Cushman

Philip Cushman

Karen Cushman

By now, at the time of her Newbery Award, my time on earth with my wife Karen has been longer than my time on earth without her. I've gotten to know her pretty well. And there is something I can tell you that you won't find by reading about her on the inside flap of dust jackets: before she began to devote most of her work week to writing, there was always about Karen the sense of something desperate trying to come out. This wasn't usually a noisy or panicky desperation, and in fact one had to know Karen pretty well in order to notice it. It didn't so much appear as a disturbance as it did an absence: Karen was like an ear waiting for a song. In retrospect, we should have realized what was missing, but sometimes the most important things are the most difficult to see.

Karen grew to womanhood and set out to find a job in the years when the word career was still reserved for men. She graduated from Stanford with a degree in classics and no money for graduate school; in those days, job opportunities for female liberal arts grads pretty much revolved around two possibilities: stewardess or secretary. She hated the thought of being a waitress at thirty thousand feet, and she saved herself from the fate of being a secretary by her first "career" strategy: she refused to learn how to type. The strategy worked, sort of: she was hired at several low-level, low-paying administrative, clerk-type jobs—but at least they weren't (too) secretarial.

We found each other in graduate school, me as rabbinical student, Karen as assistant-clerk-administrator. There was from the first moment I talked to her the sense of a special and remarkable person imprisoned inside the deeply sad and wary bluegray eyes that were so stunningly intelligent and beautiful. Yes, she was physically beautiful, but her beauty was more than that; it was the kind that shone forth from a deep warmth and intelligence.

We were strange, similar, different, and very bonded very fast. It was the winter of 1968 in Los Angeles; we have been together ever since.

We made many plans about the life we would make, in the world we would have a hand in shaping, after the revolution. We dreamed about babies and organic corn, apple trees and wild blackberry jam, political sanity, rainy Oregon days, and peaceful snug nights with warm wood stoves. First we dreamed about it, and then we made it (well, some of it) come true. We built a big, beautiful dining-room table out of hardwoods from the four corners of the earth, around which all our children, students, and friends could sit while eating and arguing and making music together. Needless to say, the dreams weren't quite as great in reality as they were in the planning. The revolution failed, and political sanity—even in Oregon—continued to evade us, but the corn grew sweet and the jam was spectacular. Also, however, the baby was expensive, and teaching jobs dried up. We reevaluated, made new, slightly more realistic plans, clung to each other, and tried again.

The baby grew into a wonderful young girl, dogs and cats came and went, and my hair grew increasingly thin. Finally, we found Berkeley, learned to live with disappointment and without the revolution. We made new friends, and struggled to become reconciled, reluctantly, to being adults in a permanently unredeemed world.

But even these many changes could not shake from Karen the sense that something was not right. Many jobs, many graduate schools, many new ideas, new plans, new starts. Even our child, smart, beautiful, and much loved, could not allow Karen to shake the sense of something not yet expressed, not yet done. Over the years she tried many different careers, from organic gardening to a job as administrator of a community arts program, from two master's degrees to a position as editor of the *Museum Studies Journal*. These were all interesting and informative to her, and she was an engaged, conscientious, and remarkably efficient worker. But with all the variety and action, something still was not right.

The quiet torment and absence are gone now, as long as Karen has time to write. The stories that used to intrude, unbidden and unwanted, into her consciousness can now be researched, written out, crafted, sculpted, and gifted to others. They are no longer something to be, avoided or put away, but joyfully embraced.

Now we know why good jobs and respected graduate degrees, friends, family, and good times were not enough. It was not as though the jobs were bad; they just weren't the job she was born for. She was destined for a different kind of work, and she had the honesty and integrity to face her despair until she figured out what that was. In our world today, it is not easy to choose to be an artist. Innumerable seekers read do-it-yourself job-change books and see career counselors and go to informational interviews until they are blue in the face, but rarely does the pilgrim "realize" she is a novelist. Karen did. And thank God she did.

Karen did not, of course, proclaim herself a novelist. She just found the courage to let herself try what she knew she was meant to do from her first breath: write. It is one thing to write when one is a child, before one knows the risks. It is quite another, at fifty, to take up what one has been longing to do all of one's life, and do it publicly. To write, instead of just dream of writing, to actually put the words on paper, for everyone to see and evaluate—that is difficult.

Pretty much everyone tried to dissuade Karen from trying. They told her that history books do not sell, that adolescents are not capable of understanding the concept of the past, that boys would never read a novel with a female protagonist. They told her that she would never find an agent, and if she did, the agent would never find her a publisher. They told her to write cutesy little books about boring subjects, or vulgar little books filled with action and violence. They told her to write what would sell, what would not offend, what would be marketable and merchandizable. No one told her to write what was in her heart; no one told her to search her soul and write what she saw there; no one told her to listen to her voices, and bring them to life. No one, that is, except Ray Bradbury. Once, in the mid-seventies, we traveled to a big book fair, not sure why we were going except that we loved books, and there he was making the most inspirational speech I have ever heard. I watched Karen as he talked, and I've never seen anyone absorb the spoken word quite like she did that day. She never forgot what he said (and in fact tells you in her Newbery speech)—it just took her a while to know what to do with it.

Well, Karen didn't listen to "them," thank God; she listened to Ray instead. A dozen or so years later, she decided to write, and write from her heart. She decided to write what wanted—no, demanded—to be written. Now that she writes each day, it is easy to see the difference it makes in her life. But of course it was not simply a matter of deciding, or of finally realizing something relatively easy. To write the way Karen writes, about the issues Karen writes about, one has to be wise and courageous. It takes time to learn all the things that go into making up one of Karen's novels, and I don't just mean the painstaking historical research. Writing takes living, and soul-searching, and a deep love of humanity. Karen's writing is also motivated by sadness and anger, responses to the greed and deceit and mean-spiritedness that often overwhelm our meager attempts at kindness and political change.

Through a lot of hard work, and despite a sizable amount of self-doubt and fear, Karen Cushman found the courage to let herself write. Fortunately for us. Now, the whole world, not just me, can get a sense of the compassion and intelligence that lie deep in those blue-gray eyes. She deserves to be known by you, and you—children, parents, teachers, and librarians—deserve to know her and her stories. I am glad to share her with all of you. In fact, I am relieved to do so. I have been waiting for so long to tell you about her. Now you, and she, can take it from here. Enjoy.

The Caldecott Medal 1997

Golem

written and illustrated by
David Wisniewski

published by
Clarion Books, 1996

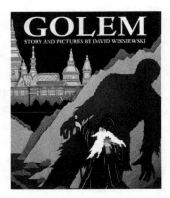

Horn Book Review

A monumental story of good and evil—and the gray areas in between—
receives a dramatic presentation through Wisniewski's intricately cut
colored-paper collage. The story takes place in sixteenth-century
Prague, where Jews are being attacked mercilessly following the general
acceptance of the "Blood Lie," a rumor that Jews are making their
Passover bread from flour, water, and the blood of Christian children.
To protect his people, Rabbi Loew decides to invoke the Golem, a giant
made of clay. After creating the giant, the rabbi places the word *emet*
(truth) on Golem's forehead. Every night Golem leaves the walled
Ghetto, catching the men planting false evidence of the Blood Lie, and
delivering them to the authorities. When Golem grows larger and
more violent, killing many of his enemies, the emperor guarantees the
Jews' safety if the rabbi will destroy Golem. Golem tries to hold on to
his animated state, but the rabbi erases the first letter from the word
on his forehead, changing *emet* (truth) to *met* (death), and Golem col-
lapses into a mound of clay. Despite his violence, Golem is a sympathetic character; like King Kong or the monster in Mary Shelley's
Frankenstein (which this legend may have influenced), Golem is young
and innocent, with a childlike ability to love and trust. The crisply cut
colored-paper illustrations have been painstakingly created to show
both small details and large landscapes. At times, some fussy detailing
can distract the eye away from the main action, but not enough to
dilute the power of the central character or the story. An extensive note
provides origins and variations of the legend.—*Lolly Robinson*

Booklist Review

Drawing on Jewish legends, two very different versions tell the story of
the giant monster of sixteenth-century Prague, created by the holy

Rabbi Loew from the clay of the river to help protect his people in the ghetto against racist persecution.

Rogasky tells it in 13 expansive chapters, with a colloquial warmth and a Yiddish idiom ("Why? Who knows why?") that makes you read it aloud. There's terror when the Poles come after the Jews, especially when they accuse the Jews of killing children to drink the blood, a lie used for centuries to fuel anti-Semitism. In a foreshadowing of the Holocaust, the evil priest Thaddeus, being led away to prison, curses the Jews ("I will return and you will not recognize me . . . I will tell the same lies . . . You will burn, burn as if in the ovens of hell"); a picture of the gates of Auschwitz ends the chapter. Some of the plotting and counterplotting gets convoluted. But the terror is framed by the rabbi's wise control and by uproarious episodes of domestic farce when the golem takes his household orders literally. Hyman's illustrations in shades of brown and blue, some tall and full-page, some small and unframed, reveal the ordinary and the mysterious in the ghetto community. From the rabbi in his library among his piles of books to the golem rampaging through the streets of Prague, there is a depth of perspective, an expressive sense of character, and an exquisite detail of line. Both author and illustrator provide endnotes about sources in Jewish mysticism and history.

Wisniewski's large picture-book version is stark and terrifying. His extraordinary cut-paper collages show and tell the shape-shifting and changing perspectives that are the essence of the story. Chanting spells from the holy books of the Cabala, the rabbi creates the giant, whose task is to protect the Jews and catch those planting false evidence of the Blood Lie. When the mob storms the gates of the ghetto, the golem is a huge Frankenstein monster who smashes the people and their weapons. But Wisniewski adds an element of melancholy to the creature (just as Mary Shelley did). This golem can talk, and when his work is done, he begs to be allowed to go on living. The pictures of the desperate giant trying to prevent his hands and face from dissolving are scenes of horror and sorrow. Wisniewski ends with a long, detailed background note about the religious roots and folklore and about the history of Jewish persecution through the ages.—*Hazel Rochman*

1997 Caldecott Acceptance Speech
David Wisniewski

Back when I was a circus clown with a tent show, there was a guy called the Arrow Man. His job was to tack up paper signs with red arrows

printed on them all along the route to the next town, so the perform-
ers and crew could find their way. This fellow did his job very well. He
never made a mistake. And he really secured those signs; even in the
worst weather, the red arrows could be seen flapping from lightposts
and exit ramps, bedraggled and torn but always there, a tattered assurance to all concerned that they were on the right track.

Despite his excellent record, there were times I doubted the Arrow
Man. Not on the well-posted hops between neighboring towns or
within big cities, but on the long hauls, over flat, featureless plains and
twisting mountain roads, whenever there were scores of miles between
pointers.

And sometimes that doubt got the better of me. I'd turn off the
highway, looking for local assurance. Eventually, a rusty gas pump
tended by a wizened elder named Slim, Buzz, or Junior would come
into view. After absorbing my request for guidance, Slim-Buzz-Junior
would squint, spit, wipe his hands on an oily rag, and always say the
same thing: "Son, it's the next exit."

And, sure enough, the next exit would be festooned with red
arrows.

In a career that's careened from circus-clowning to shadow puppetry to picture books, early off-ramps have been a great temptation.
Sometimes, there weren't any red arrows. Other times, the road disappeared.

But here's a terrific indication that, despite numerous detours and
stop signs, I'm on the right track. Being awarded the Caldecott Medal
for *Golem* is a wonderful honor and I'm very grateful for it. It's much
prettier than a beat-up red arrow. And the people who give it are so
classy. At dinner tonight, not one of them used an oily rag, squinted,
or even spat.

After the announcement, many people asked me if I was excited. I
was, but the initial burst soon dimmed. As more folks inquired, I
began to wonder if I was excited enough. Then, I realized, "Yes, of
course, you are." It had simply transformed—to a steadier, more quiet
glow, just as satisfying but easier to sustain.

My wife, Donna, and I have been self-employed in the arts for
almost twenty years. We've managed to maintain a steady upward
course despite changes, challenges, disappointments, and victories. It
helps to keep good things in perspective as much as bad.

Donna is excellent at this.

One time at home, she took a breathless call from a teacher totally undone by the fact that we answer our telephone like all other mortals.

"Is this where David Wisniewski lives?" she queried.

"Yes," Donna replied.

"Oh, my!" said the teacher. "Are you his secretary?"

"No," said Donna. "I'm his wife."

"Gracious!" said the teacher. "That must be so exciting!"

Donna said, "Occasionally."

Another reason for perspective is that I'm still new at this in a lot of ways. Yes, *Golem* is my sixth book, but it and all the others have been achieved without standard training. As a self-taught artist and writer, I rely on instincts developed through years of circus and puppet performance to guide a story's structure and look. It's worked well so far, but there's still plenty to learn. At least I don't doubt the outcome as much as I used to. When my first effort, *The Warrior and the Wise Man*, got great reviews, I said to Donna, "Gee, I hope they don't find out that I'm not a real writer."

But the greatest rationale for perspective concerns the nature of awards. The Caldecott Medal, like all other honors, isn't a glorious destination. It's a glorious indication, brightly marking a turning point on a continuing course. Gold rather than red, metal instead of paper, it serves the same purpose (albeit in much grander terms) as those weathered signs that guided me across the country earlier.

Cheering as it was to spot those red arrows, I didn't pull over, set out a deck chair, and wave to the show from the median strip. The boss wouldn't have liked it. It's still not a good idea, because now the editors wouldn't like it. Treating the Caldecott as an end in itself would mean the journey's over and complete, and—my goodness—there's still an awful lot to do.

Backstage at Ringling Brothers, I overheard a reporter question Gunther Gebel-Williams, the animal trainer who headlined the show for decades, about his energetic performances and nonstop training schedule.

"Don't you ever relax?" she asked.

Gunther looked at her as though she had three heads.

"You can relax when they throw dirt in your face," he replied.

I take a similar attitude toward book illustration. Actually, with my obsessive-compulsive art style, I have no choice. It's the only way to meet a deadline within the decade specified by the publisher.

Though demanding, making words and pictures fit and flow in narrative harmony is enormously satisfying. Few other professions are as metaphysical: the thoughts and images of one mind are transformed into a solid object, which, when opened, conveys them to thousands of other minds. What a privilege! What an opportunity! What a responsibility . . .

That's why I enjoy epic tales. There's so much to them; huge canvasses teeming with character, adventure, and romance which, when flung back, reveal an equally luxuriant superstructure of history and culture. When properly balanced, epics operate like enormous machines, with the thoughts and actions of individual characters meshing with the giant gears of society and civilization in perfect synchronization.

And they take you places.

When I was a kid, I remember so well being transported by big stories. The first was in first grade: Dr. Seuss's *McElligot's Pool*, an undersea tale of bizarre creatures that had me gazing suspiciously at puddles and bathtubs for months. Comic books came next; sometimes short on character, but with enough interplanetary upset to make up for it. These were followed by Classic Comics, simplified graphic versions of novels by Charles Dickens, Jules Verne, and H. G. Wells, inspiring me to tackle the densely printed pages of the real things later on. By fourth grade, I was a regular commuter to other worlds: *20,000 Leagues under the Sea, A Journey to the Center of the Earth, The War of the Worlds, The Time Machine,* and everything ever written by Ray Bradbury, Robert Heinlein, and J. R. R. Tolkien.

So, I figure that if I'm going to lavish all this time and energy designing a ticket, it should take the buyer someplace worthwhile.

The first ingredient in constructing that someplace is *language.* The words must serve the world of the story. And because that world is other than our own, the words seldom have the comfortable cadence and vocabulary of contemporary English.

Sometimes that causes complaint. "Why do you use such big words?" some students and teachers ask.

Actually, the words aren't so much big as underused. On that basis, they can be unfamiliar. I'm not a fan of using big words when little ones will do. However, as a culture, we're rather lazy with language. Lack of variety and imprecision abound. Books are the last repository of specific language. So, when a more exotic word refines a phrase or adds subtlety and grace to a sentence, I'll give it the nod over its more common cousin.

The second ingredient is *mission*. The characters must engage in something that matters greatly—to them and to the family, village, clan, or nation they love and are part of. The execution of this mission forces the characters into a conflict, which, to resolve, demands they stand, if not on their own resources, on principles beyond themselves. Then, if I've adequately humanized the characters in the few broad strokes allowed within the text limits of a picture book, the readers will not only willingly suspend disbelief, but give the story their heart. They will invest themselves emotionally. An author cannot be granted a greater gift than this.

When creating this emotional fulcrum, I often think of an excerpt from Percy Bysshe Shelley's *Prometheus Unbound*, a piece committed to memory for its simple and majestic reasoning:

> To suffer woes which Hope thinks infinite,
> To forgive wrongs darker than Death or Night,
> To defy Power which seems omnipotent,
> Neither to change, nor falter, nor repent,
> This is to be good, great and joyous, beautiful and free.
> This is, alone, Life, Joy, Empire, and Victory.

This thought has powered all my books. At one point, I got concerned about it. I asked my excellent editor, Dinah Stevenson, if I was writing the same story all the time and just changing the characters' clothes.

She replied, "No. The individual against great odds is one of the great themes of literature, and you can spin endless variations off a theme. And, besides that, I would be the first to tell you if you were repeating yourself."

The final ingredient is the *happy ending*. Not for its own sake and the pleasant conclusion of a comfortable tale, but because a principle has been called into action, and that principle must prove itself. Life has laws, and these laws of life must stand by the one who requested their assistance as truly and faithfully as the one willing to sacrifice everything for their aid.

Of course, one might reasonably say, "Well then, you really blew it with *Golem*. There's no happy ending there."

On the contrary, there is: the persecution of the Jews of Prague ended, at least for a time, and the community survived. But this triumph is deeply shaded by sacrifice: the melancholy demise of the clay giant who was the flawed instrument of their salvation.

In his wonderful essay "On Fairy-Stories," J. R. R. Tolkien writes,

> the joy of the happy ending . . . does not deny the existence of
> . . . sorrow and failure: the possibility of these is necessary to
> the joy of deliverance; it denies (in the face of much evidence,
> if you will) universal final defeat . . . giving a fleeting glimpse
> of Joy, Joy beyond the walls of the world, poignant as grief.

I regard striving for and transmitting these glimpses of Joy to be the highest calling of this profession. It's for this reason that a Japanese sage is awarded the kingdom when wisdom overrules force; that a blind Viking girl's bravery regains her stolen vision; that a Maya ballplayer's skill saves his people from disaster; that a prince of Mali overcomes overwhelming odds to lead an empire; that a desperate rabbi successfully calls upon divine salvation.

And it's also the reason for the Caldecott—to point beyond the walls of the world, to wrest attention away from the extraordinary hustle and bustle of everyday life in order to acquaint an eager audience with the quiet beauty of a book—a book that, for the duration of its spell, may provide a fleeting glimpse of an existence more pure and powerful than the one we presently know.

I've had a lot of help achieving these stories. The greatest has been and continues to be from my wife, Donna, whose loving support has been constant, even when I didn't deserve it. This honor is hers.

I want to thank Dilys Evans, the resolute artist's representative who was gracious enough to look at a fledgling artist's meager portfolio ten years ago and say, "Why not? Give it a go!" And who has been a source of great encouragement and advice ever since.

Dorothy Briley of Clarion Books has my great gratitude for agreeing with Dilys Evans and giving an untried artist a chance.

Dinah Stevenson, editor extraordinaire, has been instrumental in refining six books of my words and pictures with the fiery red of her flashing pencil. My deep appreciation for your grand sense of story and unwavering eye for composition.

Thanks are also due art director Anne Diebel, production supervisor Andi Stern, photographer Lee Salsbery, and the indefatigable staff at Berryville Graphics.

And, of course, thank you to the members of the 1997 Caldecott commitee for choosing *Golem*.

David Wisniewski
Dilys Evans

David Wisniewski

I met David Wisniewski at a children's book conference in Washington, D.C., in 1987. 1 had just finished a speech about the fine art of children's book illustration and had moved on to the portfolio review section of the program. David's portfolio was the high point of the entire day. I went carefully through his samples of cutpaper illustrations with an occasional remark from him—but words were really immaterial. He had said everything in his pictures. I asked him what he most wanted to do with this remarkable art form, and he said, "Tell good stories." We talked about the technical aspects of his work and about his graphic art experience, and that was all I needed to know about this earnest young man with a ready smile.

Even then he knew the importance of story and the power of the picture. He had a great sense of fun and a definite goal in mind, and his artwork was quite simply magnificent. My advice to David Wisniewski that afternoon was: "Go home now and call Dorothy Briley at Lothrop, Lee & Shepard and tell her I told you to make an appointment to see her." Meanwhile, I called Dorothy to tell her to expect his call, and to let me know what she thought about his work. *The Warrior and the Wise Man* was published by Lothrop in 1989, and now, eight years and six books later, *Golem* has captured the 1996 Caldecott Medal.

When David was in high school, he concentrated on both the performing and visual arts, and then went on to the University of Maryland to study drama. While there, he attended a talk about Ringling Brothers and Barnum & Bailey Circus Clown College, and he was so intrigued that he knew he had to find out more. He spent the next two years with the circus and found it to be fascinating, hard work, and tremendous fun! He traveled around the country the next year with the Circus Vargas, the largest tent show in the nation, but by the end of the season he realized that the solitary traveling life was not for him.

Returning home to the Washington area, he found a puppet theater troupe and was interviewed for a position by Donna Harris; six months later, they would be married. It was in this environment, under the guidance of his future wife, that he learned all about puppetry, costume making, set design, and finally shadow puppetry, an ancient performance art where flat jointed characters perform against a screen lit from behind to create the shadow forms. David was now able to explore his sense of drama and storytelling to the fullest, and he learned new and exotic folktales that would later fuel his picture books.

In 1980, David and Donna left the troupe to form their own company, the Clarion Shadow Theatre, for which they created thrilling adaptations of "Rikki-Tikki-Tavi" and "Kaa's Hunting" from Kipling's *Jungle Book*. They even ventured into puppet pantomimes set to classical music, and by the end of their first year they were performing at the Smithsonian Institution's Discovery Theater and the Kennedy Center's youth and family program.

In 1984 the troupe was awarded its first Henson Foundation grant, an award established by the late Jim Henson "to foster excellence in the field of American puppetry." This grant enabled them to stage a grand adaptation of Mussorgsky's Pictures at an Exhibition, which was highly acclaimed at theater festivals in California and Florida and won a citation of excellence from UNIMA (Union International de Marionette).

By 1985 they were awarded a second Henson Foundation grant and were commissioned by the Smithsonian to create a production of "Peter and the Wolf." It had been a thrilling five years, but the hectic schedule brought both David and Donna to yet another turning point in their lives. It was now time to concentrate on raising their family. They established Clarion Graphics, a graphic design company, which enabled them to work at home.

With Donna's previous training as a graphic designer and David's growing skills in illustration, they pursued clients in the performing arts and education areas. Their daughter Ariana was now four years old, and son Alexander was born that year. At this point David felt he needed another creative challenge to fill his life, and he began to work on some ideas for a children's book. He had a wealth of information and story to draw upon from his life experiences, and the portfolio I saw that day in Washington reflected a remarkable diversity coupled with natural intelligence. I knew he was bound to succeed, not only by the contents of his portfolio but by the intensity of purpose that was evident in our conversation. So I am particularly happy that my friend David proved me right! And also because this year's Caldecott committee recognized a book created with cut paper and collage, the most demandine of disciplines. To be able to take such an exacting medium and translate a tale with great scale and drama, color and passion, is a formidable achievement, and it proves that this art form truly embraces the standards of the fine art of illustration.

In the creative process, David Wisniewski is first and foremost a storyteller. When the manuscript for the text is deemed perfect, he proceeds to do the first pencil sketches on layout paper, followed by more detailed black ink. Once the drawings are approved by the editor, he uses a color marker to establish color consistency, adding to the growing mood of the book. Then detailed tracings are made, one for each spread, and these are the final compositions. Each spread is then transferred, with carbon, to colored papers, and the cutting, positioning, and assembling with double-stick photo-mounting and foam tape takes place. For each book David uses between eight hundred and one thousand blades for his X-Acto knife.

The final and most important step in the procedure is the lighting. Working closely with Lee Salsbery, who has photographed all of his books, David carefully lights each spread for the full dramatic effect. The lighting must be perfect to ensure that depth, illusion, and color are at their best in the final transparencies that will be sent to the printer. In the tradition of all great artists, David Wisniewski makes it look so easy, and he tells me there are still more surprises ahead.

The Newbery Medal 1997

The View from Saturday

written by
E. L. Konigsburg

published by
Atheneum/Simon, 1996

Horn Book Review

Mrs. Olinski's sixth-grade Academic Bowl team, self-named "The Souls," has made it all the way to the state finals. Each of the four Souls must answer a question, and their answers blossom from their surprisingly intertwined lives and aspirations. As the Souls tell their stories we learn, for example, that Nadia's grandfather married Ethan's grandmother, and fellow soul Noah was the best man—all the way down in Florida, no less. The interlockings are clever, but they contribute to an aura of artifice that haloes the book: nothing seems and no one sounds quite real. Characters speak archly and aphoristically, and while we are given to understand that these students are "gifted" (although Konigsburg's good sense and wit would never allow her to use such a word without irony) and therefore quirky, they sound too much alike. (Mrs. Olinski, in fact, emerges as the most rounded character, and in some ways the book is about her more than it is anyone else.) Smart readers, though, may be drawn to this story of smart kids who win—on many levels.—*Roger Sutton*

Booklist Review

Four sixth-graders are chosen by their teacher, Mrs. Olinski, to be the class representatives for the Academic Bowl team. When the team goes on to perform amazing feats of erudition, including winning the state championship, people keep asking Mrs. Olinski how she chose the participants. Although the questioners never get a real answer, the story, told from different perspectives, lets readers in on the secret. Konigsburg's latest shows flashes of her great talent and her grasp of childhood, but the book is weighted down by a Byzantine structure that houses too many characters and alternating narratives that will confuse readers. The story begins at the wedding of two senior citizens in which young Noah is the best man. Two of the other team members, Ethan and Nadia, are grandchildren of the bride and groom, and the fourth member, new boy Julian Singh, cements the group when he invites the others for tea (yes, tea). Mrs. Olinski, who is wheelchair bound, only thinks she is choosing the quartet, when it is just as true they are choosing her. Overriding themes of civility and inclusiveness add interesting elements, but this is more ambitious than it is successful.—*Ilene Cooper*

1997 Newbery Acceptance Speech
E. L. Konigsburg

As I was saying, four days and twenty-nine years ago, thank you.

Between the banquet in Kansas City, where I received what my family currently refers to as Newbery I, and this evening's glorious celebration for the award we are calling "Newbery Eye Eye" [Newbery II], you have taken me on a journey. You invited me to many places. They were places where I could have grown-up conversations, places where I could shed the burden of my personal self and become part of the community of children's books.

And those places became my Third Place.

The Third Place is where we go that is neither work nor home. It is where we are taught to measure up in a different way from home and from work. The Third Place is the destination of people who want to meet, to mingle, and to participate, both as individuals and as part of a community. It is a place where we feel accepted for ourselves and where we learn to conduct ourselves as grown-up members of a larger community. The Third Place attaches us to the human tradition.

Civilized society has always had a Third Place. It is as ancient as the agora of Greece where Socrates walked among the youth of Athens. It is as old as the forum in Rome where Marc Antony came to praise Caesar. The Middle Ages had the church; the Renaissance the piazza. At the turn of the century, Vienna had its coffeehouses. Between the two world wars, New York City had the Algonquin for the New Yorkers, and Paris had Shakespeare and Company for the expatriates, and after the wars, there was the Café Des Deux Magots for the existentialists. Ireland has its pub, England its club. Colonial America had its town square. Suburban America has—what? The workout center? The sports bar? Could it be—Barnes and Noble? I don't know if suburban America even has a Third Place. But I do. I have a Third Place, and it is the one you opened for me after Newbery I and have kept open ever since.

My first Third Place was Cleveland. The Ohio Association of School Librarians was meeting there at a time when Dorothy Broderick was on the faculty at Case-Western Reserve in their School of Library Science (of blessed memory). Broderick was scheduled to be in the audience when I spoke. The Third Place demands that we test our-selves, and I knew that this audience would not have much patience with an author ramble—a talk that was not properly dressed as dis-course—so I extended the thoughts of my Newbery address wherein I had spoken about my love of words, and I spoke about language, and how language is God's gift to us as humans, and how we must take care of it as we would any treasure, for it not only reflects our culture but also helps to shape it. Language demands that we treat it with dignity. It makes demands, but it also delivers rewards, for precise language helps shape precise thinking.

The Third Place also makes demands, and it also delivers. From the Third Place we give something, and we take something, and we return with our lessons transplanted and transformed. From the agora Plato took the teachings of Socrates and returned with the academy. From the Piazza della Signoria in Florence Michelangelo took the spirit of the Renaissance and returned it in the heroic figure of David.

To my surprise and delight, I have found traces of my Third Places in *The View from Saturday*. Here is how the echo of that talk on lan-guage plays back.

> It is the day before the contest with Knightsbridge for the dis-trict championship of the Middle School Academic Bowl. Mr. Connor LeDue, the principal, visits Mrs. Olinski, the Epiphany coach, and says: "I heard a rumor that your team is expecting to blow mine out of the water." His smile was as genuine as a Xeroxed signature. "I told our coach that she could expect to be hung if she lets your sixth-grade grunges beat us out."
>
> "Well then," Mrs. Olinski replied, "much as I respect your coach, I recommend that you start buying rope." She added, "By the way, Mr. LeDue, in our grunge neighborhood, we say hanged, not hung. Check it out."

The first call I ever received from a reader of my published work was from Amy Kellman, a children's librarian who lived in Rye, New York, the town neighboring Port Chester, where we lived at the time.

Both Amy and I had once called Pittsburgh home. In 1976, when I was invited to speak at the Fall Festival of Children's Books in Pittburgh, Amy had returned and was at the Carnegie Library there, but I had moved to Florida. So Pittsburgh was now a Third Place for me.

The Third Place is where we go to talk about what is current but not necessarily quotidian. In our bicentennial year, the classics of children's literature were being re-reviewed for political correctness. Language that was once merely colorful was being attacked as racist or sexist or both.

The Third Place is where we learn to listen to different voices and where we learn how to agree to disagree, so in the auditorium of that great Carnegie Library on Forbes Street in Pittsburgh, I spoke about how it is important to maintain color in children's literature, that true diversity does not prescribe, proscribe, or circumscribe language, and that for the sake of accuracy as well as poetry it is best not to skew or skewer language to be current or to be politically correct.

And I found that those thoughts, too, have surfaced in *The View from Saturday*.

Mrs. Eva Marie Olinski always gave good answers. Whenever she was asked how she had selected her team for the Academic Bowl, she chose one of several good answers. Most often she said that the four members of her team had skills that balanced one another. That was reasonable. Sometimes she said that she knew her team would practice. That was accurate. To the district superintendent of schools, she gave a bad answer, but she did that only once, only to him, and if that answer was not good, her reason for giving it was.

Mrs. Olinski's bad answer is her response to political correctness.

Part of that Fall Festival was the dedication of the Elizabeth Nesbitt Room. That's Nesbitt with two t's, named for a children's librarian, not a children's book writer. In the wonderful way that the world of children's books has of circling back on itself, the Third Place that Pittsburgh had become has once again become home, for the Elizabeth Nesbitt Room in the Library School at the University of Pittsburgh is now home to my manuscripts and illustrations.

Pat Scales and I met over the telephone when her students at Greenville Middle School called me for an author interview. The degree of preparation, the quality of the questions, and the courtesy of that interview were a prelude to not only another Third Place but to a friendship as well.

It was upon the recommendation of Pat Scales that I was invited to address a joint conference of the Southeastern and Southwestern Library Associations when they met in New Orleans. New Orleans is an American city that retains a downtown. As I grew up in small towns in Pennsylvania, downtown was the Third Place for townfolk, but it was also home for me, for we almost always lived over the store.

I thought about the homes I had known as a child. I thought about how I had always looked for home in the books I read, and how I still look for home in the books I read. I talked about that and about how, now that I am grown up, I have a chance to create homes in the books I write.

All of us long for home.

Nadia's story in *The View from Saturday* is about that. Her need for finding home is there when she says that her mother moved the two of them from Florida "to upstate New York where she had grown up [because she] needed some autumn in her life." And it is there in Nadia's account of how the turtles, after decades of absence, return to their home shore to nest.

My friendship with Pat Scales that began with a telephone call is maintained by phone, and our late-night, long-distance calls have come to qualify as a Third Place, for—sometimes sooner, sometimes later, but always—our conversation gets around to what is current in children's books. But we usually begin our marathon phone visits by talking about home. We discovered that we have a lot in common. We were both raised by Jewish mothers even though Pat's Jewish mother happens to be a Methodist. We are both the middle child, and we both have an older sister. During one long call, Pat told me about her sister's taking the family dog to an audition for the part of Sandy in the play Annie. Daisy not only got the part, she made the front page—above the fold—of the Leisure section of the Anderson, South Carolina, *Independent-Mail*. Pat sent me the clipping. I still have it in my files. It is dated September 15, 1983.

Daisy is now in Dog Heaven enjoying the company of other celebrities like Lassie, Rin Tin Tin, and Toto. But I hope those other stars realize that, unlike them, Daisy led the life of a real dog and was the inspiration for a character named Ginger. I wish Daisy a long afterlife in Julian's story, "When Ginger Played Annie's Sandy."

Simmons College was my next Third Place. The theme of the institute that summer was "Do I Dare Disturb the Universe?" I thought about how every creative act disturbs the universe and how every creative act requires risk.

Addressing the theme, I used the example of Galileo to show that those who dare disturb the universe must first have the courage to dare disturb the neighborhood. It sometimes takes more courage to disturb the neighborhood than it takes to disturb the universe. I discovered that kind of courage in Julian Singh.

At the state finals of the Academic Bowl, the commissioner of education reads the question, "An acronym is defined as a word formed from the initial letters of a series of words . . . Can you give me two . . . examples of acronyms that have entered our language as words?" Julian answers, "Posh and Tip."

> The commissioner looked over his list of possible answers. "Posh and tip?" he asked.
>
> Julian quickly answered, "Posh means fashionable and is the acronym for Port Out, Starboard Home . . . And tip, meaning the small sum of money given for services rendered, is the acronym for To Insure Promptness."
>
> The commissioner laughed. ". . . I don't have either of those acronyms on my list. We'll have to check with our advisory panel." He nodded to the three people sitting at a table on the far side of the room . . . The three of them conferred briefly and passed a note to the commissioner.
>
> "We can allow posh, but we do not find a reference for tip."
>
> Julian said, "With all due respect, sir, I think you ought to check another source."

In *The View from Saturday* Mrs. Olinski says, ". . . sometimes to be successful, you have to risk making mistakes . . . [and] sometimes we even have to risk making fools of ourselves."

The structure of *The View from Saturday* was a risk. The Third Place is where we learn to take risks. Newbery banquets [are] where we learn whether or not we have made fools of ourselves.

It is in the Third Place that we learn to wear a mask or risk taking one off because it is here that we learn to identify—or not identify—with people whose lives are not our own.

Nineteen eighty-nine was designated "The Year of the Young Reader." The Florida Center for the Book invited me to speak at a conference on writing for young readers. I gave a talk entitled "The Mask beneath the Face." I believe that a writer wears a mask every time she sits down to write, and readers try on masks every time they read. I also believe that children design the masks they will wear by the time they finish sixth grade.

In that talk I asked my husband, the psychologist, Dr. David Konigsburg, "Do you think wearing a mask allows a person to be someone else, or do you think that a mask allows a person to be that which he really is?" And my husband, the psychologist, Dr. David Konigsburg, answered, "Yes."

Now listen to what Ethan Potter, a sixth-grade "Soul," has to say in *The View from Saturday*.

[I]t was dark when I left Sillington House. Mrs. Gershom had offered to drive me home, but I wanted to walk. I wanted to walk the road between Sillington House and mine. I wanted to mark the distance slowly. Something had happened at Sillington House. Something made me pull sounds out of my silence the way that Julian pulled puzzle pieces out of Nadia's hair.

Had I gained something at Sillington House? Or had I lost something there? The answer was yes.

Maureen Hayes ("Mo," of blessed memory) recommended that— even though I was going to Rochester, New York, on a different assignment—I ought to speak to an assembly of children's librarians there. Mo was an extraordinary matchmaker, the Dolly Levi of author appearances. She knew that I needed to meet Julie Cummins, who was Children's Services Consultant in Rochester at the time. Following our meeting, Julie, a few other librarians, and I went to lunch. This was not the Café Des Deux Magots, and this was not the Round Table at the Algonquin. This was better. Not even the chocolate dessert was as rich and savory as our conversation.

In 1992 Julie Cummins was at the New York Public [Library], and she invited me to give the Anne Carroll Moore lecture. It was here that I chose to explore the relationship between reading and the brain. I learned that the human brain must be jump-started with experience. For example, a baby kept blindfolded may have all his equipment in perfect order but will never function as a seeing person, even when the blindfold is removed, because the pathways that allow him to interpret what he sees will not have been carved out. Experience is necessary to start function, and more experience is necessary to refine it. A child must see in order to be able to see. A child must speak in order to speak.

I also learned that there is, for each of these senses, a critical age by which these nerve pathways must be carved out if they are ever to be reinforced. For most developing brains, that critical age comes before adolescence. I came to believe that there is a critical age for establishing the nerve pathways that allow us to interpret the printed word. We must read in order to read.

I found those thoughts—that the human brain must be jump-started with experience as well as the thought that there is a critical age for experience to shape our brains—translated in *The View from Saturday*. But here it is an emotion that must be experienced to be expressed.

After the state championship of the Academic Bowl has been decided, Mrs. Olinski and Mr. Singh are driving home from the state capital, and Mr. Singh speaks:

"How can you know what is missing if you've never met it? You must know of something's existence before you can notice its absence. So it was with The Souls. They found on their journeys what you found at Sillington House."

"A cup of kindness, Mr. Singh? Is that what I found?"

"Kindness, yes, Mrs. Olinski. Noah, Nadia, and Ethan found kindness in others and learned how to look for it in themselves. Can you know excellence if you've never seen it? Can you know good if you have only seen bad?"

A person must experience kindness to recognize it. He must recognize it in order to develop it. Being kind makes us kind. And just as there is a critical age by which we must speak in order to speak, there is a critical age by which we must experience kindness to be kind. And that critical age is before adolescence. That critical age is in the cruelest year—grade six.

There are some Third Places where I have been three times. Call it an exponential three. Or three to the third power. These three-times Third Places have all been very kind to me.

I have been to Oklahoma, and I have been to Maine three times. Conversations with Donna Skvarla in the former, and Mary Peverada in the latter, reassured me that a writer can trust the kindness of readers. Librarians who work with children as well as books know that young readers want to connect and are willing to reach down and up and into a book that has more to it than meets the eye.

Herb Sandberg and Hughes Moir invited me to the University of Toledo three times, and each time I went I met not only with kindness at that university but also with kindness in the community, for through their efforts the Children's Literature Institute has become a Third Place for the people of the town. Every year lay citizens support the institute by participating in the events, both social and educational. In Toledo I learned to trust an informed community. Herb Sandberg knows that an informed community fears its children's not finding books more than it fears what they might find in them.

I met Ethel Ambrose in the mid-seventies when she and Esther Franklin invited me to their Stockton/Sacramento gig. Ethel left California for Little Rock, Arkansas, and where Ethel goes a Children's Literature Festival follows. On one of those days in Little Rock, I was in Ethel's office signing books when the custodian came in to "redd up," as we ex-Pennsylvanians say. Out of sheer enthusiasm Ethel picked up a copy of one of my books and began to read it out loud. She had hardly turned a page before the young man had bought the book. He had to, of course. Whether he had children or not, he had to. Ethel Ambrose's enthusiasms are not to be denied and neither is her commitment to excellence. There is no greater kindness to readers or to writers than the commitment to excellence of an outstanding children's librarian.

The Third Place is neither work nor home, but would have little meaning without them. Had I not found trust and kindness at a critical time at work, would I have ever been able to recognize them in the Third Place?

Jean Karl has been my editor since she took a risk on a manuscript called *Jennifer, Hecate, Macbeth, William McKinley, and Me, Elizabeth* that had come in over the transom. We have worked together on eighteen books since, and she has never been less than brilliant as an editor. Over the course of our association, through waves of political no-nos, Jean has demonstrated such intellectual integrity that never once has she asked me to shape my text to the times. That is trust. Thank you, Jean Karl.

It is Jon Lanman, as editorial director, whose understanding of the head of an author, as well as the head of a publishing house, has maintained the flow of thought as well as the flow of paper from manuscript to bound book. His understanding of the book-making process borders on the Talmudic. If genius is an infinite capacity for taking pains, Jon is a genius. And he is kind. Thank you, Jon.

I believe that courtesy is the threshold to kindness, and I believe that courtesy begins at home—in the First Place—and I also believe that in a forty-five-year-old relationship, courtesy is no longer the threshold to kindness, but is maintenance. And in a forty-five-year-old, empty-nest relationship courtesy is mandatory. And in a forty-five-year-old, empty-nest relationship where one's husband is one's agent, courtesy is a miracle. But I'm here to tell you, miracles do happen. Thank you, David, for the pretty thing our years together have been.

In the thirty years since my first books were published, the children of our children are now the same age that Paul, Laurie, and Ross were in 1968—a little in-house guarantee for a long shelf-life for one's books. Thank you, kids.

In his 1997 State of the Union message, President Clinton said, "As the Internet becomes our new town square, [we need] a computer in every home . . . ." The Internet may be the new town square but it can never be my Third Place. The Third Place is community; the Internet is isolation. The Third Place is dress-up; the Internet is dress-down. The Third Place is learning to interpret a wink, a blink, a flick of the hand; the Internet is learning to keyboard. The Internet is not a Third Place.

But I discovered that Sillington House is.

In *The View from Saturday*, when Ethan Potter tells his story, he says:

> Something in Sillington House gave me permission to do things I had never done before. Never even thought of doing. Something there triggered the unfolding of those parts that had been incubating. Things that had lain inside me, curled up like the turtle hatchlings newly emerged from their eggs, taking time in the dark of their nest to unfurl themselves. I told jokes I had never told before. I asked questions I had never asked before.

In *The View from Saturday* I told a story I had never told before, for Sillington House is not only the Third Place for Ethan and The Souls and Mrs. Olinski, it is my return on the Third Place you have given me. It is my statue returned to the piazza. It is my rendering of the place you gave me to see in order to see, the place you gave me to speak in order to speak.

Ethan again:

> One Saturday afternoon . . . as we sat around the table-for-four where we had had our tea, I broke the silence by asking—I really don't know why—except that it was something I had been thinking about, "If you could live one day of your life all over again, what day would it be? . . ."
>
> When it was my turn to tell what day I would like to live over . . . The Souls . . . were not embarrassed to hear, and I was not embarrassed to say, "I would like to live over the day of our

first tea party. And, look," I added, "every Saturday since, I get to do just that."

Now, in a paraphrase of Ethan Potter's desire, "I am not embarrassed to say, and you are not embarrassed to hear, I would like to live over the evening of my first Newbery party. And look," I can add, "after a fulfilling twenty-nine years, I get to do just that."

Thank you, John Edward Peters—I love all your names—and all the members of the 1997 committee—I love all your names, too—thank you for letting me do just that. Thank you, members of the American Library Association for then. Thank you for now. Thank you forever.

E. L. Konigsburg
Laurie Konigsburg Todd

E. L. Konigsburg

Readers frequently ask where E. L. Konigsburg, my mother, gets her ideas. I'll tell.

Although Mom can detect the most subtle nuance in painting or prose, she never developed a musical ear. Knowing that, my brother Paul purchased several classical records and proceeded to give her a course in music appreciation. It is not surprising that Mom's interpretation of music took on a literary dimension. After hearing the first movement of Mozart's Symphony #40 in G Minor, she knew she would one day use it as a model for a book. Like that movement, her book would have a short opening, a recurrent theme, and a melody that was separate yet intertwined, repeated, and extended. The result was *The View from Saturday*.

Discord, not harmony, motivated Mom to conceive *From the Mixed-Up Files of Mrs. Basil E. Frankweiler*. As she listened to Paul, Ross, and me complain about insects and heat during a family picnic, she concluded that her suburban children would never run away from home by opting for a wilderness adventure. Instead, we would seek the comfort and splendor of the Metropolitan Museum of Art.

Although the inspiration for these Newbery books was as disparate as the three decades which separate their publication, their theme is the same. In fact, every one of E. L. Konigsburg's fourteen novels are about children who seek, find, and ultimately enjoy who they are.

Despite this common denominator, E. L. Konigsburg's writing is the antithesis of the formula book. Her characters are one-of-a-kind. They include Jamie Kincaid, who likes complications and cheats at cards; Ned Hixon, who turns the finding of fossilized sharks teeth into a competition as fierce as Wimbledon; and Chloe Pollack, who learns to put bad hair days and other people's opinions into perspective.

Mom always lets her characters speak for themselves. At the same time, she persists in having them speak to the core of her readers. Thirty years has not changed the fundamental identity of Mom's audience—middle-aged children who crave acceptance by their peers as desperately as they yearn to be appreciated for their differences. E. L. Konigsburg's success can be attributed to the fact that when children read any of her novels, they see themselves, and they laugh.

Since readers recognize themselves in E. L. Konigsburg's books, they frequently ask how she discovered her own identity as an author. The answer is that her writing career began when she was a graduate student in chemistry.

Both science and art demand discipline and imagination. The laboratory protocol that compelled Mom to log and monitor experiments developed into the self-control she exercises when she forces herself to sit at her desk and write. Conjecturing how molecules fit together during chemical reactions became training for creating character and plot. Indeed, chemistry showed that transcending intellectual boundaries is prerequisite to true discovery. How else did a former student of architecture, Friedrich Kekule, dream that a snake was biting its own tail, and so discover the ringed structure of benzene?

Today, there is less recognition that skills can be transferred from one discipline to another. The current crop of help-wanted ads demand specialized degrees and mastery of specific computer programs. They don't mention imagination. It's a good thing E. L. Konigsburg has found success as an author, because she's out of sync with today's narrowly defined careers. She has a terrific sense of design, but what firm would hire a graphic artist who's never heard of CORELDRAW, and has trouble double-clicking a mouse? Mom would also have difficulty as an administrative assistant. She'd comply with requests to organize office records, but nobody else would be able to retrieve them. The process her brain goes through to store and retrieve information is as mixed-up as Mrs. Frankweiler's files (and uncovers as much treasure).

So the entire Konigsburg family is grateful, truly grateful, that readers and the Newbery committee admire and recognize E. L. Konigsburg's talent. By coincidence, my family and I arrived to visit my parents the very day they learned that she had won the 1997 Newbery Medal. She had only five minutes to spend with us before she left to be on the *Today* show in New York. We spent those moments jumping for joy.

While Mom was in Manhattan, Dad answered dozens of phone calls, and the condominium filled with floral arrangements. I was moved by how proud Dad was of her. For forty-five years, he has been her sounding board, and throughout her career, he has been her business adviser. I was also touched by how many well-wishers were friends who had helped our family celebrate the 1968 Newbery. Now, some of their children called with congratulations.

Mom came home, exhilarated from her trip. Soon, she was returning phone calls and writing thank-you notes. She had already returned to being wife, mother, and grandmother. After learning that my thirteen-year-old son was wearing a stocking cap to prevent his hair from curling, Elaine Konigsburg took her grandson to a hair salon and bought him styling mousse. That evening, she heated up the brisket she had made to celebrate our visit. We enjoyed our meal, and I thought about how receiving a second Newbery has made Mom's life come full spiral. After twenty-nine years, that's better than full circle.

The Caldecott Medal 1998

Rapunzel

written and illustrated by
Paul O. Zelinsky

published by
Dutton, 1997

Horn Book Review

Reduced to its plot, the story of "Rapunzel" is the ultimate melodrama: a hapless child, because of her mother's longing for a particular herb, is given to a sorceress to be raised in a formidable tower until an undaunted prince breaches the defenses. Pregnant, she is banished; he is blinded by a fall. Both must wander through a desolate wilderness until their final triumphant reunion. But, as Zelinsky's extensive notes reveal, the tale is far more than a folktale version of a long-running soap opera. Dating back to *Basile's Il Pentamerone* (1637), it underwent several metamorphoses before being included by the Brothers Grimm in the first edition of their *Household Stories* (1812). Various retellers obviously knew a good story when they found one-and "Rapunzel," with its roots in the human psyche, is all of that. But it takes a scholar's mind and an artist's insight to endow the familiar with unexpected nuances—which Zelinsky does with passion and dazzling technique. Given the story's Italian origins, his choice of a Renaissance setting is inspired, allowing for many allusions to the art and architecture of the fifteenth, sixteenth, and seventeenth centuries. Yet these are not slavish imitations of masterpieces; rather, he has assimilated the sources and transformed them, giving depth to the characters and endowing the story with an aura of otherworldliness that enlarges upon the historical references. There is both love and menace in the sorceress's face; the landscape through which Rapunzel and the prince wander is both beautiful and desolate. Simply put, this is a gorgeous book; it demonstrates respect for the traditions of painting and the fairy tale while at the same time adhering to a singular, wholly original, artistic vision.—*Mary M. Burns*

Booklist Review

After his wildly exuberant illustrations for Anne Isaacs' tall tale *Swamp Angel* (1994), Zelinsky turns to the formal beauty of Italian Renaissance art as the setting for his glowingly illustrated version of an age-old story. And, like Donna Jo Napoli's YA novel *Zel* (1996), this story is as much about the fierce love of mother for child as it is about the romantic passion between the imprisoned Rapunzel and the prince. Drawing on the Grimms' and earlier versions of the tale, Zelinsky begins with a childless couple, who are thrilled when the wife finally becomes pregnant. She develops a craving for the herb rapunzel, and when her husband is caught stealing it for her, the sorceress makes a terrifying bargain: if she can have the baby, she will allow the wife to live. The stepmother raises Rapunzel, "seeing to her every need," then locks her in a tower away from the world. Only the sorceress can enter the tower, by climbing Rapunzel's flowing hair. Then one day, the prince hears Rapunzel sing, falls in love with her, and learns to climb into the castle. They marry secretly. When Rapunzel becomes pregnant, the furious sorceress drives Rapunzel out, cuts off her hair, and blinds the prince. The lovers wander separately in the wilderness, where Rapunzel gives birth to twins; then the couple find each other, her tears make him see, and they come home to the prince's court.

The rich oil paintings evoke the portraits, sculpture, architecture, and light-filled landscapes of Renaissance art. The costumes are lavish, the interiors intricate. Rapunzel is both gorgeous and maidenly. The sorceress is terrifying: the pictures also reveal her motherliness and her vulnerability, especially in the two double-page narrative paintings that frame the drama. One shows the sorceress taking the baby—and we see how she lovingly cradles it in her arms; in the climactic painting, when Rapunzel, the prince, and their children find each other, the whole natural world of rock and sky and tree seem to close around them in a loving embrace. Children—and adults—wll pore over the intricate detail and glowing colors; they will also be moved by the mysterious tale of nurture and passion and terror.—*Hazel Rochman*

1998 Caldecott Acceptance Speech
Paul O. Zelinsky

Members of the Caldecott committee, librarians, publishers, and all who have wished me so well and who make me feel so welcome and happy and important here today: what a day this is for me and my family! I—we—are so proud to be given this great honor.

I have a confession to make: this is a moment I have staged in my imagination, any number of times, when I've needed cheering up. I stand at a podium in a vast room. Surrounding me, a festive crowd fills a sea of round tables and disappears off into the misty distance. The image of this transcendent scene, I'm embarrassed to say, has lulled me to sleep during troubled times that accompanied more than one book. The best part of my vision was that I didn't even have to write a speech! The scene began and ended before I opened my mouth.

But here I stand, in real time, with my mouth open in no small disbelief. It's hard enough to believe that I actually finished *Rapunzel*. I started thinking about this book long ago. Something in the story kept pulling at me. For years those fertile images—of garden, tower, wilderness, hair, and more hair—were taking root in my mind. I talked about a "Rapunzel" with my editor, Donna Brooks, as far back as 1987, when *Rumpelstiltskin* was in progress. The two books would clearly be related in style. But when the *Rumpelstiltskin* paintings came out in a way that surprised and pleased me, I had no confidence that I could paint at that level again. I found myself extremely reluctant to try. Intriguing projects came up and came first: *The Wheels on the Bus, Strider, The Enchanted Castle, More Rootabagas, Swamp Angel,* and other books allowed me to put off *Rapunzel* again and again. It was eight years before I felt ready to approach the girl with the long hair. By then, signs had been gathering: in the window of a top floor apartment across the street from us, someone set a wig stand with a long blond wig on it. I found myself trying to memorize all the cupolas and turrets I saw on the tall buildings around me. And altogether too many people, appreciative of my work in *Rumpelstiltskin,* came to me and said, "I loved your book *Rapunzel.*"

So I set out to discover what my book *Rapunzel* was going to be. Soon I uncovered Rapunzel's colorful past: how in France, under the name of Persinette, she had resided luxuriously in a fairy's silver tower; how before that, as Petrosinella, she'd carried on wildly in Naples with her prince, right under the nose of a live-in witch; and how in both places she was named after parsley, not rapunzel. (It was the whim of a German translator to rename her for the salad herb known in English as rampion.) My first challenge was to find a way to tell the strong story I felt lurking among these versions, a many-leveled story about children and mothers, about coming of age, about home and the world outside. After many attempts, and with lots of help from the intrepid Donna, *Rapunzel*'s text gradually pulled its strands together. We brushed and braided them and they began to look like writing.

My second first challenge was to figure out the pictures. Ever since the paintings for *Rumpelstiltskin* came out looking a little less Northern European and a little more Southern European than I had intended, I knew that something Italian in me was trying to show itself. Evidently, it was this *Rapunzel*. The story was like a many-layered onion. And a nice onion, with its elegant, round shape and lustrous surface, embodies most of the qualities I cherish in Italian Renaissance painting. Such a solid, symmetrical shape, the onion. Set in a pure light, it defines a clear space with its simple geometry, like the simple geometry of Perugino, or Raphael. This would be the perfect space in which to set my *Rapunzel*. And then the tower, that staple of Italian architecture, could be a thing of beauty like the marble campanile of Tuscany. It seemed inevitable: my *Rapunzel* pictures would have to look like paintings from fifteenth- or sixteenth-century Italy.

If I had let myself think realistically about what I was getting myself into, I might have put *Rapunzel* off for another decade. The list of what I couldn't do was endless, if I hoped to emulate even the least of the Renaissance painters. Could I quickly learn how they painted cloth? Or, harder still, faces? How they laid down paint so smoothly, yet with such form and shape? (When I try to smooth brushstrokes away, my shapes lose all definition.) Not to mention the bigger picture: the simplicity and grandeur of the images. I had set myself a goal I had no prospect of achieving.

So I moved hesitantly, wrestling with my limitations. When figures refused to come out right in my sketches, I would make another trip to the Metropolitan Museum, buy another Renaissance art book, spend more mornings at Minerva Durham's figure drawing and anatomy workshop in SoHo to whip my fingers into shape. Sketch by sketch I crept forward, but there was always that odd detail needing research: the shape of a sixteenth-century scissors, or the underside of a cuckoo in flight. In most of my books there is a moment after which the work starts to come easily. I never reached that point here. At least, thank goodness, most of the attempts I made to improve the pictures seemed to help. But they helped—oh, so slowly.

Keeping a picture book interesting in all the right ways is a little like keeping four or five juggling balls in the air. You have to follow them all with your mind's eye. I constantly struggled not to get too distracted by any one of them. Technique, for example: I had to limit the time I spent trying to make leaves on bushes and trees as patterned, yet as leaf-like as Raphael's (did his oak leaves always go: one up, three across, two down?). Obsessing on technique, I'd risk losing sight of whether the pictures work to tell the story, and whether the story flows as you turn from page to page. There should be no forgetting that on each page the feeling must be the right one, that it be expressed through literal means, such as facial expressions and body language, as well as abstract means—the way the picture is constructed, its colors, its shapes. When these means combine to tell a vivid story, that's good illustration. But the abstract elements operate on another level as well: a structural level where something other than storytelling takes place, something that can turn illustration into art.

The storytelling in pictures is more natural to me than the art. This dawned on me during my first drawing course at Yale with my great teacher, Bernard Chaet. He looked at the pen-and-ink pictures I had brought to show him and said, "You can already do what those guys at *Esquire* do, but, Paul, you really have to learn how to draw." I was shocked to hear this. I most certainly could not do what those guys at *Esquire* could do—slick, deft work—and what did he mean I couldn't draw?

You can't really draw or paint, said my teachers, Mr. Chaet and William Bailey, unless you can make pictures "work formally." You have to "make the form work." And what on earth does that mean? I would wonder. What is form, and how does it work? Here is what I've come to believe: form is what you would see if you had brand new eyes and no names, no real-life associations for things. Form is what your retina takes in before your brain starts recognizing. You see colors and shapes. You see lights and darks, textures, lines, patterns. You see indications of depth, of space. Everything drawn has form. And form creates motion, speed, influence. Shapes and colors act on each other. Dramas are played out in the realm of form. Beauty—pictorial beauty— arises from form. I have never been sensitive enough or creative enough to completely get through to it. But when form works very well, I have faith that everyone who can see, children as well as adults, will respond to it. When shapes perform dances with other shapes, when colors play up and down scales, when they fall into chords, when lines move in patterns that look inevitably right, we will all feel it.

When form works, something profound happens. Art happens. All stories move us with the emotions they provoke. We feel sad when Rapunzel and the prince suffer in the wilderness, and happy when they reunite. But art moves us on another, complementary level as well. My friend Rika Lesser, the poet and translator who wrote the words for my

Hansel and Gretel, and also helped me with *Rapunzel*'s text, told me a Swedish neologism for the part of us that responds to art: tänkehjärta. I think it's wonderful; in English it would be the "thought-heart." Not the heart that fills with sentiment, and not the mind that judges ideas; this is a separate organ. It gives us the emotion of thought and the logic of feeling. It lies deep inside all of us, I am certain. Hoping to sense its pulse, I sit in my studio day after day, and strive to make my pictures engaging as form. When I need to show how intrusively a prince bursts into the ordered life of a Rapunzel, I want to make the shapes show it along with the characters: the prince's straight lines jutting forward and Rapunzel's curves wheeling out of their way. To the degree that I succeed, form and content of the picture will become one thing, and you'll feel it in your thought-heart.

I've been convinced that classical artists thought about their creations just as formally as Mr. Chaet does ever since I saw one drawing by a pupil of Rembrandt in an exhibition at the Chicago Art Institute. A group of figures were clustered at the bottom of the drawing, and an angel filled the upper left corner. Rembrandt himself had marked up this composition with a bold line to show his pupil how the angel's wing should look. And the difference made by that one line was beyond remarkable: it not only gave strength to an unstable little pen-scratch, it made an empty, formless space around the wing into a shapely compartment of air. It made the wing a better wing, it charged the angel with a sense of direction, and the drawing with a spirit it hadn't had before.

It made a better angel's wing. Who here has ever seen, much less judged, an angel's wing? How do I know a better one when I see it? What was it but perfect form at work, making me think I knew, assuring me that this was right. Children, especially little children, have never seen many things. To them, so much of the world is no different from angels' wings. And what makes a child respond to a picture in a book? Is it accuracy of depiction? Is it photographic realism? No! It might be an instinctual button being pushed—bright colors, cute animals—but it's also compelling form, form that works. Then, after that, it's what's particular to the child, whatever happens to appeal to her or him, as with any person of any age.

Many artists in children's books are masters of form. Maurice Sendak, my first and only illustration teacher, is one. He raised a curtain for me on the workings of the picture book when he applied the word rhythm to it. Others whose work has helped me to see in new ways are Garth Williams, Marc Simont, Evaline Ness, Margot Zemach, Irene Haas, Robert Lawson. I'm leaving out so many whose drawings get me in my thought-heart.

I, too, was aiming for the thought-heart one Monday morning last January, working and reworking an old sorcerer's right hand for a paperback book cover. I was also aware that the ALA was meeting then, but I can never remember days or dates. I asked my wife Deborah, who always can, if she remembered what day of the week the call had come telling me that *Swamp Angel* had won a Caldecott Honor. It was a Tuesday, she said.

So I went to work Monday morning concerned with other things. I was eager to check for e-mail, and maybe look into the Internet, a brand-new treat for me. My new computer had been failing to go online through two weeks of grueling phone calls for technical support from AT&T, my service provider, but on Friday, things had seemed to work. First thing Monday, the software couldn't locate the modem. Which was the reason I was working on a painting that morning, and my telephone line was clear.

It's about 9:15 A.M. The phone rings. A male voice asks for Paul Zelinsky. Now, this can mean one of two things: someone hawking financial services, or a salesman for a long distance phone company. "Who's calling?" I ask, not admitting to my name, and ready to bite the head off of anyone connected with AT&T.

"This is John Stewart," the man seems to say. I know of no John Stewart. "What is this about?" I ask, icily.

Then came the words, "I'm calling for the Caldecott committee here in New Orleans"—and the world reshaped itself around me. My heart went to my throat; my throat went to my head. I think I said "Oh!" And John Stewig said, "Is Paul Zelinsky there please?" Oh, yes, that's me after all. And suddenly there was only one thing more I wanted to know, which John was about to reveal. "We're happy to tell you," he continued, "that we've voted *Rapunzel* the book of the year." A magnificent thrill and a cheer welled up inside me, but didn't quite make it out of my mouth.

Instead, I burbled, "I don't believe it!" This, after all, was the wrong day!

But when I heard the entire committee cry "hooray" in the background, I had to believe it. I think I thanked them, hung up, and out came the cheer. "YOWEE!" Immediately, I called Deborah at P.S. 8. "Interrupt her class," I told the school secretary, "it's urgent: *Rapunzel*

won the Caldecott Medal!" Deborah says that when she saw the secretary enter her classroom, pink message-paper in hand, she started to
cry. She had known all along that Monday was the day; she had wanted
to give me an easy weekend. My weekend had been just fine, but hers
hadn't. She had prayed and stewed and tossed and turned. I thank her
for the kind deception she played on me.

After the fact, the signs all seem to have shown that *Rapunzel* was
marked for something special. Mind you, I am not a superstitious person. I'm as rational as they come. But I like the attitude of Niels Bohr,
the father of quantum theory, who kept a horseshoe over the door of
his country house. When guests saw it, they would say, "You of all people don't believe in this primitive superstition, do you?" And he would
answer no, he didn't, but he understood that it's supposed to work even
if you don't believe in it. In this spirit, I would like to tell you some of
the indications that *Rapunzel* might have been specially blessed.

The first sign happened just before the ALA Annual Conference
last year. I had managed to buy rapunzel seeds by mail, and Deborah
raised the plants on the roof deck of our apartment building. I wanted
to portray the plant and its flowers accurately, and also to know what
it tasted like. (Knowing the flavor, I thought, would help me in some
indefinable way with the illustrations.) Rapunzel is a biennial; in its
first year it grows only leaves; in its second year, mainly flowers; and
then it dies. I started to work on the book in 1995. That summer we
ate lots of rapunzel salad. It was crisp and spicy. I hadn't gotten nearly
far enough along in the painting by the summer of '96, but we had
plenty of rapunzel flowers. The following summer was last summer,
1997, and we planted other plants in the rapunzel pots. I was supposed
to have finished *Rapunzel* long since, but I hadn't. There had been a
deadline, then an urgent deadline, then a dead-and-buried-line and a
brutally-murdered-line, and I missed them all. I completed the book in
a sustained rush the likes of which I hope never to repeat. Not for the
first time, I put my family and myself through quite an ordeal.

The rush lasted right up until the ALA Annual Conference itself.
Deborah and I were to leave for San Francisco on a Saturday, and not
until Thursday did I finish the back of the book jacket, the last piece
of art. I delivered it to Dutton, then returned home half dazed. In the
elevator I met our neighbors, ninety-three-year-old Janet and her daughter Nancy, both avid roof-deck gardeners, who said, "Have you been to
the roof today? We think your rapunzel is blooming."

I said, "No, there is no rapunzel this year. It's a biennial."

Nancy said, "Well, why don't you come up and look? We thought it was your rapunzel." So instead of getting off on eight, we all went up to the penthouse. There on the roof deck, in the center of a large clay pot full of marigolds, one slender stalk of rapunzel was poking up, with four purple flowers, newly opened, nodding on their stems. What a sign that was, don't you think?

And what am I to make of the fact, which I perceived during a bout of procrastination three-quarters of the way through the *Rapunzel* oil paintings, that my full name, Paul Oser Zelinsky, is an anagram for "Rapunzel's key oils?"

By the way, is this related to the fact that in the Library of Congress cataloging code, the call numbers for children's stories all begin with PZ? How could I have gone into any other line of work?

Clearly I belong with you, the children's librarians who have taken so enthusiastically to the books I have been lucky enough to work on. My gratitude belongs to you. And it belongs to my dear friend and longtime editor—we have collaborated for almost half my life!—Donna Brooks, to whom I owe more than I can say, starting with *How I Hunted the Little Fellows* and *The Maid and the Mouse and the Odd-shaped House* and going on and on. And it belongs to my glamorous wife of almost equal tenure, whom I love. Deborah, a teacher of uncanny understanding, bestows beauty and order on the life of our family, and makes it rich with her love of music. And my gratitude goes to our children, Anna and Rachel, for being so terrific. I know they can't help that, but they did put up with a sometimes-absent and distracted father in exchange for seeing their cat Skimbleshanks made a supporting actor in a picture book. I'm prouder of them than of any product of my hand. And if my parents had not brought me up with a love of the arts, I would surely not be here tonight. I am thankful to them for a childhood full of trips to the Art Institute, among other things. And I wish to thank Amy Berniker for being a patient collaborator on all questions of *Rapunzel*'s design, and Laurence Tucci for conjuring a magical tower of a production schedule: somehow he squeezed more stages of proof into this book's preparation than there was space on the calendar to fit them in. And thank you, Alissa Heyman, for doing so much of the extra work brought on by my tardiness, and many others at Dutton Children's Books.

The Caldecott call has made me feel like the prince at the end of the French Rapunzel tale, "Persinette," when the sorceress rescues the prince's little reunited family from certain death in the wilderness. John

Stewig and the committee play the part of the sorceress to my prince. Imagine that you're hearing courtly seventeenth-century French:

> She transported herself to the place where they stood; she appeared in a chariot resplendent with gold and precious stones. She had them climb in, placing herself between the fortunate lovers, and setting their lovely children on magnificent cushions at their feet. And in this manner she drove them to the palace of the king, father to the prince. It was there that joy burst all bounds: the prince, who had for so long been thought lost, was received as if he were a god. And he was so happy to find himself at peace after having been so agitated by the storm that nothing in the world was comparable to the felicity in which he lived with his perfect spouse.

I think that nothing in the world is comparable to this. Thank you very much.

Paul O. Zelinsky:
Geishas on Tractors

Donna Brooks

Paul O. Zelinsky

When Paul's elder daughter, Anna, was thirteen months old, Paul made a "Dictionary of the Anna Language" for her great-grandparents on their sixtieth anniversary. A little book, carefully hand-lettered on marbled paper from India and bound in leather (from an old briefcase he found in the garbage), it contained fifty-five entries for twelve letters. Except for a colophon drawn on the title page (a small rubber duck with the word dah under it), the dictionary was unillustrated. It is a tender example of the considerate attention with which Paul enters into the world of another person, and of the delicacy and humor he brings to bear on what he finds there. Here are a few entries.

> Bub • buh (bii'ba) n. button. *interj.* "Get me something to drink!" (lit., bottle).
>
> Dad • dy (da'de) n. *l.* Daddy 2. doggie; dog 3. donkey.
>
> Mom • my (mo'me) n. Mommy; occas., Daddy.
>
> Nnollonono (nononono) *interj.* 1. no 2. yes.

Pap • pa • doo (pa pa doo) *interj.* meaning obscure.

Ta(t) (ta-) *n.* cat; also chihuahua.

Tah • toe (Ya'to) *interj.* "Take this away from me!" (lit., thank you).

Tup • py• tup • py• tup• py (td'pd-td'pe-tu'pe) *interj.* expression denoting a cheerful mood and the desire to kill time.

Such faithful, amused appreciation of a baby's utterances has to please a children's book editor. Anna's wants, her confusions, her economies, her delights—here they all are, given to us with gentle wit, orderliness, grace.

The dictionary reminds me of Paul's own personal gentleness, which you can hear in his voice as well as feel when you are with him, and which permeates his studio and heightens the perceptions of any-one who spends time there. I have seen this quality persist under great pressure, when he is exhausted, even suffering from illness, painting to meet a deadline that has passed. His gentleness takes his less gentle impulses and casts them as humor. Given an assignment to build a box in seventh-grade woodshop, he created a small guillotine with a stor-age area underneath. The weight of the dropping blade (a thick piece of stainless steel that he sawed and filed) opened the lid. I asked him if he ever cut anything with this guillotine. "No," he replied sadly. "I didn't have the strength to make it really sharp."

I first watched Paul draw when he was working on the pen-and-ink illustrations for *How I Hunted the Little Fellows* by the Russian author Boris Zhitkov, translated by Jemma Bider. But I didn't realize how much everything he drew was infused with character until I looked at a page of doodles in his studio. Whether a goblin head resting in a gob-let or a cat playing its own fiddle-body, each had a distinct energy and personality, each seemed to suggest an invisible world behind it. "How do you do this?" I asked, unable to draw even an apple myself and make it look round. He shrugged. "It just comes out that way."

Perhaps this ability to animate is simply innate. Some years back Paul told me that when he was two and his family lived in Japan, he fell madly in love with geishas. He drew them over and over. "Their white, white faces; their black hair; the rich colors of their costumes—their otherworldliness." Perfect, I thought, seeing my vague idea of geisha beauty and Japanese art in some of the geometrical forms that I love in Paul's work. This spring *Publishers Weekly* reproduced a geisha drawing of Paul's (age three years) that *Highlights* had unearthed from the pages of their November 1957 issue. The drawing was tiny, but I've seen a larger one of similar vintage. This geisha, too, is holding open the sleeves of her kimono, a delicate motion implied in the lines of her arms and the tilt of the fan she holds. She's looking at us and her face is lovely, with wide-set eyes, a sweet, modest smile, no nose, and a hair ornament slanted just right. Sure enough, even in this drawing by a not-yet-four-year-old illustrator, a person—poised, appraising, friendly—is peeking out.

As the geisha drawings surfaced, I learned more of their story. After the year in Japan, Paul's family moved to Princeton, New Jersey, where they lived across the street from a construction site. Again Paul fell madly in love, this time with tractors and steam shovels. Did he desert the geishas? By no means. In his new, obsessive drawings of tractors and steam shovels, the geishas were the drivers.

Even then, Paul brought together what gave pleasure to his eye and mind. He is a maker of things, an assembler of worlds. At Yale, he thought about becoming a set designer, and you can see that interest in his books. Costumes, furnishings, buildings, interior space, landscapes—the set of elements represents coherent choices yielding drama and beauty. He has something of the director in him as well. I've seen this in the way he works with models or revises his sketches, feeling out the possibilities in their poses, expressions, compositions.

I often go to Paul's studio when we are working together. Early on, his studio was his apartment—a large, high-ceilinged unit in a brownstone in Brooklyn Heights. His drawing table, surrounded by doodles, supplies, and a radio, stood near the window in a tiny room that served as his bedroom. In the main room were his easel, a few paintings, a small table and chairs, and a big oak bookcase with intricately carved molding that Paul had patiently stripped of paint using a sharp-pointed instrument the size of a crochet hook. Against the wall lay a round, reflective blue glass tabletop, suggesting magic and sorcery. And indeed, it seemed to me, over the years, that Paul was a conjurer. "As adults we have lost that equality of belief in what we see and what we don't," he once wrote in a piece about a fellow painter. For Paul, illustrating a book must summon up that lost belief. Projects begin to develop a power that recasts the physical world around him, drawing whatever or whomever is useful toward the studio. A friend from college, the poet Rika Lesser, was pressed into service—between pillows—as a model for a grandmother. I was recruited to wear a tablecloth as a skirt and lead my children briskly into the forest; and another time to stand hunched over and, thinking like a witch, hold my hand out to an imaginary Hansel. A lovely young woman Paul spied in a Chinese restaurant visited the studio to model for the miller's daughter in *Rumpelstiltskin*. (Paul's wife, Deborah, assured her of his honorable intentions.) Fresh from class, Alexandre Proia, a ballet dancer, trekked downtown to be tucked into a tunic held together with staples and masking tape, crowned with an inside-out beret, and made to emerge and reemerge from Paul's bathroom as the king coming into a room full of gold. From time to time his family might lend a hand, an ear, a pair of legs, or whatever else had to be drawn.

Often Paul constructed what he needed to see—a boat of papiermache, a grandmother's head in clay, a tiny Swamp Angel out of bent wire wrapped in paper tape. He built the front half of the top quarter of Rapunzel's intricately patterned tower out of cardboard. (Later, at a party, he reproduced the tower as a table-long arrangement of different cheeses.) And if he could not make what he needed to look at, he journeyed to find it: to the woods to examine lichen, the Museum of Natural History to look at drawers full of cuckoos, Coney Island to find the perfect Russian boy. Or he brought what he needed back: grass to dry into straw; rapunzel seeds to grow; books of all sorts; a live mouse, which he attempted to coax onto a toy motorcycle. Somehow Paul would assemble these homemade objects, improbably draped models, and piecemeal, jerrybuilt sets and transform them into a seamless and ravishing new world. When enough illustrations had been completed—a kind of critical mass—a moment would arrive that never failed to stagger me. The effects of the separate pieces would suddenly express their coherence, and I would finally grasp the power of the book (and the world) that was emerging. That it was once again a new and different look, that Paul had been struggling toward this all along, and that I had blithely "helped out" without realizing what was underway, all fueled my feeling of amazement. If I expressed my astonishment and regard to him in terms that suggested he had been painting what he saw in his mind's eye, he was careful to correct me. He didn't necessarily know what he was doing, he worked his way moment by moment, and it could be wonderful and flow, or it could go nowhere.

The streak of scientist in Paul (he might have majored in physics, but "I liked it better than I could do it") and his fascination with ingenious construction allow him to face down complicated technical challenges. He charged intrepidly into the paper engineering for *The*

Wheels on the Bus. For *Swamp Angel* by Anne Isaacs, he experimented until he had systematized a way to prepare cherry veneer for oil paints. (Getting the veneer was another story.) And in the olden, budget-conscious days of preseparated art for all but the most famous illustrators, Paul figured out how to use silk-screened gray paper to achieve flat background colors—a lot harder than it looks—for *The Maid and the Mouse and the Odd-shaped House.* It doubled his work, but it came in at the right cost.

All of this research and pursuit of precision rarely derails Paul's nimble sense of humor. He has an elastic wit that stretches from the sublime to the silly (or worse). A sly bathos always brings things down to earth. One day when he was cross-hatching the illustrations for *How I Hunted the Little Fellows,* a story set in nineteenth-century Russia, I showed up to see the drawings. There, amidst all the carefully researched and finely rendered details of the grandmother's room-wallpaper, rugs, door-handles, picture frames-stood Mickey Mouse, waving out at the reader from between the plates on Grandmother's armoire. Paul explained that it was a joke; Mickey was carefully positioned to disappear into the gutter when the book was side sewn. I instantly fantasized reviewers ripping the binding apart, finding Mickey Mouse on a shelf in a St. Petersburg apartment in 1896, and writing damning reviews about smart-aleck illustrators and their publishers. Or worse—thinking we didn't know better! Finally my mind went to the printers. What if they thought Mickey was supposed to show, and actually cut and split the art so as not to lose him? That possibility held sway with Paul, and the mouse was sanded away.

I love getting birthday cards from Paul. Often these cards are little books themselves, sardonically recapitulating our most recent project together. Here he can express all the inevitable feelings of aggravation, frustration, and yes, even rage, that he never lets loose in the actual working process. His cards offer me a sidesplitting view of the ridiculous extremes that go into making a children's book. The birthday card I received after *Hansel and Gretel* (where much effort had been expended to find the earliest Grimm versions) bore these words on the title page: "Three hitherto undiscovered very early and even more authentic versions." The illustrations were colored pencil in a smart-looking Bauhaus style. In the first version, the children were eaten by wild animals in the forest. From behind a tree a little bearded man peeked out, saying, "Ach, Wilhelm—perhaps dis ist too harsch? Mebbe ve try again." At the end of the second version, Gretel shoved the witch into the oven, and "when they reached home their father said, 'Your mother is dead and this is one great story. Sell the rights and we can live happily and prosper to the end of our days.' Early the next morning, they set off into the forest. They walked and walked. Finally they reached Frankfurt. A gnarled old man came out from behind a desk, 'I'm sorry, folks,' he said, 'You're in the public domain.'" In the third version, the mother turned nice, the children stayed happily at home, and Wilhelm cried, "Dis time I tink I got it."

After *The Maid and the Mouse and the Odd-shaped House*, a picture book adapted from an old tell-and-draw story, Paul made me a small tell-and-draw book called "The Cat" as a birthday card. In the actual book, a maid and a mouse make improvements in their odd-shaped house, unwittingly "drawing" a cat's face (the new chimneys become ears; the windows, eyes; and so on). The body of the cat is created by the path the maid takes when she goes looking for the source of a hissing sound. Once she realizes what their house has become, she races back to snatch the mouse from the jaws of this now animated feline. "Matter enough, my mouse so fat! / Oh, dear! Alas! It is the CAT!" The book works as a kind of puzzle; though the viewer can tell that something is being constructed, the full picture of the cat is withheld as long as possible for maximum surprise.

The card Paul made has illustrations that are simple, energetic, and dead-on funny. The whole thing mimics the real book—its meter, its pacing—with a few significant plot alterations. The maid's roommate is not a mouse but a rat, and the two live not in a pentagonal house but a cat's stomach. "The rat was young, the maid was old. / The Cat, of course, was rent-controlled." The maid and the rat get busy taking their revenge on the cat—lopping off its head, disguising the stump of a neck, stretching out its legs like rubber bands. Then the maid goes out to investigate a bothersome noise. "'It sounds,' announced the little hag, / 'like paste extruding from a bag.'" Again, what all this decapitation and transmogrification amounts to is withheld from the viewer until the very last, when the maid, hurries back inside. "What she had seen to prompt her flight / was this most unexpected sight: / The Cat, expressive in its looks, said:". . . and here you turn the page to a picture of what the cat has finally become—a big beautiful birthday cake with frosting letters spelling out . . . "Happy Birthday, Donna Brooks!"

In my own tell-and-draw story, had I Paul's clever command of line and form, a gold-colored cat would by some means be squashed into a perfectly round, flat shape except for a slight feeling of embossment left over from its bones. The maid and the mouse would have gone out to investigate a loud noise. Upon discovering that the source of the sound was a cheering crowd, the maid would exultantly return on mouseback, riding sidesaddle across the golden circle. The last lines of my story would go something like, "And so, dear Paul, a cat it's not. / This time it's the Caldecott."

The Newbery Medal 1998

Out of the Dust

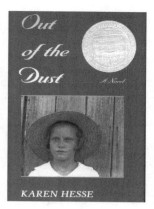

written by
Karen Hesse

published by
Scholastic Press, 1997

Horn Book Review

Prairie winds dark with dust blow through this novel—turning suppers gritty, burying tractors, and scouring lungs. Even the pages of the book, composed solely of first-person, free-verse poems, have a windswept appearance as fourteen-year-old Billie Jo Kelby relates her Depression-era experiences in the Oklahoma panhandle: "We haven't had a good crop in three years, / not since the bounty of '31, / and we're all whittled down to the bone these days." Billie Jo's world is further devastated when a kitchen fire causes the deaths of her mother and newborn brother and severely injures her hands, stalling the fledgling pianist's dream of a music career. A few of the poems are pretentious in tone or facile in execution, and some of the longer, narrative-driven pieces strain at the free verse structure, but the distinctive writing style is nonetheless remarkably successful. Filled with memorable images—such as Billie Jo's glimpse of her pregnant mother bathing outdoors in a drizzle—the spare verses showcase the poetry of everyday language; the pauses between line breaks speak eloquently, if sometimes melodramatically. The focus of the entire book is not quite as concise. As tragedies pile up over the two-year timeline (a plague of grasshoppers descends, starving cattle need to be shot, Billie Jo's father develops skin cancer), the pace becomes slightly numbing. Billie Jo's aborted escape from the dust bowl almost gets lost in the procession of bleak events, instead of serving as the book's climax. Yet her voice, nearly every word informed by longing, provides an immediacy that expressively depicts both a grim historical era and one family's healing.
—*Peter D. Sieruta*

Booklist Review

"Daddy came in, / he sat across from Ma and blew his nose. / Mud streamed out. / He coughed and spit out / mud. / If he had cried, / his tears would have been mud too, / but he didn't cry. / And neither did Ma." This is life in the Oklahoma dust bowl in the mid-1930s. Billie Jo and her parents barely eke out a living from the land, as her father refuses to plant anything but wheat, and the winds and dust destroy the crop time after time. Playing the piano provides some solace, but there is no comfort to be had once Billie Jo's pregnant mother mistakes a bucket of kerosene for a bucket of water and dies, leaving a husband who withdraws even further and an adolescent daughter with terribly burned hands. The story is bleak, but Hesse's writing transcends the gloom and transforms it into a powerfully compelling tale of a girl with enormous strength, courage, and love. The entire novel is written in very readable blank verse, a superb choice for bringing out the exquisite agony and delight to be found in such a difficult period lived by such a vibrant character. It also spares the reader the trouble of wading through pages of distressing text, distilling all the experiences into brief, acutely observed phrases. This is an excellent book for discussion, and many of the poems stand alone sufficiently to be used as powerful supplements to a history lesson.—*Susan Dove Lempke*

1998 Newbery Acceptance Speech

Karen Hesse

Let me begin by extending my heartfelt congratulations to my fellow Newbery and Caldecott winners, past and present. And to all the hardworking, dedicated authors, illustrators, and librarians among us, please know, you are all winners, we are all winners. Because your work makes a difference. I celebrate every one of you.

For those of you who are wondering, here is the truth. Winning the Newbery could give a person heart failure. Even now, months after Ellen Fader phoned my once-so-quiet apartment overlooking the Connecticut River, even now my heart thunders when I think of that phone call.

I can't tell you how many hours of my childhood I spent tucked in a corner of the Enoch Pratt Free Library, devouring books, particularly Newberys. And look at me now. Members of the ALA, members of the Newbery committee, do you have any idea how extraordinary it is for me to be standing here, on this occasion?

There are so many to thank: My zadi, who sold his ticket on the Titanic and took the next boat over; my bubi Sara; my mom, Fran; my aunts, Esther and Bernice; my whole delicious family; a legion of dedicated teachers and librarians; my writing groups; my prince of a husband, Randy; Kate and Rachel, my extra-ordinary daughters; Katherine Paterson, my unwitting mentor; Brenda Bowen, my dazzling editor; my dear friends at Henry Holt and Puffin Books; the terrific team at Scholastic, led by Dick Robinson, Barbara Marcus, and Jean Feiwel; and my inspiration for *Out of the Dust*, Lucille Burroughs, who stared out at me from the pages of *Let Us Now Praise Famous Men*, imploring me to tell her story, even if I had to make it up.

I was told once that writing historical fiction was a bad idea. No market for it. I didn't listen. I love research, love dipping into another time and place, and asking the tough questions in a way that helps me see both question and answer with a clearer perspective. *Out of the Dust* is my third historical novel. In the first two, Rifka Nebrot and Hannah Gold brought me back to my Jewish roots. But Billie Jo Kelby brought me even deeper. She brought me back to my human roots.

I can't think about roots of any sort without thinking of my husband, Randy. We have had nearly thirty years together, to listen to each other, to learn from each other. Among his many gifts, Randy has a marvelously green thumb. I, unfortunately, do not.

Once, accidentally, I watered one of Randy's favorite house plants with vinegar. The plant looked thirsty. I thought I was doing my husband a favor. I didn't know the bottle held vinegar until I had soaked the soil, until the sharp acid filtered down through the rich dirt toward the roots. The plant died. It couldn't have done otherwise.

The innocent substitution of one liquid for another . . . it happens. In *Out of the Dust*, when Billie Jo's mother reaches for the pail, she thinks she, too, is reaching for water, pouring water to make coffee. She doesn't realize her mistake, that she is pouring kerosene, until the flames rise up from the stove.

Readers ask, could such a terrible mistake really happen? Yes. It happened often. I based the accident on a series of articles appearing in the 1934 *Boise City News*. That particular family tragedy planted the seed for *Out of the Dust*, as much as the dust storms did.

Let me tell you: I never make up any of the bad things that happen to my characters. I love my characters too much to hurt them deliberately, even the prickly ones. It just so happens that in life, there's pain; sorrow lives in the shadow of joy, joy in the shadow of sorrow. The question is, do we let the pain reign triumphant, or do we find a way to grow, to transform, and ultimately transcend our pain?

The first traceable roots for *Out of the Dust* reach back to 1993 when I took a car trip out to Colorado with fellow author Liza Ketchum. When we entered Kansas, something extraordinary happened. I fell in love. I had never been in the interior of the country before. Our first day in Kansas, we experienced a tornado. I watched, awestruck, as the sky turned green as a bruise and the air swelled with explosive energy. The second day in Kansas, we walked in a town so small it didn't have a name. It grew up beside a railroad track and never fully pulled itself from the earth. The wind never stopped blowing there. It caressed our faces, it whispered in our ears. The grass moved like a corps of dancers. The colors were unlike any I had ever encountered on the east coast or the west. And the sky and land went on to the horizon and beyond.

It took me three years to internalize that experience enough to write about it. I had been working on a picture book in which a young inner-city child longs for rain. My writing group loved the language but had problems with the main character's motivation. The question, as it usually does, came from Eileen Christelow. She asked, "Where's the emotional line here? Why does this child want it to rain so much?" I later captured the motivation, the emotional line of that picture book, even to Eileen's satisfaction, but at that moment, instead, my mind slid precipitously back sixty years to a time when people desperately wanted rain, to the dirty thirties.

A week or two later, Brenda Bowen, during a phone conversation, asked what I was working on. Either she should stop asking or I should stop answering. I know it's not good for either of us. When I replied I was researching agricultural practices on the Great Plains, the silence on the other end of the line was deadly.

"Oh," Brenda said at last. But then she said "oh" again, and this time it had a decidedly up side to the end of it. Not "oh," like "oh, no." "Oh," like "oh, yes." Brenda trusted me. She had faith that if I was excited by dust, there was a good chance that she—and, ultimately, young readers—would be, too.

But how could I recreate the dust bowl? I was born in 1952, in Baltimore, Maryland. What did I know from dust? I knew alley dust, I knew gutter dust, but what did I know of dust so extensive it blew from one state to another, across an entire nation, and out over the ocean where it rained down on the decks of ships hundreds of miles out to sea?

I phoned the Oklahoma Historical Society and asked for help. I'd found, in one of the very dry treatises on Plains agricultural practices, a reference to the *Boise City News*, a daily paper published in the Oklahoma Panhandle during the period in which I was most interested. The Oklahoma Historical Society allowed as how there had been such a paper. I asked if I might get copies of it. Yes, they said, it was available on microfilm. So off went my check to purchase the film, and when the package arrived, with giddy excitement, I rushed to my local library, and took possession of the microfilm machine, proclaiming it my exclusive property for weeks, while I dug in and lived through day after day, month after month, year after year of life in the heart of the Depression, in the heart of the dust bowl. I saturated myself with those dusty, dirty, desperate times, and what I discovered thrilled me. I had thought it never rained during that period. In fact it did. Only rarely did the rain do any good. But it did rain. And through that grim time, when men jumped to their deaths from tall buildings and farmers shot themselves behind barns, I discovered there was still life going on, talent shows, dances, movies. Daily acts of generosity and kindness. Living through those dirty years, article by article, in the pages of the *Boise City News*, supplied the balance of what I needed to re-create credibly that extraordinary time and place.

I gave the manuscript to my daughters first. A novel in free verse, I didn't know if anyone would understand what I was trying to do. But both Kate and Rachel handed the limp pages back, hours later, their eyes welled with tears. Okay, I thought. They must have understood a little bit. I revised the manuscript based on Kate and Rachel's comments, and gave it next to Liza and Eileen. They asked a lot of questions, but for once they didn't ask about emotional line. I revised the manuscript again, according to Liza and Eileen's comments. The next time I sent it to Brenda Bowen. She phoned after reading it. "Agricultural practices on the Great Plains?" she asked. And then she laughed. And I felt that first flush of joy. But still there was shadow. I knew how much Brenda had loved *The Music of Dolphins*. "Could you love this as much?" I asked. "When it's all finished, could you love it as much?" And Brenda never hesitated. "It'll be great," she said. That's my Brenda. "It'll be great."

"But I want you to think," she said. "What is it about, really. What is going on with Billie Jo and Pa, what is going on with Billie Jo and Ma. And what is going on with Billie Jo herself?"

And I knew. It was about forgiveness. The whole book. Every relationship. Not only the relationships between people, but the relationship between the people and the land itself. It was all about forgiveness.

I began my literary life as a poet. When I was expecting my first child, my ability to focus on the creation of poetry diminished as my need to focus on the creation of human life increased. For seventeen years, my brain continued to place the nurturing of my daughters above all other creative endeavors, and I forsook poetry. Not that prose is easy to write. But for me, at least, it required a different commitment of brain cells, a different commitment of energy and emotion. Part of my mind always listened for my children during those years. And that listening rendered me incapable of writing poetry. But something inexplicably wonderful happened. My daughters grew up. They reached an age of independence and self-possession that for the first time in seventeen years permitted my brain to let go of them for minutes, hours at a time, and in those minutes and hours, poetry was allowed to return and *Out of the Dust* was born. I never attempted to write this book any other way than in free verse. The frugality of the life, the hypnotically hard work of farming, the grimness of conditions during the dust bowl demanded an economy of words. Pa and Ma and Billie Jo's rawboned life translated into poetry, and bless Scholastic for honoring that translation and producing *Out of the Dust* with the spare understatement I sought when writing it.

I have so much respect for these people, these survivors of the dust, the Arley and Vera Wanderdales, the Mad Dog Craddocks, the Joe De La Flors. I discovered Joe in WPA material on the Internet and wove him in, a Mexican-American cowboy, hardworking, unacknowledged. I put him up high in the saddle where he belonged, where Billie Jo could look up to him.

Occasionally, adult readers grimace at the events documented in *Out of the Dust*. They ask, how can this book be for young readers? I ask, how can it not? The children I have met during my travels around the country have astounded me with their perception, their intelligence, their capacity to take in information and apply it to a greater picture, or take in the greater picture and distill it down to what they need from it.

Young readers are asking for substance. They are asking for respect. They are asking for books that challenge, and confirm, and console. They are asking for us to listen to their questions and to help them find their own answers. If we cannot attend always to those questions, to that quest for answers, whether our work is that of librarian, writer, teacher, publisher, or parent, how can they forgive us? And yet they do, every day. Just as Billie Jo forgave Ma. Just as Billie Jo forgave Pa. Just as Billie Jo forgave herself. And with that forgiveness Billie Jo finally set her roots and turned toward her future.

Often, our lives are so crowded, we need to weed out what is essential from what is not. Reading historical fiction gives us perspective. It gives us respite from the tempest of our present-day lives. It gives us a safe place in which we can grow, transform, transcend. It helps us understand that sometimes the questions are too hard, that sometimes there are no answers, that sometimes there is only forgiveness.

Hodding Carter said, "There are only two lasting bequests we can hope to give our children. One of these is roots, the other wings." Ellen Fader, members of the Newbery committee, members of ALA—from the girl who devoured Newberys in a corner of the Enoch Pratt Free Library, thank you.

Karen Hesse

Brenda Bowen

A profound and visceral sense of place is one of the qualities that is most memorable about Karen Hesse's writing. As I think about my relationship with Karen Hesse, I think not about what things happened, but where they happened. The sense of place in Karen's books is so strong that, as her friend and editor, when I think of Karen, I think of places.

Photo credit: Cheryl Liston ©1992

Karen Hesse

My first experience of Karen was in a small, crowded cubicle at Scholastic, where I worked as an assistant editor. It must have been early in the day (I was on the east side of the building), and it must have been summer, because I remember light pouring in from the window. There was light; there was a plain brown envelope, and there was an address that made me want to read on. What kind of author lived on "Star Route" in a small town in Vermont?

Alas, this was an author who had written a story about a family's encounter with Bigfoot. It was impossible to believe the plot, and the Yeti angle was just plain weird. I didn't believe in that monster for a second. I very nearly packaged the manuscript up and sent it back to the author with a polite form rejection letter, but something in it made me keep reading. I could see that family, crowded into an old green station-wagon, hopes high, driving through the Vermont hills. I can still recall it clearly. The story was not credible, but the time and place were palpable. The voice was something to remember. I thought: This is a writer.

I wrote an encouraging letter, but declined to publish the manuscript, and I invited the author to send me more when she was next ready to submit.

I didn't see any more from her for many years.

In a different office, at a different publisher, with more oblique sun (facing east again, probably late winter), another package arrived at my desk. This one was from an agent, with four or five slender stories inside. I looked at the place from which the manuscript had been sent. There, on the title page, was Karen's name, which I didn't remember, and Star Route, which I did.

Could this be the Bigfoot lady?

One of the slender stories just four pages long was called "Wish on a Unicorn." "Hannie and I were walking home from school when we saw a unicorn in Newell's field." Now there's a sentence to get a story going. But at only four pages in length, there was no room for the author to explore the characters, the situation, the magic of the story. Could she revise? I asked the agent. Oh yes, she could.

That four-page picture book became Karen's first novel, which held in it so many seeds of her later work: an underprivileged family; a child who has had to shoulder more responsibility than she should; a longing to fix things for people who can't fix them for themselves. And that strong sense of place.

Where do those seeds come from? Karen—typical writer—unfailingly uncovers more about her interlocutors than she reveals about herself. I've known her fifteen years, and my sense of her childhood is sketchy at best. She was born and raised in Baltimore, Maryland; she has an older brother who fought in Vietnam; she dearly loves her mother, her aunt, her sister, her stepfather; and when she was nineteen she married her husband, Randy, and they took off to find a home for themselves, stopping only when they got to Vermont.

But though the names and dates are sketchy, here are the things I know for sure about Karen Hesse: as quiet as she appears, she's a born performer, and once she's on stage—whether on a panel at IRA, or in a cafeteria crowded with a hundred and fifty Long Island fifth-graders—she shines.

She's empathic to an extent I have never before witnessed—no nuance is too subtle for her to pick up and feel herself.

She makes everyone feel cherished—from the taxi drivers in New York who are startled by such unprovoked kindness; to her family, her publishers, her friends.

And, lest she sound like a complete Girl Scout, she has a backbone of steel.

Her books give her away, too. *Phoenix Rising* reveals that she loves the land, and has a profound respect for it. She is unafraid of taking chances—witness *The Music of Dolphins*. She values independence—look at the wonderful Rifka, who makes that long, long journey all alone. Sable and Lavender show that family is important. Her Jewish heritage has shaped her greatly—Rifka again, and Hannah, from *A Time of Angels*. She knows that death is a part of life from being a hospice volunteer—that's in nearly all of her books. She has an ear for language, and is meticulous about word choice—*Out of the Dust*. Plus, she loves chocolate, though that book has yet to be written.

Two years after Holt published *Wish on a Unicorn*, when the manuscript from *Letters from Rifka* had been delivered, I met Karen Hesse in New York City for the first time. I took her and Barbara Kouts, her agent at the time, to a fashionable Italian restaurant on 18th Street, because I wanted to impress Karen with my taste. Another warm, sunny day—we were seated outside, and bees hovered menacingly above our food. As I looked at Karen's stricken face when the oversized carta del giorno was presented—her discomfort at being at such a pretentious place on such a lovely day, her dismay that a meal for three people could cost so unreasonably much—I learned something about her that I should have understood through her writing: with Karen, I couldn't fake it. Bertolt Brecht has some words that, for me, sum up Karen's emotional honesty:

> And I always thought: the very simplest words must be enough.
> When I say what things are like
> Everyone's heart must be torn to shreds
> That you'll go down if you don't stand up for yourself
> Surely you see that.

A cold memory this time: up in Vermont, late fall, past peak, at her home. My husband and I were up there, visiting with Karen and Randy and their two wonderful daughters, Kate and Rachel. We saw where Karen wrote, spent some time where she lived, got a sense of the texture of her life. I'd say we were in the garage when Karen told me the subject of her next book, but I don't think that's true, because I'm not even sure there is a garage up there.

But I felt as if I were in a garage—cold and hollowed out—when Karen said that her next book was going to be about a nuclear accident. I pictured a story with screaming headlines; desperate teens trapped in bomb shelters; a *Lord of the Flies* post-apocalyptic over-the-top nightmare of a book. We had just published, at Holt, Karen's two beautiful chapter books, *Sable* and *Lavender*, to excellent reviews. They were gentle, sweet, satisfying family stories. What's wrong with more of the same? the publisher inside me cried.

Of course, Karen saw right through me, but she didn't let it stop her. *Phoenix Rising,* or "Forever, Ezra," as it was called at the time, was to be the next book. I edited *Phoenix Rising* with the manuscript propped up on my pregnant stomach that next spring. It was a difficult book, and I drew on my colleague, Donna Bray, to help me help Karen sort it out. This was not the sensationalized story I had anticipated, not in the least. Karen had reached very deep inside herself for Nyle's story, and to me it marked a maturity in her writing that we are all now privileged to witness with each new book she writes.

Phoenix turned out so well that I can't recall where I was when Karen told me she was writing a book about speech development (*The Music of Dolphins*) or, of all things, soil erosion (*Out of the Dust*). I guess I trusted her by then.

But I do remember reading *Out of the Dust* for the first time. And I know where I was. I may have appeared to be sitting at my desk at Scholastic Press, turning the pages of a typewritten manuscript, tuning out the office noise. But I was in Oklahoma in 1934. 1 was tasting the grit in my mouth. I was burying the dead. I was hopping a train and running away (to Hollywood, in that first draft!), out of the dust with Billie Jo.

I chose that powerful photograph by Walker Evans of Lucille Burroughs for the jacket of the book to evoke and reinforce the time and place of *Out of the Dust*. (It was only later that I discovered that Karen was looking at the exact same photograph as she was writing the manuscript.) The jacket was originally slated to be a more conventional painting, commissioned from a commercial illustrator. But such an approach would not have done the book justice. The jacket needed to show someone who had witnessed that terrible time, that arid place— just as Karen had, just as we all do when we read her unforgettable book.

A last Karen place-memory: her first ALA, in Chicago, in an airless, beige, convention hotel room. We were going to the Newbery- Caldecott banquet, and she didn't know what would be appropriate to wear. I came up to her room, and she tried on an emerald-green, princess-style dress she had bought for the occasion. It was lovely, but Karen looked in it the way she had looked at that Italian restaurant— desperately uncomfortable, trying to be something she just is not. "Wear that when you win," said I, the ever-optimistic editor, and she changed into an outfit I don't remember now, and went down to her first Newbery banquet looking plainer, but feeling just fine.

I am grateful to Karen Hesse for many things, not least for how she has given me a sense of place in publishing. Her first submission was my first "find." Her first published book was my first "discovery." And her first Newbery—well, I've always hoped that a book I'd edited would win the Newbery, too.

I don't believe Karen will wear an emerald-green princess dress at the Newbery-Caldecott banquet this year. She doesn't need to dress the part. She's found her place now.

The Caldecott Medal 1999

Snowflake Bentley

written by
Jacqueline Briggs Martin

illustrated by
Mary Azarian

published by
Houghton Mifflin, 1998

Horn Book Review

A warm period look at a cold subject—snow—and one self-made scientist, Wilson A. Bentley, affectionately known as Snowflake. Bentley made an appearance in Johanna Hurwitz's recent novel *Faraway Summer* (rev. 7/98); Martin's book more completely gives a portrait of the man who discovered, among other things, the fact that no two snowflakes are alike (something that the book design sometimes contradicts). The book exhibits a beautiful blend of Azarian's splendid woodcuts, a lyrical text, and factual sidebars. Bentley's dedication to his research is clearly evident, and the ridicule to which he was sometimes subjected is appropriately down-played for a young audience. The illustrations, tinted with watercolors, depict the people, homes, meadows, and woods of turn-of-the-century Vermont countryside in accurate detail. Sources for the factual material are credited, and a final page features photographs of Bentley at work and three of his actual snowflake slides.—*Elizabeth S. Watson*

Booklist Review

From the time he was a little boy, Wilson Bentley loved snow. Yet snow was frustrating to him. He could pick flowers for his mother or net butterflies, but he couldn't hold on to snowflakes. First, Bentley tried drawing snow crystals, but they would melt too quickly. Then, as a teenager in the 1870s, he read about a camera with a microscope. His family were Vermont farming folk, but they scraped together the money to buy him the camera. From then on, there was no stopping Bentley, who was nicknamed Snowflake. He spent winters photographing the intricate flakes. At first no one cared ("Snow in Vermont is as common as dirt"); but Bentley found fame as a nature photographer, and even today his photo book of snowflakes is considered a primary source. Martin has chosen her subject well; Bentley's determined life will have innate inspiration for children. Just as important, all parts of the book work together beautifully. The text is crisp and engaging, using word imagery to good advantage: "[his new camera] was taller than a new-born calf and cost as much as father's herd of ten cows." Azarian's woodcuts are strong and sure, just like Bentley himself, and also, like him, show a love of nuance and detail. The book's design allows for snowflake-touched sidebars that offer more specific details about camera technique or Bentley's experiments with snow. There will be so many uses for this book—not the least of which is simply handing it to children and letting their imaginations soar like Bentley's.—*Ilene Cooper*

1999 Caldecott Acceptance Speech
Mary Azarian

January 31, 1999, was a beautiful clear winter day in Vermont. The sky was that dark shade of blue particular to late January. After a winter in which every promised snowfall came in the form of freezing rain or sleet, resulting in a foot of solid ice, we had finally gotten four inches of glorious, fluffy snow. In the afternoon, a friend and I went to a "house concert" given by a local classical pianist to celebrate his new grand piano. The music was superb, and we left the concert nourished in both spirit and body (the pianist's partner, a caterer, had provided goodies). Later in the evening, we decided to forego watching the Super Bowl in favor of a moonlight ski. The moon, just risen, was enormous. The stars glittered in the sky. The snow sparkled. The conditions were so good it was like skiing on velvet. It had been a perfect day.

The next morning, the temperature was twelve below zero. My friend left for town, and I settled into my chair by the fire with a cup of tea and my current book for my favorite hour of the day. I heard the door open. It was my friend, with the joyful news that his car was stuck in the snow. I sighed and donned parka, mittens, boots, etc., and headed out to the car. It wasn't too hard to push it out of the snow-bank, but then we discovered that a tire was flat. Twenty minutes later, we gave up trying to loosen the lug nuts and headed into the house to

call the garage. The phone was ringing. My fingers and toes were sting-
ing from the cold; my nose was dripping. I was annoyed. It wasn't even
8:00 A.M., my hour of reading was shot, and some insensitive idiot was
calling me!?

I run my printmaking studio out of my home and get business calls
at all sorts of inappropriate hours. Ordinarily, I let the machine handle
such calls, but since this was obviously going to be a BAD DAY, I
thought I'd better answer it. As you've no doubt guessed by now, it was
THE CALL. A very pleasant sounding woman told me that *Snowflake
Bentley* had won the Caldecott Medal. I have no idea what I said, something about feeling that such a joke was in poor taste, but eventually I
was convinced that the impossible had indeed happened. I really
couldn't quite believe it, and, in fact, when I called my eldest son in
Austin, he said, "Well, don't get too excited, Mom, they'll probably call
back to tell you they miscounted." All in all, it was not that bad a day.

I realize that it is something of a cliché to include the "where were
you when . . . ?" part, but I still love telling the story, because winter
in Vermont plays such an important part in my life and in Snowflake
Bentley's story.

I think you'd have to say that I got into children's book illustration
through the back door. In the early sixties, my husband, Tom, and I
moved to a small hill farm in northern Vermont. I had always wanted
to live in a place that got plenty of snow, and as we drove down roads
lined with snowbanks so high we couldn't see over them, I knew I had
found the spot. We yearned to live a simple, self-sufficient life; surely a
cow, a flock of chickens, maybe a team of horses, and a big garden
would do the trick. Ha!

It quickly became obvious that a source of income would also be
necessary. With a serious teacher shortage, I soon found myself hired
to teach grades one through eight in a small one-room school. I had
had no education courses, and I was scared stiff. A visit to the school
did little to calm my fears. Besides reading and math texts and an old
set of encyclopedias, long outdated, there were no books in evidence.
Nothing except a picture of George Washington "in the clouds"
adorned the walls. Since I had no idea how I would approach the
actual teaching part, I sought a distraction to keep myself from dwelling
on the dreaded first day of school. So I made a large, colorful, and very
simple (school was due to start in a few days) set of alphabet posters to
decorate the room. It was the first of many alphabets I have created,
and I am still fascinated by the possibilities.

That first year was a challenging, exciting, and exhausting one. In those days, Vermont was still an agricultural state; there were actually more cows than people. The children I taught came from a close-knit community of farm families. In some cases students walked miles to school after helping milk the cows by hand. We had a cook who came in every day to prepare "hot lunch." She and her children, students in the school, had picked blackberries in the summer, and they became the basis for many a cobbler that first winter. Since there were no text-books for history and science, there was no set curriculum, and I had a great deal of freedom in those areas. I am fairly hopeless at math, but fortunately several of the older students were whizzes, and I relied on them to teach when I wasn't up to the task. One of the glories of a one-room school is that education becomes a collaborative effort and depends on everyone's participation. Those kids were great. They learned, I learned, and we all had fun besides.

Eventually, with our second child on the way, I decided to try to run a business out of my home. I had studied both printmaking and painting. I had the great good fortune to study woodcut and etching with Leonard Baskin. Since it seemed important to produce works that were affordable to my neighbors (the thought of trudging around the city trying to find a gallery that would exhibit my paintings was a depressing one), I decided to concentrate on woodcut prints. The busi-ness was immediately modestly successful and continued to grow steadily. In the late seventies, the Vermont Council on the Arts announced a series of grants, funded by the federal agency CETA, for artists to produce a body of work based on Vermont themes. I decided to apply, proposing to design a set of alphabet posters chronicling the fast-disappearing rural way of life that had attracted me to Vermont. A group of ten was chosen, two each of writers, photographers, crafts people, musicians, and "fine" artists. We met every month for a "show and tell" and became a close, supportive group. The Vermont Depart-ment of Education liked the posters and printed a set for every Vermont classroom, K–3.

"Ah ha!" I thought, "these posters look ideal for a children's book." So I scheduled a week of interviews with art directors, bought a classy-looking burgundy faux-leather zippered portfolio, and headed for the big city. Polite indifference is about as enthusiastic a response as I got. One art director even told me that woodcuts were hopelessly passé. At least I got to spend a week in the city. I was a little disappointed, but not too surprised. Actually, an immediate offer to publish wouldn't have surprised me all that much either.

I returned to print production in Vermont and forgot all about book illustration. About a year later, I got a call from David Godine, ever the champion of woodcut and wood engraving, saying he had heard of the woodcut alphabet and would like to take a look at the prints. This eventually became my first children's book, A *Farmer's Alphabet*. In the following years, a few more illustration jobs came my way. Then in the early nineties, I got a call from Jeff Dwyer and Elizabeth O'Grady (I should invest in telephone stock) asking me if I would be interested in having them represent me as a children's book illustrator. We met and immediately hit it off. I was excited at the chance to illustrate more books.

People tend to think that artists have an ideal existence—after all, we supposedly get to be playful and creative on a daily basis. But I can tell you that the working life of a production craftsperson can be downright boring at times. I often feel like a particularly inefficient small factory—everything done by hand: carving, printing, painting, packing, shipping, and bookkeeping all constitute aspects of my work day. While carving the block is pure bliss to me, I am not fastidious enough to be a good printer. Operating my ancient proof press is physically quite tiring. Since I work at home, I never really get to leave the job behind. And, of course, woodcut blocks can be printed practically forever, or perhaps I should say ad nauseum. While I design many new prints each year (I have carved well over a thousand blocks), much of my working life is devoted to production work. As you might imagine, the prospect of working on a book, which is a one-time effort that usually requires learning lots of new stuff and challenges my drawing ability, fills me with joy.

And so, when Jeff called me to say that he would be sending me a manuscript about Snowflake Bentley to read, I was quite pleased. Being a resident of Vermont—even after thirty-five years it would be presumptuous to call myself a Vermonter—I was, of course, aware of Bentley's work with snow crystals. The manuscript arrived. I read it and liked it. The writing was simple yet elegant, and I was eager to do the illustrations. After signing the contract, however, the doubts began. Initial excitement over a new project is, for me, inevitably followed by a feeling of dismay. I wish I were one of those people whose enthusiasm and optimism propel them into a whirlwind of productivity. I am not. I suddenly develop an urgent need to clean the cellar, reorganize the bureau drawers—anything to avoid working on the new project. In this case, I was especially worried because so much of my subject matter has dealt with images of rural Vermont. And winter is my favorite season to depict. I doubted that I could bring much freshness or energy to the woodcuts.

Fortunately, after meeting with my editor, Ann Rider, at Houghton, Mifflin, and the art director, Bob Kosturko, some of my fears were allayed. We talked about the form the book might take and decided that sidebars would be useful to add some technical information without disturbing the text.

Once the format was established, the work began to progress. My research took me to Jericho, Vermont, and I spent one October afternoon in the Jericho Historical Society's unheated reading room poring over Bentley family photos and memorabilia. The adjacent museum houses an exhibit that included Wilson Bentley's camera and many of the incredibly beautiful photographs of snowflakes that he made during his seventy-year obsession with snow. Vermont has always loved its eccentrics, and Snowflake Bentley certainly met the qualifications. He was also a dedicated scholar and scientist, largely self-taught in the nineteenth-century tradition, who placed more value on satisfying his intellectual curiosity than on earning money. His neighbors and many of his own family members thought that he was, at best, foolish. But he was such a thoroughly likable human being that he became a valued member of the community.

As I worked on the initial drawings, I began to realize what an important message this book could convey. So often children (and adults) are told that their dreams and passions are impractical. By many people's standards, Bentley would be considered a failure. And yet, in the most important aspects, his life was a roaring success. He found as much joy in a snowstorm at age seventy as he did at age ten. If that isn't success, what is? So, in the end, it was the extraordinary Wilson "Snowflake" Bentley himself who came to my assistance. I had developed a great fondness and admiration for him, and I wanted to help tell his story.

My approach to the creative process is to clear the decks, get out of the way, and let things happen. As a result, I am not given to analyzing or intellectualizing about my work. Although I believe that drawing is important in that it forces one to really look at the object in question, I rarely do detailed drawings as preliminary work. I prefer, instead, to do my designing directly on the block. Once the final drawings are on the block, everything goes smoothly, at least from a technical point of view. Although apprehensive in the initial stages of every book I illustrate, when the knife begins to "sing" on the block, all doubts vanish. As I cut, I do many revisions, and sometimes, if I have really turned off the voice in my head, amazing (at least to me) things appear. After printing the carved blocks, the final painting of the illustrations begins. This part is the most fun, or perhaps the least stressful. The difficult work is over. The possibility of making a serious carving error no longer exists, and deciding on colors and painting techniques feels like play.

The thing that especially pleases me about *Snowflake Bentley* is that it is a real collaboration in the best sense of the word. My editor, Ann Rider, provided direction when needed while allowing me the maximum freedom to develop the images and expressing confidence in the work I was doing. Bob Kosturko developed a wonderful design for the book, including the idea of the snowflake sidebars, and, of course, Jacqueline Briggs Martin wrote the lyrical text.

In addition to thanking Ann, Bob, and Jacqueline, I would like to thank the Caldecott committee for choosing *Snowflake Bentley*. It is an unimaginable honor.

I also thank all libraries everywhere. As a child, I used to get an actual physical thrill of excitement when I entered a library. Books were my companions during my somewhat lonely and isolated teenage years. I still feel that thrill.

Thanks to Jeff Dywer and Elizabeth O'Grady for representing me and for their friendship and unfailing cheerfulness.

Finally, I thank my parents. I can't imagine more supportive parents. Although neither one of them was an artist, they were delighted when I decided to try to earn my living as a printmaker. They never suggested that something else might be more practical. They would have been so proud.

I'll close with a final story. In the whirlwind aftermath of winning the Caldecott, I spoke to many local groups. I always tried to emphasize that the central theme of the book was to follow one's passion, regardless of how difficult, impossible, or impractical it may seem. After one of these informal talks, a woman came up to me and told me she had read the book to her children and discussed it with them, adding that she would be proud if they grew up to be like Snowflake Bentley. Her four-year-old daughter looked increasingly distressed. Finally, she burst into tears and wailed, "But I don't *want* to photograph snowflakes!" I know this led to further discussion, and it is my fervent hope that *Snowflake Bentley* may inspire both children and adults to follow their own unique paths in life.

Mary Azarian
Terry J. Allen

Mary Azarian

Like the Vermont landscape she draws on for subject matter and inspiration, Mary Azarian has an integrity that is both gritty and appealing. For the last thirty-five years she has been turning out woodblock prints that now hang in nearly half the houses in Vermont and in tens of thousands more around the country. They are framed on walls, displayed in classrooms, magnetted to refrigerators, and thumbtacked in children's rooms. People who would otherwise never imagine buying original art, and others who thought they could never afford it, enjoy her articulate, accessible portraits of the pleasures of daily life.

Mary is a tall woman in her mid-fifties, with long graying hair pulled back and fastened in a utilitarian twist. With strangers she can seem intimidatingly confident or, adopting the flat Virginia smile she learned as a good little girl, blandly polite. With friends, though, she is funny, generous, and richly opinionated. She is well read and well informed and integrates gracefully what appear to be strange contradictions: her politics are progressive, but she watches football; she is anti-consumerist, but indulges gleefully in a little retail therapy and makes her living from selling; she is not particularly competitive or ambitious in her work, but is a cutthroat bridge player. Throughout, she retains a certain remoteness, drawing a careful line around her emotional privacy.

In fellow Vermonter Snowflake Bentley—who died in 1931, a decade before Mary was born—she has found an uncannily good match for her ethical and artistic values. A passionate yet practical eccentric, Wilson A. Bentley found his life's work in studying and photographing the uniqueness, symmetry, and beauty of single snowflakes. Neither selfish nor selfless, he simply devoted his days to work he loved: capturing the transient elegance of a snow crystal. But Bentley was no self-indulgent artist; he was a competent farmer who did not ignore the practical necessities of survival. He also published his work in academic journals and promoted sales of the photographs he made.

Mary has much in common with this craftsman farmer. In her own way, she is somewhat of an eccentric. She adheres to her own path, which sometimes conforms, and sometimes does not, to conventionality and fashion. A back-to-the-lander in the early 1960s, she and her husband, Tom, moved to Cabot, Vermont, and embraced the state's virtues—both mythic and real. They raised three sons and much of their own food, and their daily lives reflected the tasks and turnings of the seasons.

In her first years in Cabot, Mary was a teacher, but as her family grew, she tried to figure out a way to stay at home. Soon she turned her woodcarving skills into a small income and then a small business. That evolution coincided with the craft boom of the late sixties and early seventies that an invasion of city-weary hippies had brought with them to the Vermont countryside. As that tumult swirled around her, Mary worked. She honed her skills; kept her family in wood, taxes, and car repairs; laid the best table for miles around; maintained an independence of thought and vision; and tried to carve out a good life.

She also carved out a good number of increasingly fluent woodblocks. The posters she began printing and painting by the hundreds and then thousands reflected the Vermont values of home and hearth and celebrated the beauty of garden and landscape in a way that was nostalgic without being sappy, personal with being self-referential. (She also contributed biting political posters opposing U.S. intervention in Central America and donated graphics to scores of organizations promoting social and economic justice.)

And the prints sold, at small craft fairs and local shops. Some of her neighbors shook their heads. "Seven dollars," noted one, with a gasp of wonder and a touch of irritation, "for a piece of paper."

Well, a little more than just a piece of paper. The craft of woodblock printing goes back to the Middle Ages. Mary, who incorporates Japanese and European techniques, starts with a finegrained board. She sketches a fairly detailed design on the board in dark ink and then covers the whole surface with a light wash of color. Using razor sharp U- and V-shaped gouges of varying degrees of fineness, she carves away the wood around the black lines to expose again the light wood color beneath. When the process is finished, the lines of the sketch remain as a raised surface.

When Ann Rider, an editor at Houghton Mifflin, read Jacqueline Martin's text for *Snowflake Bentley*, she knew that Mary's style would be a fine match. The choice was perhaps even more fortunate than Rider knew. Not only was there a sympathy of geography and temperament between Mary and Wilson Bentley, but there was a historical precedent for using woodblocks to capture snowflakes. The first observer who tried to record the stark beauty of snow crystals did so in woodcuts. The crude representations were published in 1553 in Rome, in a book by Olaus Magnus, bishop of Uppsala.

Like Bentley's workshop, Mary's current studio in Calais, Vermont, looks out on snow for much of the year. In a good winter, the windows frame white fields spread wide in the pale light; in a bad winter, they expose the gray bones of the land and the threat of global warming. (Don't get her started!) Summer reveals another world, a soft land of green fields and flower and vegetable gardens carefully arranged for color, light, and season, but appearing lushly overgrown and randomly extravagant to the untutored eye.

But unlike Bentley's necessarily frigid room, Mary's workshop is warm. It fills a large, well-windowed room on the second floor of her old farmhouse. A new Macintosh computer and a nineteenth-century press sit side by side. The fax machine shares space with a fat, good-natured tabby and crusty palettes of paint.

On a stool facing the outside view, Mary carves and paints the prints. Her quick, sure strokes have the rhythm of scything, the sureness of surgery. True to the cliche of competence, she makes it look easy as she strips away all that is extraneous and leaves behind what is vital, what gives meaning. It is not a bad metaphor for the ideal of living that drew her to Vermont and still shapes her life.

The next step is printing the block. Mary squeezes a worm of viscous black ink onto a large tray. Working with a speed and determination that appears angry in its intensity, she uses a breyer, a soft rubber cylinder on a handle, to roll the ink back and forth until it is smoothly spread. Once the ink is the proper consistency, Mary rolls the breyer over the surface of the carved block, places it ink-side up onto the bed of the press, and lays a sheet of paper squarely over the block. Her old Van der Cook proof press is a heavy cast-iron contraption that requires considerable strength to manipulate. Using a large wheel, like the pilot's wheel in a ship, she turns a heavy iron cylinder so that it rolls firmly from one end of the block to the other. Under the weight of the roller, the inked uncarved portions of the wood print black, while those areas chipped away by the gouges do not make contact with the paper and remain white. She then repeats the process with a fresh sheet of paper, sometimes for hours at a time.

After the black ink has dried, Mary paints around the lines with acrylic paint, watered down to rich translucency. Taking a pile of black and white prints, she applies the same color on each of them in turn and then adds another color: all the blue skies, for example, on each print, then the green leaves, then the red blossoms. Like a river boat gambler dealing aces, she flips the wet prints around the room until all available surfaces are covered. By now, Mary's hands and nails are stained; her apron and jeans are lined with black finger marks and wipe streaks from color-charged brushes.

Whether she is producing multiple prints from a carving or one-of-a-kind illustrations for books such as *Snowflake Bentley*, the process and care she brings to her craft remain the same. Woodblock printing is a mass-production process from a pre-industrial age that marries a mindless rhythm with a mindful aesthetic. And like the flowers from which she draws inspiration, all the prints look the same until you look closely and realize each one has the kind of subtle variation Bentley found within his snowflakes. And each embodies the pleasure and sweat of good work well done.

The Newbery Medal 1999

Holes

written by
Louis Sachar

published by
Foster/Farrar, 1998

Horn Book Review

Many years ago I heard a long—very long—shaggy dog story involving a couple of grumpy people, a plane, a train, a brick, a dog, and a cigar. It must have gone on for forty-five minutes or so, involved several false starts and stops and intense manipulation of the listener, but it was worth it.

Louis Sachar has written an exceptionally funny, and heart-rending, shaggy dog story of his own. With its breadth and ambition, *Holes* may surprise a lot of Sachar fans, but it shouldn't. With his Wayside School stories and—this reviewer's favorite—the Marvin Redpost books, Sachar has shown himself a writer of humor and heart, with an instinctive aversion to the expected. *Holes* is filled with twists in the lane, moments when the action is happily going along only to turn toward somewhere else that you gradually, eventually, sometimes on the last page, realize was the truest destination all along.

The book begins, "There is no lake at Camp Green Lake," and we are immediately led into the mystery at the core of the story: "There once was a very large lake here, the largest lake in Texas." We soon learn that there is no camp here either, not really, only a boys' detention facility to which our hero, Stanley Yelnats, is headed. Stanley has been convicted of stealing a pair of shoes donated by baseball great Clyde Livingston to a celebrity auction. The fact that Stanley didn't steal the shoes, that indeed they fell from the sky onto his head, is disbelieved by the judge, and even deemed immaterial by Stanley, who blames the whole misadventure on his "no-good-dirtyrotten-pig-stealing-great-greatgrandfather!"—a favorite family mantra. And as the book goes on to show, with great finesse and a virtuoso's display of circularity in action, Stanley is right. His destiny is as palindromic as his name.

We soon learn about that pig-stealing great-great-grandfather and the curse that has haunted Stanley's family, even though the hapless elder Yelnats, like Stanley, didn't steal anything, and the curse is more of an ordination, a casting of the die. Stanley's great-grandfather found his place in the pattern when he encountered Kissing Kate Barlow, neé Miss Katherine Barlow, who became a ruthless outlaw of the Wild West when her love for Sam, the Onion Man, became cause for small-town opprobrium—and murder. Miss Barlow's recipe for spiced peaches also plays a large part in the story.

Heck, it all plays a large part in the story. Those peaches show up more than a century after they were canned, and their efficacy remains unchallenged. Just like Sam's onions. Just like the lullaby, sung, with telling variations, by the Yelnats clan:

> "If only, if only," the woodpecker sighs, "The bark on the tree
> was as soft as the skies." While the wolf waits below, hungry
> and lonely, Crying to the moo-oo-oon, "if only, if only."

As for the title: when Stanley gets to Camp Green Lake, he discovers that every day each boy, each inmate, must dig a hole five feet by five feet by five feet. (Why? Too bad you can't ask Kissing Kate Barlow.) Stanley makes a friend, Zero (nicknamed thus because this is exactly what the world finds him to be), with whom he eventually escapes the camp. These boys have a date with destiny and, trust me, it has everything to do with the pig, Kissing Kate, the lullaby, the peaches, the onions . . . even the sneakers. Sachar is masterful at bringing his realistic story and tall-tale motifs together, using a simple declarative style—

> Stanley Yelnats was given a choice. The judge said, "You may
> go to jail, or you may go to Camp Green Lake."
> Stanley was from a poor family. He had never been to camp
> before.

—that is all the more poignant, and funny, for its understatement, its willingness to stay out of the way.

We haven't seen a book with this much plot, so suspensefully and expertly deployed, in too long a time. And the ending will make you cheer—for the happiness the Yelnats family finally finds—and cry, for the knowledge of how they lost so much for so long, all in the words of a lullaby. Louis Sachar has long been a great and deserved favorite among children, despite the benign neglect of critics. But *Holes* is wit-

ness to its own theme: what goes around, comes around. Eventually.
—*Roger Sutton*

Booklist Review

Middle-schooler Stanley Yelnats is only the latest in a long line of Yelnats to encounter bad luck, but Stanley's serving of the family curse is a doozie. Wrongfully convicted of stealing a baseball star's sneakers, Stanley is sentenced to six months in a juvenile-detention center, Camp Green Lake. "There is no lake at Camp Green Lake," where Stanley and his fellow campers (imagine the cast from your favorite prison movie, kid version) must dig one five-by-five hole in the dry lake bed every day, ostensibly building character but actually aiding the sicko warden in her search for buried treasure. Sachar's novel mixes comedy, hard-hitting realistic drama, and outrageous fable in a combination that is, at best, unsettling. The comic elements, especially the banter between the boys (part scared teens, part Cool Hand Luke wanna-bes) work well, and the adventure story surrounding Stanley's rescue of his black friend Zero, who attempts to escape, provides both high drama and moving human emotion. But the ending, in which realism gives way to fable, while undeniably clever, seems to belong in another book entirely, dulling the impact of all that has gone before. These mismatched parts don't add up to a coherent whole, but they do deliver a fair share of entertaining and sometimes compelling moments.—*Bill Ott*

1999 Newbery Acceptance Speech
Louis Sachar

Thank you very much. I am truly honored to be here speaking to you today. I felt a great deal more pressure in writing this speech than I ever felt writing *Holes*. I'm a lot more comfortable writing a book than I am speaking about it. But I'm especially glad for this very public opportunity to acknowledge and thank some very nice and smart people.

Thank you, Frances Foster. Frances is the editor and publisher of *Holes*. We had worked together on four other books in the 1980s when she was an editor at Knopf, and it was a great pleasure to be able to work with her again. I write five or six drafts of each of my books, and by the time I send it to a publisher, it's not that I feel I finally got it right, but rather, I can't tell what it says anymore. I lose all perspective on my work. It's like reciting a word over and over again. After a while you wonder if it has any meaning. So it's very gratifying to be able to work with

Frances, a very smart and also gentle editor whose opinions I know I can trust. She uses her talent not to turn the book into her book, but rather to help me realize my vision. At least I think that's what she does.

Everyone I've met at Farrar Straus and Giroux, including Michael Eisenberg, Margaret Ferguson, Kate Kubert, and Jeanne McDermott, have proven themselves to be intelligent and professional, and on top of that, they're nice people too. The same can be said about Beverly Horowitz, Craig Virden, and Michelle Poploff at Bantam Doubleday Dell (now part of Random House) who will be putting the book out in paperback . . . eventually.

My agents, Ellen Levine and Susan Schulman, have been terrific. I'm not sure if many writers say that about their agents, but they definitely stand out as being bright, highly professional, and nice people, too.

Thanks also to the members of the Newbery committee for selecting *Holes* to receive the award this year. These last five months have just been wonderful. I don't know any of the committee members, at least at the time of the writing of this speech, but I have little doubt that they must be extremely intelligent, and nice, too. I'm just sorry I'm not a screamer. I was awakened by a phone call at seven o'clock in the morning on February 1 and was told the great news. I could tell I was on a speaker phone and knew they were eagerly awaiting my reaction. I felt I was letting everyone down by not screaming. Sorry.

Speaking of smart and nice people, I received this note of congratulations just as I was finishing the writing of this speech.

> Louis,
>
> Enjoy every moment, every kindness extended in your direction. Once the Newbery talk is written and recorded, you're home free. It will be impossible, but try to write in the 3½ minutes of peace and quiet you get every month or so. Remember to drink plenty of water, eat your vegetables, and get some sleep.
>
> What a lovely "hole" you've dug for yourself.
>
> Karen Hesse

Now, I also want to thank my late father, Robert Sachar, my mother, Ruth, her husband, David Furman, and my brother Andy, for all your support and encouragement over the years. Thanks for giving me a childhood to which I happily return every time I write a book. I'd always looked up and tried to emulate my older brother. Andy has had more of an influence on my tastes and my outlook than anyone. If he had been the type of person who had gone to business school and went to work for a Big Eight accounting firm, I doubt I would be here today.

Finally, I want to thank the first two people who read *Holes:* my daughter Sherre and my wife Carla. I never talk about a book while I'm writing it. It took me a year and a half to write *Holes.* During that time, neither Carla nor Sherre knew anything about what I was writing, except for an occasional announcement that I had finished the first draft, or the second draft, or third or fourth or fifth draft. Thank you for your patience and understanding; for leaving me alone when I needed to be left alone. Sherre was in the fourth grade when I finished the manuscript. I found your comments to be very helpful, Sherre, especially hearing what parts you liked and what parts didn't make sense to you. Sherre is a very smart person, and I knew if there were things that didn't make sense to her, I needed to clarify them. And thank you for putting up with some of the burdens of being the daughter of a well-known children's author. I know sometimes it has made you feel proud and excited, but I also know it's not always been easy.

Thank you, Carla, for all your support and understanding from the very beginning, including the many years when we lived on your salary as a teacher, while I had this perfectly good law degree collecting dust in the closet. Carla never once even suggested that I might . . . er, perhaps . . . look for a . . . you know . . . JOB! Before Sherre was born, Carla and I lived in a one-room apartment in San Francisco, and during the summer, when she wasn't teaching, Carla would still get up early and leave the house so I could be alone to write.

Thank you.

It's fitting that this conference is being held in New Orleans in the summer. I've been interviewed quite a lot in the past several months, and one of the questions I kept being asked was, "Where did I get the idea for *Holes?*" And when I answered "from the hot Texas summer," the interviewer always looked at me oddly, as if I misunderstood her question or she misunderstood my answer. I'm not sure what kind of answer the interviewer expected—that I lived next door to a juvenile correction facility?

But my neighbors who saw me on the *Today* show knew what I was talking about. Anybody who ever has tried to do yard work in Texas in July can easily imagine Hell to be a place where you are required to dig a hole five feet deep and five feet across day after day under the brutal Texas sun.

I've never liked hot weather. I enjoy taking walks on cool foggy mornings or drizzly afternoons. I feel truly lighthearted whenever I see snow. But for a variety of reasons—none of which I quite understand— in 1991 Carla, Sherre, and I moved from San Francisco to Austin, Texas.

We had thought about moving to Colorado or maybe the Northeast, but as much as we liked visiting places where there was snow, we weren't sure how we'd feel about living in it. We considered the fact that if we moved to Austin, we'd have to spend the summer inside in air conditioning. We figured that would be the same as if we lived in a cold climate where we would have to stay inside during the winter.

(I'm using the word "we" loosely. Sherre was only three years old at the time we made our decision, and though she's always been quite opinionated, I don't think she should share any of the blame for this decision.)

I now know there's a big difference between spending winters in places like Minnesota or Buffalo, and summers in Texas. It doesn't snow every single day in Minnesota. There are breaks in the cold weather, when the sun shines and the sky's blue, and you can bundle up in a cozy, warm coat, and go out and play.

There are no breaks from the Texas summer heat. It starts, if we're lucky, in late May and continues until almost Halloween. September and October are the worst. In July and August you expect it to be hot. That's part of the bargain. But then it just keeps going on, week after week, while you know that in other parts of the country people are enjoying crisp fall air and colorful leaves.

In 1995 Carla, Sherre, and I spent the summer in Maine. I had finished writing *Wayside School Gets a Little Stranger* in 1993, and for the next two years I had been working on an adult novel. While there were parts of the novel I liked a lot, it just never seemed to come together for me. The plot never grabbed me. The characters never came alive. So while we were in Maine I made the difficult decision to throw away two years of work and quit the novel. When we returned to Texas I was ready to begin something new.

I'm going to have to digress a moment, and explain my computer software. There's actually a point to this digression, although I'm not sure the point is actually worth the trouble of this explanation—but bear with me anyway.

My word processing program is called WordStar. If I was at a convention of computer programmers, instead of librarians, that would have just gotten a big laugh. They'd be rolling in the aisles. I have lots of friends who are computer programmers, and they always laugh when they hear I still use WordStar.

In any case, it's an old program. I don't have Windows, and I don't have a mouse. However, I know every command without thinking, and that's what's most important to me. When I'm working on a story, and my mind has transported me to Camp Green Lake, or wherever, the last thing I want to think about is how to execute a command on my computer. But now I'm digressing from my digression.

When I'm ready to start a new book, the first thing I have to do is set up a directory on my computer. Then I have to name that directory. Then when I begin writing, I have to create and name files for that directory. The entire book will be on the directory, and each file will contain a few chapters.

When we returned from Maine, and I was ready to start a new project, I had no idea what that project would be. I never plan ahead. I don't make an outline. In many ways I'm like an elementary school student whose teacher has just told the class that everyone has to write a story. I sit at my desk and think, "What am I going to write about?"

Usually I spend up to a month brainstorming. I'll get an idea, write a few words on my computer, think, "That's stupid!" and delete it. I'll try something else—"That's dumb!"—and try again. Sometimes I may get an idea that intrigues me, and I may work on it for a week before realizing it isn't going anywhere. Then at some point I'll get an idea which may not seem very special at first; however, as I write it immediately starts to grow. One idea leads to another idea, and that idea leads to another idea, and that idea leads to another idea, until I have a story going.

This was the process I expected I would go through when I returned from Maine in 1995. Still, first I had to create and name a directory. Since I expected to spend a month or so trying out different ideas, I named the directory "TRY" (t-r-y).

Now, when I say we spent the summer in Maine, that's the "Maine summer." The Texas summer was only half over. I began writing about the oppressive Texas heat.

While every other story I'd written had begun with a character, this story to me has always been about a place. Camp Green Lake—where there was no lake, and hardly anything was green. I thought of the place first. The characters and plot grew out of that place.

This was my very first idea, and the story took off quickly. Perhaps it was a result of the frustration of having worked two years on a novel that lacked strong characters and plot. As soon as I came up with the idea that the juvenile inmates of Camp Green Lake would be required to dig holes, almost immediately I had the idea that there would be buried treasure somewhere out there. I decided it was buried by a famous outlaw named Kissin' Kate Barlow, although I didn't know anything about her yet, and I decided that the warden would be the granddaughter of Kate Barlow, who was using the juvenile delinquents as slave labor to look for her grandmother's buried treasure. And I made up the deadly yellow spotted lizards, lurking somewhere out there, although I didn't know what I'd do with them yet.

(Later on, after I began writing about Kate Barlow, I realized I liked her too much for her to be the warden's grandmother, so that was changed. And yes, the yellow spotted lizards were made up by me. I've been amazed by the number of people who have asked me if they are real. I just thought it should be obvious that the lizards characteristics fit the story too conveniently for them to be real.)

Most reviewers have remarked on the clever name of the main character, Stanley Yelnats, whose name is spelled the same frontwards and backwards. That's not clever. That's just spelling a name backwards. I did it because I was so caught up in creating the story, I didn't want to stop my train of thought to think of the main character's last name. So I just wrote his first name backwards and went on, figuring I'd change it later.

For a variety of reasons I ended up keeping that name. It helped create the surreal tone of the book, and it also became important for Stanley to have the same name as his forefathers. This was a way for me to let the reader know he had the same name as his great grandfather without causing the reader to wonder why I included that detail. But I still don't think it's especially clever, not compared to the much more difficult challenge of writing the story.

After working on this story for a week or two, which, as I said, was the very first idea I tried, I knew I'd be sticking with it. So I sort of regretted having named the directory "TRY." Not that it really mattered, but I would have preferred having called it "CAMP" or "STAN-

LEY" or "DIG" or something else. However, I was afraid that if I tried to change the name of the directory, I might delete everything I'd written, so I kept it as it was.

The book took a year and a half to write. Every day I would begin by turning on my computer and typing the word TRY.

This turned out be very helpful, psychologically. This was the most ambitious book I'd ever tried to write. There were times when it seemed hopeless, when the story got so bogged down that I didn't think I could ever make it work—and this after spending two years on a novel that I'd never finished. So it was very comforting to begin each day by telling myself just to try.

People often ask me how I managed to tie everything together at the end, but that wasn't the hard part. I knew how everything was going to fit together. The hard part was laying out the strands throughout the story—of telling the story of Kate Barlow, and of Elya Yelnats, and Elya's son without it getting in the way of Stanley's story. And then trying to make Stanley's story interesting, when all he does is dig holes, all day, every day. How many times did I write, "He dug his shovel into the dirt"?

I work in the mornings, about two hours a day. During the first draft I may only write forty-five minutes a day. Then I have to let it sit twenty-four hours, like a lab experiment, and see what grows from it. And then I write a little bit more, and do the same thing. As with the directory, I have to name the files, before I begin writing. As I mentioned earlier, each file contains several chapters. Some of the files on my early drafts of *Holes* were named "NOWWHAT" and "ANDTHEN," because I had no idea what would happen next.

Most days I felt like I'd accomplished nothing. If on any given day when I was working on *Holes*, Carla had asked me, "How did the writing go today?" which she would never do, and if I answered, which I wouldn't, but if I did, I would undoubtedly have said, "It was a wasted day." I'd spent somewhere between forty-five minutes and two hours writing very little that was worth reading.

The work seemed like an exercise in futility, kind of like digging a hole, five feet deep and five feet wide.

But everyday I would type TRY and then do just that.

Incidentally, in writing this speech for today, I returned to the same directory. And once again I found some comfort by writing TRY before I began writing this very important speech. However I made the mistake of naming the file, "NEWBERY," and all the pressure instantly returned.

So what exactly was I trying to accomplish with *Holes*? That's something else I've been asked by a number of different reporters over the last several months. What do I want kids to learn from the book? What was my message? What morals am I hoping to teach children?

I seemed to give a particularly good answer when I spoke to the *Houston Chronicle*. The reporter reported that I said, "The best morals kids get from any book is just the capacity to empathize with other people, to care about the characters and their feelings. So you don't have to write a preachy book to do that. You just make it a fun book with characters they care about, and they will become better people as a result."

I always have a difficult time answering interviewers' questions—especially on TV where I'm given thirty seconds to tell the audience what my book is about—but I also have trouble with newspapers as well. So I was proud that I was able to come up with a good answer to that question, and, in fact, I believe it's true. I think I heard Jim Trelise say it once. But that certainly was not on my mind when I was writing *Holes*. I was just struggling to write the story.

It's hard to imagine anyone asking an author of an adult novel what morals or lessons he or she was trying to teach the reader. But there is a perception that if you write for young people, then the book should be a lesson of some sort, a learning experience, a step toward something else.

It's not just reporters who feel this way. Some teachers and possibly even the students themselves believe this. Some fan letters read like class assignments. I received one recently which said something like, "Your book taught me that the acts of your great-great-grandfather can affect your life." Here, it seemed, the teacher required the students to write a letter to an author and say what lessons they learned from the book.

Well, I didn't write the book for the purpose of teaching kids that something their great-great-grandparents did long ago might have cursed them and their descendants for all eternity. I included the curse only because I think most adolescents can identify with the feeling that their lives must be cursed.

The book was written for the sake of the book and nothing beyond that. If there's any lesson at all, it is that reading is fun.

I know when I finish reading a book that I love I feel somehow enriched by it. My favorite books have become a part of me. That's so much more significant than anything as mundane as a moral or lesson.

I'm thinking about this now in this moment of reflection. It's not something I think about while I'm writing a book. I'm too caught up in just trying to write the story to worry about its significance. As I type the words on my computer, it's hard for me to even imagine that real people will actually read them someday.

Mostly when I write I'm just trying to please one reader—myself. I try to write a story I like. And knowing myself as I do, I would not presume to try to teach myself a lesson. Just ask my mother. She'll tell you. You can't teach me anything.

Although I often do surprise myself.

I feel a bit awkward, after spending the year and a half inside my shell, writing, with myself as the only reader, to step out into the public glare and receive this tremendous award. Maybe that's why I didn't scream. I'm still waking up.

But I'm very grateful and thankful to the members of the committee, and all the wonderful people whom I've been fortunate to work with over the past three years, and especially my readers. Thank you.

Thank you.

Louis Sachar

Sherre Sachar

"Are you really Louis Sachar's daughter?" A fifth-grader asked me that my first week of kindergarten. Word spread rather quickly on the playground, and I was suddenly thrown into the world of people who really loved my dad's books. Until then, I didn't realize that his books had so much influence on that many people.

Photo credit: Carla Sachar

Louis Sachar

My dad sees himself as two different people: a writer and a dad who just happens to have the exact same name. I consider myself very lucky. I come home every day after school to find him waiting for me to play, because his work day is over. He likes to challenge me in video games, pinball, basketball, or to help me with his favorite thing of all, my math homework. When he travels, he calls every night, even if it's from an airport, the waiting room of a restaurant, or his hotel room, to see if I need help with that day's assignment. Dad loves logic problems and pretty much anything that deals with numbers, other than taxes. That's something we have in common (the numbers—not the taxes).

Dad loves to play duplicate bridge at a local bridge studio or on his computer. He used to play a lot of chess when we lived in California. He is very competitive, so he often played in tournaments. Now his love is bridge. He didn't even know he liked it, until one day he was invited to play in a weekly game. He and his partner (who is very good) won . . . and that was the beginning of his new hobby. Another game of numbers! It didn't take him long to earn all the points he needed to be a "life master." When he is in Austin, if he isn't in his office working, you can find him at the bridge studio.

When I was little, Dad sang his favorite songs to me at bedtime. Some adults thought it was strange that I was singing Bob Dylan and Randy Newman music by the age of two. Because I was so young, Dad knew I wouldn't understand the more adult subject matter of the lyrics, but these were the songs he knew by heart, so he sang them. As I grew older, I pressed him to explain the stories of the songs to me. I've learned a lot about love and life and war and peace from these musicians and my dad. We share a love for their unique styles of writing and singing (and protesting).

Getting fresh air and exercise are important to my dad. He used to run every day in San Francisco, but it was the foggy weather there that inspired that bit of fitness. Here in Texas, there are few days he feels are cool enough to encourage running. The dogs insist on outside activity, though, so besides their daily morning walks, we enjoy taking long family hikes in a neighborhood park with them. The whole family volunteers weekly at the Austin SPCA, walking those homeless dogs and giving them a few minutes of hugs. (You could definitely refer to us as dog people.)

One of my dad's toughest rules is that he will not talk about anything he is writing while his story is evolving. We might know it is a Marvin Redpost book or another Wayside School book, but that's it. He doesn't want anyone giving him suggestions; he says it interferes with his creative process. When a book is finally complete, he'll let Mom and me read it. I tell him if something is hard to understand or just doesn't work. My mom gets caught up in looking for all the errors like the school teacher she is. We both love the day when Dad says, "OK, my book is finished. Anyone want to read it?" It's really neat to be the first to get to make comments to him about his work. He gets very nervous while we are reading and paces around the house. If it's a long book, he just finds something else to do while we read. He always wants lots of comments from us as soon as we finish reading it. He likes to hear us talk about what we think is funny and waits patiently to see if we really "get it," since some of his humor is kind of deep.

"Are you related to the Sachar who writes children's books?" "Did your dad write those Sideways Stories?" These are questions I've heard all my life, from teachers, other students, librarians, clerks in bookstores, even people we meet on vacations. These phrases have become as common to me as "hello" or "what's your name?"—especially since *Holes* has been winning so many awards and Dad has been in the news. I have also learned that I have to share part of my dad with all the other kids in the world. We just love him for two different reasons.

Louis Sachar

Carla Sachar

When I met Louis, he was already a published author, had just passed the California Bar exam, and was preparing his first court case. I learned very quickly that he had mixed feelings about what he really wanted to do with his life. He had just spent a lot of time and effort earning his law degree and knew he could probably support himself doing law work. He had also had the good fortune of having his first two books accepted for publication. Common sense told him he should proceed with his career as an attorney, but his heart pushed him to keep writing. Thank goodness his heart won the battle.

Writing is his love. How unbelievable to have a chance to do something every day that you relish doing. Creating a story never seems laborious to Louis, and his self-motivation—he sits in his office at his desk five days a week—is incredible. His morning routine is especially important to him; that's what gets his mind ready to be creative. He has had to make adjustments to that routine a couple of times: first, when we married, and later, when Sherre was born. In turn, we have learned what Louis needs and how to make sure he gets it.

When people come to visit us while Louis is working on a book, they soon learn that he doesn't sit and chat over the breakfast table. Each morning he showers, dresses, makes himself a glass of freshly squeezed grapefruit juice, boils water for his tea, and prepares his breakfast. If there are other things going on in the house at this time, he just tunes them out. After eating and reading the morning paper—taking time to solve the daily bridge column—he heads upstairs to close the door of his office and do who-knows-what. When he is first getting started on a new book, we can often hear the rumble of his pinball machine in his office after only an hour or so of work. We're always surprised when he says he is almost finished with a new book. Those few hours a day can really add up to time well spent for his readers.

Louis has a terrific workspace upstairs at the end of the hall, where he is less likely to be disturbed. The only others allowed in the office with him are our two dogs. They seem to know how important his task is, because they protect his closed door with determination. They each have a specific place to sit while they wait for Louis to finish his writing for the day. If they're lucky, they all go for a refreshing walk when the work time is over. Every morning around nine o'clock they slowly make their way into his office and spend the next few hours lying on the floor staring intently at their master. Lucky and Tippy have insisted that they receive credit for their help in writing *Holes* and the Marvin Redpost series. Oh, what they could tell us of stories started but never completed!

Louis is a kid at heart. He loves playing games, being outside, and not working. (He doesn't consider writing "work.") All of us who enjoy reading his books wonder just how he is still able to tell stories from a kid's point of view and be so on the mark with children's feelings and attitudes. He vows that his characters are not based on himself or anyone he knew as a child, but once you know him, you can see a bit of him in everyone he creates. The situations he puts his characters in are so everyday that adults can remember being there. Children who read his books have either been through similar situations, hoped they would never go through anything like it, or have witnessed someone else living through it. His work crosses the boundaries of age and is enjoyed by young and old alike.

Although it becomes more and more time-consuming with every newly published book, Louis never fails to respond to his fans. The letters may sit in a pile on the floor across from his desk for weeks at a time. The class assignments to "interview your favorite author" may come in waves, but Louis always takes time to personally answer all of the mail from his readers. Most of the letters ask the same questions over and over, year after year, but still he answers them. Each child is important to him, so he is determined to give them all the respect they deserve.

For the last eight years, I have felt a little guilty for bringing Louis closer to my part of the world—Texas. He hates heat. Often just walking out of the air-conditioned house into a summer day can take your breath away. Imagine baking in that hot Texas sun, day after day, standing in a dry lake bed, with a limited supply of water . . . digging holes! It can only be your worst nightmare. We had no idea Louis's loathing of this heat would be just the emotion to encourage him to create his latest book. His imagination never ceases to amaze me. He can twist and turn an extremely clever, complicated plot and return to tie up all of the loose ends. Only Louis could find the humor and the words to concoct such a tale as this latest book. The Sachar family is very excited that the Newbery committee has recognized *Holes* as an outstanding piece of children's literature. We're always proud of what he writes, and we know that others love his books because of the response of children and their parents when a new book is published. It is wonderful for him to be honored in such a way for doing something he most wants to do. Our family has enjoyed the special recognition that the Newbery Medal and the National Book Award have given to Louis. He and his mom have had calls and letters from friends they haven't heard from in years. Everyone shares in the pride of this special accomplishment for Louis . . . much as if they were somehow a part of it all. And somehow, they probably were.

The Caldecott Medal 2000

Joseph Had a Little Overcoat

written and illustrated by
Simms Taback

published by
Viking, 1999

Horn Book Review

"Joseph had a little overcoat. It was old and worn. So he made a jacket out of it and went to the fair." So begins this adaptation of a Yiddish folk song (a newly illustrated version of a book Taback first did in 1977). The text is simple to the point of prosaicness—nowhere near as inventive and jazzy as the illustrator's riff on *There Was an Old Lady Who Swallowed a Fly*—but the art sings with color and movement and humor and personality. Taback employs die-cuts with the same effectiveness and cleverness as he did in *There Was an Old Lady* to tell the story of resourceful Joseph, a farmer/tailor of Yehupetz, Poland, who recycles his worn overcoat into ever-smaller elements (jacket, vest, scarf, tie, handkerchief, and button). Taback incorporates detail after detail of Jewish life—the Yiddish newspaper the *Morning Freiheit*; references to Sholom Aleichem and other writers and philosophers; Yiddish proverbs and Chelm stories—to create a veritable pageant of pre-WWII Jewish-Polish life. (In fact, the book is as much a tribute to a vanished way of life as it is a story, but the tribute only enriches the tale.) Broad comedy plays an important part of the pageant: Joseph looks so unhappy and gets such expressively reproachful looks from his animals when his garments become "old and worn"; in contrast, he is all smiles when, each time, he makes something new out of the old. (The exceptionally clever cover design—which incorporates die-cuts to show first a distressingly full-of-holes and then a jauntily patched overcoat—echoes this satisfying pattern.) Double-page spreads employ a mixture of painting and collage to somewhat surreal but delightful effect, such as the one in which Joseph is standing in a field covered with photographs of fruits and vegetables of every kind, from watermelons to jalapeño peppers. In the end, Joseph loses his button, his last bit of overcoat; left with nothing, he makes one more item—this book. Don't you lose it: clever, visually engrossing, poignant, it's worth holding on to.—*Martha V. Parravano*

Booklist Review

This newly illustrated version of a book Taback first published in 1977 is a true example of accomplished bookmaking—from the typography and the endpapers to the bar code, set in what appears to be a patch of fabric. Taback's mixed-media and collage illustrations are alive with warmth, humor, and humanity. Their colors are festive yet controlled, and they are filled with homey clutter, interesting characters, and a million details to bring children back again and again. The simple text, which was adapted from the Yiddish song "I Had a Little Overcoat," begins as Joseph makes a jacket from his old, worn coat. When the jacket wears out, Joseph makes a vest, and so on, until he has only enough to cover a button. Cutouts emphasize the use and reuse of the material and add to the general sense of fun. When Joseph loses, he writes a story about it all, bringing children to the moral "You can always make something out of nothing."—*Tim Arnold*

2000 Caldecott Acceptance Speech
Simms Taback

Tie-er-er menschen-ah shayhem donk. Thank you very much.

I want to begin by saying here and now that I'm not going to get a swelled head about all of this, which is what I promised everyone at the Penguin Putnam party back in February. I said everything was happening so fast: my Hollywood agent had called that morning to say that he had signed with Miramax for "Joseph, the Movie!" and that Bruce Willis was considering taking the role of Joseph, except that he wasn't comfortable with the sewing part (didn't fit his persona) and they were thinking about casting Meg Ryan to play his wife and she would be the one mending the coat. I just want to make clear that I was only joking—yes, I was—and I'd like to apologize. I didn't mean to call Meg Ryan a *shiksa.*

What's really wonderful about getting this award is that I feel like a relative newcomer to the world of illustration, as if I have only just arrived as a practitioner of this craft. But actually, I have been illustrating for forty years, making pictures for just about everybody: Eastern Airlines, McDonald's, Kentucky Fried Chicken, American

Express, CBS, NBC, ABC, many national consumer magazines, Sesame Street, and Scholastic's "Let's Find Out."

I also illustrated about thirty-five books during this time, although sometimes I was careless in my choice of manuscript and material. Only a few of these sold well. My father used to ask, "From this you can make a living?" Well, he wasn't far wrong, yet I always knew I would end up being a children's book illustrator. And if the Caldecott committee has any doubts at this point about awarding me the medal, let me assure you that I really deserve it. Let me tell you why.

I did my very first children's book for Harlan Quist and I was very excited. It was called *Jabberwocky and Other Frabjous Nonsense* (selected poems from *Alice in Wonderland*). I was quite pleased with the results and it was reprinted in several languages. The only problem was that Harlan Quist, the editor, ran off to Europe with all the royalties.

I illustrated a book called *Thump, Thump, Thump* for Mister Roger's Library, a start-up, independent imprint. On the day I delivered the artwork—four months of work—Mister Rogers had second thoughts and cancelled the whole project.

I was offered a book on concrete poetry for children. I was convinced to take it on as a special favor. Everyone knew it was a dud. I said to the editor, "You will always remember me for this book and never offer me another." Well, you couldn't give this book away. I was never offered another.

I illustrated a picture book called *A Bug in a Jug*. All the artwork was lost before it was printed and I had to create all new illustrations.

I illustrated a book called *Please Share That Peanut!* Though I had a lot of respect for the author, Sesyle Joslin, I didn't quite understand the title. That is—until I received the royalty statement. And I could go on from here, but I'll spare you.

But I did have some success; I won't deny it. I have a piece in the Smithsonian collection. This is the very first McDonald's Happy Meal box, which I designed and illustrated with riddles, puzzles, and old Henny Youngman-type jokes. "It's raining cats and dogs. I know, I just stepped in a poodle." I bet this is the first time anyone has tried to impress librarians with a McDonald's Happy Meal.

But there is a downside to this experience, too. It was presented to me as a low-budget assignment because it was only going to be a test print run. It turned out to be seven million boxes.

I know the Caldecott committee does not give its prestigious award for failure—or even a string of failures. But what you should understand here is that I am making a *kaynahora*, that is, I am warding off the evil eye. Up in the Bronx, where I lived, if you praised someone, he or she would say, "Don't give me a canary."

If I had told my mother, "Ma, I won the Caldecott Medal," she would reply, "Yeah! I should live so long." And when it finally sinks in that perhaps it's true, she would add, "Caldecott, Shmaldecott . . . will it put some food on the table?" Any other reaction and you are courting disaster. The old-world Jews understood not to take themselves too seriously.

There is an old joke, told in Yiddish, about a very religious, pious man who complains to God one day: "I go to *shule* and pray every day. I study Talmud for hours and hours. Why, O Lord, do you reward my brother, and not me, with riches, when he is a *gonif* (a thief), and a person of low morals?" There is a long moment of silence and then God replies, "Because you bother me too much!"

But I will break with tradition here because what is even more wonderful is that you have awarded me the medal for this book—this book which is set in a world I heard so much about as a child and tells a story which is so personal to me. This book is filled with my family and I am *kvelling*, which means to feel immense pride and pleasure.

Joseph Had a Little Overcoat is adapted from a Yiddish folk song and is a good example of Yiddishkayt, meaning "Jewish life or Jewish worldview." It embodies the values and struggles of life in the *shtetl*—the small villages where Jews lived in Eastern Europe. These were not big-city Jews, but families of farmers and tradesmen of mixed economic classes. The Kohn (or Cohen) family lived in one of these villages where my *zada*, my grandfather, Meyer Kohn, earned his living as a blacksmith. I use the Kohn name in the book as Joseph's family name—Joseph Kohn of Yehupetz, Poland. The painting of Joseph having his tea is inspired by a fond memory of my *zada*, the way I remember him, placing a cube of sugar under his tongue and sipping his glass of tea, reading his Bible with a handkerchief always tied loosely around his neck.

Yiddish was my first language. I know little of it now. But most American *goyim* speak some Yiddish or some Yiddish inflection, whether they are aware of it or not; Yiddish has become so much a part of everyday English. Goy means Gentile or non-Jew. To the Jews of the *shtetl* there were only two ethnicities—either you were Jewish or weren't Jewish. This is typical of how an oppressed people see the world. Goy is also used as a put-down, as in *Goyishe Kup* (non-Jewish brain) meaning that you're not very smart. Here is a sample of the words we all use:

Chutzpah	Schlock
Megillah	Kibitzer
Yenta	Klutz
Nosh	Nebbish
Kvetch	Mishmash
Tchotchke	Shmo
Shlep	

I hear that *Webster's Unabridged Dictionary* contains some five hundred Yiddish words. And who has not heard some of the following phrases and used them:

Get lost.

All right, already.

I need it like a hole in the head.

So, who needs it?

It should happen to a dog.

OK by me.

He knows from nothing.

A person could go bust.

Excuse the expression.

Go fight City Hall.

I should have such luck.

It's a nothing of a dress.

You should live to a hundred and twenty.

As long as she's happy.

The following could be overheard in any Hollywood restaurant, "Listen, bubeleh, that guy is a shlepper. What's his shtick anyway? All he has is cockamamy ideas." The use of the suffix nik, as in nogoodnik, is very common. We say beatnik and peacenik. The *Wall Street Journal* once carried a headline: "Revolution, Shmevolution." This was found in a review in the *Times Literary Supplement*: "Should, schmould, shouldn't schmouldn't." This was seen on a button worn at a university campus: "Marcel Proust is a yenta."

OK, enough already. I don't mean to knock your head against the wall. But what about the influence of Yiddish inflection in the telling of a joke or story, or only to make a point? Leo Rosten in his *Joys of Yiddish* reminded me of this joke: During a celebration in Red Square after the Bolshevik Revolution and after Trotsky had been sent into exile, Stalin stood beside Lenin's tomb and read the following telegram from Trotsky: "Joseph Stalin, Kremlin, Moscow. You were right and I was wrong. You are the true heir of Lenin. I should apologize. Trotsky."

In the front row sat a little Jewish tailor. "Psst . . ." he whispered to Stalin, "Such a great message, Comrade Stalin, a statement for history, but you didn't read it with the right feeling." Whereupon Stalin quieted the crowd and raised his hand to say: "Comrades, here is a simple worker and a loyal communist who says I have not read this statement with enough feeling. Come up to the podium, comrade, and read this historical statement." So the tailor took the telegram from Stalin and read: "Joseph Stalin, Kremlin, Moscow. You were right and I was wrong? You are the true heir of Lenin? I should apologize? Trotsky."

And finally, there are at least a dozen words to describe a fool, like *shlimazel, shlemiel, shmegegge, shmendrik,* etc., but "Yiddishists" would agree that there is no Yiddish word for disappointment.

When I started school, I forgot all the Yiddish I knew as a child. So when I started to do the artwork for Joseph, I knew I had research to do. I started at the Workmen's Circle bookstore on East 33rd Street in Manhattan. I found five or six books on Jewish life in Poland and Russia with many wonderful photos and a video of the Jewish section of Vilna in Poland before World War II. I visited the Jewish museum to see articles of clothing and other artifacts. The clothing was quite drab, probably faded, though beautifully sewn, and the patterns were quite plain and simple. For the book, I decided to take some artistic license and mix it up with more traditional Polish and Ukrainian designs. This made it more like the *shtetl* of my imagination. I illustrated the ethnic clothing by using collage fragments from various catalogues. So even as I created the artwork for Joseph, I was making something new from something discarded.

I listened to klezmer and Jewish liturgical music, looked at old family photographs, and did all I could to immerse myself in this old-world culture. I wanted to reflect its emotional life, yet I needed it all to be upbeat. I sang. I danced. I did the troika.

I grew up in a working-class neighborhood in the Bronx, made up mostly of socially aware Eastern European Jews. Even though it was the Depression, they built their own cooperative housing project. It was called the Coops. The people who lived there were called coop-niks. We were all poor, but it was a very special place for me. We had a community center, science and sports clubs, art classes, and even our very own library. I spent my summers at Camp Kinderland (Land of Children) and Camp Nish-ka-dieget (No need to worry). These camps were supported by Jewish labor organizations like the Amalgamated Clothing Workers, the IWO, and Workmen's Circle. They were secular camps. You could attend Yiddish classes there, but it wasn't compulsory. It was here in these camps that I was encouraged to develop my talent and to go to Music and Art High School, even though I hated leaving the neighborhood. Upon reflection, I see my old neighborhood as an extension of the *shtetl* life these European Jews had experienced as children. They left Europe for a new life in America, Der Goldenah Medina (Streets Paved with Gold), far away from pogroms, but still with a sense of community, humor, and values learned from generations of family.

I don't know how many *shtetl* communities existed in Eastern Europe (the word *shtetl* does not appear in the *Encyclopaedia Britannica*) but they are all gone now. So is my neighborhood in the East Bronx. It is said that Yiddish is a dying language . . . and perhaps that is true. But as long as I can say, "I am making a *gontse megillah* (a big deal) here," and as long as a good number of people here tonight understand me, who knows? Enough already.

I have many to thank here this evening:

To Music and Art High School and Cooper Union who trained me and gave me a free education; my thanks.

To the Caldecott committee: Thank you so much for saying that a book with a novelty aspect is worthy of this prestigious medal and that *yiddishkayt* can be of interest to young children if presented in an appealing way. Thank you for this *mitzve*, and Ah *mazaltov* to you!

To my editor and publisher Regina Hayes: Thank you for seeing the possibility of successfully redoing a story I had published before.

It took some *chutzpah* to let me do this. Thank you for your confidence and optimism.

To my art director, Denise Cronin: You are a real *mensch* and just a pure pleasure to work with. Thank you for guiding Joseph through a difficult production process.

Thank you Nina Putignano, Janet Pascal, Elizabeth Law, Stephanie McCarthy, and the rest of the Viking staff. Thank you Doug Whiteman for your support. And to my wife, Gail Kuenstler, *Az meir binst du shayne, Der einer oif der velt.* And to everyone here tonight: *Zayn gezundt* and may you live to be one hundred and twenty. Thank you.

Across the Drawing Board from Simms Taback

Reynold Ruffins

Simms Taback

For twenty-eight years, I shared a studio with Simms Taback. He's innovative, creative, warm. He sees the overview, the underview, and the details. He cares. But his work habits are a strange symphony of beauty and agony. First the many, many exploratory drawings using a lead pencil. Then a colored pencil. Then trying the same subject in crayon or with ballpoint pen. Then pen and ink. Or a number 6 brush with watercolor and two-ply kid-finish Strathmore. Perhaps a number 10 brush over the ballpoint on color paper with the pastel smudge would be more interesting. Or the texture of the Arches with watercolor and pencils would lend a certain something. In the process, this patient perfectionist produces a thousand gorgeous sketches of a character or a scene for a forthcoming gem of a book. That's the beauty. The agony comes with the whistling that accompanies the creation. Sometimes the whistle is meandering. Sometimes it is piercing. It is a sound in search of a song. Perhaps it's a sound that is necessary, like the sound that comes before a fine cup of tea. Perhaps it's as integral to his creative process as the grinder to the sausage factory. Perhaps it is the agony of creation. Simms Taback, like Giovanni Bellini, Hans Holbein, and Pieter Bruegel, is the son of a painter. But unlike those earlier artists, Simms did not study painting under the tutelage of his father. In fact, it can be said with some certainty that most of Leon Taback's work is now covered by fresh coats of Benjamin Moore—or even wall-paper. The younger Taback was, instead, privileged to study art with the best and brightest at two of the finest art institutions in New York City—the High School of Music and Art and the Cooper Union. Although Simms's application of paint was different from his father's, Leon's sense of fairness and the family's deep interest in social issues shaped the young artist. They strongly influenced his direction and the sensibility he brought to his work and to the business of his work. In the 1930s and 1940s, Leon Taback had been a union organizer in his trade. Simms's mother was a proud member of the ILGWU. In 1974, Simms began organizing illustrators. He could see so clearly the need for freelancers, who worked in isolation, to be in touch with one another and to be informed about current business practices. His efforts resulted in the formation of the Illustrators Guild, which, in 1976, affiliated with the Graphic Artists Guild. He conceived of, led, art directed, and gently shepherded *Pricing and Ethical Guidelines,* a publication central to the Guild's mission—to raise standards and protect the interests of the freelancer and, in fact, of all art professionals. Simms served as president of the Illustrators Guild from 1975 to 1977 and of the Graphic Artists Guild from 1989 to 1991. He sat on the Guild's national board for over twenty years. He was chair of the Society of Illustrators' groundbreaking show and book, *The New Illustration.* Simms dedicated himself one hundred percent to every Guild endeavor—generating ideas, selecting staff, organizing and chairing meetings, art directing publications, and dealing with the management of minutia. As a freelancer, he also dedicated himself one hundred percent to creating unique, beautifully conceived and executed illustrations for advertising and publishing. Impossible, you say? That's Simms Taback, I say. Simms's work has given pleasure in so many varied areas over a long, successful career. He has won many awards from the Art Directors Club and the Society of Illustrators for work done in advertising and publishing. He has worked as a designer for the *New York Times,* Columbia Records, various advertising agencies, and his own studio and greeting card business. His strength as a designer is manifest in all his work. He is designer, illustrator, letterer, and typographer on all his projects. All these accomplishments come despite Simms's ongoing battle with an addiction that threatens his brilliant career and clear complexion. Often, working late into the night, poor Simms is seized by an all-consuming craving. All attempts to dissuade him are futile. It's a sad and tragic thing to see an otherwise sterling man sneaking out to his supplier and hungrily requesting "a Hershey with almonds, please." Simms once did a series of posters for children published by Scholastic. One in particular expresses his philosophy of life. It is called "Giving and Sharing," and it depicts those acts in simple imaginative ways that cross the lines of gender, ethnicity, disability, and age. No better person could have been chosen to illustrate what might have become joyless or trite in other hands. Simms combined sensitivity and humor—without being maudlin or cartoony—to create engaging, well-designed teaching tools. He has done this many times over in books and posters that sometimes deal with difficult social or scientific topics. He has the enviable ability to take any subject and infuse it with his own personality. Simms's hand is always evident, enlivening without intruding on the subject. Two very different assignments come to mind: one, illustrating construction equipment in the book *Road Builders*; the other, depicting insects on a large poster called "Bugs, Beetles, Flies & Wasps." Engineers and entomologists alike would be impressed and, perhaps, surprised by his accuracy. Certainly, they would be charmed by his style. Simms is genetically programmed to be generous. He deals with an open hand with family and friends, clients and colleagues, students, strangers, and stray dogs. He is always giving. Simms offers more—more interest, more time and attention, more care. A bit like a loving mom with a pot of hot soup. Although his talent has been commissioned countless times in the service of advertising and publishing, it's particularly magical when performed for family and friends. When Simms's kids were away at camp or when they were separated from him for any period, he would always write, draw, or paint the perfect personal postcard. (Often they were part of a series, "Believe It or Don't.") He has often had to work late into the night because he spent the day finding just the right gift, illustrating just the right sentiment, decorating the paper and wrapping the present in the most perfect personal way. He couldn't do less. Randolph Caldecott's name is synonymous with excellence in illustration. Caldecott gave up the life of a bank clerk to become a freelance illustrator. Simms Taback put aside an early interest in engineering to study art. How fortunate their career choices were for the rest of us. The Caldecott committees of 1998 and 2000 are to be praised doubly for twice recognizing and rewarding Simms Taback for his very special and tradition-breaking work. The good people on the 1998 Caldecott committee wisely chose to award a Caldecott honor to Simms Taback for *There Was an Old Lady Who Swallowed a Fly*. It should be noted, however, that if there are a few holes to be found in the fabric of Simms's nurturing, empathetic nature, they appear in this book. Usually caring to a fault, Simms barely managed to squeeze out a tear as he coolly, deftly, and humorously documented the demise of an elderly and obviously demented woman who kept swallowing things she must have known were not good for her. Children and teachers, parents and pastors find themselves in paroxysms of laughter as the dear, unfortunate, omnivorous woman topples over with a large Equus caballus clearly seen inside her. Simms's transformative magic goes into high gear with *Joseph Had a Little Overcoat*, this year's Caldecott winner. Simms makes ingenious use of die-cutting, drawing, design, collage, and exciting color to move the story with a surprising focal point on each page. The book is a Möbius strip of creation and re-creation: Joseph is Simms, Simms is Joseph. In this hole-y book, Joseph, using the wit and wisdom given him by his creator, shows us that "you can always make something out of nothing." If that's true—and Joseph convinces us it is—imagine what we can look forward to from Simms, a man who has so much of so many things—and who gives so generously.

The Newbery Medal 2000

Bud, Not Buddy

written by
Christopher Paul Curtis

published by
Delacorte, 1999

Horn Book Review

In a story that's as far-fetched as it is irresistible, and as classic as it is immediate, a deserving orphan boy finds a home. It's the Depression, and Bud (not Buddy) is ten and has been on his own since his mother died when he was six. In and out of the Flint, Michigan, children's home and foster homes ever since, Bud decides to take off and find his father after a particularly terrible, though riotously recounted, evening with his latest foster family. Helped only by a few clues his mother left him, and his own mental list of "Rules and Things for Having a Funner Life and Making a Better Liar Out of Yourself," Bud makes his way to a food pantry, then to the library to do some research (only to find that his beloved librarian, one Charlemae Rollins, has moved to Chicago), and finally to the local Hooverville where he just misses hopping a freight to Chicago. Undaunted, he decides to walk to Grand Rapids, where he hopes his father, the bandleader Herman E. Calloway, will be. Lefty Lewis, the kindly union man who gives Bud a lift, is not the first benevolent presence to help the boy on his way, nor will he be the last. There's a bit of the Little Rascals in Bud, and a bit more of Shirley Temple as his kind heart and ingenuous ways bring tears to the eyes of the crustiest of old men—not his father, but close enough. But Bud's fresh voice keeps the sentimentality to a reasonable simmer, and the story zips along in step with Bud's own panache.—*Roger Sutton*

Booklist Review

Bud, 10, is on the run from the orphanage and from yet another mean foster family. His mother died when he was 6, and he wants to find his father. Set in Michigan during the Great Depression, this is an Oliver Twist kind of foundling story, but it's told with affectionate comedy, like the first part of Curtis's *The Watsons Go to Birmingham* (1995). On his journey, Bud finds danger and violence (most of it treated as farce), but more often, he finds kindness—in the food line, in the library, in the Hooverville squatter camp, on the road—until he discovers who he is and where he belongs. Told in the boy's naive, desperate voice, with lots of examples of his survival tactics ("Rules and Things for Having a Funner Life and Making a Better Liar out of Yourself"), this will make a great read-aloud. Curtis says in an afterword that some of the characters are based on real people, including his own grandfathers, so it's not surprising that the rich blend of tall tale, slapstick, sorrow, and sweetness has the wry, teasing warmth of family folklore.—*Hazel Rochman*

2000 Newbery Acceptance Speech

Christopher Paul Curtis

First I'd like to extend my congratulations and joy to my fellow Newbery honorees, Audrey Couloumbis, Tomie dePaola, and Jennifer Holm, and to Caldecott winner Simms Taback and honorees Molly Bang, Jerry Pinkney, Trina Schart Hyman, and David Wiesner. And an especially hearty "Go Ahead, Bruh!" to one of my heroes, the winner of the first Printz Award, Mr. Walter Dean Myers, upon whose shoulders I stand.

What an honor! This is the speech so many authors dream about making, and I admit that ever since *The Watsons Go to Birmingham—1963* won a Newbery Honor in 1996, I've hoped that one day I would be standing in front of the gathered throng of the ALA accepting this beautiful medal.

Several firsts are taking place here tonight, some very well known, others not so well known. Among the latter is:

I've done quite a bit of research on the subject and I feel quite confident in saying that I'm the first person with dreadlocks to be presented with the Newbery. Actually what I have are not dreadlocks; dreads are much more organic, much wilder. What I have are more accurately known as Nubian Locks. Webster's defines Nubian as "originating in or pertaining to North East Africa." But ever since I received a phone call from San Antonio, Texas, at 9:20 A.M. Eastern Daylight Savings Time on January 17, 2000, the word *Nubian* has acquired an entirely different spelling. From now on, for me, Nubian will no longer be spelled N-U-B-I-A-N, but N-E-W- (as in Newbery) B-I-A-N.

So many family members and friends, old and new, are responsible for my being here today, and you can only imagine how thrilled I am that many of them are here to share this moment. If I were to start naming them this would be a very long night indeed, but I would like to make special mention of Lynn Guest, my Aunt Joan and Uncle George, and my sister, Cydney. The four of you have made everything so much easier for me, thank you! Also to Liz Ivette Torres, Mikial Wilson, Michael, Lonnie, and Ara Curtis, Lindsey Curtis, Terry Fisher, Janet Brown, Aunt Nina and Uncle June and all of my wonderful siblings, my cousins, my aunts and uncles—thank you for years of kindness.

Thanks to the many teachers and librarians I have met over the past five years for making me feel so special. Pauletta Bracy, Joan and Ray Kettle, John Jarvey, Gary Salvner, Smoky Daniels, Jean Brown, Elaine Stephens, Kylene Beers, Teri Lesesne, Lois Buckman, Len Hayward and the many other people who have so warmly opened their schools and libraries to me, thank you for making me feel at home whether I'm in Cleveland, Chicago, Saginaw, or Houston.

And to my family members at Random House, Pearl Young, Terry Borzumato, Beverly Horowitz, Kevin Jones, Michelle Poploff, Jeannette Lundgren, Tim Ditlow, Craig Virden, and particularly Andrew Smith, Mary Raymond, and Melanie Chang, I've seen how hard all of you work and I know I've seen only a tenth of what you do. All of the Curti (the plural of Curtis) thank you.

And to my children, Steven and Cydney, thank you for your contributions to both of the books. Steven, you are directly responsible for the *Watsons* going as smoothly as it did. You're the best first reader an author could ask for. And Cydney, many people have told me that their favorite part of *Bud* is the song that you wrote. "Mommy Says No" is a classic, thank you so much.

I also would like to extend my sincerest thanks to Carolyn Brodie and this year's committee for their selection of *Bud, Not Buddy* as 2000's medal winner. I once judged a short story contest with forty entries, and after reading the tenth one I thought I'd lose my mind. I'm amazed at the dedication, the time, and the strength it took for these members to complete their assignment. Thank you from the bottom of my heart. I'm well aware of the incredible honor that has been bestowed upon me.

I'd also like to thank the Newbery committee from 1996 for honoring *The Watsons Go to Birmingham–1963* and, more importantly, for not holding a grudge. Let me explain.

In January of 1996 there was talk that my first novel might receive some recognition from the Coretta Scott King committee and, less likely, from the Newbery committee as well. I had read somewhere that the committees called the authors who had won on Sunday night before an announcement was made to the general public on Monday morning.

That Sunday evening in the Curtis household was horrible. The phone never rang. I even picked it up several times to make certain we had a dial tone. Finally at 11:00 I called it a night. Kay stayed up, sure that the time difference was delaying any word. The last thing I said to her as I went upstairs was, "Aww, who wants those old awards anyway?"

The next morning I headed off to the library to write. At around 9:00 the phone rang, waking Kay up. It was Mary Beth Dunhouse from the Newbery committee. I have to explain here that Kay is not a morning person. She doesn't really begin to wake up until ten-ish, so in her defense she wasn't really sure what was going on.

Ms. Dunhouse told Kay *The Watsons* had won a Newbery Honor and asked if I was home. Kay told her, "No, he's gone to the library to write." When Ms. Dunhouse relayed that fact to the librarians, they screamed wildly! Around this time, the call waiting clicked. As I've said, Kay was still half-asleep. She said to Ms. Dunhouse, "Could you hold for a minute, there's another call coming in."

It was Carolyn Garnes of the Coretta Scott King committee. Kay finally woke all the way up and began chatting enthusiastically with Ms. Garnes. About ten minutes into that conversation, Kay remembered the other line. When she went back, the Newbery committee was long gone.

So as you can see, I really am grateful that librarians didn't hold that against me.

Not that I'd ever suspect that they would. I've been involved with librarians all of my life, and I, just like Bud, have always known where to go for a sympathetic ear or for information or for the key to the magical world of books. Libraries and librarians have always played such an important role in my life.

A rite of passage for me occurred at the Flint Public Library. My siblings and I used to spend Saturday mornings at the library with my father. We'd go into the children's section while Dad, who at the time was in Labor Relations, went to the part of the library that was filled with books about unions and contracts. One day Dad took David and Cydney into the youth section and told me to come with him. We walked across the hall into Adult Fiction and Dad said, "You're a good enough reader to start here now."

From that day on I remember the pride and accomplishment I felt when on Saturdays we'd go to the library and David and Cydney would turn left into the world of Dr. Seuss and *Harold and the Purple Crayon* and I'd turn right into the world of Langston Hughes and Mark Twain.

Both of my books were written in the Windsor, Ontario, libraries. When I started writing *The Watsons*, I found that once again the children's section was the place where I was most comfortable. I'd write for three or four hours every day and was always made to feel right at home by everyone who worked there. One of the librarians in particular, Terry Fisher, took me under her wing.

One of the most difficult things for a new author to do is to find someone who can offer informed criticism of your work. When I'd finished *The Watsons*, I figured, Who better to review it than a children's librarian? Terry was the logical choice. I asked her if she would read my manuscript, and even though she had no idea if the 220 pages I handed her would be the least bit readable, she never hesitated, she said of course.

A couple of weeks later I was back in the library and steeled myself to get Terry's criticism. I walked over to her desk. She looked up at me and tried to say something, but instead she was wracked with sobs. She finally said she loved my book, and I nearly broke into tears, too.

And now this.

I don't even have to look at the table where she is, because I'll bet you dollars to doughnuts that she's crying all over again, but Terry, could you please stand up? Thank you, once again, for all of your encouragement and support, you are such a librarian!

One of the proudest moments of my life happened this year, and once again the library was involved. In late January I received a call from the Flint Public Library and was told that if a millage tax didn't pass in Flint, the same library that my father took us to on Saturdays, along with every other public library in the city, would be permanently closed. I was asked if I'd be willing to make a commercial for the millage. I said yes, but first I called my editor, Wendy Lamb, and told her what was going on. The next day, Craig Virden, my publisher at Delacorte Press, sent a substantial check to the Friends of the Library Fund. I also called my agent, Charlotte Sheedy, and the next day Charlotte also sent a very generous check to the fund. In two days, the fund's advertising budget tripled. I am so proud to be involved with people like Charlotte and Wendy and Craig. The millage passed overwhelmingly.

Soon after graduating from high school, much to my mother's dismay, I began working in an automobile factory in Flint called Flint Fisher Body Number One. The factory was historic, for in 1936 and 1937 the workers took over the plant when General Motors refused to recognize a union.

One of my political science professors at the University of Michigan-Flint, Dr. Neil Leighton, made this period come alive. His descriptions of the tensions and fears and tremendous danger to which these auto workers were exposed seemed the stuff of high drama to me. I knew there had never been a book for young readers about the Sit-Down Strike, so in early 1996 I began researching the labor movement and the Great Depression.

By November of '96 I'd written three chapters of the novel when Kay, Steven, Cydney and I went to Grand Rapids to my family reunion. At the reunion, the main topic of conversation was my father's father, Herman E. Curtis, who in the 1930s led a Big Band called Herman E. Curtis and the Dusky Devastators of the Depression. The stories of Grandpa's exploits had everyone dying with laughter.

When I went back to the library in Windsor to write, I began taking notes about my grandfather; the notes turned into vignettes; and the vignettes finally overwhelmed the Sit-Down Strike book and evolved into *Bud, Not Buddy*.

One of the questions I was constantly asked between the time that *The Watsons* was published and the time that *Bud* came out was a variation of, "Goodness, your first book did so well, what on earth are you going to do to top that?"

Early on I made a conscious effort not to try to top that.

I remembered the fun I had writing *The Watsons* and decided that *Bud* would be no different. I decided I had a story to tell, that I was going to tell it the best way I could, and that I'd give no consideration whatsoever to how it would be received. I figured Wendy Lamb could worry about that.

Here's another first that is taking place tonight. Many very famous people have been quoted and had their names dropped in past Newbery speeches, but Craig Virden has confidently agreed to provide either a six-figure advance and a two-book deal or one of the typically high salaried, glamorous jobs in the world of New York publishing to anyone who can conclusively prove that the person I'm about to quote from has ever been cited in a Newbery speech before. Mr. Sylvester Stewart. No need to rummage through old copies of the *Horn Book*;

Mr. Virden's money is safe. Sylvester Stewart is better known as Sly, from Sly and the Family Stone.

> Sly said,
> Lookin' at the devil, Grinnin' at his gun.
> Fingers start shakin', I begin to run.
> Bullets start chasin' I begin to stop.
> We begin to wrestle I was on the top.
> I want to
> Thank you falettinme be mice elf
> Agin.

The pertinent line is the last one, "I want to thank you for letting me be myself again."

I'm not exactly sure what Sly had in mind when he wrote that, but it rings of the highest truth to me tonight. I really do have the need to tell several people thank you for letting me be myself, starting right at home.

To my mother and father, Herman E. Curtis Jr., and Leslie Lewis Curtis, thank you for letting me be myself. It wasn't until I had children of my own that I truly understood my parents. It wasn't until I too worried about what the world had in store for my young black children that I appreciated my mother's protectiveness. And protective she was.

Momma was convinced that our neighborhood in Flint was the poison capital of North America. As such, we were not allowed to go out trick-or-treating. Momma had it on the highest authority that every apple given out at Halloween had a razor blade in it, that every Hershey bar had been dusted with enough rat poison to bring down an elephant, that each NutChew was chock-full of the ground-up glass from a six pack of Faygo Red Pop. This is not to say that we didn't go trick-or-treating, just that we didn't go *out* to go trick-or-treating.

So we wouldn't feel totally left out of the festivities, Momma developed a brilliant plan. What the Curtis children would do was gather in a whiny, pouting group, go to a closed bedroom door in the house, yell "trick or treat," and, lo and behold, Momma would open the door and drop some candy in our bag. We'd then wait while she moved to the next bedroom and the sad little scene played itself out again. By the time we reached the bathroom door, I've got to tell you, the thrill was gone and all whining about going trick-or-treating ceased.

In addition to being protective, my mother and father have always been supportive and encouraging. I remember writing an article for a school paper in the sixth grade. I brought it home to do the final touches, and when I was done I gave it to Momma. After reading my work, she said, "Oh dear, I wish you'd left this at school, your teacher is going to think it was written by an adult." I've had a starred, boxed review in *Publishers Weekly* and glowing reviews from *The New York Times*, but neither of them has meant as much to me as those words from my mother. Momma, thank you for letting me be myself.

Wendy Lamb, who is blessed with the perfect name for children's literature, thank you for letting me be myself. I never understood or appreciated how much a book is a collaboration between an author and an editor until Wendy took both of my books in hand and improved them immensely.

I've worked in an automobile factory for thirteen years, I've hauled garbage, I've mowed lawns, I've worked for the census, I've been a maintenance man, I've unloaded trucks and spent hours sorting through and recycling paper, but I think I'd rather go back to any one of those jobs than be an editor. I can't imagine a more difficult profession. Not only is a good editor technically on top of what she is doing, she also must be able to deal with a writer, a person who can range from frighteningly insecure to unbelievably cocky. Often in the same conversation.

After seeing how hard she worked on my books, I asked Wendy why the editor wasn't at least given an acknowledgment on the copyright page. She told me that the editor's job was to be invisible, merely another set of eyes for the author. And Wendy's touch *has* been invisible.

After each of my books has been published, I think to myself, "Why is Wendy Lamb making that big, cushy, typically high New York publishing house salary? It doesn't seem to me like she did very much on this book." Then I make the mistake of reading through our correspondences or, worse, reading the actual first draft of the book.

I end up saying things such as "Wait a minute, I could swear *I* was the one who thought of doing it that way," or "Ooh, that's right, Wendy *did* say it would make more sense if Buphead said . . ." or "Yikes, she's right again, 'booger' is mentioned a couple of dozen times too many on this page."

I remember going to Wendy's office for the first time and being absolutely crushed. I screamed, "Wendy, I thought I was the only one!" I was shocked to see that she actually worked on other people's books! Though I didn't want to believe it, the evidence was irrefutable. On her desk was a well-thumbed-through Graham Salisbury manuscript, and in a pile that nearly reached the ceiling was a stack of fourteen or fifteen novels. I rushed over to see whose they were and can still remember the searing pain in my heart as I cried out, "Oh, Wendy! Not Gary Paulsen! Tell me it's anyone but Gary Paulsen!"

I'd always pictured Wendy sitting around in her office napping or biting her fingernails or playing solitaire while she waited for me to send her my latest re-write, but I guess the old saying is true, the author's always the last one to know.

Wendy Lamb, thank you for pulling *The Watsons Go to Birmingham—1963* out of a pile of nearly four hundred other manuscripts entered in your contest, the Delacorte Press Prize for a First Young Adult Novel, and thank you for letting me be myself.

Finally, Kaysandra Anne Yasmine Sookram Curtis. KayBee Baby, thank you for letting me be myself. In 1993 Kay took a tremendous leap of faith and said to me, "Look, I know you hate your job, and I don't think you're doing everything you can with your life. I've read some of the things you've written and I bet you could be a writer. So why don't you take a year off work and see if you could write a book?"

Kay got me writing and is probably the person most responsible for me standing here tonight. That's an easy story to tell, but it leaves a lot of the gory details out, and believe me there are gory details when you take a year off work to write a book. Perhaps the biggest gory detail is fear. There was the fear that the year would be wasted, the fear that I wouldn't be able to produce anything worthwhile, and the all-encompassing fear when I realized I was being given a chance to have no excuses. There was also the fear of admitting to people that I was going to try to make a career as a writer. I knew that the looks this would draw from friends and family would be somewhat akin to the way they'd look if I announced I was quitting my job to be either a brain surgeon or a ballerina. But Kay even had me covered there.

When money would allow, we would make our one family trip a year to Toronto to attend the Caribbean festival known as Caribana. In 1993 we ended up at a party with a group of five or six other couples. My worst nightmare developed right in front of my eyes—everybody began taking turns telling what they did for a living. Before I could excuse myself and run to the bathroom to hide, all eyes turned to me. I hung my head and whispered, "I'm a writer." I don't know which was worse, the embarrassing silence that followed my announcement or the snicker that someone couldn't contain. All the women in the group looked sympathetically at Kay.

Kay never missed a beat, she said, "That's right, he's a writer and a very good one and one day all of you are going to know who he is." The women in the group still looked at Kay with sympathy, but now it was sympathy colored with a touch of pity.

In 1993 an essay I'd written and an early draft of *The Watsons Go to Birmingham* won Avery and Jules Hopwood Awards at the University of Michigan in Ann Arbor. While I waited on stage to accept my prizes, Kay sat next to the mother of another winner. I don't know what their conversation was, but afterward the woman came up to me and said, "You know, with a wife like that you don't have any choice but to be a success as a writer."

I didn't understand what the woman meant at the time, but now I do. It's much like Bud Caldwell's mom told him: with the right love and care and hope, miraculous things can happen. A confused, lost Bud can blossom into a beautiful flower; an unhappy, unfulfilled factory worker can bloom into an author who realizes his dream, can become someone who doesn't have to just *imagine* what it feels like to stand before a gathered throng of the ALA and accept this beautiful medal.

Kay, thank you for providing that love and care and hope. Thank you for letting me be myself.

In January of 2000 there was talk once again that my novel might receive some consideration from both the Coretta Scott King committee and the Newbery committee. This speculation does not make for an easy Sunday night's rest.

On the morning of Monday, January 17th, Kay took our daughter, Cydney, to school, leaving me to field any calls that came in. 9:00 came and went. At about 9:10 I repeated my lines from four years earlier. "Aww, who wants those old awards anyway?" At 9:16 the King committee called, and at 9:32 the Newbery committee called.

When Kay came home around 10:00, I'd had plenty of time to compose myself. She opened the door, found me sitting on the couch reading, and said, "You didn't hear anything?"

I said, "Well, just as a hypothetical let's say I won honors from both committees again. Would that mean I could be excused from doing all housework for the next year?"

Kay said, "Huh. You'd have to win the gold from both of them before that would happen."

After we hugged and cheered and cried, Kay said, "You know I was only kidding about the housework, don't you?" Thank you, Kay, for letting me be myself.

Bud Caldwell coped with life by developing a set of Rules and Things for Having a Funner Life and Making a Better Liar Out of Yourself. Christopher Curtis has coped with the attention and exhilaration of winning the Newbery and Coretta Scott King Awards by developing a set of Rules and Things for Keeping Your Ego in Check and Your Feet Firmly Planted on the Ground.

Rules and Things Number 541:

Don't Worry about Getting a Big Head. Friends, Family, and Total Strangers Will See to It That There Is No Way in the World You Will Be Allowed to Become Too Full of Yourself.

Two examples. *Time* magazine started its article about me by stating that I am six feet two inches tall and weigh 240 pounds. When I was interviewed by *Essence Magazine,* the reporter told me he'd seen those statistics, and he stated, "I don't know why they had to put that in there, I'm kind of tall and husky myself, they didn't have to tell everyone that stuff. I mean the brother can't help it if he's got tall genes in his family. The brother can't help it if he likes a sandwich every now and then!" Ouch!

The other example took place in New York City in March. Melanie Chang, my publicist at Random House, and I were walking through the lobby of the Doubletree Guest Suites in Times Square when a woman spotted me and came up to us very excitedly and said, "Oh my God, I don't believe it, aren't you the guy who wrote that book?"

I smiled humbly and said, "Yeah, that's me!"

Melanie asked the woman if she was in New York to attend the NCTE conference.

The woman replied, "No, I'm here on vacation and I'd heard about your book and picked it up for the flight. I love it!"

"Thank you!" I replied even more humbly.

The woman said, "I've got my copy right upstairs, is there any way I can get you to sign it?"

Melanie told her, "We're going to lunch here in the hotel, we'll be here for the next hour or so."

The woman beamed and said, "Thank you so much, I'll be right back."

I don't know which of us was more pleased—Melanie because the Random House publicity machine was so potent that here was a non-teacher, nonlibrarian who had heard of her author, or me because I'd been recognized in the heart of New York City. I mean it's one thing to be recognized in downtown Flint, Michigan, but it's a whole 'nother world to have a stranger know you in the Big Apple.

Melanie and I went to the restaurant and sat at a table where our fan could easily spot us. A few minutes later the woman came squealing and gushing to our table and handed me her book.

It was *Monster*, by my hero Walter Dean Myers.

Once again, thank you, thank you, thank you to the Newbery committee for giving me the freedom to be myself. Thank you so much to the many librarians and teachers who have through their recognition also encouraged me to be myself, and who have permitted three voices from Flint, Michigan—Kenny Watson, Bud Caldwell, and Christopher Curtis—to be heard across this land.

Christopher Paul Curtis
Wendy Lamb

Photo credit: photo courtesy of James Keyser

Christopher Paul Curtis

One morning in January 1994, I stood in a small office at Delacorte Press, surrounded by hundreds of manila envelopes and boxes, opening and logging in submissions to that year's Delacorte Press Prize for a First Young Adult Novel Contest. Gray fuzz from the innards of exploding jiffy bags drifted onto everything, including me. I opened yet another envelope and pulled out yet another manuscript and looked at the title: *The Watsons Go to Birmingham–1963*, words that filled me with curiosity and dread; words that instantly evoked the church bombing where young girls died in Sunday school. Well, I thought, this person was ambitious, trying to write about something terrible, something important. I logged it in as a "hold" for a special look later. One Saturday in February, I pulled the envelope out of a box I'd sent to my home in New Hampshire. It was a bright morning, about twenty below, and I laughed when I read the first words, "It was one of those super-duper cold Saturdays." I kept laughing, chapter after chapter. As I read I thought, "This novel is too funny—no one's going to die, are they?" I was amazed by many wonderful details, one of them a moment when Kenny looks inside Joetta's shoe as she sleeps on the drive south and sees Buster Brown's face printed on the heel. After the bombing, Kenny looks inside the shoe he finds at the church and sees Buster Brown. I stopped reading. Not Joetta! I turned the page face down. I thought, "Wow. Look what he did with a shoe. Who is this guy?" When I got to know Christopher, it became clear that not only could he write a great story, but his life was a great story. He was born in Flint, Michigan, in 1953, the second of five children. His father, Herman E. Curtis, was a chiropodist, and his mother, Leslie, who attended Michigan State, was a homemaker. Both of his parents were great readers, and so was Christopher. But he didn't find books "that were about me." When poor patients could not pay, Dr. Curtis went to work at the Fisher Body plant. Christopher graduated from high school in 1971 and went to work on the assembly line with his father. He'd been accepted at the University of Michigan–Flint, so it was supposed to be just a summer job, but the money was too good. Christopher spent thirteen years on the assembly line, hanging eighty-pound car doors on Buicks, going to school at night and working toward his degree part time. He met Kaysandra Sookram, a nursing student from Trinidad, at a sports event in Hamilton, Ontario, Flint's "sister city." During their courtship, Christopher wrote her letters about his job, family, and friends, and Kay said, "You're good at this. You could be a writer." At Fisher Body, Christopher and his partner worked out a plan: instead of taking turns, so that each of them would hang every other door, instead each man would hang every door for half an hour while the other took a half-hour break. Christopher used this time to write, as a way to escape the noise and boredom. Christopher left Fisher Body and worked at many other jobs while continuing school. Meanwhile, Kay and Christopher had married and had two children, Steven, now twenty-one, and Cydney, eight. In 1993 Kay, an intensive-care nurse, offered to support the family while Christopher took a year off to write *The Watsons*. "She had more faith in my writing than I did," he says. (Christopher's sister, also named Cydney, "knew by his fibs" that he could be a great writer.) He sat in the children's room of the Windsor Public Library and wrote in longhand. Steven typed his father's drafts into their computer and served as first reader. Clearly, family is a rich source for Christopher. Kenny Watson is a combination of Christopher and his brother David, and one incident—when Momma tries to cure Byron of setting fires by threatening to burn his fingertips—really happened. Luckily, sister Cydney rescued Christopher. One of the photos on the cover of *The Watsons* is of Cydney; another is of their parents. The story in *Bud, Not Buddy* is an invention, but it was inspired by his two grandfathers, Earl "Lefty" Lewis and Herman E. Curtis, and by Herman's band, The Dusky Devastators of the Depression. And Christopher's daughter Cydney contributed the unforgettable lyrics to the song "Mommy Says No" in *Bud, Not Buddy*. Since Christopher is so big on family, he treats me like family, too. This means I get teased. All the time. My birthday is fourteen months ahead of his and he scrupulously defers to me because he is so much younger. In May 1994 he wrote: "Richard Peck told me you were a real toughie, are you wimping out as you get older?" Working with him is like working with a brother—but without the punching. Early on, I told him that I hate it when people use the verb "to pen." I received a fax: Here is the essay I promised, it was penned two years ago. I've also included the first short story I ever penned. Hope you enjoy them. I really enjoyed penning them. Unre-pen-tantly yours, Christopher. Working with Christopher means I laugh a lot—I have to, when we're having yet another discussion of how many times Bud should mention snot, boogers, and "vomick." Christopher's second novel was going to be about the sit-down strike of 1937 in Flint. In the first draft of *Bud, Not Buddy* Bud had a glimpse of tanks and strikers in the street, but that story will have to wait for another book; in this one, the strike boiled down to the box of flyers in Lefty's car. Bud had amazing adventures that also wait for other books, as do some terrific characters. Stories leak out of Christopher like laughter, along with hilarious asides, dialogue, and wonderful details. Most of the editorial process (i.e., struggle) is about trying to control these elements so that the story doesn't lose momentum or tension. I marvel at his use of slapstick, humor, and "gross" things kids love, like backwash in a bottle of pop. Or his shorthand with the details: Bud's first meal in a restaurant, or Kenny's description of breathing in the pomade on his little sister's hair, or that moment, after the bombing, when Kenny looks at the shoe. Each book is carried along by the exaggerated tone and the heightened childlike energy of the voice, and by the tension created when Christopher sets each boy up against a great, dark force: the bombing; the Depression; racism. In *Bud, Not Buddy* the rules are funny and to the point, but they also show us what inspired them—Bud's hard, hard life in the hands of strangers. Christopher's readers learn how history affects ordinary people like the Watsons and Bud—and about other ideas, such as the importance of music, whether it's Yakkity Yak on the Ultra Glide or the subtle "vocal stylings" of Miss Thomas in 1930s Grand Rapids. And they learn about family: family is the goal; family is the salvation; family is Bud's right and he must demand it from the world. Publishing *The Watsons* changed Christopher's life, and certainly winning the Newbery has set him and his family upon another new course. But one of the first great changes in his life is related in the following excerpt from the essay mentioned earlier, which he faxed me soon after we met; an essay which brought him his first recognition as a writer, a Hopwood award at the University of Michigan in 1993. It's about the day, after thirteen years on the job, that he walked out of the factory and just stopped, "amazed into nothingness."

> The light changed to green, the herd bolted, and I stood there, staring at the backs of the other workers, watching the swinging lunch pails, the work boots being lifted and put back down, seeing the gray pinstripe coveralls running toward the bars and cars that waited to take them to whatever would carry them away. I felt that every dream, every hope, every talent I ever had was being melted away by the numbing horror, the endless repetition, the daily grind of that factory. I had been suddenly and unexpected amazed. I was amazed that I had hated crossing this street for thirteen years, amazed that I was no closer to getting out of it than I had ever been, amazed that I was so unhappy and wasn't crying. Red . . . green . . . red . . . green . . . I stood there getting brushed now and again by other members of the herd who didn't expect or understand my reluctance to step into Saginaw Street. The light changed to red, the herd filled up around and beside me again, jostling and laughing, paying careful attention to the crossing signal. It was one thing to get hit by a car and killed coming into work; it was a whole different level of tragedy to get nailed on the way out after having given your last nine-and-a half hours to General Motors. REDGREENREDGREENREDGREENREDGREEN The first time I'd felt this way was soon after I hired in and had to start working in the Jungle. The Jungle is where the whole body of the car gets started, it's where they take a couple of sheets of steel and coerce them into the beginnings of a twenty-thousand-dollar Buick. To do this they use spot welding guns that look like two giant, black fingers that end in long, thin copper fingernails. The guns are about four feet long and hang off ceiling-high beams on heavy cables and balancers. There must be several hundred of these guns hanging along the assembly line,

and when you see all of those cables and balancers and fixtures hanging down looking like vines, and when you see all of the smoke hugging the ground looking like a dirty mist or fog, and when you see all of the welders in their dingy gray coveralls walking around like some type of ghost in a forest, making all of those quick moves as they dance from one welding gun to the next, and you hear all of that noise, all of the screaming that the metal makes when the guns melt the pieces together sounding like some gigantic animal is down there being ripped apart and dying hard, and when you hear all the squeals and groans the line makes as it drags the car through the workers and you hear the workers hollering above the noise trying to talk to the person next to them and you hear the KERCHUNKA-KER-CHUNKA-KERCHUNKA sound of all the welders pounding their guns into the steel sounding like the largest elephant ever born is crashing through the bushes and stomping the hell out of anything in the way or sounding like drums pounding out some message that you don't get, then you can understand how the name Jungle fits so well. REDGREENREDGREEN Saginaw Street yawned in front of me like a grand canyon, I felt as if one step into it would be the end. I felt an arm go 'round my waist, it was Muley, the man who hung deck lids one place up the line from me. "Christopher, you all right? Need some help to your car?" Muley was taking me across the street, he'd picked up my jacket and the book I'd been reading and tucked them under one huge arm and me under the other, we floated across Saginaw and down to the lot where my car was parked. Muley looked at me and said, "If I was you I wouldn't come in tomorrow, I know how you feel, some of the time it's just too much, isn't it?" I had to agree, it had become too much, but more importantly it had become too little, it had become nothing.

I am fervently glad that this man has found the right work. And grateful, always, that Delacorte Press became part of Christopher Curtis's story on the day his manila envelope landed in our contest.

Index

"Illus." *following* an author name within parentheses refers to the name in the entry heading.